LANDSCAPE AND IMAGES

JOHN R. STILGOE

LANDSCAPE
AND IMAGES

University of Virginia Press   Charlottesville and London

University of Virginia Press
© 2005 by the Rector and Visitors of the University of Virginia
All rights reserved
Printed in the United States of America on acid-free paper

First published 2005

9 8 7 6 5 4 3 2 1

LIBRARY OF CONGRESS CATALOGING-IN-PUBLICATION DATA

Stilgoe, John R., 1949–
   Landscape and images / John R. Stilgoe.
      p.   cm.
   Includes bibliographical references and index.
   ISBN 0-8139-2321-2 (cloth : alk. paper)
   1. Landscape—United States. 2. Landscape photography—United States. 3. United States—Geography. I. Title.
   E161.3.S754 2005
   917.3—dc22

2004020122

For Eleanor Norris

CONTENTS

PREFACE

Walking proves pleasant in a mediated age. Away from cinema, television, video, and computer screens, and away from headphones and cell phones too, the walker courts discovery.

Encountering landscape involves little more than glancing around, even while driving a car or sipping a drink aboard Amtrak. Bicycling, canoeing, horseback riding, and cross-country skiing enable observation, discovery, and delight. But walking especially opens on so much that the surfeit almost stuns.

Landscape designates shaped land. Here follows no paean to wilderness, although land unshaped by people gets some cautious examination. Here follows no praise of wholly shaped structure and space either, and especially no analysis of indoor space. But everything else, rural, suburban, and urban, is fair game, and the astonishing amount of space, and range of variation, lure the walker who can never walk it all.

Physical exercise needs space, but a little spice helps it along. Walking and looking around flex muscles and lungs, and eventually stretch the mind too. Anyone who realizes landscape, who notices carefully enough to make it discrete and real, encounters a subject worthy of lifetime study in the open air and in libraries alike.

ACKNOWLEDGMENTS

Boyd Zenner, acquiring editor at the University of Virginia Press, conceived this project. Without her initial idea and continued gracious support, it would have remained not even a dream.

The editors in whose journals appeared earlier versions of the chapters deserve much credit, and I happily provide it here. Editors not only refine the ideas of writers, but by their very existence cause at least some writers to think more than twice about concepts and prose alike.

My students deserve much credit too. Many of the essays began in direct response to student questions, sometimes shouted from the back of lecture halls or tentatively asked around the seminar table, but far more often posed in office hours. Sometimes questions produce a new lecture for a course, and in time the lecture becomes a journal article.

Friends and colleagues deserve mention here, especially Daniel Aaron, Thomas Armstrong, Robert Belyea, Steve Forti, Suzanne Jevne, Arthur Joseph, Phillip Joseph, Eleanor Norris, and John Opie. As young boys, Stephen DuLong, Joseph McGuire, Richard Newey, Chester Paskow, and the late Harry Merritt went exploring with me in sandpits and salt marshes and old fields and cutover woods, all of us ranging constantly over the little coastal town in which I still live. In later years Suzanne Jevne and Marcia Zottoli Stone wandered around with me too, enjoying the freedom of bicycles, then a very-high-mileage 1950 DeSoto in which each enjoyed a wreck caused by my inattention to stumps and swamps. Theodore Baldwin, friend, neighbor, and retired police officer, began instructing me in looking acutely when I backed the DeSoto into his sparkling new car, and still suggests landscape elements that I might investigate.

My family deserves much credit too, not only for observations shouted or whispered to me but for enduring thousands upon thousands of stops to make photographs. Adam and Nathaniel, our grown twin sons, proved to be extraordinarily patient, intrepid, and sometimes serendipitous explorers of landscape, and they still make extremely useful suggestions. My wife, Debra, not only makes all exploration special, but remains the reason I come home.

A NOTE ON THE ILLUSTRATIONS

Except as noted, all of the illustrations either are in the author's collection or are photographs made by the author. Exploring the national landscape produces haphazard encounters with rummage sales, flea markets, barn auctions, and trash set out for collection. Two of the period illustrations included here turned up in a late-eighteenth-century volume of sermons purchased at a farm sale on a Pennsylvania back road. Libraries prove integral to landscape and image research, but a mass of old books and ephemera at a farm machinery auction can be useful too.

INTRODUCTION

Landscape inveigles. Trees and highways, rivers and villages, hills and urban sprawl become more than view or setting altered by weather or slant of light or ideology. Looking at landscape, realizing it, perhaps ordering it in painting, photography, and other representation reward a willingness to be cajoled, surprised, reassured, ensnared, but often misled. Analyzing landscape slams traditional academic inquiry against serendipity and intuition. Always analysis begins in just looking around, noticing the nuance that becomes portal.

Just looking around drifts out of fashion nowadays. Frenzy scars too many over-long workdays, and high-speed or congested highway traffic makes pleasure driving rare. Cell-phone calls interrupt the walker and distract the motorist and the railroad passenger. Walking and running become merely physical exercise often taken in such harried, collision-prone locations that health-club treadmills satisfy more completely. In sinister ways, suspicion attaches to watchers. The walker stopped to examine an old building, the motorist pulled over to scrutinize the last suburban farm fields, even the shopper stopped to watch playground activity becomes suspect. People ignore landscape and its constituent elements, but they see observers as potential thieves, kidnappers, land developers, Environmental Protection Agency operatives, and worse. Since the terrorism of September 11, 2001, citizens and law enforcement officers alike scrutinize anyone who gazes too long at railroad trains, bridges, water-supply towers, chemical plants, oil refineries, industrial waterfronts, skyscrapers, airports, or even the rights-of-way of natural gas lines buried beneath a forest. Paranoia worsens if the observer makes a photograph, even a sketch or a painting. Despite constitutional guarantees and a surfeit of laws protecting looking and photography, once-innocent and honorable activities now require commendable guile.

Underlying suspicion lurks distrust of anyone who observes what most miss. Americans learn in kindergarten to not look from classroom windows. Even looking around the classroom becomes forbidden, evidence of an undirected mind or a willingness to cheat. Since 1900 formal education has involved chiefly learning to listen to words and to manipulate numbers and written words. The Scholastic Assessment Test includes no visual-acuity section to complement the sections that evaluate verbal and quantitative reasoning. Despite a century of cinema, and the explosive growth of television after World War II, despite the subtle and provocative power of video, animation, and video-based games after 1980, despite the astounding power of hypertext-based Internet imagery after 1990, formal education includes almost nothing visual. By third grade students figure out that art is far less important than mathematics, and that looking around produces admonition.

Mediated reality seduces the young. Post–World War II houses usually have windows set so high toddlers cannot look out at streets and yards and squirrels. But most houses offer television to toddlers, and once hooked on the drug, many young children thereafter look chiefly at screens. Adults watching suburban intersections will notice minivans and other domestic vehicles fitted with videocassette and videodisc players that produce images on monitors mounted above front seats. Young children, strapped in car seats that make looking from side windows uncomfortable, stare at the monitors rather than watch the passing show.

Surely the collapse in teaching geography during the 1950s Sputnik-inspired shake-up of American public education still deflects attention from landscape. An important school subject into that decade, geography alone focused student attention on visual representations of real places. Mixing words, numbers, symbols, and images on maps taught much now forgotten, even by experts. Students learned to read maps, but also to look at paintings, photographs, and other images. Reading maps meant realizing cartography as one expression of three-dimensional topography, and reading and making maps well meant first seeing landscape acutely. Art might or might not strike any student as important, but mapmaking struck most as an important corollary of outdoor play and map reading a useful codicil to the first adult certification, the driver's license. Sooner or later, everyone would need a road map, and sooner or later, students knew from family vacation trips gone awry, maps would be twisted and turned and read in relation to intersections, bridges, rivers, and other landscape constituents beyond the windshield. By 1970 geography had vanished from high school curricula, and had nearly disappeared from universities and elementary schools too, shoved aside by ferocious attention to physics, mathematics, and high-speed driving along interstate highways perfectly marked with green signs.

Becoming lost or scared or in desperate need for information often focuses attention on context, especially if maps fail and cell phones catch no signal. On a rural road locked in winter night, the glimmer of the low-fuel warning light becomes potent. At the next fork or intersection, the motorist must distinguish the road most likely to lead to an open gas station. In a strange city, the taxi traveler leaving the airport must eventually judge if the driver has diverted from the shortest route to the convention hotel. In times of earthquake, fire, terrorist attack, perhaps especially warfare, discerning particular meaning in landscape becomes vitally important, literally effort that preserves life. Even summoning help by cell phone often demands immediate assessment of location, and if that fails, description of location accurate enough to direct emergency personnel. Often only calamity focuses attention on landscape.

Artists and other makers of images focus attention on landscape too. But lately formal art education devotes only infinitesimal attention to the landscapes that comprise the ostensible subject of so many images. Students learn to discern massing of color, the play of light within a photograph, the angles of shadows and subjects. Only rarely do observers question subtleties of subject. Strong seacoast prevailing winds distort tree growth, something many painters depict but others neglect. Turning radii of automobiles have increased dramatically since 1940, something that leads to miscalculation of distance, road width, and angles in photographs of parked cars. Idiosyncratic knowledge often produces sparks of insight concerning paintings and other images, but formal education submerges such knowledge in cloying methods of engagement derived from literary theory, not the visual acuity that predates learning to read.

Advertising imagery becomes almost all powerful, skewing much understanding of landscape. More than a century after the triumph of mass advertising, especially visual advertising, neither schoolchildren nor university students learn how to analyze images crafted to sell. That so much advertising uses landscape as background, and sometimes as the subject in advertising for real estate or resort vacations, concerns anyone inquiring into the source of landscape attitudes. In American advertising, farming remains the small-scale, mixed-crop-and-livestock operation it was circa 1920. Its wood barns, narrow fields, and wide-porch farmhouses form a background that suggests tradition, adaptability, security, and family-focused effort, all apparently useful in advertising pickup trucks, jeans, margarine, and political candidates. Modern, industrial-scale agribusiness rarely informs mass-circulation advertising, and cross-country motorists discover jarring disjunction in the so-called heartland. Almost anywhere thoughtful observers of landscape explore, they discover disjunction between the real and the advertised.

Mediated reality becomes the standard by which so many Americans scale hyper-reality. Something truly exciting, a bank robbery shoot-out or even a high-speed car crash, enters conversation as "just like in the movies" or perhaps on television. Not surprisingly, many landscapes now please simply because they resemble advertising landscapes seen so many times that viewers unwittingly accept them as ideal. A little coastal village, a valley of small farms, a low-storied city street of compact store-fronts, all may be discerned as quaint or attractive by visitors almost un-aware of personal landscape standards. Sometimes well understood by local tourism-development or planning officials, and perhaps especially by real estate developers and boutique owners, often the attractive or unspoiled places exist unvalued by locals lulled by geographical remoteness. Millions of Americans see advertisements supposedly set in Montana or Louisiana or the upper peninsula of Michigan, but few residents of the East or West Coast now drive back roads across the country. They fly, and watch videos at thirty thousand feet. Only rarely do they look from windows, let alone take a long-distance train ride or extended walk away from their neighborhoods.

Perhaps something has vanished from childhood. But as the first essay suggests, perhaps children still possess the ability to wander in spaces adults dismiss, and to shape those spaces in ways that shape lives. In childhood exploration and shaping began the lifelong effort that produces these essays.

Time, inclination, and just looking around shape these essays. But exploration always leads to libraries and archives. Landscape studies is scarcely a scholarly field, but rather a part of the larger discipline loosely designated visual and environmental studies that embraces geography, landscape architecture, and visual assessment. That discipline descries such shadowy think-tank and secret-government-agency efforts as critical infrastructure analysis, scenario forecasting, and topographic change assessment, and scans their traces outdoors and in libraries. Looking around often satisfies, and sometimes almost satiates, but usually it grates too. Close scrutiny of landscape invariably raises questions, sometimes almost inchoate ones at first, that nudge inquirers into libraries.

Some of the inquiries involve the very deep past. Why Americans merrily carve pumpkins at Halloween is a question leading back to pagan Europe. That most Americans see the landscape of the forty-eight states as continental rather than archipelago requires some understanding of the old French view of North America as islands connected by rivers. Such issues involve others, including the way nineteenth-century painters struggled to produce a national landscape motif from colonial preferences. Only rarely do museum visitors learn that paintings of landscape once had political significance, especially before the Civil War and trans-Mississippi settlement, or that aesthetic sensibility has taproots extending into agricultural land-classification systems about which suburban gardeners still know fragments.

Others involve rural space. Population concentrates on the seacoast, and the marges of the Great Lakes: half of the United States population lives within fifty miles of the coasts, and three-quarters of the population lives within seventy-five miles of them. So-called national media, including news media and especially television advertising, consequently focus on people living in very confined areas, and much mediated landscape imagery is now distinctly parochial. Rural America is not only vast, but for most well-educated adults, almost wholly unknown. Yet rural America is the national attic. Fundamental values find spatial expression in rural places: such values endure obviously. City dwellers accustomed to traffic congestion and urban sprawl discover that tolerance of diversity, for example, seems almost casual when neighbors live miles apart, or that the traffic law obtains easily on roads traveled by five cars a day. Most of the national landscape remains rural, and attracts settlers in the quasi-suburbanization process that so perplexes spatial planners. As the essays in the second section demonstrate, since the eighteenth century many thoughtful observers have found the values codified in the Constitution best expressed in rural places. Right or wrong, their thinking shapes what analysts nowadays call lifestyle values.

Certainly one lifestyle value involves shaping personal or family space. Rural landscape remains the greatest triumph of landscape planning, but not planning by government-employed planners. Instead the concatenation of farms, woodlots, small towns, and roads reflects a fundamental United States belief in personal physical expression. Sometimes individual personal expressions coalesce in similar ways, particularly in the context of recreation and other shared experience, creating the landscapes that attract tourists, advertising experts, and, especially, retirees, homeschoolers, and the wealthy. Individual expression involves the shaping of space to produce personal goods (especially crops), microclimate, and privacy, but also demi-independence from utility grids and other communal networks coastal people accept as norms. Spatial privacy leads to more creativity and often to more dramatic impacts than the wardrobe-styling efforts of young urban dwellers, but since most rural effort involves little or no cash outlay, advertisers ignore it. Only when the deep past, even the pagan past, slivers into rural thinking in large-lot suburbs do observers realize hobgoblins still twitch magic.

Contemporary landscape focuses the third section of this book. In the twenty-first century subtleties of landscape demand new metaphors of analysis and rethinking accepted notions of everyday behavior. Some landscapes seem smooth, like jellies, but nonconforming uses punctuate others, like seeds in jam. Thinking of landscape as food seems ordinary enough when critics speak of sprawl devouring countryside, and leads to analyzing other words. Automobiles shattered the urban magic of chance encounters, disappointing women beyond words. Whatever young bachelors ask each other when one reports meeting a woman, women almost invariably ask each other, "Where did you meet him?" The where of meeting grew important as urban automobiling reduced serendipitous meeting of strangers, and also curtailed the designing of rendezvous. Bumping into new people, including people one wanted to meet, became something rare, and sometimes involving the collision of cars.

Derelict cars often join others across rural America, comprising elements in ordinary countryside self-appointed improvers want to eliminate although they never question their dislike of wrecked cars. The clash between upscale urban landscape aesthetics and downscale rural values involves more than landscape analysis. It suggests the growing force of pre–Civil War thinking, especially the arguments of Thoreau, in a high-tech urban age. Perhaps too it presages a suspicion that technology fails to solve problems of metropolitan crowding and density from which more and more wealthy citizens escape geographically. Small towns now begin to understand themselves as citadels resisting urban failure, welcoming upscale, astute, and often ruthless escapees. Number-crunching government departments, insurance companies, think tanks, and above all marketing and advertising firms study the demographic shifts in the context of class and values division.

Such shifts sometimes reveal themselves in imagery. The human eye evolved to look at reflected light, fire, sun, and stars excepted. Even when illuminated at night by streetlights and neon signs, landscape is studied by observers under reflected light, not the blue light emitted from television and computer monitors. So consuming and exhausting are moving images now that few busy individuals scrutinize period still ones, especially daguerreotypes and photographs. But old images reward scrutiny, especially when examined in conjunction with what else is known about period landscape and about contemporary space and structure too. In the deep past, looking acutely frightened the common folk. Those who saw or professed to see around the curve of time became known as seers, and sometimes condemned as witches. Even now, professional lookers at landscape, surveyors and police officers for example, make the timid slightly afraid, but scryers scare even the police. Someone disciplined to look at landscape eventually sees what many want to keep hidden, perhaps most lately not terrorists lurking around critical infrastructure but law enforcement personnel poorly camouflaged. Scrying means at least the chance of seeing through landscape, perhaps into the deep pagan past, or even into long-unvisited courtyards of traditional religion. Limbo must have a landscape every bit as bizarre as Xanadu, but only disciplined vision glimpses it. Before the Civil War, Hawthorne and others mused about the dangers implicit in the daguerreotype. The new technology not only mimicked divine sight but at any moment threatened to escape the control of the daguerreotypist. The separation of soul and character from each other, and perhaps both from body, the uncanny ability of the daguerreotype to pull secrets through the eyes of subjects and from seemingly innocent, ordinary landscapes loomed as another presentiment of disunion, war, and chaos.

Modern photography now shapes landscape aesthetics and even landscape planning and design. Americans no longer distinguish easily between landscapes and photographs of landscapes. So much photography originates in anything but artistic endeavor that few methodologies of art analysis apply. Popular photography derives from sophisticated film, paper, and cameras produced by companies that also educated photographers through proprietary instruction manuals and advertisements. Children and adults alike learned to make snapshots and much higher quality images, but not necessarily as art at all. The beach became not only landscape especially fitted for photography but very quickly a place for any photographer to explore the relationship of natural environment, landscape, nature, and human form. In time beach became studio, and the beaches of California became the prism through which Americans understand beaches. They unthinkingly accept sunset over beaches as far more beautiful and attractive than sunrise there, devoting as little attention to the origin of beach aesthetics as they do to issues of beach culture and beach behavior, especially the baring of skin. Nor do they consider scale, population density, and the intractable issues of personal freedom, crowding, congestion, and openness implicit in any image-making in so much of the High Plains part of the nation. Sparsely settled landscape proves as photogenic as any beach, but few consumers of advertising, calendar imagery, or Internet imagery pause to inquire why lonely beaches figure in so many advertisements and lonely High Plains roads figure in almost none.

In the end, and at the end, lies interdisciplinary library research. A spectacular university library system supports my just looking around. But sometimes it pays to consider libraries as landscapes. The replacement of card catalogues by computers ended the serendipity of meeting colleagues and students in the catalogue room, and perhaps the computer now means something to middle-aged scholars that resembles what the automobile meant to young women in 1910-era cities. Chance encounter happens far less frequently in libraries nowadays, and only interdisciplinary subjects like landscape thrust inquirers, faculty and students alike, from one floor to another, and then from one library to another. A pleasant thing about a decentralized library system is that research efforts mean striding across campus from one library to another, and realizing that in the midst of an afternoon of library research a bit of fieldwork might happen accidentally, as it did in boyhood in the fields and woods and beaches around the old farmhouse in which these words began.

TREASURED WASTES

Spaces and Memory

The Bog, The Pit, Mrs. Norris's Woods, The Swamp, Fuller's Dam, The Landing, all linger as landmarks in a landscape of childhood. Adults in the 1950s and 1960s knew the places treasured by boys growing up in a small New England coastal town but used other designations, if they applied designations at all, to a collection of semi-used or long abandoned spaces. Only one bog deserved "the" in its name; perhaps fifteen acres in extent, it produced few cranberries but innumerable wild ducks, frogs, herons, and the big snakes eventually identified from junior high school nature guides as the common northern water snake, *Natrix sipedon sipedon*. Beaver now and then dammed the brooks flowing through the worn dike built in the early part of the century; if the beaver stayed "up bog," boys rolled fieldstone into the breaches, insuring a tiny pond all summer and, with luck, a larger skating pond by Christmas. Three miles away, south by southeast, endured The Landing, a ragged gash in salt marsh opening into the estuary. From the 1650s to the 1920s, boatbuilders, fishermen, and farmers used it, making it common land; its steep slope and slick mud defeated cars and trucks, however, and as the age of the horse passed, bayberry and sumac crowded the lane. Officially if occasionally visited by the Highway Surveyor, used by fishermen seeking striped bass, and rare summertime canoeists, it remained the possession of boys bored with the well-kept gravel and asphalt of the densely populated town landing slightly seaward. Hidden by second-growth forest, defended by twisting, muddy paths and rotted bridges, The Bog, The Landing, and other constituent elements of the intricate landscape of childhood thrived within an equally complex landscape of adults.

Now and then intersection of interest shattered peaceful coexistence. Forest fire signaled the arrival of the volunteer firemen, adult onlookers, and the boys, breathless on bicycles. Always the fire chief barked the same question: "Boys, what's the best way in?" Then followed the frantic flinging down of Indian pumps—four-gallon, Army surplus handpumps worn on the back—to the boys, filling the pump tanks by a fireman nearly knocked down by boys with pumps and too-small boys screaming for

"Treasured Wastes: Spaces and Memories" appeared in *Places* 4, no. 2 (Fall 1984): 64–74.

Poised at the edge of the pit it excavated over decades, this derelict power shovel presided over the exploits of boys attracted to a wasteland bereft of adults.

the honor of a pump, then dragging the hose along the trail known only to boys thrilled to be guiding the townsmen and squirting tiny streams on smoldering white pines or smoldering canvas hoses. Day after day, however, after school, in the frigid winter vacations, the landscape of boys remained almost untrodden by adults. Separate, protected, and regularly modified by its stewards, it passed eventually to younger boys when the wonders of driving family automobiles in distinctly adult space deflected sixteen year olds from marshes, swamps, and the forgotten plantation of balsam fir designated Christmas Tree Land.

Of course, men return now and then, even a landscape historian weary of typewriting and determined to improve the last of a November afternoon by following the old route to The Bog. Windfalls and poison ivy have deflected the path a bit, but the long vista across the now overgrown sandpit remains. And in the gray light, at the crest of the drumlin, the historian descries a man walking as he walked a quarter-century earlier. In the hollow, now thick with chokecherry, the old friends meet, the historian asking the lawyer dressed for court what brings him onto the path to The Bog. "She just told me. She wants a divorce. Somehow I just wound up out here."

Discreteness distinguishes a landscape from landscape. A landscape

INTRODUCTION

typically acquires discreteness from natural or artificial boundaries or as it evolves peculiar spatial and distinguishing characteristics. The landscape of Nantucket Island or Sombrero Key extends to the low tide mark and is easily bounded by any observer on foot or equipped with a map or chart. Even the landscape of Missouri or Montana can be delineated by political boundaries. But more often geographers and other dedicated students of the built environment identify a landscape not only by tracing its edges but by defining its distinguishing characteristics. Bank barns, double-pen cabins, adobe wall construction, and a thousand other characteristics serve to define landscapes. In the past two decades, landscape identification and definition have grown sophisticated. Edges and details, cherished by discoverers, dovetail with frameworks evolved by philosophers, economists, and mathematicians.

Landscape is not *a* landscape. As I define it in *Common Landscape of America, 1580 to 1845,* landscape is not cityscape but essentially rural, essentially the product of tradition.[1] To discern and define *a* landscape means knowing what landscape is in general, then devising a system for noting the important edges and other features of the place under study, be it a suburb, a valley devoted to cattle ranching, a Great Lakes resort island. Scholars have lately devised such systems; many prove immediately useful, others suggest modifications or adaptations to specific landscapes.[2] Implicit in most are prisms, however, prisms that subtly distort the usefulness of the system in the work of others.

Consider scale. What is a long vista across an overgrown sandpit? To a native of Moab, Utah, perhaps two or even three miles; bright sunlight, clean air, and unobstructed views combine in Utah to produce attitudes toward distance alien to West Virginians. In Norwell, Massachusetts, it means about two hundred yards, a figure not surprising for a heavily wooded town. But what, then, is the impact of a town's coastal location? What influence has the sea, stretching away flatter than any Wyoming wheat field? Such are the issues that perplex the reader of undergraduate and graduate term papers. What local values, unrecognized by their bearers, distort visions of landscape?

The question lies at the heart of landscape analysis. "In certain of its fundamental features, our rural landscape," asserts the French historian Marc Bloch in *The Historian's Craft*, "dates from a very remote epoch." But in order to examine the rural landscape of the past, "in order to ask the right questions, even in order to know what we were talking about, it was necessary to fulfill a primary condition: that of observing and analyzing our present landscape." Bloch says little about the actual observation and analysis; he does, however, liken the task of the historian to that of someone examining a roll of photographic film. "In the film which he is examining, only the last picture remains quite clear. In order to reconstruct the faded features of the others, it behooves him first to unwind the spool in the opposite direction from that in which the pictures were taken."[3] The state of the last negative, therefore, determines the whole study of the prior ones. And as any surveyor or navigator knows, the slightest error at the start of a long course produces increasingly serious errors as the course is run.

J. R. R. Tolkien, the British folklorist who produced *The Hobbit* and *The Lord of the Rings* for fun and in so doing created one of the richest of fantasy landscapes, wondered about the start of landscape perception, about the very frame that worried Bloch least. "If a story says, 'he climbed a hill and saw a river in the valley below,' the illustrator may catch, or nearly catch, his own vision of such a scene," Tolkien argues in *Tree and Leaf,* "but every hearer of the words will have his own picture, and it will be made out of all the hills and rivers and dales he has ever seen, but specially out of The Hill, The River, The Valley which were for him the first embodiment of the word."[4] If Tolkien is correct, the landscape of childhood has immense meaning for the student of landscapes, for that first landscape remains—despite training, system, and years of fieldwork— a prism through which actual landscapes are viewed and through which long vanished landscapes are reconstructed using the written documents favored by Bloch and other historians. And as all prisms do, the prism distorts, perhaps dangerously.

Innocence suffuses the landscape—or cityscape—of childhood. To the child not yet aware of thermonuclear fire, landscape is permanent. It is no accident that landscape history is largely a postwar phenomenon; the work of Maurice Beresford and W. G. Hoskins in Britain and J. B. Jackson in the United States evolved out of wartime experience and technique.[5] The devastated landscapes of continental Europe advertised the fragility of built form, spurring interest among people ever less certain of permanence.[6] "The city has never been so uncomfortable, so crowded, so tense," wrote E. B. White of New York in 1949. "The subtlest change in New York is something people don't speak much about but that is in everyone's mind. The city, for the first time in its long history, is destructible. A single flight of planes no bigger than a wedge of geese can quickly end this island fantasy, burn the towers, crumble the bridges, turn the underground passages into lethal chambers, cremate the millions."[7] World War II destruction and the subsequent threat of atomic warfare did not create the field of landscape history and the profession of historic preservation, but they urged them onward. If Tolkien is correct, if the last frame of Bloch's film is seen through the prism of childhood, it may be simply because the landscape of childhood is the last safe place, the refuge to which adults can never return.

A landscape, therefore, can certainly be what geographers or landscape historians so frequently say it is: a discrete area. It may also be something else, something defying photography. It may be a prism, or a pipe dream.

Prism

In autobiography lies the shadow of the prism, if not the prism itself. Often writers of autobiography stare backward at some well-remembered space, the details of which remain crisply clear. "In the foreground lay a marvelous confusion of steel rails, and in the midst of them, on a vast cinder-covered plain, the great brick roundhouse with its doors agape, revealing the snouts of locomotives undergoing surgery within," writes Russell Baker in *Growing Up*. "Between the mountains that cradled the yard there seemed to be thousands of freight cars stretching back so far toward Harpers Ferry that you could never see the end of them." Baker recalls the long approach to Brunswick, "as distant and romantic a place as I ever expected to see," the toll bridge with its loose boards, the "incredible spectacle" of an express passenger train "highballing toward glory," a department store, movie house, and drugstore. For the boy from the farm, Brunswick is a "great smoking conurbation," a "metropolis."[8] But for the town-bred boy, the country is equally exciting.

"I realized at once that we had been transported into a different world, far from the dust and heat we had left behind," muses Gerald Warner Brace in *Days That Were*. "It is always in my memory a pure summer morning with white sunlight glinting across the eastward bay, the waters all calm except for the long heave of the groundswell that reared and creamed along the rocky shores of the islands on our port hand, and the air is faintly redolent with the fragrance of fir and spruce." For Brace, entering Rockland Harbor aboard the *Bangor* or some other coastal steamer proves as memorable as arriving in Brunswick by flivver proves for Baker. Brace recalls every vacation "rediscovering" the town's "perfect harmony of function, where everything seemed to fit into a natural design," but clearly Baker savors the memory of the industrial order of the railroad town so unlike his own.[9]

Memories of Brunswick and Rockland Harbor endure so strongly simply because they originate in what the novelist-philosopher Walker Percy calls a "rotation," a successful escape from daily routine, something different. For students of landscape, however, it is the concept of repetition, not rotation, that proves of more lasting value in defining a landscape. "A repetition," argues Percy in *The Moviegoer*, "is the re-enactment of past experience toward the end of isolating the time segment which has lapsed in order that it, the lapsed time, can be savored of itself and without the usual adulteration of events that clog time like peanuts in brittle." The narrator of the novel provides an example: in glancing at a newspaper, he sees an advertisement identical to one he saw twenty years ago in a magazine on his father's desk. For a moment, "the events of the intervening twenty years were neutralized," and "there remained only time itself, like a yard of smooth peanut brittle."[10] The concept of repetition explicates the prismatic function of remembered childhood landscape.

Baker recalls his boyhood in the agricultural town of Morrisonville, "a poor place to prepare for a struggle with the twentieth century, but a delightful place to spend a childhood." He describes it almost in shorthand. "It was summer days drenched with sunlight, fields yellow with buttercups, and barn lofts sweet with hay. Clusters of purple grapes dangled from backyard arbors, lavender wisteria blossoms perfumed the air from the great vine enclosing the end of my grandmother's porch, and wild roses covered the fences."[11] Such memory remains strong because it is grounded in sensory experience, a range of sensory experience extending well beyond sight. Baker recalls sounds, smells, and textures, the heat of the sun on his skin. As Edith Cobb and other researchers have noted, children experience space through all senses, achieving, for a few years at least, a powerful intimacy.[12] Smell acquires an importance in childhood that it quickly loses, perhaps with the discovery of reading and the consequent emphasis on vision. Just as Brace recalls the fragrance of Maine coast conifers, Baker savors the lingering aroma of newly stacked hay and the perfume of wisteria. As sensitive adults know, smells trigger repetition more quickly, more directly than visual stimuli. The traveler alights from an airliner, smells the odor of the floor wax used in his kindergarten room, and is momentarily transported across time with awesome immediacy. Children—or some children, at least—know a landscape as they know the back of their hands, not only through sight but through the other senses as well.

Certainly rural and small-town children have the "back-of-the-hand" knowledge; so much autobiography springs from such roots. About urban children, the young inhabitants of cityscape, not landscape, the evidence is much less clear. City life may be qualitatively different for children; researchers have only begun to examine it.[13] In deciphering the mysteries of landscape, however, the role of childhood space in rural and small-town America acquires importance in proportion to the degree of repetition it engenders. The landscape of childhood can function exactly as Tolkien suggests, by becoming a prism; it can also evoke repetition.

Many scholars—and artists—agree on the importance of memory in the intellectual life of creative adults. Indeed Cobb suggests that powerful memories of childhood may be the roots of genius. Powerful memories, vibrant enough to frequently stimulate repetition, often involve landscape or interior space. "Memories are motionless, and the more securely they are fixed in space, the sounder they are," muses Gaston Bachelard in *The Poetics of Space*. "Each one of us, then, should speak of his roads, his crossroads, his roadside benches." After describing how powerfully his memories of a childhood attic inform his thinking, he continues, "each one of us should make a surveyor's map of his lost fields and meadows." Bachelard argues that such remembered space, whether attic or "familiar hill paths," is somehow "creative," that to visit it in dreams or daydreams is to partake again of its energy.[14]

Artists rarely deal explicitly with this issue. Even Wordsworth's "The Prelude; Or, Growth of a Poet's Mind" or Whitman's "There Was a Child Went Forth" are many-layered constructions, not simple autobiographical statements.[15] From time to time, of course, artists do write explicitly about the significance of memory of childhood landscape, and their work bears scrutiny, for some artists understand the prism.

Eudora Welty perhaps understands the prism better than most other writers of fiction. In *Place in Fiction*, Welty suggests that place can focus the eye of genius and so concentrate its energy. "Place absorbs our earliest notice and attention, it bestows on us our original awareness; and our critical powers spring up from the study of it and the growth of experience inside it," she asserts after insisting that place is the fundamental component of successful fiction. "Imagine *Swann's Way* laid in London, or *The Magic Mountain* in Spain, or *Green Mansions* in the Black Forest."[16] Throughout the slim book, she insists on the absolute importance of place in ordering all else in fiction, character, plot, period.

In *One Writer's Beginnings*, published twenty-seven years after *Place in Fiction*, Welty sharpens her argument, focusing on her own childhood. The first sentence of the book introduces the striking of clocks; the first paragraphs introduce the "elegant rush and click" of her brothers' electric train, the rocking chair that "ticked in rhythm" to the stories read aloud by her mother, the appearance of illustrations in her first storybooks. Early in *One Writer's Beginnings*, Welty suggests that "childhood's learning is made up of moments," and offers a catalogue of hers, beginning with sitting in a kindergarten circle of chairs and drawing three daffodils just picked in the schoolyard. The middle third of the book, "Learning to

See," lovingly describes a series of discrete landscapes, the landscapes that eventually appear, sometimes in altered shape, in her fiction.

By "a landscape," therefore, the artist may designate a concatenation of images remembered in the creative moment, indeed somehow merging with the creative moment, perhaps in a near-magical repetition. "But it was not until I began to write, as I seriously did only when I reached my twenties, that I found the world out there revealing," writes Welty near the close of her book, because "*memory* had become attached to seeing, love had added itself to discovery."[17] Welty italicizes the word *memory* because memory sparks the creative process; love receives no such emphasis.

Baker and Brace, Cobb, Bachelard, and Welty assert or imply the importance of remembered childhood landscapes in the creative process. For them, landscape can be a prism through which they look at present experience and space. But landscape may also be pipe dream, not prism, and the distinction is subtle.

Pipe Dream

Urbanization in the years following the Civil War prompted many Americans to savor the memory of rural childhood, of childhood in landscape abandoned for cityscape, or at least for the built environments of towns and villages. The last decades of the nineteenth century consequently witnessed the appearance—and acceptance—of nostalgic works concerning rural childhood. *Being a Boy,* an 1878 volume by Charles Dudley Warner, not only represents the genre, but hints at the genre that replaced it.

Being a Boy describes a farm boyhood to readers intimately familiar with such experience. Haying, weeding, woodchuck baiting, firewood toting, all the experiences of farm boys, Warner sites in an environment focused on house and barn and encompassing fields, dirt roads, and woodlots. And Warner is aware of repetition, of the immediacy with which an urbanite may be momentarily transported to another time and place. "But that which lives most vividly in his memory and most strongly draws him back to the New England hills is the aromatic sweet-fern; he likes to eat its spicy seeds, and to crush in his hands its fragrant leaves; their odor is the unique essence of New England."[18] No description of overgrown, half-wildered pasture or shaggy roadside prefaces the sweet fern sentence; Warner assumed an audience familiar with the habitat of the shrub.

Twenty years later no writer could so easily assume a once rural audience; indeed the turn-of-the-century era witnessed a new scorning of farmers, a scorning evident in words like *hayseed* or *clodhopper.*[19] No longer did farm boys grow up to prosper in professions other than farming: the new generation of male urbanites recalled a boyhood spent on the fringes of farming, in villages or small towns. Between 1880 and 1930, American authors turned out a staggering literature focused on small-town life; for many writers, the small town represented the best of all possible worlds, a place free of the new evils of corporate industrialism and massive urbanization, but for others it exemplified a sterile, conformist, dull existence useful only as a starting point for urban splendor.[20] Social and literary historians continue to examine the wonderfully rich, markedly divided literature ordered about small-town life, and they reach only rare accords.[21]

One window on late-nineteenth-century small-town life remains oddly unstudied. The small-town weekly newspaper, for all its biases and inaccuracies, endures as the voice of the moment. Consider, for example, the May 8, 1880, issue of the *Saturday Evening Journal* of Crawfordsville, Indiana. In 1880, the *Journal* had published for thirty-three years, apparently always weekly. The left-hand column of its front page consists entirely of advertisements for pianos, groceries (including nine varieties of coffee), ornamental poultry, and patent medicines. Five additional columns of fine type report stories involving the circus stranded by debt, changes of railroad schedules, the organizational meetings of an equal suffrage society and a baseball club, the twenty-five-dollar fine levied on a man convicted of attempted murder, an Illinois rapist reported to have given Crawfordsville as his address, a drunk rescued from a railroad track. Beyond the front page lies more news, similar in content and tone. Only a few back-pages advertisements for McCormick reapers and other field machinery aim at farmers. Clearly the *Saturday Evening Journal* is a town paper.

More than a century after its appearance, the May 8 issue fuels two interpretations of small-town life. On the one hand, it is evidence of a closely knit, friendly community; most articles emphasize names—everyone organizing the baseball club, for example—and demonstrate the essential quietude of Crawfordsville. Trouble comes from outside, and internal difficulty is immediately confronted, if not by bystanders, then by the town judge. On the other hand, the articles make easy the argument that the town is stuffy, nosy, and determined to maintain close scrutiny of all activity. For the landscape historian concerned with landscape perception and the role of childhood landscape perception in particular, however, the newspaper proves at first glance less than useful.

The *Saturday Evening Journal* reports almost nothing of landscape, indeed of space. To name a person or business is sufficient; scarcely one address intrudes in news stories or advertisements. Just as Warner assumes an audience familiar with the habitat of sweet fern, so the newspaper editor assumes a readership familiar with the town landscape. And with the exception of a brief story concerning school enrollment and another describing the abandonment of a baby by a city woman who arrived in Crawfordsville for that purpose, stories involving children are lacking too. Landscape and children deserve no notice by the editor because they are simply part of the scene.

What the *Saturday Evening Journal* provides so exquisitely is the official, adult view of things in Crawfordsville on May 8, 1880. To discover the other view, one need only examine the memories recorded decades later by boys who recalled the landscape and the escapades it hosted.

More than many writers, the cartoonist Clare Briggs scrutinized the childhood small-town landscape left behind by city residents. Throughout the first decades of the twentieth century, Briggs's sketches delighted readers of the New York *Tribune*.[22] Briggs recalled all the spatial details so lacking in small-town newspapers, and he knew exactly the thousand and one familiar places so vitally important in the lives of children. His sketches depict boys playing on railroad tracks, playing follow the leader through an orchard, playing in lumber yards, old barns, half-finished houses, on rooftops, and in a hundred other places. Now and then the boys tolerate the company of girls, but in the many sketches focused on swimming holes, girls—and women—are conspicuously absent. Briggs's drawings of boys running past haunted houses, dreaming of hopping freight trains, and taking a thousand shortcuts now and then include urban backdrops, but chiefly they memorialize the small-town landscape out of which so many New York City men had come, a landscape of boyhood, a landscape of innocence. They memorialize the landscape of Reedsburg, Wisconsin, the late-nineteenth-century boyhood home of Briggs himself.[23]

Autobiography savors the landscape of small-town boyhood. The most cursory survey of American autobiographical writing uncovers hundreds of twentieth-century books extolling the intricate world unreported by the *Saturday Evening Bulletin*. Now and then, as in Edmund G. Love's *The Situation in Flushing* and Loren Reid's *Hurry Home Wednesday: Growing up in a Small Missouri Town, 1905 to 1921,* most or all of the book focuses on the boyhood environment, but more often, only the first chapter records the timeless details of intimately known small-town space.[24]

"The golden age of childhood can be quite accurately fixed in time and place," begins a typical autobiography, Dean Acheson's 1965 *Morning and Noon.* "It reached its apex in the last decade of the nineteenth century and the first few years of the twentieth, before the plunge into a motor age and city life swept away the freedom of children and dogs, put them both on leashes and made them the organized prisoners of an adult world." Morning for Acheson is life in Middletown, Connecticut, in the 1890s, a place where "nothing presented a visible hazard to children," where "no one was run over," where only his mother fleetingly worried when she saw him hooking a ride on the ice wagon. As do so many other male authors, Acheson catalogues structures and spaces, some certainly noticed by local newspaper reporters, but many part of the invisible landscape of boys. "An open field of perhaps three acres" where the boys refought the Boer and Spanish-American wars, the dentist's "large, round bed of luxuriant canna plants" in which baseballs vanished, "the maze of backyards and alleys." Acheson recalls the importance of naming spots like the pond "too muddy and choked for bathing and appropriately called by 'Polliwog Pool'" and shaping and reshaping places like the three-acre field and the caves in the wooded hills just west of town. Acheson concludes that "life in the golden age was the very distillation of that place and time," a distillation whose essence, at least, lingered with him through the decades.[25] Safety, spatial freedom, the power of naming, the power of shaping and reshaping space, such are the attributes so frequently catalogued in male autobiography of the mid-twentieth century.

Only rarely does an intrepid observer long departed from his boyhood small-town landscape return and scrutinize contemporary space. Eric Sevareid's long, incredibly detailed 1956 *Collier's* account of his own return to a small North Dakota town illustrates so forcibly the shock of confrontation and the meaning of memories strong enough to provoke repetition.

Sevareid catalogues smells, sounds, and a wealth of boyhood spaces remembered clearly enough and describes the strain of finding some smells and sounds absent, and many once familiar, once cherished spaces changed beyond recognition by the building of a small office building or the demolition of the town water tank. At first profoundly disappointed— *disenchanted* perhaps designates better his melancholy shock—he gradually discovers some boyhood elements, a faded lumberyard fence, for example, still unchanged, and recognizes in the movements of boys the existence of an equally rich space. Eventually, Sevareid uses a photographic metaphor to explain his new perception: "I could run through the film exposed this day of 1955 and see it all, the hills, the rapids, the bridge and the house and the streets, all of it as it *is,* in black and white, exact, life-size, no more, no less. Then I could run off the old, eternal negative, larger than life, in its full color and glory—the same scenes and trees and faces—and there was no fading or blur of double exposure." He emphasizes the photographic nature of memory: "I had both reels now, sealed in separate cans, and I knew I could keep them both, as long as I lived." What then of Marc Bloch's notion, of the historian unwinding the film backward in order to study the rural landscape of time past? Sevareid answers the question, albeit obliquely.

"In stark clarity I remember running away from home at the age of four, crossing the Soo Line tracks, trudging up South Hill and then, suddenly confronting the sky and the plains; I was lost, alone in the eternity of nothingness." In the era of his boyhood, towns had definite edges, edges of genuine significance to the people who lived "in town" and to those farmers or ranchers who lived "outside." In walking back from "outside," the adult Sevareid recalls the one terrifying incident of brutality of his childhood, the senseless, deliberate shooting by a farmhand of his friend's dog. As he recounts burying the dog in a weed patch, "across from our island," Sevareid enters the town, and his essay immediately changes subject and tone. With the prairie at his back, the adult Sevareid "felt for a moment, faintly, the joy this passage had brought me at each re-entry into the oasis with its familiar shapes and smells and sounds, its thousand secret delights, cool water and shade, and home and safety." And suddenly, he pierces the veil of mystery that shrouds so many autobiography first chapters. "I understood then why I had loved it so and loved its memory always; it was, simply, *home*—and *all* of it home, not just the house, but all the town. That is why childhood in the small towns is different from childhood in the city. Everything is home." Walking the old path across the edge of town, turning his back on the place where he had witnessed evil, he perceives the childhood reality of town as oasis, as refuge, as home.

"We are all alike, we graying American men who were boys in the small towns of our country," he muses. "We have a kind of inverted snobbery of recollection and we are sometimes bores about it, but that's the way it is."[26] Of course, for Sevareid, for Acheson, for Baker, the way was not permanent residence; the way led to the corners of the earth, to success not only in great cities but in national and international arenas. For such men, the landscape of small-town boyhood is in Robert Frost's terminology, a fixing point, a place in which later life is moored, however long the mooring line.[27]

For others, for many according to the most recent federal census, the landscape of small-town boyhood is a contemporary, accessible place. In *Return to Main Street: A Journey to Another America,* Nancy Eberle chronicles and analyzes her family's move from a Chicago suburb to a rural small town. Before its appearance in 1982, portions of the text appeared as a long article in *McCall's* magazine in which Eberle argues that small-town life redirected her two sons toward richer, simpler living. *McCall's* and so many other so-called "women's magazines" focused on middle-class audiences have lately emphasized child-rearing issues. Eberle, in her article and subsequent book, argues explicitly that small-town physical and social environments strengthen both individual and family character. "It's never wondering if storekeepers think you're a shoplifter and never being asked to produce your driver's license," she asserts in her final chapter. "It's a swimming hole, a haunted house, a Halloween Parade, and a nickname."[28] *Return to Main Street* emphasizes not only the physical and social setting so casually presented in the May 8, 1880, *Saturday Evening Journal* but that of the cartoons of Clare Briggs. Eberle delicately balances the adult view of small-town life—and space—with that of her sons, the stewards of shortcuts and swimming holes.

In her first chapter, entitled "Main Street," Eberle begins her balancing with a command: "Picture a primitive." She then describes the buildings and spaces along Main Street, the residential streets adjacent to them, the farms at the edge of town. For Eberle, it *is* primitive, and as her argument evolves, one learns that it is Edenic. Galena, Illinois, in 1982 is prelapsarian America, the Republic before the fall, the United States of America before urbanization, industrialization, Viet Nam, drug abuse, divorce, even before the nuclear bomb. In her last chapter, the balance kept poised, Eberle asserts that "quality of life" is increasingly important to thoughtful men and women, often more important than social status, salary, professional advancement. And Eberle grounds her argument, her balancing of adult and child view, in space, in the landscape of small-town America.

Eberle is no lonesome soothsayer. As she correctly points out, periodicals like *Mother Earth News* now boast circulations over the one million mark, suggesting that even many urban and suburban families feel a tug toward rural living and small-town residence. The tug is more than emotional. Harley E. Johansen and Glenn V. Fuguitt demonstrate in their 1984 study, *The Changing Rural Village in America: Demographic and Economic Trends Since 1950,* that the growth rate of small towns in the countryside has surpassed that of suburbs and metropolitan regions.[29] As the 1960 census hinted, as the 1980 census proves, something important, something massive, now looms in the American psychological horizon. A geographic shift of staggering implications is under way. As Sevareid suggested in the middle 1950s, the small town remains the American home, the cultural cradle. And if the statistics indicate anything, they indicate that many Americans are going home.

Perhaps they go for the reasons Eberle, Johansen, and Fuguitt catalogue: fear of urban crime, distrust of new forms of community, disgust with unhealthful air, water, and food. Perhaps they go for such reasons and for many more. But perhaps they also go for a more elemental reason. Perhaps they search for the landscape of childhood.

If they go to rediscover the full-color photograph Sevareid describes, to experience not only fleeting repetition but permanent repetition, to restore themselves with the energy of place about which Welty orders her fiction and autobiography, to experience a place known in the years before they recognized that the atomic bomb destroys all, then indeed they are in search of the landscape described not in the *Saturday Evening Journal* but in the nostalgias of the heart. One popular prime-time television series, *The Waltons,* drew energy from this concatenation of thought and feeling, each show concluding with an epigraph extolling not only childhood security but the importance of childhood space enduring into adulthood: "Forty years have passed, but that house still stands, and the solace and love that we knew there as children still sustain us." Solace and love, important as they are, gather strength from the *still existing house,* the physical manifestation of family life.

What underlies the power of boyhood landscape, what attracts so many men—and women—to the small town today, is not only the memory so strong it engenders repetition. It is the recapturing of the right, the freedom to shape space. The small-town boyhood landscape is not simply enjoyed by boys. It is maintained and changed by boys. As Clare Briggs depicted in so many of his sketches, as so many graying men remember in their autobiographies, the small-town landscape permitted and rewarded shaping. Boys felled trees to make rafts, cut saplings to lace together as huts or duck blinds, begged slabs from the sawmill to make tree houses so high in the white pines that even the lighthouse could be seen through field glasses borrowed from fathers' dresser drawers. No one, not even the Highway Surveyor, considered the field-stones rolled into the bog dam spillway an act of vandalism; no one, not even the Coast Guard crew chugging seaward, looked askance at the boys laboriously pounding a newly cut cedar tree into the salt marsh to make a mooring bollard at The Landing. Men who had long ago shaped the boyhood places expected new generations of boys to shape them, and so long as real estate developers stayed clear of the abandoned, half-forgotten acreage, the boys did shape space and do so still.

And as long as bits and pieces of the boyhood landscape endure, grown men can visit them, sometimes in the panting rush of the volunteer fire department, grunting under the weight of hoses, "Used to come here when I was a kid, huge tangle of barbed wire under those wild grapevines, stay left"; sometimes they come alone, seeking the solace of innocence. For that landscape is, as Sevareid so accurately saw, home, all

Unchanged over the decades, this landing remains a muddy opening in salt marsh, its wharf a couple of planks, its promise an estuary opening on the North Atlantic and the South Seas.

of it is home, for it flows into back yards and barnyards, to back steps and screen doors. And home, as Frost discerned in 1914 in a poem entitled "The Death of the Hired Man," is indeed special: "'Home is the place where, when you have to go there,'" one of the poem's narrators says; "'They have to take you in.'"[30] The landscape of boyhood, if it endures in an age of suburbanization, condominium development, and shopping malls, is perceived by many grown men as Sevareid perceived it, as being somehow obligated to give solace, rest, repetition. And even when modernization has obliterated it, it can survive as a prism or even as a pipe dream, changing the perceptions of grown men or luring others, with their families, back to small towns.

Understanding landscape must, I think, involve coming to terms with the power of boyhood landscape. Tolkien is correct: words like *river, hill, wooded valley, salt marsh* mean in part the visual image adults first associated with them. Consider the words *steam shovel.* Now used by nearly everyone to designate diesel-powered equipment, they carry special meaning in my little coastal town. For decades, boys old enough to explore the abandoned sandpits bordering the cranberry bogs—not The Bog—have found The Steam Shovel, a derelict diesel-engined vestige of long vanished activity, a derelict still standing watch over sandpits growing up in chokecherry and now green with sweet fern. For many Norwell men in their late thirties, now graying and wondering about their own children, *steam shovel* evokes memories of The Steam Shovel, of races ending at it, of precarious balancing on its outstretched boom, of shaping the abandoned sandpits and bogs around it, of living in an innocent summer afternoon free of The Bomb, of living at home.

Notes

1. New Haven: Yale University Press, 1982, pp. 3–7, 339–346, and passim.
2. See, for example, Yi-Fu Tuan, *Topophilia: A Study of Environmental Perception, Attitudes*

and Values (Englewood Cliffs, NJ: Prentice-Hall, 1974); D. W. Meinig, ed., *The Interpretation of Ordinary Landscapes: Geographical Essays* (New York: Oxford University Press, 1979), especially Peirce F. Lewis, "Axioms for Reading the Landscape: Some Guides to the American Scene," pp. 11–32; Annette Kolodny, *The Land Before Her: Fantasy and Experience of the American Frontiers, 1630–1860* (Chapel Hill: University of North Carolina Press, 1984); and Tadahiko Higuchi, *The Visual and Spatial Structure of Landscapes,* translated by Charles S. Terry (Cambridge, MA: MIT Press, 1983).

3. Translated by Peter Putnam (New York: Random House, 1953; reprinted 1964), pp. 46–47.

4. Boston: Houghton Mifflin, 1965, p. 80.

5. Jackson is especially eloquent about the role of war; see "Landscape as Seen by the Military," *Discovering the Vernacular Landscape* (New Haven: Yale University Press, 1984), pp. 133–137.

6. World War I had, perhaps, a similar effect, at least on Edith Wharton; see her *A Backward Glance* (New York: Appleton-Century, 1934), pp. 362–363.

7. "Here is New York," *Perspectives USA* (Summer 1953), p. 44.

8. New York: Congdon & Weed, 1982, pp. 50–53.

9. New York: Norton, 1976, pp. 66–67.

10. New York: Avon, 1960; reprinted 1980, p. 68.

11. *Ibid.,* p. 42.

12. *The Ecology of Imagination in Childhood* (New York: Columbia University Press, 1977).

13. See, for example, Kevin Lynch, *Growing Up in Cities* (Cambridge, MA: MIT Press, 1977); Irwin Altman and Joachim F. Wohlwill, *Children and the Environment* (New York: Plenum, 1978); George Butterworth, *The Child's Representation of the World* (New York: Plenum, 1977); and Charles Zerner, "The Street Hearth of Play: Children in the City," *Landscape* (Autumn 1977), pp. 19–30.

14. Translated by Maria Jolas (Boston: Beacon, 1958; reprinted 1962), pp. 10–12.

15. William Wordsworth, *Complete Poetical Works* (Boston: Houghton Mifflin, 1904), pp. 124–222; Walt Whitman, *Leaves of Grass* (New York: Random House, 1950), p. 287. One critic has discerned the role of childhood space in the poetry of Hart Crane; see Sherman Paul, *Hart's Bridge* (Urbana: University of Illinois Press, 1972).

16. New York: House of Books, 1957, n.p.

17. Cambridge, MA: Harvard University Press, 1984, pp. 3–7, 10, 76, and passim.

18. Boston: Osgood, 1878, p. 177.

19. Eric F. Goldman, *Rendezvous with Destiny: A History of Modern American Reform* (New York: Vintage, 1956), pp. 30–31; see also Warner Berthoff, *The Ferment of Realism: American Literature, 1884–1919* (New York: Free Press, 1965). The place of farm boyhood in the American spatial and cultural imagination deserves separate, detailed study.

20. For an introduction to the arguments still swirling about small-town life, see Carl Van Doren, *The American Novel* (New York: Macmillan, 1920), pp. 294–302 and *Contemporary American Novelists, 1900–1920* (New York: Macmillan, 1922), pp. 146–171; Richard Lingeman, *Small Town America: A Narrative History, 1620 to the Present* (Boston: Houghton Mifflin, 1980); Anthony Channell Hilfer, *The Revolt from the Village, 1915 to 1930* (Chapel Hill: University of North Carolina Press, 1969); and John R. Stilgoe, *Metropolitan Corridor: Railroads and the American Scene* (New Haven: Yale University Press, 1983), pp. 191–220. One of the most thought-provoking studies is John A. Jakle, *The American Small Town: Twentieth-Century Place Images* (Hamden, CT: Shoe String, 1981).

21. Since very few farm children grew up to be writers, there is a consequent dearth of written evidence explicating the farm child's view of the town, however, something frequently overlooked by literary historians.

22. After his death, a multivolume memorial edition of his drawings was published: *When A Feller Needs a Friend* (New York: Wise, 1930); *That Guiltiest Feeling* (New York: Wise, 1930); *The Days of Real Sport* (New York: Wise, 1930); et al.

23. *National Cyclopaedia of American Biography*, XXIII, p. 317.

24. Respectively, New York: Harper, 1965; and Columbia: University of Missouri Press, 1978. To the best of my knowledge, there is no parallel development of autobiographies by women who grew up in small towns.

25. Boston: Houghton Mifflin, 1965, pp. 1–24.

26. May 11, 1956, pp. 38–68.

27. "Take Something Like a Star," *Poetry* (New York: Holt, Rinehart & Winston, 1969), p. 403.

28. New York: Norton, 1982, pp. 19–23, 214–224, and passim; portions of the book appeared as "A Good Place to Live," *McCall's* (October 1981), pp. 127–131. When Eberle finished the book, her daughter was only three years old and not roaming the small-town landscape (pp. 206–207).

29. Cambridge, MA: Ballinger, 1984.

30. *Poetry,* p. 38.

THE DEEP PAST AND IMAGES

At Halloween Americans carve pumpkins into effigies of Jack-of-the-lantern, the goblin who pulls up boundary markers, creating confusion in landscape and disputes among neighbors. Few carvers know why they hollow a pumpkin, and fewer still seem inclined to ask. Almost all memory of the goblin, indeed of any goblin, has long vanished.

Centuries ago British peasants carved turnips, and even now a few Americans hollow out a turnip deliberately grown monstrous in a neglected corner of the vegetable garden. Far larger than grocery-store turnips, the craggy turnip replete with leafy stem unsettles children trick-or-treating. The flickering candle inside transforms the vegetable into a lantern, but the shape of the turnip jars. Unlike the pumpkin, the turnip seems more like a pointed head. Samhain, All Hallows Eve, and pagan understanding that boundary markers keep peace among landowners swirl beneath nylon costumes, giggles, and candy. And as children leave they glance back at the turnip.

Landscape evolves slowly. It constricts even powerful people. Once shaped into rough form, landscape begins to shape its makers and maintainers. Kings and city councilors find it difficult to realign a road, and everyone finds it tricky to imagine a landscape without roads and paths. Agriculture biases most casual thinking about landscape. After the trees are felled and the stumps uprooted in the effort western Canadians still call *making land,* agriculturists plow the soil and plant crops in the new-made fields. Well into the Middle Ages, European and Asian peasants lived in villages surrounded by fields, each concatenation of structure and space functioning roughly free of larger concerns. Only the narrow track through the forest beyond the fields linked villagers with other villagers, but ordinarily only peddlers, carters, and other wayfarers moved along the rutted road that drifted almost free of government control.

Nowadays for most American adults, landscape consists of nodes, usually the single-family house on a discrete lot of land, sometimes a condominium in a cluster, often a neighborhood focused on a school, church, and grocery store, perhaps a small mall, and a tracery of roads connecting to other nodes and to interstate highways. Nodes focus the energy and affection of most Americans. Comparatively few devote most of their time to lines, but railroad and towboat crews, long-distance truck drivers, and other professional wayfarers remain subtly different. They know junctions and bends and edges, truck stops and motels, diners, toll booths, and bridges, and most of the time they are passing through, but are neither in nor of, one node after another. They suspect most Americans of geographical dullness, if not worse. Most node-focused Americans suspect them of lacking roots and perhaps values involving front lawns, fences, porches, and backyards, and they appoint highway troopers to police them.

The dichotomy between the landscape views of British, African American, and Spanish colonists of what is now the United States and the French view of the continent as a cluster of islands linked by rivers endures. So does the agrarian origin of so much landscape aesthetics embraced by the former group of colonists. The aesthetics of nineteenth-century landscape painting originate both in an intellectual effort to order the spatial juxtaposition of rivers and fields and villages and in an emotional enterprise aimed at composing on canvas something that celebrates and reinforces civil order. Viewing landscape painting embroils the contemporary museum visitor in long-ago ideological conflict focused on wilderness and shaped land.

The backyard gardener spading up soil in springtime unwittingly shares in the traditional riches of land and landscape evaluation. Ascertaining color and texture of soil means more than a trip to the garden-supply store for fertilizer, or a long-term effort to enrich the ground with compost. It thrusts contemporary gardeners not only into an ancient alchemy that transforms specific types of wilderness but into specific types of landscape. It nudges the gardener toward the very foundations of landscape aesthetics.

Amateur painters and photographers still seek the supposedly traditional agricultural, nodal landscapes medieval peasants valued so deeply. Their seeking produces the restlessness that nowadays characterizes all sorts of efforts at landscape planning and design, particularly those aimed at controlling urban sprawl.

LANDSCHAFT AND LINEARITY
Two Archetypes of Landscape

Older Americans dislike the man-made environment. They call it monotonous, homogenized, commercial, or chaotic. Their adjectives presume a standard of judgment with which contemporary "built space" is compared and found vexingly inferior. The standard is a remembered spatial order so complete and so perfectly reflective of the good life that it survives as an unqualified archetype in the national memory.[1] It is the primary essence of landscape.

Landscape is a slippery word. In the sixteenth century *landschaft* defined a compact territory extensively modified by permanent inhabitants. A *landschaft* was not a town exactly, nor a manor or a village, but a self-sufficient, fully-realized construct of fields, paths, and clustered structures encircled by unimproved forest or marsh.[2] The modern word is transformed, abused in phrases like "the landscape of injustice," which deny its ancient relations to land and to shape.[3] Vestiges of the archetypal *landschaft* endured well into the nineteenth century across Europe and the United Sates, and while the form no longer orders space or language, its memory controls men's imaginations.

Landschaft (or *landskap* or *landschap*) made perfect sense to Germans, Danes, and Dutchmen accustomed to compact, discrete space, but seventeenth-century English merchants and sea captains smitten with Dutch scenery painting took home only its sound. Thus, *landschap* entered the English language as *landskip,* and referred at first only to the pictures imported from Holland. Very quickly, though, it was used in new ways. Soon it defined any natural or rural view that approximated those painted by the Dutch, but by mid-eighteenth century signified the ornamental gardens of great country estates. Gardeners, reshaping fields and woods according to picturesque standards, made it a verb, and artists made it a synonym for *depict*.[4] Implicit in every definition is the old-country awareness of knowable space, however, and the contemporary critic reviewing "the moral and intellectual landscape" vaguely apprehends it.[5]

Landscape endures and thrives because the English language is par-

"Landschaft and Linearity: Two Archetypes of Landscape" appeared in *Environmental Review* 4 (Autumn 1980): 3–17, copyright by the American Society of Environmental History.

ticularly unsuited to topographical discussion. In the early years of the seventeenth century, the English countryside changed so dramatically that men abandoned their traditional spatial vocabulary. *Vill,* for example, once defined something like a *landschaft,* a collection of dwellings and other structures crowded together within a circle of pastures, meadows, planting fields, and woodlots. Like the Anglo-Saxon *tithing,* and like *landschaft,* it connoted the inhabitants of the place and their obligations to one another and to their land. By 1650, however, *village* had supplanted *vill;* the encircling ring of improved land and its involved maintenance were far less important to men moving freely from one cluster of dwellings to the next. Like *hamlet* and *town, village* soon defined only the built-up nucleus, not the surrounding fields or the intricate web of interpersonal association implicit in earlier arrangements of space.[6] Traders and other travelers thought in spaces larger than vills, and seized on *landscape* to define their vague perceptions of places now dependent on roads and long-distance commerce. In their eyes, a landscape was an extensive, cultivated expanse dotted with villages, towns, and cities; it was best seen from a mountain top, and best depicted in a painting or on a map, not in prose.

Travelers found it difficult to describe landscapes because their view was either too broad or too narrow. From a distance many structures and land forms seemed insignificant; up close they were extremely complex. Eighteenth- and nineteenth-century spatial description falls into two categories: the sweeping catalogs of large regions written by observers confined to well-traveled roads, and the intimate depictions of compact places penned by residents or long-time visitors.[7] Until late in the nineteenth century, the built environment easily accommodated the two schools of observers and descriptions multiplied. But suddenly, at the close of the century in the United States and a few years later in Britain, the rate of spatial change accelerated and observers learned that old perceptions no longer applied to space transformed beyond comprehension.

Henry James made the discovery for himself, when he returned to the United States in 1904, after an absence of twenty-four years. Twelve months later he left for England, defeated among other things by space he no longer recognized. Despite his misgivings, he published *The American Scene* in 1906.[8] It is a cryptic travelogue, filled with misadventure, disappointment, and disgust. Unwittingly, he had arrived in the United States near the end of a forty-year transformation. The nation was changing from a pedestrian to a vehicular orientation.

The American Scene is crucial because it identifies the transformation. James did not understand the changes he described, but his book enumerates the most significant of the time, and orders them against a backdrop of traditional space. James oscillated between backward areas and the most up-to-date cities, between Berkshire farmhouses and Manhattan hotels. He landed in New York, was astonished by its skyline, and fled after several days to the quiet of New Hampshire, Cape Cod, and Cambridge. From there, his wits collected, he returned to New York and plunged into the Bowery, Lower East Side, and Manhattan, striving to experience a city wholly reshaped. After several exhausting weeks he retreated to the unchanged stillness of Newport, and after a second rest set out for Boston. His last exploratory thrust into the booming resort areas of Florida forced him home to England for a final recuperation. American space overtaxed James's powers of observation and ability to control composition. In the end, description and analysis proved impossible.

James was secure in compact places—the abandoned farms of New Hampshire or the fishing villages of Cape Cod or the small towns of the Berkshires, each with its elm-lined street, white-painted houses, and quiet. In such places, he remarked, "the scene is everywhere the same; whereby tribute is always ready and easy, and you are spared all shocks of surprise and saved any extravagance of discrimination." Harvard College drowsing in the early September sunlight, Newport deserted in off-season, George Washington's monumental Mount Vernon, and "the old Spanish Fort, the empty, sunny, grassy shell by the low pale shore" of Saint Augustine are all pedestrian places. James walked about them, around their perimeters as was his custom with European towns, then strolled through them, pausing to compare present with past, or to marvel at details missed on earlier, less leisurely visits.[9] Such places, for good or bad, were "finished," and acquiring a thin patina of time.

No such patina concealed the new roughness of urban and suburban form; most of *The American Scene* documents James's excursions in understanding it. New York was like a pin cushion, he noted after his return from New England, studded with skyscrapers "grossly tall and grossly ugly" that overpowered churches and funneled winter gales along streets jammed with electric cars. The trolleys, "cars of Juggernaut in their power to squash," terrified him, and in a moment of desperation he determined that they were "all there measurably *is* of the American scene."[10] They prevented his crossing streets, surrounded monuments, destroyed any hope of quiet, and at times kept him from entering his hotel. New Yorkers skirted death at their fenders and fought for life at their doors as frantically as they did at elevators. Wherever he stopped, James was jostled and shoved or warned by gongs and by shouts to get out of the way. In New York he took refuge in Central Park, in Boston he rediscovered the twisting, peaceful residential streets of Beacon Hill, and in Baltimore he explored the hall and court of Johns Hopkins University, searching constantly for pedestrian islands in vehicular space. Bridges, especially New York's bridges, "the horizontal sheaths of pistons working at high pressure day and night, and subject, one apprehends with perhaps inconsistent gloom, to certain, to fantastic, to merciless multiplication," are his symbol of urban form and existence.[11] He could not walk in the way of pistons and view space at his leisure.

So James began touring on wheels. Much of New York he saw from inside trolleys, and elsewhere he traveled by train and by automobile, at first fascinated by "the great loops thrown out by the lasso of observation from the wonder-working motor car." But soon he tired of his moving vantage point, and delighted in discovering a small village while his automobile underwent repair. Most of the time, however, he traveled by train, "the heavy, dominant American train" which he said made the countryside exist for it and whose great terminals made the cities' only portals. Railroad schedules determined his itinerary; one told him when he must desert Salem, and another allowed him only fifteen minutes in which to glimpse Savannah. In the small hours of the morning, during a two-hour layover in a deserted Charleston station, James set out to examine the workings and meaning of the great junction. He turned back, convinced in the gloom lit only by signal lamps and flaring fireboxes that the wisest course was "to stand huddled just where one was."[12] Later, as he raced south in a well-upholstered Pullman, he was suddenly aware that he could not recall when Florida began, so uniform was his highspeed view. Caught between two kinds of space, and between two ways of seeing, James determined to go home.

Unlike earlier observers of the United States, James was forced to travel at high speed, and to interpret space ordered about lines of transportation. Astute as they are, the commentaries of his predecessors were of little use. Timothy Dwight's four-volume *Travels in New England and New York,* for example, is superb topographical analysis. At the beginning of the nineteenth century, however, its author moved almost as slowly as seventeenth-century English travelers, walking his horse while he scrutinized his environs, and discovering local history each evening at an inn. Dwight paused to inquire into crops and wildflowers, to examine soils and industries and ferries, and to question fellow travelers about the road ahead. He gazed from hilltops on towns below, criticizing their dwellings and street arrangements, and enjoying countless moments of "profound contemplation and playfulness of mind."[13] Fifty years later, Frederick Law Olmsted explored the slave-states: like Dwight, he rode horseback, following back roads and trails into the center of the South, talking with storekeepers, teamsters, and children, and puzzling over structures and fields.[14] For Dwight and Olmsted, travel was a succession of minor discoveries and observations for deciphering vague maps, and of stopping again and again to examine clusters of dwellings or a new mill or a run-down farm. Olmsted's volumes, like Dwight's, chronicle self-paced travel in knowable space, the essence of the Central Park experience Olmsted devised for New York City. Travel according to his own terms, in space immediately intelligible, was denied to James; later writers such as Post, Dreiser, and Stewart, adopted automobile speed and perspective as unthinkingly as Dwight and Olmsted had adopted theirs.[15] *The American Scene,* then, perceives pedestrian and vehicular space through a paradigm congruent with neither.

Pedestrian Space

Smallness was both absolute and subjective in the typical medieval *landschaft.* The twelve- to fifteen-square-mile area was home to perhaps three hundred people satisfying almost all of their own wants. Every rod of ground was fully recognized as vitally important. Meadows, arable fields, and pastures were precisely divided and bounded by paths and balks, and everyone spoke a vocabulary of landmarks.[16] Space was symbol. A family's dwelling bespoke economic and social status as clearly as its fields expressed skill at husbandry; every spot was invested with memory or some other significance—the copse where someone saw the Devil, the corner where the cart collapsed, the hill struck twice by lightning long ago. To move about the *landschaft* was to move within symbol, to be always certain of past and present circumstance. The laborer, woodcutter, baker, and husbandman understood each other's responsibilities and associated each responsibility with a specific place. By place, men understood social position and spatial location: the woodcutter's place was hewing timber in the woodlots, not directing apprentices at the bakeshop. Cycles of birth, marriage, and death, of sowing and reaping, of building and rebuilding all found expression in space.

Individuals were subordinate to the group. Nowhere was the subordination more clearly objectified than in the common fields. Here fields of wheat, rye, or barley were plowed at the same time, planted to the same crop, harvested at the same moment, and opened at the same time to all livestock. Each householder owned one or more "strips" in the fields and was entitled to their produce, but he accepted the will of the majority concerning their care.[17] Common-field farming was never innovative. Most husbandmen distrusted new seeds and plowing techniques, and forbade would-be innovators from experiments that might destroy the harvest of all. The most respected husbandman was he who best kept the corporate tradition, not he who hoped to fence off his strip from his neighbors' and selfishly experiment.

Inside the ring of fields stood a cluster of houses and perhaps a church, all focused about a roland, that aged tree, hewn shaft, or market cross that objectified the idea of *axis mundi,* the armature about which *landschaft* lived revolved. But each dwelling was of extraordinary importance too, for it alone confirmed status and rights. No one might reside in the *landschaft* unless he was a householder or under a householder's oversight, and no one might possess strips in the common fields unless he also owned all or part of a dwelling.[18] House-building, and admission to the *landschaft,* were strictly controlled. If the fields could be expanded and greater harvests obtained from them, new houses might be authorized for the younger sons who would not inherit their parents' dwellings and strips. Forests and swamps made any expansion difficult while slow illnesses kept populations almost static. New houses and new householders were few: every *landschaft* grew slowly. Like the gypsies, discharged soldiers, and other suspect vagrants of European folktales, drifters were rarely invited to settle, but instead urged onward, away from the place of settled men.

Houses were hardly private. In fact, privacy was scarcely understood as a concept, let alone a right. Dwellings were crowded with extended families, and rooms served many purposes. Gossip made much indoor activity known outside as well, and priests and elders were empowered and expected to enter dwellings unannounced if they suspected wrongdoing. Almost every resident of a *landschaft* accepted community values and standards as his own, however, and while domestic mischief and sin were common, major offenses were few. For such misdeeds the *landschaft* had a terrible punishment. It banished the offender and broke down his dwelling, erasing all memory of him and his crime.[19] Broken men were few in medieval Europe, but they testified to the power of group values. Position in society and in space was the essence of individual identity, and banishment and house-breaking destroyed identity completely.

Chaos surrounded every *landschaft,* whether or not the forest actually enclosed the fields and dwellings. Away from the *landschaft* individual identity diminished, and men were thought to succumb to the lure of the wild. Woodcutters, huntsmen, and others who moved between ordered space and pathless wilderness were slightly distrusted by their stay-at-home neighbors. Many folktales begin at a woodcutter's hut, already removed from strict community control on the edge of a forest. Children and young women enter the forest and discover good or evil according to their character.[20] Helpful, obedient, self-sacrificing children, those who have internalized group values, discover piles of silver, magic herbs, or other treasure after triumphing over witches and robbers, and return to the *landschaft* wiser and richer. Selfish, misbehaved children and beautiful but self-centered maidens find ashes, dragons, and sex fiends, and are punished or destroyed, or else join the evildoers of the wild. In the folk imagination, the *landschaft* is more than the objective correlative of order and safety. It is a continuous reinforcement of character, and its inhabitants desert it with trepidation.

Sometimes, of course, chaos intruded upon order. Any field left untilled grew up at once in weeds and brush, and wolves and wild boars sometimes foraged among sheepfolds and fields, occasionally slaying a husbandman trudging home after dusk. But it was the human evil of the forest that people feared most, the eldritch robbers and traders and wanderers who practiced goety, rape, and theft, and who infected children with new ideas. Out of the forest came every evil, from sorcerers to plague, against all of which the *landschaft* was almost powerless. The order of the *landschaft* was never secure, no matter how strictly enforced from within. External disruption was always imminent.

The *landschaft* was, therefore, the spatial expression of identity, order, and value, a kind of collective self-portrait of small-group life, and a great instrument of social control. Like an island, the *landschaft* was a defined place, across which a privileged traveler walked without hesitation and without danger.

Roadsides

The integrity of the *landschaft* was broken by princes and kings intent on consolidating their rule. From the fifteenth century onward, at first hesitantly and then decisively, they made forests and other wastes safe for travel. Pacification was far more advanced in some realms than in others by the end of the sixteenth century, but everywhere alert men sensed new possibilities for adventure and profit.[21] The new concern for roads, and for exploration, developed as slowly as political unity and long-distance overland commerce, but eventually it entered the popular imagination as *strassenromantik*. The romance of the road found expression in ballads and tales and, most importantly, in wandering. The newly safe roads which passed from *landschaft* into forest promised excitement and fortune. Folktale after folktale begins with a ploughman or tradesman accosted from the highway by a traveler and enticed into adventure. The highway clearly expressed an authority beyond that of *landschaft* elders. It announced the rule of kings and promised royal protection from danger. Highway robbery was infinitely more than theft by violence—it was an affront to royal power and a disruption of the new order of the road. By any name, *camino real, Richtstrasse,* or king's highway, the long-distance road was a new sort of space.

Unlike the path between fields or woodlots or dwellings, which belonged to its abutters and was limited in use, the road belonged to the wayfarer and to the king. Each *landschaft* along the highway was commanded to maintain its share of roadbed in order that armies and couriers—and merchants—might not be delayed.[22] Self-sufficiency vanished as capitals and large towns drained surrounding regions of talent and produce and flooded local markets with fashionable goods. Roads became ever more important to the places they linked, for along them flowed wealth and ideas greater than those of any one *landschaft.* Local values contested with those of the road; the husbandman prized honesty, but the peddler prized sharpness. As roads grew safer and more passable, carts and wagons and finally coaches replaced pack horses, and the flow of wealth and information increased further still. No longer was the traveler an oddity to be welcomed or turned away; he became an expected figure in—but not of—every *landschaft.*

Professional travelers—merchants, peddlers, carters—had only the road as home, although they often claimed residence in some place along it. They had a new view of the countryside, for they saw only what was visible from the road and they used only what was immediately accessible from it. Increasingly, the roadside was adapted to their needs. First came inns and stables for pack animals, then corrals for driven herds, and then bridges and toll houses and eventually directional signs and mileposts. It was at this time that *village* replaced *vill* because fields and woodlots and responsibility for them interested travelers far less than a good inn and perhaps a blacksmith shop. Eventually, the *landschaft* surrendered its identity to the highway, and was known not as a unique place but as one of many settlements along a well-known road.

For the sedentary inhabitants of the *landschaft,* the wayfarer was personified *other,* against which they evaluated themselves. In the days when roads were so few that traveling was almost unknown—and German folktales collected at mid-nineteenth century mention such times—adolescents had only their parents and adult neighbors as models. The absence of different values and exotic behavior made internalization of *landschaft* mores simple. Only when travelers provided new standards to any youth astute enough to linger about the inn or stableyard after nightfall did socialization break down. Travelers were anonymous, and their larger experience was approached with a mixture of distrust and deference by adults and adolescents alike. The road introduced the kind of marked change in interpersonal relationships which one usually associ-

Away from any *land-schaft*, especially in forest, highway robbery became a fearsome possibility, as this seventeenth-century image, found interleaved in an eighteenth-century dictionary, suggests.

ated only with city life.[23] Strangers met knowing they might not meet again, judged each other as types according to dress and occupation, and talked of matters of importance only among themselves. It was a rare carter who was deeply interested in the state of the crops, and a rarer husbandman who cared about the weak bridge thirty miles to the east. But traveler and native alike were interested in conversation, the traveler to pass his evening and the native to learn something of the larger world. While at first no one noticed, the web of corporate ties connoted by *landschaft* and *vill* was torn.

Until the nineteenth century, *landschaft* and road coexisted, but ever more fitfully. It was not that travelers were murdered in inns or daughters ran off with teamsters, but that the life of the highway was becoming removed from the life of the *landschaft*. Road signs made asking directions unnecessary, and the improved maps, road surfaces, and police ordered by stronger governments permitted travel even after nightfall.[24] The turnpike avoided some settlements in its quest for directness, and mailcoach passengers scarcely glimpsed villages far from the route.[25] Railroads only sharpened the dichotomy between traveler and inhabitant already implicit in turnpike design. Trains followed their rights-of-way too quickly for casual communication between passengers and spectators, and forced riders to look sideways at a silent blur. Soon space was ordered about the track; towns focused on stations, water towers, and grain elevators which blocked passengers' views of the towns. As factories and warehouses moved next to the rails, trains ran for miles through a tunnel of structure. The railroad traveler was denied a long-distance view and the opportunity of stopping to analyze nearby space. The inhabitants of trackside areas could in turn only gape at the faces staring behind the glass.

Increasingly, travelers suffered from a curious *anomie* described as early as 1798 in Coleridge's "The Rime of the Ancient Mariner":

LANDSCHAFT AND LINEARITY

Like one, that on a lonesome road
Doth walk in fear and dread
And having once turned round walks on,
And turns no more his head;
Because he knows, a frightful fiend
Doth close behind him tread.[26]

The fiend snuffling at the heels of every traveler is the fiend of home-lessness, of lack of place in the world of men. Most travelers fix their heart and eye on a refuge somewhere ahead—though criminals may look back in desperate horror at homes forsaken—and ignore the road-side world in their haste to arrive.

What they see from the road is landscape, the not-quite-understood complex of dwellings, fields, factories, and other artifacts of human work placed among natural landforms and vegetation or in totally modified space. If the view is chiefly natural or rural it qualifies as scenery, and the traveler choosing a "scenic route" knows he should appreciate it, if only as a relief from man-made complexity. But all too often, man-made, not natural shapes and spaces dominate his route, and the hurrying ob-server is stunned by elaborate man-made forms having no immediately-apparent use or arrangement or uniqueness. He looks away and thinks on that place which he does understand but which no word, not *community*, not *neighborhood,* and certainly not *landschaft* accurately identifies. There only is his personal being congruent with man-made form.

James defined the power of high-speed, long-distance travel in the title of his book. *The American Scene* is concerned not with scenery but with scenes, places transformed by man. James could not avoid such places because the highway and railroad constantly directed him to them. While he was honest enough to look at them, to describe them, and to try to appreciate them, he judged them by older, far different places, the backward vestiges of America's *landschaft* past. He longed for discrete, knowable territories where social order and man-made space coincided, where the disruption of highway was unknown.

Utopias

James was not alone in his search for knowable space. Dozens of other observers rejected America's late-nineteenth-century spatial order and re-treated into historical, local-color, or nature writing.[27] The reorganization of space about railroads and motor highways sparked a flurry of futurist thought in utopian novels and polemics. Earlier Americans knew little of the genre, perhaps because experimental communities had once flourished in fact, on cheap, backcountry land away from censorious eyes. By the 1870's, however, most of the communities had disbanded in the face of mechanized agriculture and manufacturing, and the dream of social harmony in ordered space reappeared in the writings of utopianists.

Most of the fictional utopias are characterized by social and economic systems derived from the theories of Herbert Spencer, Henry George, or the Bible, and are served by mechanical devices—electric motors, air-conditioning units, and even automatic bed-makers—predicted in scores of magazine articles. No master plan or consensus of opinion inspired the shaping of utopian space, however, and the American visionaries were left to their own imaginations. It is startling, then, that the same spatial features, curious as they are, occur repeatedly. The striking uniformity of utopian built environments is not a matter of vagueness; most writers were lavish with detail and many delighted in engravings of city plans and building elevations. It was a shared conviction that space was no longer knowable, and a shared dislike of several especially pernicious features in particular, that prompted nineteenth-century writers, like Thomas More four centuries earlier, to envision perfection.

A geometry of well-being informs almost all utopian space. Wildernesses, mountains, and dangerous seas usually surround the perfect place and protect it from the profane world; chaotic nature rarely intrudes. The Martian utopia described in Henry Olerich's *A Cityless and Countryless World* (1893) is seemingly without hills or valleys, its topographical monotony broken only by buildings.[28] The future United States of Edward Bellamy's *Looking Backward* (1888), Bradford Peck's *The World a Department Store* (1900), and Edgar Chambless's *Roadtown* (1910) likewise lacks great forests or swamps.[29] Most of the territories are completely gardened. There is little construction or other modification because social perfection has engendered perfection of space. Every problem confronted by industrializing America is neatly solved.

In nearly every vision the marriage of country and city is consummated without the trauma of suburbia. Olerich's Martian visitor tells his American hosts that noisy, dirty cities are "detrimental to an orderly, well-regulated society," though he is quick to add that farm life is a social and economic waste too. The orderly solution to urban congestion and rural isolation, he explains, is the "community," an arrangement of apartment houses carefully sited along the perimeter of a great agricultural enclosure. Peck and Bellamy bring rural joy to everyone by filling their airy cities with shade trees and promenades, Peck by throwing together back yards and demolishing offensive structures, Bellamy by judicious planting of open squares. Chambless's Roadtown extends indefinitely across farm land, a sinuous chain of two-story road houses, each with a flower garden in front and a vegetable patch behind, and public buildings linked by a basement railroad and roof-top walks. In each utopia, farmers share in the charms of reformed city life, and all residents enjoy gardened nature—but not wilderness.

Single-family housing, except in Roadtown, is gone, along with home cooking, parlor entertainment, and housework. Communal restaurant facilities provide choice food and conversation, and the theater is the focus of recreation, though amusement parks, athletic fields, and gymnasia are scattered everywhere. A new—or very old—sense of community finds expression in malls, shopping spaces, and public parks. Even the telephone and musicphone, while providing solitary entertainment of highest quality, are poor substitutes for social visits and the theater. Free time in Cooperative City and Roadtown is never private time, but time devoted to public affairs. The loner and the hermit are unknown, and indeed have no place in the *landschaft*-like utopian world.

Work is stimulating and deeply satisfying. Everyone takes turns at the boring jobs—serving in the communal restaurants or driving sightseeing carriages—though most arduous tasks are lightened by such machines as Olerich's electric-powered farm tractor. The drudgery of housework in particular is vanquished, partly by mechanical invention and partly by communal laundries, kitchens, and furnaces.[30] Women are free to garden, read, visit, sew, or cook, though many choose to attend the theater with friends. Factory work is meaningful too, even if it is given over to an army of young citizens, by its association with community advancement. Repeatedly, the importance of small workshops— Chambless locates a workroom in the lower level of every Roadtown house—is emphasized as the spatial manifestation of pleasant, soul-satisfying work. There is little or no separation of workspace and home in the utopias. The smokeless, noiseless electric machinery is as unimportant in the utopian vision of work as creative play. It is the small group companionship, healthful workspace, and beautifully finished products that satisfies the workers, not gadgets.

The companionship of the theater and shop extends beyond each citizen's immediate acquaintance to the larger community, finding expression in monumental building. Theaters are, after all, recreational, and most writers, terrified of offending sectarian readers, substituted the lecture hall and government building for the cathedrals which might otherwise order utopian space. Citizens gather for education and decision-making in the grandest structures of utopia, almost invariably sited in exquisitely-planted public squares. Education is rational and politics are straightforward and honest; children enter school buildings happily and adults administrative halls without hesitation. Peck's Cooperative City, for all its squares, avenues, and diagonal streets, focuses on a great administration complex, "situated in the center of several acres of land laid out by leading landscape gardeners in the most artistic manner, setting off the magnificence of the enormous building which accommodated the numerous offices and legislative halls of the executive boards."[31] At the center of almost every utopian place, rationality and right government take physical form.

Roads, and sometimes railroads, monorails, and trolley lines, touch every part of every utopia, making the monumental center immediately accessible. Nearly every writer resolves communication difficulties first with telephones, and then with highways, boulevards, and service streets. Roadtown, of course, is a road, the epitome of Chambless's determination to order linear settlement. Beneath its gently curving superstructure run several railroads for long-distance and local transportation of freight and passengers. Its continuous roof is devoted to a steam-heated, glass-enclosed promenade paralleled on each side by bicycle and roller-skating paths, benches, and jogging tracks. It is on this recreational street, Chambless predicts, "that Easter hats will be shown and neighbors' crops discussed and new acquaintances made and local pride developed."[32] The less ambitious plans of other writers also stress roads both as recreational and social places, and as boundary lines. Bellamy's futuristic Boston succeeds as an artistic device because of its broad streets and grand vistas, and Peck's utopia is crisscrossed with extravagant avenues. But the roads and railroads, and even Roadtown itself, lead nowhere in particular. They are not strands in larger networks, and are rarely used for long-distance travel. Indeed travel, except for an afternoon's diversion, is uncommon, for there is no place better worth seeing. Strangers, except for the nineteenth-century narrator-visitors, are unknown, for the broad avenues terminate in dimly known regions inside the wall of mountains or seashores that ring the utopian places. For all the width and beauty, utopian roads are really paths.

Thomas More would have found himself at home, for the utopian spaces are little different from his own. In 1516 More abandoned the utopian vision which had satisfied Europeans for fifteen centuries. Unlike Heaven, his Utopia was just over the horizon, somewhere beyond the New World discoveries. Like his American counterparts four centuries later, More was troubled by social and spatial changes. Feudalism was giving way to capitalism, and the old rhythms of rural life deteriorated. Intellectual authority weakened before the onslaught of empirical science, and the unity of the church was threatened. Order lay beyond imagined equatorial regions filled with wild beasts, serpents, and savage men, in an ideal commonwealth where good sense, sound learning, and

LANDSCHAFT AND LINEARITY

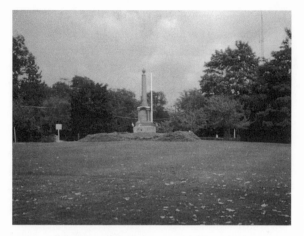

Small New England towns still reflect much older notions of spatial ordering. Here a flagpole and Civil War monument on a tiny green mark the center of civic space.

mercy find expression in space. His fifty-four city-states, "all spacious and magnificent, identical in language, traditions, customs and laws," are "similar also in layout, and everywhere, as far as the nature of the ground permits, similar even in appearance."[33] Each is intimately associated with the life of its agricultural land, for every inhabitant shares in the farm work. Utopia's capital, the walled town of Amaurotum, rivals Peck's Cooperative City as a paradigm of order. Each of its three-story row houses fronts on a broad avenue and opens in the rear on a great common garden. A market building for the storage and sale of family handicrafts and the distribution of farm produce orders each quarter of the town, and common dining and recreation halls order every block. There are no hermits or idlers; everyone finds his community life and work satisfactory. The off-island world of Abraxa, the Indies, and all of Europe is only so much chaos in comparison.[34]

More's book had several successors, but by mid-seventeenth century the genre was moribund. For two hundred years, utopian writing was displaced by travel narrative. Europeans and Americans, distracted by exotic customs and topography and lulled by faith in progress, paid little attention to the continuing disruption of small-scale community existence and space. Not until the impact of railroads was fully felt, and the meaning of trolley cars and automobiles surmised, did intellectuals discover that imageable space was fiction. Distraught and baffled by the seeming chaos of society and the built environment, most shut out the confusion by concentrating on bits and pieces of personal significance— the family or circle of friends, the isolated village or farm. Others turned to utopia and city planning, reinvoking the memory of *landschaft*.

The *landschaft* is the controlling spatial metaphor in most sixteenth- and nineteenth-century utopian writing, and in city planning literature of all ages, including our own.[35] Like the *landschaft*, the utopian place is ringed by wilderness. It is also fully realized by its inhabitants, characterized by home-based farm work and handicrafts, focused about a symbolic center, and interlaced with short-distance paths. Nineteenth-century city and regional planners, like their utopian contemporaries, fastened on the *landschaft* archetype too, finding utopia in long-lost New England villages or in Main Street towns. Their successors see it in green belt suburbs or in circular condominium complexes.[36] It is always the circular, clustered archetype that reigns as standard, be it a remembered and often romanticized *landschaft* or a perfectly contrived utopia.

Archetypes

In comparison with the archetypal standard, the man-made environment of the United States seems almost chaotic. The vehicular traveler is overwhelmed, then stupefied; views change too quickly, too dramatically for sustained high-speed study. Passengers close their eyes and doze, while drivers focus on the pavement ahead and grimly ignore the roadside scene.[37] Meaning escapes the pedestrian too. There is so much detail and so much variation that the walking seer edits his surroundings at once; he knows his house clearly enough, and his hotel and the museum, but he does not realize the buildings between.[38]

Passenger and pedestrian alike have a snapshot vision of the built environment. They see bits and pieces of greater or less importance, but continuously significant space, because they see through the prism of *landschaft*.

This is the power of the ancient archetype of *landschaft*. It controls visions of what the built environment is, and shapes dreams of what it ought to be. It prevents men from realizing—and from loving—the space they inhabit.

But its power is weakening. The present post-industrial, post-modern age is also post-*landschaft*. The old significance of defined, imageable space is lost on today's children. They can hardly conceive of a medieval *landschaft* isolated from a wider world by feared wilderness, fully realized by every inhabitant, and space is defined by the road, and linearity shapes their vision of what space ought to be.[39] In their *strassenromantik* of exploring and wandering, and in the fantasy and science fiction they so frequently read, the road and the quest are dominant metaphors. Thoreau and Henry Beston are suspect; they stay too much at home. Hobbits, apprentice magicians, and neophyte priests, on the other hand, are respected for searching in space, for following roads however dangerous and indistinct, and for confronting Coleridge's frightful fiends.[40] It is no accident that America's young people are not disturbed by interstate highways, shopping strips, and vast suburban sprawl. They are children of landscape, and see in the built environment a symmetry, order, and beauty scarcely visible to Henry James and to their parents.

The old archetype of *landschaft*, then, no longer wholly shapes images of home, neighborhood, and utopia.[41] Its resiliency, however, should not be underestimated. Archetypes are not created by the conscious, and they cannot be destroyed by it. They can only be submerged, ignored for a limited time. To ignore the archetype of *landschaft* and unthinkingly accept the landscape of linearity is as dangerous as to see all man-made space through the prism of *landschaft*. Implicit in the concept of landscape are two archetypes, the ancient one of *landschaft* and the venerable but younger one of the road.

Notes

1. On archetypes see C. G. Jung, *The Archetypes and the Collective Unconscious,* trans. R. F. C. Hull (Princeton: Princeton Univ. Press, 1969), pp. 1–36; Jung mentions spatial archetypes in *Mandala Symbolism,* trans. R. F. C. Hull (Princeton: Princeton Univ. Press, 1969), pp. 93–94.

2. For other definitions see Robert E. Dickinson, "Landscape and Society," *The Scottish Geographical Magazine,* 55 (January, 1939), 1–15; J. B. Jackson, "The Meaning of 'Landscape,'" *Kulturgeograft,* 88 (1965), 47–50; Josef Schmithusen, "Was ist eine Landschaft?" *Erdkundliches Wisen,* 9 (1964), 7–24; and Gabriele Schwarz, *Allgemeine Siedlungsgeographie* (Berlin: Walter de Gruyter, 1966), pp. 162–220. Perhaps the most comprehensive analysis of the medieval landschaft is found in three works by Karl Siegfried Bader: *Das Mittelalterliche Dorf als Friedens–und Rechtsbereich* (Weimar: Bohlaus, 1957); *Dorfgenossenschaft und Dorfgemeinde* (Koln: Bohlaus, 1962); and *Rechtsformen und Schichten der Liegenschaftsnutzung im Mittelalterlichen Dorf* (Wien: Bohlaus, 1973).

3. Stephern Miller, "Politics and Amnesty International," *Commentary,* 65 (March, 1978), 58.

4. *Oxford English Dictionary* (New York: Oxford Univ. Press, 1971). I, 1566–1567.

5. Robert Coles, "Telic Reforms," *The New Yorker,* 54 (March 13, 1978), 141.

6. *OED,* II. 3630–3631.

7. John Conron, ed., *American Landscapes* (New York: Oxford Univ. Press, 1971).

8. (New York: Harper and Brothers, 1970), pp. v–vi; hereafter cited as James.

9. James, pp. 38, 442, 50; in his novels James writes lovingly about pedestrian places; see *The Ambassadors* (1903; rpt. New York, W. W. Norton, 1964), p. 24.

10. James, pp. 105, 98, 122.

11. James, p. 73; for another use of the metaphor see Hart Crane's *The Bridge* (Paris: Black Sun, 1930).

12. James, pp. 46, 49, 385.

13. (1822; rpt. Cambridge, Mass.: Harvard Univ. Press, 1969), III, 221.

14. Frederick Law Olmsted, *A Journey in the Seaboard Slave States* (New York: Dix and Edwards, 1856); *A Journey through Texas* (New York: Dix and Edwards, 1857), and *A Journey in the Back Country* (New York: Mason, 1861).

15. Emily Post, *By Motor to the Golden Gate* (New York: Appleton, 1917); Theodore Dreiser, *A Hoosier Holiday* (New York: John Lane, 1916); and George R. Stewart, *U.S. 40: Cross Section of the United States of America* (Boston: Houghton, 1953).

16. Adalbert Klaar, *Die Siedlungs- und Hausformen des Wiener Waldes* (Stuttgart: J. Engelhorns, 1936).

17. Marc Bloch, *Land and Work in Medieval Europe,* trans. J. E. Anderson (Berkeley: Univ. of Calif. Press, 1967); G. G. Coulton, *The Medieval Panorama: The English Scene from Conquest to Reformation* (Cambridge, England: Cambridge Univ. Press, 1938); Joan Thirsk, *The Agrarian History of England and Wales* (Cambridge, England: Cambridge Univ. Press, 1967); Warren O. Ault, *Open-Field Farming in Medieval England* (New York: Barnes and Noble, 1972).

18. Jacob Grimm, *Deutsche Rechtsalterthumer,* eds. Andreas Heusler and Rudolf Hubner (Leipzig: Dietrich, 1899), I, 557–675.

19. Edward Chamberlayne, *Angliae Notitia; or the Present State of England* (London, John Martyn, 1669), pp. 76–77.

20. Jacob and Wilhelm Grimm, *German Folk Tales,* trans. Francis P. Magoun, Jr. and Alexander Krappe (1857; rpt. Carbondale, Illinois: Southern Illinois Univ. Press, 1960).

21. Geoffrey Hindle, *A History of Roads* (Secaucus, N.J.: Citadel, 1971), pp. 46–56; Hans Hitzer, *Die Strasse* (Munchen: Callwey, 1971), pp. 105–185; and Lewis Mumford, *The Culture of Cities* (1938; rpt. New York: Harcourt, 1970), pp. 26, 80.

22. Emmerich Vattel, *The Law of Nations* (Dublin: Luke White, 1787), pp. 80–82.

23. On the role of the city streets as meeting place see Pierre Lelievre, *La Vie des Cités des l'Antiquité a nous Jours* (Paris: Bourrelier, 1950), p. 11 and Richard Senett, *The Fall of Public Man* (New York: Knopf, 1977), p. 36 and passim.

24. See, for example, Nikolaus Lenau, "Der Postillon" for a description of the nightjourneying: *Sammtliche Werke* (Stuttgart: Gottascher, 1855), I, 200–203.

25. Thomas De Quincey, *The English Mail Coach* (Boston: Ticknor, 1851).

26. (Oxford: Oxford Univ. Press, 1930), p. 29. See also Arnold Van Gennep, *The Rites of Passage,* trans. Monika B. Vizedom and Gabrielle L. Caffee (1906; rpt. Chicago: Univ. of Chicago Press, 1972), pp. 15–25.

27. As examples, see the writings of Thomas Nelson Page, George W. Cable, Sarah Orne Jewette, George W. Sears, John Muir, and Dallas Lore Sharp.

28. (1893; rpt. New York: Arno, 1971). The following paragraphs are based on extensive study of approximately fifty-five utopian works, many of which are listed in Allyn Bailey Forbes, "The Literary Quest for Utopia, 1880–1900," *Social Forces,* 6 (December, 1927), 179–189.

29. (rpt. Boston: Houghton, 1966); (Lewiston, Maine: The Author 1900); (New York: Roadtown Press, 1910).

30. Such communal facilities are frequently well described; they are not simply mentioned.

31. Olerich, p. 61.

32. Chambless, p. 53.

33. Thomas More, *Utopia,* ed. Edward Surtz (1516, rpt. New Haven: Yale Univ. Press, 1968), p. 61.

34. On the form of utopia see Louis Marin, *Utopiques: Jeux D'Espaces* (Paris: Editions de Minuit, 1973) and Wolfgang Biesterfeld, *Die Literarische Utopia* (Stuttgart: Metzler, 1974), esp. p. 11.

35. See Douglas Fraser, *Village Planning in the Primitive World* (New York: Braziller, 1968);

Joseph Rykwert, *The Idea of a Town: The Anthropology of Urban Form in Rome, Italy, and the Ancient World* (Princeton: Princeton Univ. Press, 1976); Mircea Eliade, *The Sacred and the Profane,* trans. Willard R. Trask (New York: Harcourt, 1959), pp. 1–65; and Werner Muller, *Die Heilige Stadt* (Stuttgart: W. Kohlhammer, 1961).

36. Benton MacKaye, *New Exploration: A Philosophy of Regional Planning* (New York: Harcourt, 1928); Paul and Percival Goodman, *Communitas: Means of Livelihood and Ways of Life* (New York: Random, 1947); for a powerful visual linking of the archetypal *landschaft* with the crafted utopia, see Pare Lorentz's film *The City* (1939).

37. Despite the picture windows provided on buses and trains, most riders talk or read or sleep; it is the rare adult or child who stares outward for long.

38. See Carl Steinitz, "Meaning and the Congruence of Urban Form and Activity," *American Institute of Planners Journal,* 11 (July, 1968), 233–248; Kevin Lynch and Malcolm Rivkin, "A Walk Around the Block," *Landscape,* 8 (Spring, 1959), 24–34; and Kevin Lynch, *The Image of the City* (Cambridge, Mass.: MIT Press, 1960).

39. This conclusion is based on my reading of several hundred Harvard University student term papers.

40. See, for example, Ursula K. Leguin, *The Wizard of Earthsea* (New York: Bantam, 1975); Herman Hesse, *Sidhartha, eine indische Dichtung* (Berlin: Fischer, 1922) which has been translated into English several times: Robert M. Pirsig, *Zen and the art of Motorcycle Maintenance* (New York: Morrow, 1974), and most importantly, J. R. R. Tolkien, *The Hobbit, or There and Back Again* (1937; rev. ed. 1966; rpt. New York: Ballantine Books, 1973). The dominant spatial feature in Tolkien's Middle Earth is the road.

41. Heiner Treinen, "Symbolische Ortsbezogenheit," *Kolner Zeitschrift für Sociologie und Sozialpsychologie,* 17 (1965), 73–97; Alexander Mitscherlich, *Die Unwirtlichkeit unserer Stadte* (Frankfurt am Main: Suhrkamp, 1965); and Hans Oswald, *Die Überschatzte Stadt* (Olten: Walter, 1966).

JACK-O'-LANTERNS TO SURVEYORS
The Secularization of Landscape Boundaries

The lighting of Halloween jack-o'-lanterns is one of the last pagan ceremonies performed by modern man. For almost all Americans the meaning of the custom is lost; few know that the jack-o'-lantern is the ghost
of a long-ago remover of landmarks forever doomed to haunt boundary lines.[1] The defining, marking, and keeping of property lines has preoccupied family and community for at least three thousand years, and
the persistence of the jack-o'-lantern tradition illustrates how deeply
man perceives his private piece of landscape by the boundaries he creates about it. Indeed one chief distinction between the medieval and
modern views of the natural environment is the difference in attitude toward landscape boundaries. The flickering, hollowed pumpkin is all that
remains of a great folklore of boundary-keeping practice which dis-
solved in the late seventeenth century. Nowhere is the dissolution better
recorded than in early New England documents, because the English
colonists straddled the break between ancient custom and modern technological innovation. For them the jack-o'-lantern was both specter and
superstition.

Terminus was a powerful deity in classical Rome. Everywhere citizens
met boundary stones, some sculptured with his likeness and all erected
in his honor. The Roman new year feast of beginnings and endings was
consecrated to the god of bounds, and before they exchanged gifts among
themselves, men showered the stones with wine, food, and flowers. The
termini guarded each field against trespass and illegal encroachment;
those who dislocated the stones and altered property lines broke both
civil and religious law. The farmer who plowed under a *terminus* was im-
molated along with his team in expiation of the sacrilege.[2] Each family's
territorial integrity was sacred according to the precedent of ancient
Greece, where men early equated political stability with an ordered landscape.[3] Plato's ideal boundary law derived from the real one of Athens;
both stressed the social necessity of landscape delimitation.[4] The dividing line between classical houses and planting lots was not infinitely thin

"Jack-o'-lanterns to Surveyors: The Secularization of Landscape Boundaries" appeared in *Environmental Review* 1 (Autumn 1976): 14–30, copyright by the American Society of Environmental History.

As this 1906 *Suburban Life* image suggests, the making of jack-o'-lanterns from pumpkins has long pleased children, even if they fail to ask why they practice the custom. A monstrous turnip (*inset*), grown especially for Halloween, proves more historically accurate, and perhaps more frightening, than the ordinary pumpkin.

as it is in many cities and Austrian common fields today. In Greece and Rome dwellings could not touch each other and could share no common walls. Lots were separated by narrow spaces consecrated to the boundary gods; Roman law fixed the sacred space at two and one-half feet.[5] The unowned and unimproved spaces separated the domains of family gods and allowed each household to worship free from profane interruption. Each city was in turn surrounded by a circle of sacred bounds,

THE DEEP PAST AND IMAGES

"a horizon of its natural religion and of its gods."[6] Unlike private boundaries, city frontiers were rarely marked. The range of each city's protecting deities ended a few miles from the city center, and while occasional shrines might mark the limit, most travelers found it difficult to tell when they left city territory and entered the intervening spaces of godless waste. Throughout the classical world whatever was protected by gods or owned by man was somehow defined by boundary markers or invisible but real limits.

It was the Roman *robigalia* which eventually linked pagan boundary customs to Christian practice. Once a year the citizens of Rome marched to a grove five miles outside the city and begged the god Robigus to spare their crops from blight.[7] Early Christianity assimilated the *robigalia* with ease; church fathers simply altered the focus of the prayers. Not until the late sixth century did St. Gregory regulate the rite; he retained the traditional date of April 25 and only codified the prayers used in the procession. A century earlier the Bishop of Vienne in Gaul had introduced a three-day rite of supplication in response to earthquakes and volcanic eruptions in Auvergne, and within four decades the three days preceding Ascension Day were solemnized in the church calendar across Europe.[8] By the year 600 Christians celebrated the Major and Minor Rogations by following their parish priests into the fields to beg (*rogare*) God's blessing upon their crops. In 707 the Council of Cloveshoo introduced the three-day minor festival to England, and for more than eight centuries Englishmen all but ignored the April 25 holy day and celebrated the "gang-days" with fervent enthusiasm, perhaps because they were already accustomed to "gang about" their newly-plowed fields in honor of pagan gods.[9]

Rogationtide made the entire village what the Romanian philosopher Mircea Eliade calls a hierophany, an irruption of the sacred world into the everyday space of men.[10] After prayers at the church, priest and people proceeded about the village fields singing hymns and stopping occasionally for Bible readings and homilies. The reason for some parts of the old service was long forgotten; probably no Englishman remembered that earthquakes had prompted the Bishop of Vienne to include Psalm 103 among the required readings. Other portions of the order were more to the point; the richly geographical imagery of Psalm 104 had very real significance to the marching villagers.[11] In Anglo-Saxon times it was customary for religious relics to be carried in the processions, and while that practice eventually fell into disuse, great banners, crosses, and standards were common into the sixteenth century; even after the Reformation, the days were sometimes called crossdays.[12] Special rogation processions were occasionally made when crops suffered from particularly inclement weather; as late as 1543 Henry VIII ordered them to be made throughout England in August because of prolonged rains.[13] The gang-days and special rogations emphasized God's particular concern with the land; one mid-sixteenth-century writer noted that "by virtue and operation of God's word, the power of the wicked spirits which keep in the air may be laid down, and the air made pure and clean, to the intent the corn may remain unharmed."[14] In a time when the supranatural world and its attendant malignities hung very near the heads of rural Englishmen, the outdoor Rogationtide ceremony provided protection for the land and an explicit connection between village space and cosmic infinity.

The ecclesiastical custom very early acquired a marked civil character. Rogationtide was from the beginning always a local festival celebrated within each village; men might pray for a good harvest across the entire kingdom, but undoubtedly their thoughts centered on the fields beneath their feet. Priests took care to lead the processions along village bounds, and to combine praying with pointing out the limits of village land. It was to every priest's personal advantage to protect his village from encroachment; the boundaries marked as well the area whose tithes supported him. Too, the outdoor ceremony was perfectly fitted for priestly admonitions about maintaining private landmarks. The Bible speaks eloquently and often of the sin of moving boundary markers (Deuteronomy 27:14 is perhaps most succinct: "Cursed be he that removes his neighbor's landmark. And all the people shall say, Amen.") and the lessons were quickly incorporated into the service, parts of which came to be read beneath marker trees or beside boundary streams.[15] Children were sometimes rudely bumped against the trees or held head-first in the water so that they might better recall the location of boundaries; at some places men from neighboring villages played at tug-of-war across boundary streams.[16] Slowly the gang-days acquired a festive air distrusted by a clergy increasingly aware of Puritan warnings; as early as 1542 in "A Sermon in the Cross Days or Rogation Days" Richard Taverner bemoaned the loss of piety and claimed that the processions were given over to merrymaking. Taverner was not alone in his attempts to restore the religious fervor of earlier times, but the efforts were doomed to failure. Even the Puritans could not conquer the good feeling; Robert Herrick caught the flavor of Puritan festivities in a 1648 love sonnet:

Dearest, bury me
Under that Holy-oak, or Gospel Tree
Where (though thou see'st not) thou may'st think upon
Me, when thou yearly go'st Procession.[17]

By the mid-seventeenth century, Herrick's use of the word procession was outmoded; the custom was increasingly called perambulation out of respect to its civil worth. In a time when maps and other written records were few, the annual boundary lessons were vital in maintaining accurate memories of land divisions and ownership privileges. But still the earthly boundary markers were consciously related to divine precept, and their destruction was a sin as well as a crime.

So important was the civil character of the perambulations that religious reformers very rarely interfered with them. Queen Elizabeth deliberately exempted Rogationtide ceremonies from her 1547 and 1559 prohibitions of religious processions.[18] Bishops frequently asked about the status of the perambulations during their annual parish visits, and while by 1571 banners, handbells, and other accessories were being denounced as Popish to an unseemly extent, the festivities endured almost unchanged.[19] The Puritans abolished the accoutrements and set-prayers, but the perambulations continued throughout the Interregnum. In 1632 the Puritan clergyman George Herbert enumerated the "four manifest advantages" of the perambulation custom in *The Country Parson*. He found it procured God's blessing on the fields, preserved boundaries, brought neighbors together in good fellowship, and provided an opportunity for assisting the poor.[20] However they differed about the ecclesiastical ordering of the custom, Catholic, Anglican, and Puritan Englishmen respected its political value.

The spatial significance of the custom cannot be over-emphasized. Perambulations followed village bounds through thickets, swamps, and marshes; had only the fertility of the fields been at stake, the marchers could have avoided the difficult passages. The English landscape historian Maurice Beresford notes in *History on the Ground* that "the Rogation procession was both a statement of the past rights of a village and the means by which these rights should be preserved in the future."[21] By the sixteenth and seventeenth centuries, villages had good reason to ensure their rights; as England became more populated and enclosure movements quickened, boundaries took on increased significance. The three-day period was scarcely long enough for the careful perambulation of large villages with perimeters of ten miles or more.[22] Religion, law, and folk custom all served to define the village outline and secure the community landscape from old and new forms of external disruption. If seventeenth-century Englishmen attached less importance to the hierophantic aspects of the perambulations, they nevertheless deeply valued the spatial implication of the annual marches. Rogation perambulations ensured every villager of his particular location within the kingdom; they defined his community space and sanctified his personal property.

Most medieval Englishmen lived in constant fear of trespass. The common- or open-field system of agriculture precluded substantial boundary markers; fences and ditches obstructed group operations during plowing and harvest, and men divided their strips with irregularly-placed stakes or stones.[23] The crimes of trespass and illegal land encroachment are everywhere in European folklore of the Middle Ages.[24] In the fourteenth century the English poet William Langland found "the fair field full of folk" he described in *Piers Plowman* beset by trespassers who stealthily guided their plows across the invisible boundaries into other men's strips of land.[25] The fifteenth-century English translation of Etienne de Besevcar's *Alphabetum Narretionum* includes two selections dealing with the moving of boundary markers. In both tales dying men are tormented by visions of landmarks about to enter their mouths; the men confess that they once moved boundary markers, and one relates how "one time he removed a stake of the same measure and length out of his own field into a knight's field that was near his, to enlarge his own ground."[26] Only when the men confess their sins to priests do the torments cease; as the clergy warned in the perambulations, boundary markers were sacred.

Until Tudor times boundary-keeping was every man's personal affair. Each villager helped in the annual perambulation of his community's boundaries, checking for trespass and encroachment, and passing on his knowledge to his children. He took care to maintain the bounds of his own property as well, and when he suspected trespass he turned to the aged husbandmen of his village to decide the dispute. But in the 1520's a new way of boundary measuring began replacing old traditions and the ancient relation among men, boundaries, and the landscape decayed.

As late as 1650 mathematical surveyors were distrusted by the English common people; that year a young land-measurer confronted an angry village parson "who raised a cry against him as a conjuror."[27] The superstitious fear of the men who measured land at a distance with strange-looking instruments dated only to the early sixteenth century; prior generations were familiar with another sort of surveyor who was sometimes disliked but never feared. As countless rural problems beset the English farmer after the Wars of the Roses, the new mathematical surveyors were seen as the incarnation of rural troubles.

Originally surveyors functioned much like contemporary insurance and tax appraisers who expertly "look over" property. Like the marine surveyor who carefully examines the hull and fittings of a ship, determines it sea-worthiness, and estimates its value, the medieval land surveyor did more than simply measure lot outlines. According to a law of 1276, the lord of any manor could convene a court of survey to inquire into the status of rents, tenures, and lot sizes. Usually the steward of the manor and a surveyor presided, and tenants were required to appear with written evidence of their leases, lot boundaries, and other rights in the land. In the absence of written documentation, as was usually the case, the surveyor accepted the sworn testimony of tenants and neighbors. After hearing testimony and carefully looking over the manor, the surveyor would apply his agricultural knowledge to the setting of new rents and land apportionments. While not uncommon in Tudor England, courts of survey were only irregularly called; when a manor was sold or many of its leases expired at once, or when a rare progressive landlord decided to learn the true value and efficiency of his estate, a surveyor was called and witnesses summoned. Like all officials who raise assessments, the surveyor was not well-loved, but since any husbandman could haggle about the worth of his land and call on his neighbors to support his view, the surveyor's appraisals were not always unchallenged.

With the beginning of enclosure the surveyor's role changed. As fields became more valuable as pasture, many landlords began forcing off tenants when their leases expired. In order that landlords might accurately know what land could be enclosed as sheep pasture and what arable fields produced the best crops on the least ground, they asked the surveyor to carefully bound and measure the many internal subdivisions of their manors, and to determine the precise limits of estates surrounding theirs. The surveyor had always been concerned with estimating lot sizes and determining boundaries, and often employed an assistant called a "land-meater" to help with the measuring. The land-meater's work was not especially important, because for generations land was measured in terms of work; the acre, for example, was held to be the amount of land which could be plowed in one day by one man. The definition made no correction for heaviness of soil or length of day, and the meaning of acre differed from place to place and season to season. As large-scale farming became more profitable in the sixteenth century, many landlords grew aware of the vagaries of old definitions and agreements, and the work of the land-meater increased in esteem. Eventually his skill usurped the older assessing tasks of the surveyor, and measurement became of chief importance.[28]

Tudor surveyors were beset with many difficulties. Only a few had the mathematical knowledge necessary for accurate area-finding; almost half of the many manuals published near the close of the century include tables where men might find answers without knowing multiplication, division, and logarithms. Extremely elementary errors were common; perhaps the most frequent involved irregularly-shaped lots of five or more sides. Surveyors customarily measured the perimeter, divided by

JACK-O'-LANTERNS TO SURVEYORS

four, and squared the result, assuming that the area of any figure could be calculated on the basis of squares and rectangles. Other surveyors suffered from a lack of perspective; many did not know that a field with a hill in it has greater area than one without. A general lack of surveying instruments further hampered most land-measurers, and when the tools were available few understood their use. Hilly or wooded ground made simple compasses and carpenter's squares almost useless, and many supposedly accurate measurements were later discovered to be wrong. About the only aspect of mathematical surveying which was clearly understood in the sixteenth century was the use of the measuring chain by which the surveyors could arrive at an accurate measurement of a boundary line. Not until 1620 were most of the mathematically incompetent retired or forced from the profession and well-trained surveyors making excellent plats of large areas.[29]

The evolution of mathematical surveying paralleled, and perhaps encouraged, the changing landscape perception of the common folk. Land came to be thought of in statistical quantities derived from area measurement, not in terms of fertility or capacity to absorb labor. In large part it was the shift in perception which brought about the hatred of the surveyor. Many tenants feared that the surveyor would discover old encroachments or an additional acre surreptitiously twisted around another's boundaries, but the quantitative view destroyed almost everyone's relation to the landscape by substituting the new language of perches, rods, and angles for the old folk wisdom of boundaries.

Still the husbandman was not defenseless against the surveyor, and in the sixteenth and seventeenth centuries developed the stratagems which still plague surveyors working in rural areas. No matter how mathematically competent and technically well-equipped, the surveyor was forced to base all his measurements on local landmarks. In 1607 John Norden explained that the surveyor should bound the manor using the old perambulation techniques: "As for the bounding of the manor, it is fittest . . . that the best experienced tenants accompany him for information, and some of the youth, that they may learn to know the bounds in times to come."[30] The surveyor was thus at the mercy of the tenants whose land he was to bound and measure; only they could explain and locate landmarks mentioned in old deeds or carefully memorized, and the surveyor was sometimes deliberately misinformed. How often he made official bounds known only by custom—or by fiction—is unknown.

The end result of the surveyor's work was a painstakingly-drawn map of the measured, bounded, and ordered manor. In 1658 George Atwell described the making of such maps in *The Faithful Surveyor*. His specifications, and the few examples which survive, suggest that the finished product was a valued and symbolic addition to any landlord's personal estate. Atwell's concern lay with accurately reproducing not only the plan of the manor but at least a hint of its landscape morphology. To that end he specified the use of a suitable scale, and the orienting of the top of the map to the north. Such landscape features as "all houses, ways, rivers, churches, windmills, arbors, great lone-trees, gates, stiles" and open soils were to be drawn in correct relation; the manor house was to be drawn in perspective. The names of abutting manors and of the lots' tenants were to be entered in the correct locations, and around the perimeter of the map were an indication of the scale, drawings of compasses, ovals, squares, and compartments, and the figure of the landlord's coat-of-arms. The map was not monochromatic; in one of the clearest extant descriptions of the visual impact of the early modern landscape, Atwell explains the mixing and applying of "colours":

> Arable for corn you may wash with pale straw-color made of yellow-ocre and white lead. For meadows take pink and verdigris in a light green. Pasture in a deep green of pink, azure, and smalt. Fens a deep green, as also heaths, of yellow and indigo. Trees a sadder green of white-lead and verdigris. For mud-walls and ways mix white-lead, and rust of iron, or with ocres brown of Spain; for white-stone take umber and white: water or glass may be shown with indigo and azure, or black-lead: for seas, a greenish sky-color of indigo, azure, smalt, white-lead, and verdigris.[31]

The instructions show Atwell's concern for realistically capturing the appearance of the landscape; there is no hint of artistic creation like that of painters of his time, but only a determination to create a functional substitute for the manor's topography.

The map was a sinister thing. Tenants and landowners no longer decided boundary disputes by appealing to the custom and the memory of aged men. They went instead to the manor-house, where they viewed a permanent, unchanging, schematic rendering of their land and boundaries. There is no estimating the impact of the maps; many viewers suddenly perceived their spatial existence in an entirely new way as they saw their houses from an aerial perspective. The maps were inviolable standards against which all customs and memories were judged. No longer did each villager carry with him a unique mental map of his land and community; once the surveyor's work was done one map alone ordered the landscape.

The map was secular as well. There is little mention of the religious meaning of boundary markers in the English surveying literature of the sixteenth and seventeenth centuries, although as late as 1705 a German treatise began with a statement of the surveyor's holy office.[32] Atwell's map is beautified only by figures of seventeenth-century technology, not by angels or Biblical quotations. The English surveyor was true only to his craft, and recognized no holy responsibilities. The landscapes he measured and mapped were never conic, but always horizontal.

In New England the ideal village landscape *was* conic; the meeting-house was both the hierophantic opening to heaven and the axis of space. The amount of land owned by an individual was usually proportionate to his social and religious rank; "saints" lived on large lots near the meeting-house, and the unregenerate owned only a few acres away from the village center. Since the landscape was intended to mirror the rigid social hierarchy, it is not surprising that the Puritan clergy, like the ancient Greeks, equated the divisions of society with divisions of land.[33] In the early 1640's the Reverend Thomas Shepard made the equation explicit: "Would you have rapines, thefts, injustice abound? Let no man know his own, by removing the landmark, and destroying property."[34] In 1645 Plymouth Colony enacted a stiff law against the removal of boundary marks and two years later the Massachusetts Bay General Court ordered the selectmen of every town to perambulate their borders once every three years.[35] The laws were responses to a growing number of trespass and encroachment problems, which by the 1640's reached a serious level.[36] In the Plymouth Colony town of Scituate men had struggled with boundary questions since the town's founding in 1633. Scituate's land records, among the most complete in New England, show the colonists' hesitant attempts to abandon age-old boundary-keeping practices and adopt the modern ones of mathematical surveying.

Scituate men did not at first perambulate the boundaries of their plantation, apparently because the natural barriers provided by brooks and estuaries seemed secure in their own right. There were no settlements beyond the town's official borders anyway, and at first the husbandmen were preoccupied only with the land immediately surrounding their village center. Like the borders of Greek city-states, the frontiers of Scituate were at first extremely vague; not for several years did the settlers explore the distant corners of their grant.[37] Only when the neighboring town of Hingham was settled in 1635 did the Scituate men become concerned with their northern border, and soon there developed a boundary confrontation which involved both Plymouth and Bay Colony governments, whose jurisdictions met at the disputed line. Scituate men pulled up the boundary stakes set out by Hingham farmers, and eventually the two colony governors met at the site and hiked inland.

Bound Brook and Accord Pond were named in honor of the colonists' agreement on a fair dividing line.[38]

Old-country perambulation customs were aimed at preserving boundaries, not creating new ones. Since only a rare Puritan, most notably Roger Williams, paid any attention to Indian boundaries, the colonists were constantly forced to create new dividing lines.[39] When Scituate men drew community boundaries they tried to incorporate existing natural barriers; sometimes they were forced to use pocket compasses to run abstract lines through dense forest. The town's western line was calculated with the aid of a compass and the husbandmen blazed trees to mark it. Once borders were agreed on, the town met irregularly with its neighbors to perambulate them according to English custom. The language of the perambulation reports is almost unchanging; decade after decade the men retained the same narrative form and precise attention to landscape features. The reports now offer extremely detailed pictures of vanished natural and man-made landscapes, and at least a suggestion of ecological succession and human intervention.[40]

The perambulations were based on memory as well as landmarks. Men were aware that the North River estuary eroded salt marshes and silted up old channels, and by 1738 the reports noted the memory of vanished salt creeks which were once official boundaries. There is no direct evidence to prove that young boys were physically reminded of the town bounds, but the 1782 report suggests that men remembered landmarks as they existed fifty years before. There were no prayers said during the Scituate perambulations, but in all other respects they differed little from English ones. Indeed there is scarcely any difference between the reports' prose style and the wording of a Saxon perambulation report of 991; as late as the close of the eighteenth century, Scituate men viewed their community boundaries in medieval terms.[41]

Individuals maintained their private boundaries in customary fashion as well, although the overgrown landscape sometimes frustrated their best attempts. Men were quick to identify abstract property lines with some physical reminder; stakes defined salt meadow lots and fences and stone walls early marked upland lot lines while enclosing livestock. Woodlots were at first surrounded by lines of blazed trees, but by the end of the seventeenth century men's initials replaced the crude hackings.[42] Scituate men respected landmarks; between 1633 and 1800 only two court cases involved their destruction, and one instance was plainly an accident.[43] So important were boundary marks in the psychological life of the town that men maintained them even when their significance was forgotten; in 1709 the town meeting complained that such markers were causing great confusion in the north end of town.[44] The intensity with which men marked property lines and tended landmarks derived from medieval fears of trespass and encroachment, which in Scituate were well-founded.

Until the 1680's almost all private property in Scituate was laid out by respected husbandmen who assigned space eunomically, by rank or merit. The land committee was almost wholly untrained in mathematical surveying; it thought of land in terms of social and economic value, and awarded more to men it esteemed and less to those it ranked lower on the social scale. There is little trace of statistical thought in the records of its actions; the committee allotted parcels from the commonly owned land of the town without mentioning boundary measurements and compass bearings. It guessed at the acreage involved and bounded lots by noting the abutting parcels by owners' names. The lack of precision led quickly to boundary debates and a passion for marking dividing lines, especially those in distant places. Far out in the salt marshes and woods men arrived to cut hay and timber to find their property already harvested. Most of the disputes evolved from honest mistakes, but contending parties did not always settle matters quietly. Men frequently came to blows and in one or two instances nearly assaulted each other with scythes and pitchforks.[45] Their fervor came from fears that the trespass would threaten their title to their land; many of the cases which were tried in Plymouth involved charges that trespass and encroachment rendered titles doubtful. In a society where a man's land both bestowed and indicated social rank, trespass was more than a crime of property; it struck at the basis of an individual's identity.

Mathematical surveying arrived late in Scituate, partly because trained professionals were scarce in the colonies, but also because the husbandmen distrusted the art. At first Scituate men used old-country lot definitions; land was described by metes and bounds, topographical features, and general location.[46] When greater precision was called for, they acquired a compass and tried determining boundary-line bearings themselves. As late as 1710, however, there was no one in town who could find the area of irregularly-shaped lots, and the town meeting required all persons selling such parcels to enter a measured sketch of their outlines in the town land book.[47] As inheritance and frequent sales made evident the need for better lot descriptions, the town hesitantly questioned the wisdom of hiring a surveyor.

Some far-sighted—and perhaps confused—individuals had hired a professional land-measurer as early as 1649, when they discovered the land committee's boundary lines to be grossly in error. So distorted were the lot lines that the owners felt obliged to forgo the usual viewing pro-

Haunted houses usually have decrepit margins. In this 1924 *New York Tribune* cartoon, the fence proves a poor boundary, except to the imagination.

THE
HAUNTED
HOUSE

cedure by respected farmers and instead have the land allotments completely revised. Despite the success of the nameless surveyor, Scituate men refrained from hiring others; not until 1683 were boundary lines so confused that the town meeting discussed a professional survey of all privately-owned lots. Some farmers at first intended doing the job themselves, and one moved that the town buy an "arttis" to accurately measure the boundaries. But the expensive instrument was not purchased, apparently because no one was sure how to use it, and someone suggested hiring a surveyor. The motion sparked one of the most heated debates in the town's history, and the meeting was unable to agree on any course of action. The discussion was so confused that the town clerk could hardly summarize it: "After much agitation about measuring the land already laid out and dividing the remainder yet undivided, it was voted whether they would act according to the warrant requesting the measuring and dividing of said land, and some voted for and some against, and some voted not at all."[48] The town intermittently debated the hiring of a surveyor until 1710, while boundary questions became more complex by the year. Eventually the town meeting sent a representative to a neighboring town to request the help of a surveyor; the professional condescendingly replied that he would not serve Scituate until his haying and harvesting were complete and enough leaves fallen from the trees that his instruments would work. The town accepted his reply, and in 1711 the professional outsider arrived and the town's longest-running internal debate ended.

The remainder of the eighteenth century saw many private parcels competently surveyed and the simultaneous decay of traditional boundary-keeping customs. In particular, the language of deeds changed;

JACK-O'-LANTERNS TO SURVEYORS

once it had consisted chiefly of natural resources, topographical features, and man-made improvements, but by 1750 most deeds were hardly more than brief mentions of surveyors' measurements and bearings. Boundary conflicts declined in the eighteenth century, perhaps because the surveyors' lines were clearly defined and easily proved, but also because lots in all parts of town were better known due to frequent use. Still, however, the professionals ignored community boundaries and worked only for private parties; the farmers continued to perambulate the town borders in the traditional manner.

Not until 1795 did a surveyor check and mark the town bounds. Christopher Turner paid no attention to the political and social effects of his dividing lines; he judged all previous boundary lines only by their degree of technical accuracy. Unlike the first surveyors hired to measure private lots, Turner was not forced to begin his lines at landmarks known only to local farmers; for the first time in Scituate's short association with surveyors, Turner used a sextant to mark the starting point of his work. His conception of Scituate's outline became the standard by which old views were measured, because he drew the town's first map. Like the village and manor maps of Tudor England, that of Scituate had immediate social effects. The town stopped perambulating its borders; the map clearly indicated the lines, and there seemed no further need for men and boys to hike across swamps and marshes.[49] Turner's map marked the beginning of Scituate's fascination with local cartography; between 1795 and 1831, map after map was drawn of the town or specific locations within it. In 1831 another Turner printed for public sale a huge map showing house locations, topographical features, and place names; it served the town's needs until the twentieth century.[50] During the thirty-six years the folk landscape became professionalized; mapped place names superseded those known only by custom, topographical features which the mapmakers declined to name lost their identity altogether, and vegetation cover in isolated areas was lost to memory. Only the longitude and latitude calculations linked the maps with the heavens; otherwise they took no notice of the town's hierophantic places, except for sketches of meetinghouses. Graveyards, battle sites, and other places of renown, in short the landscape of transcendence and remembrance, went unmapped and were soon forgotten. More and more the physical landscape was bounded and measured by professionals, and gradually men saw it only through paper sketches. A few bearings and measurements were a surer boundary than a dozen stakes or a chest-high stone wall.

Scituate's hesitant embrace of the professional surveyor was like that of many other towns settled when medieval custom still governed men's ideas of boundaries.[51] But already before the Revolution, land in west-

ern New England was surveyed and mapped at the request of speculators who sold lots in the new townships to land-hungry easterners. Most
of the purchasers visited the lots before buying, but after settlement
they found their boundaries already fixed by modern measuring techniques. By 1795, when Scituate was hiring Christopher Turner to survey
its borders, the land-hungry men in western towns were migrating into
the Northwest Territory. In the Land Ordinance of 1785, Congress had
provided for the surveying of the Territory before sale of townships and
"sections." Many immigrants bought land sight unseen because they
were familiar with surveyors' measurements and maps. Unlike the Scituate men who struggled to divest themselves of medieval perceptions
of landscape boundaries, the westward-moving settlers were prepared
to buy land bounded only by abstract lines determined by cadastral survey. Boundaries were not part of the landscape in the Northwest Territory and eventually elsewhere in the West; they were abstractions in
government land offices and surveyors' records. The sacred customs of
Rogationtide and the semi-sacred civil practices of perambulation vanished; only the jack-o'-lantern remains, the enduring effigy of a marker-
stealing goblin.

Notes

1. J. A. MacCulloch, "Landmarks and Boundaries," *Encyclopedia of Religion and Ethics*
   (New York: 1915), VII, 793, 794.
2. Fustel de Coulanges, *The Ancient City* (Garden City, New York: 1968), pp. 67–68.
3. Hannah Arendt, *The Human Condition* (Garden City, New York: 1958), pp. 56–58.
4. Coulanges, p. 69. Plato, *Works*, trans. George Burges (London: 1852), V, 338–339.
5. Coulanges, p. 63.
6. Coulanges, p. 202.
7. *Harper's Dictionary of Classical Literature and Antiquities*, ed. Harry Thurston Peck
   (New York: 1965), p. 1378.
8. Francis Mershman, "Rogation Days," *The Catholic Encyclopedia* (New York: 1912),
   XII, 110–111.
9. *The Prayer Book Dictionary*, ed. George Harford and Morley Stevenson (London:
   1912), pp. 566–567, 719.
10. Mircea Eliade, *The Sacred and the Profane*, trans. Willard R. Trask (New York: 1959),
    pp. 11–12, 24–26, and passim.
11. Maurice Beresford, *History on the Ground* (London, 1971), p. 29.
12. John Brand, *Observations on the Popular Antiquities of Great Britain* (London: 1849), I,
    197–212.
13. Francis Procter, *A New History of the Book of Common Prayer*, ed. Walter Howard
    Frere (London: 1902), p. 31.
14. Richard Taverner, "A Sermon in the Cross Days or Rogation Days," *The Epistles and
    Gospelles with a brief Postil . . .* (London: 1542), f. xxiii.
15. See also Deuteronomy 19:14, Proverbs 22:28, 23:10, Hosea 5:10, and Job 24:2; the
    parallel with Plato's view is striking.

16. Bersford, p. 30.

17. Robert Herrick, *Complete Poetry,* ed. J. Max Patrick (New York: 1968), p. 31.

18. *Documentary Annals of the Reformed Church of England,* ed. Edward Cardwell (Oxford: 1844), I, 220.

19. J. S. Stryke, *The History of the Life of . . . Edmund Grindell* (London: 1710), pp. 31, 32, 38, 168. Edmund Gibson, *Codex Juris Ecclesiastici Anglicani* (London: 1713), p. 239.

20. George Herbert, *A Priest to the Temple, or, The Country Parson* (London: 1652), pp. 157–158.

21. Beresford, p. 30.

22. Beresford, p. 30.

23. Warren Ortman Ault, *Private Jurisdiction in England* (New Haven: 1923), pp. 152–53. H. S. Bennett, *Life on the English Manor* (Cambridge, Eng.: 1937), passim. Roland E. Prothero, *English Farming Past and Present* (London: 1941), pp. 70–150.

24. For a typical instance, see Gottfried Keller, "Romeo und Julia auf dem Dorfe," *Die Leute von Seldwyla* (Braunschweig: 1856), esp. 232–238.

25. William Langland, *The Vision of William Concerning Piers the Plowman,* ed. Walter W. Skeat (Oxford: 1886), I, 152–153, 408.

26. Etienne de Besevcar, *Alphabetum Narretionum,* ed. Mary Macleod Banks (London: 1905), pp. 31–32.

27. E. G. R. Taylor, "The Surveyor," *Economic History Review,* XVII (1947), 131n.

28. Taylor, passim. H. C. Darby, "The Agrarian Contribution to Surveying in England," *The Geographical Journal,* 82 (1933), 529–538 passim. There is no history of surveying; like the above two articles, A. W. Richeson's *English Land Measuring to 1800* is chiefly concerned with surveying instruments, not the profession's social effects. Sixteenth- and seventeenth-century surveying handbooks offer the only introduction to the subject.

29. See Ralph Agas, *A Preparative to Platting of Lands* (London: 1596); George Atwell, *The Faithful Surveyor* (Cambridge, Eng.: 1658); John Norden, *The Surveyor's Dialogue* (London: 1607); Aaron Rathborne, *The Surveyor* (London: 1616); William Ley-bourne (pseudo. Oliver Wallinsky), *Planometria, or the whole art of Surveying Land* (London: 1650); and Edward Worsop, *A Discovery of Sundry Errors and Faults Daily Committed by Landemeators* (London: 1582).

30. Norden, p. 94 (misprinted 49).

31. Atwell, pp. 52–53.

32. Florinus, *Allg. kluger u. rechtsverstandiger Hauss-Vater* (Nüremberg: 1705).

33. John R. Stilgoe, "The Puritan Townscape," forthcoming in the Spring, 1976 issue of *Landscape.*

34. Thomas Shepard, *Works* (Boston: 1853), II, 260.

35. *Records of the Colony of New Plymouth,* ed. David Pulsifer (Boston: 1861), "Laws," 47. *Records of the Governor and Company of the Massachusetts Bay in New England,* ed. Nathaniel B. Shurtleff (Boston: 1853), II, 210.

36. Larzer Ziff, *Puritanism in America* (New York: 1973), p. 84.

37. The land records of the town of Scituate are kept in the Town Hall vault; while they are extremely complete they have suffered from generations of amateur antiquari-ans who have repetitively mislabelled and mispaged them. Volume numbers here refer to the numbers inked on the spines; all binding titles, including those affixed in 1975 are doubtful—one volume labelled *Roads* contains deeds, for example. *Scitu-ate Records* (hereafter *SR*), I, 1–30.

38. For a brief overview of the dispute see William Bradford, *History of Plymouth Plan-*

tation (Boston: 1912), II, 275–278; William Bradford to John Winthrop, *Collections of the Massachusetts Historical Society,* Fourth Series, VI, 274–282; John Winthrop, *Journal: 1630–1649,* ed. James Kendall Hosmer (New York: 1908), I, 287–288, 305–306.

39. Roger Williams, *A Key into the Language of America* (London: 1643), p. 93.

40. *SR,* I, 1–80, passim; 140; II, 24.

41. *SR,* I, 140; II, 24. Beresford, pp. 50–51.

42. *SR,* IV, 346.

43. *Records of the Colony of New Plymouth,* VII, 180; IV, 50.

44. *SR* ("Conihassett"), 28.

45. *SR,* I, 1–100 passim; *Records of the Colony of New Plymouth,* VII, 56, 160–161, 116, 117, 119, 193.

46. *SR,* II, 1–200 passim.

47. *SR* ("Conihassett"), 27; the meeting was especially concerned about land that lay in "nooks, corners, or triangles."

48. *SR* ("Conihassett"), 19; see also 15–49 passim.

49. Massachusetts Archives No. 1242 "Maps and Plans"; Turner's map includes a lengthy rationale for its creation.

50. Massachusetts Archives Nos. 1586, 2095, 2666, 2474 "Maps and Plans." Contemporary Geological Survey maps rely on Turner's 1831 maps for many place names.

51. See, for example, *Early Records of the Town of Providence* (Providence, Rhode Island: 1892–1915), XIV, XX, XXI passim.

ARCHIPELAGO LANDSCAPE

Any exit ramp leads away from the interstate highway corridor, away from that singular American landscape of standardized, franchised, trade-marked American space into other landscape, into elsewheres, peculiarities, oddnesses. Long-haul order rules the interstate corridor, an order of chain motels, sanitized gasoline stations, fast-food restaurants, an order of broad median strips, green-painted bridges, well-marked junctions. Inside the mowed lawns, guardrails, and chain-link boundary fences of the interstate corridor, Americans know what to expect. Broad curves, wide shoulders, gentle gradients, a million shield signs gleaming with numbers: I-40, I-95, I-20, I-283. Even-numbered routes run east–west; odd-numbered, south–north. But always the capital I stands as prefix, proclaiming interstate federal space, standardized route, announcing the long-haul sameness that infuses motels, gas stations, and restaurants just adjacent, businesses that pander to the traveler in homogeneous space, businesses that accept national credit cards. But beyond the corridor sameness ends. Sameness ends where exit ramp ends.

Beyond the exit ramp, car becomes capsule, spaceship, launched into localism. Away from home turf, every motorist turns explorer, suddenly conscious of interstate landscape left behind, of oddness just ahead. Automobilists glance at gas gauges and twist around, locking doors. Truckers downshift, test air brakes, then crane forward, checking mirror angles. Everyone slows down, expecting unannounced intersections, unmarked speed limits, potholed roads, narrow bridges, detours, local speed traps. And without warning, maps fail.

Away from smooth interstate space, every road atlas fails. Great national atlases such as the *Rand McNally Road Atlas,* the best-selling annual publication in the United States, aim only at national audiences, at long-haul drivers.[1] Intended to help drivers travel long distances, they include only the scantest local information, here an exploded map of Los Angeles, there a glimpse of southern Missouri. At the end of the exit ramp, automobilist and truck driver new to an area expect to hesitate, to watch for signs, to ask locals the best way. Everything away from the red, black,

"Archipelago Landscape" appeared in *Visions of America: Landscape as Metaphor in the Late Twentieth Century* (New York: Abrams, 1994), 72–85.

and blue lines designating interstate, state, and county highways is only so much blankness to be entered in an exploring state of mind, with doors locked and fuel tank full. Yet at the end of the twentieth century, few Americans explore as the voyageurs did, even on today's rivers of asphalt.

Landscape

"I do not know why the name 'lakes' has been given to these watery deeps of such vast extent," mused Antoine de la Mothe Cadillac in the year 1699. What other explorers of New France called the Great Lakes, he saw as one immense sea. "It will be easily understood that you can readily sail round these lakes for a distance of 1800 leagues, in fresh water and with land all around you, not only with canoes but even with barques and large vessels." An able lieutenant of Governor Louis de Buade Frontenac in the 1690–1697 war against the British and their New World colonists, an explorer and cartographer of the Upper Country, the founder of the city of Detroit in 1701, one of the pioneers of Mobile on the gulf coast of Louisiana, Cadillac ever demonstrated an angle of vision peculiarly French. Precise, convincing, always bold (at one point he argued that all New York colony should fall to the French), he saw North America as an archipelago. "No bottom can be found well out into these lakes, any more than on the high seas; near the land, there are twenty, twenty-five, thirty, forty, or fifty fathoms of water almost everywhere. In Lake Michigan there is a tide, that is, its waters ebb and flow every twenty-four hours, just as in the ocean, and the waves increase and diminish according to the course of the moon." Such a sea demands a marine point of view, for the freshwater sea opens on others, even on the Pacific itself.

"In the country of the Sioux there is a river which is known for 1,000 leagues around," Cadillac concludes near the end of his "Memoir." "Its current is gentle and it would carry a ship throughout. It is bordered on both sides by prairies stretching farther than the eye can reach, with a few clumps of trees. Its source is not yet known." But Cadillac has a hunch, a fervent feeling that he knows its source. "It runs from the west and joins the Mississippi, which runs into the Southern Sea. It is my belief that the Western Sea could be discovered by means of this river, for experience shows those who travel in this country that every river takes its rise in some lake situated on a mountain or rise of ground which has two slopes, almost always giving rise to two or more rivers." In a detailed argument mixing fact with surmise, hope with legend, Cadillac makes perfectly clear that the ease with which *coureurs de bois* (trackers) move by boat from the St. Lawrence across the Inland Sea to Chicago, then into the Missis-

The gorges of what are now Arizona, New Mexico, and Colorado forced Spanish conquistadors into time-consuming detours around rivers along which flowed French exploration.

sippi tributaries and south to the Southern Sea, will be duplicated in a western route. That route will lead the traveler from the Mississippi west along the river of the Sioux for one hundred days, and eventually to what the Assiniboine tribesmen call the salt sea "beyond which, they say, there is no more land." No Frenchman had found the "grandfather of all lakes" that the Indians located at the headwaters of the Sioux-country river (what Americans now call the Missouri), nor the river flowing west from it to the salt sea, but Cadillac argues eloquently for exploration by water. "It should be observed that one can navigate the interior of the country on fresh water in a ship" already, making only three portages in 2,300 leagues, he observes, and the unexplored western river can only open on the Pacific, offering untold advantage to France.[2]

Seventeenth- and early-eighteenth-century cartography makes clear the striking significance of the peculiarly French vision of the New World as archipelago. While British and Dutch settlers huddled along the Atlantic shore, Cadillac and other Frenchmen roamed far inland, covering immense distances in canoes, bateaux, and other small craft perfect for

THE DEEP PAST AND IMAGES

exploring promising watercourses. Louis Joliet's map, "Nouvelle découverte de plusieurs Nations dans la Nouvelle France en l'Année 1673 et 1674," offers graphic evidence of the French vision so clear in Cadillac's writing. North America lies almost wholly surrounded by ocean, especially by the Arctic, becoming essentially a giant island. Its Atlantic and gulf coasts exist in the most cursory form imaginable, perhaps not simply because they lie in British or Spanish hands, but because they offer no estuaries or rivers leading far into the interior. What leaps at the viewer, of course, is the vastness of the interior lakes that give rise to two great river systems, one opening into the Atlantic, the other into the gulf. Despite the crudities of individual details—say the triangular shape of Lake Erie—the overall intention is clear, and repeated in a letter from Joliet strategically placed to cover the unexplored country in the west.[3] The map exists as navigational chart. Viewer and letter-reader alike discover that the river running west from the Mississippi can lead only to the Pacific. Joliet knows North America as an archipelago.

Certainly the Spanish worried about the French vision as much as they worried about French exploration. In 1686, for example, Martin de Echegaray drew a map for Spanish authorities alarmed by news of René Robert Cavelier, Sieur de la Salle's colony at the mouth of the Mississippi. The Spanish naval officer knew the gulf coast and islands well enough, but only hearsay directed his interpretation of the interior. Yet he caught the significance of la Salle's colony as entrepôt to an archipelago undoubtedly connected to the Pacific, along whose coast Spain had already planted missions, and to a vast inland sea, not a chain of great lakes.[4] Quite evidently, de Echegaray understood the importance of a Spanish thrust northward, not overland, but by water, and especially along the rivers running northwest from the gulf. Delay would mean French exploration, and French settlement.

What was it that the Assiniboine told Cadillac, that Joliet heard rumored midway down the Mississippi? Had de Echegaray heard something too about a salt sea, some vast bay of the Pacific or some chain of massive lakes like those the French already knew, but salt? In 1752 a version of a map supposedly drawn by cartographer Guillaume Delisle half a century earlier appeared in Paris, a map entitled simply "Mer de l'Ouest." Perhaps the map misuses the name of the late, great cartographer as a way of introducing the geographical theories of his son-in-law, Philippe Buache, its publisher.[5] But perhaps the map reveals the best possible thinking about North American topography around the year 1700, the thinking of Cadillac and other Frenchmen conversant with tribesmen's tales. The map shows an enormous bay unbounded to the north, a sea near the size of Hudson Bay and dwarfing the lakes, a sea clearly salt. Of equal importance, perhaps greater, the map locates a wondrous River of the West, rising in a lake near what Cadillac calls the river of the Sioux country, but titled here the Missouri. Dotted lines reveal the uncertainty of its course, but its importance is unmistakable, indeed awesome. Unlike the ice-bound Northwest Passage luring the British, the great bay and the west-running river offer the French a central passage, a route through the center of the North American archipelago.

United States history properly begins with the War for Independence, of course. Before that glimmers mere colonial history, and the seamless "Time Past" of the Indians, an agelessness rammed home by ruins unknown to living tribes. Yet colonial history endures—irksome, embarrassing, seductive, lurking in bits and pieces of wiry landscape. Rural New England families still speak of "the old French wars," as nineteenth-century novelists and historians did. In the 1850s, Nathaniel Hawthorne found something to chew on in the legends distinguishing the Province of New England from the Colony of Massachusetts Bay, and a few decades later Francis Parkman found something even meatier in the struggle between France and Great Britain in North America, the "French and Indian Wars" American schoolbooks now gloss in half a page.[6] Frontenac, Cadillac, Joliet, and de Echegaray belong to "Times Before," to the times when different world views, different angles of vision, clashed for primacy, when North America remained an archipelago, not a chunky continent. As late as the end of the nineteenth century, Times Before perplexed the most acute American novelists and historians.

Deep into the nineteenth century, long after independence, United States writers mused continuously on Times Before, on geography, on culture. "Canada was at the very portal of the great interior wilderness. The St. Lawrence and the lakes were the highway to that domain of savage freedom; and thither the disfranchised, half-starved seigneur, and the discouraged habitant who could find no market for his produce, naturally enough betook themselves," argued Francis Parkman in 1874 in his *Old Régime in Canada,* juxtaposing the *coureur de bois* against the "New England man," whose "geographical position cut him off completely from the great wilderness of the interior," whose field of action remained the sea. For Parkman, the *coureurs de bois* knew more deeply than the Anglo-American settlers the great natural wonders of the continental interior, the "gulfs where feathered crags rise like castle walls" or the "stern depths of immemorial forests, dim and silent as a cavern," knew more deeply the depths of emancipation from the restraint of royal edict, "the lounging ease of the campfire, and the license of Indian villages."[7] Author after United States author gnawed the bones of Times Before, authors like James Fenimore Cooper, whose *Last of the Mohicans*

Only a handful of motorists now take the two-car ferry from Illinois across the Mississippi River to Sainte Geneviève in Missouri, but those who do make land in a fragment of New France.

(1826) ends in deaths intended only to defuse the force of incipient miscegenation, the miscegenation so easily accepted everywhere in New France and New Spain. But one author alone speaks still of Times Before, of another attitude toward wilderness, of matters beyond the ken of Massachusetts farmers.

Eleven years after Buache published his cryptic map showing a western sea, cities of gold, and a river running west from the Missouri, a French mercantile company set about surveying the streets of St. Louis. United States schoolbooks make much of the westward movement of Anglo-Americans, showing great arrows emerging from the "cultural hearths" of New England, New York, Pennsylvania, and Virginia, and emphasizing the clearing of forest and building of log cabins. But settlement proceeded not by clearing and planting, but by hunting, trapping, and exploring, by the building of trading posts fought over in the Anglo-French wars, by the building of cities. In the western interior, cities came before farms, even after the Treaty of Fontainebleau (1762) and the Treaty of Paris (1763) split the West at the Mississippi. Before farmers arrived, the Mississippi basin boasted small cities dreaming large dreams. Pittsburgh, St. Louis, Louisville, New Orleans, Cincinnati, and other small places, such as Ste. Geneviève, nestled against navigable rivers— only Lexington in Kentucky survived as a riverless inland city. At first dependent on trappers and boatmen, early fought over by warring armies, sometimes changing allegiance—usually from French to Spanish to French—these infant cities prospered mightily as ports, trading posts, and jumping-off points. Only tortuous trails at first connected them to the East, or to anywhere. Commerce moved by river.

All nations came by canoe, flatboat, bateau, and later by keelboat and

ARCHIPELAGO LANDSCAPE

barge. Each city offered a strikingly similar street pattern, a grid of streets crossing at right angles, a grid focused on the waterfront. Anglo-settled cities took their grids from Philadelphia, while St. Louis took its from New Orleans. The grid, the great rectilinear survey Congress authorized after Independence, in time covered the whole West, producing square farms, townships, and fields, the "checkerboard" that airline travelers discern miles beneath them. Grids emphasize equality—supposedly.[8] Easily extended, replicated, and duplicated in the next city to be, the grid has the sameness of graph paper laid across the wilderness, a sameness belying differences of topography, forest cover, soil fertility, a sameness that silently but eloquently welcomes newcomers. By 1810 the interior of the eastern Mississippi basin boasted cities in which all nationalities mingled, while emerging rural landscapes were almost wholly Anglo.

Rural landscape endures as Anglo landscape almost everywhere in the United States. Here and there the explorer-beyond-exit-ramp encounters exceptions—say in the hill country of northern New Mexico, where most farm families descend from seventeenth-century Spanish colonists and fields and villages show traces of Castille. But elsewhere, even where last names tend to be German, as in much of the wheat country of Minnesota and South Dakota, the framework of Federal rectilinear survey orders a mix of barns, fences, and other details scarcely different from those of Anglo-ancestry Kansas and Idaho. State after state, longitude after longitude, the pattern paralyzes most travelers into boredom. Big square farms, each with a farmstead sitting in the midst of square or rectangular fields, reach toward the horizon, interrupted now and then by a tiny small town, a handful of cross-hatched streets, one the Main Street of stores, post office, and farm-supply businesses, one or two others essentially residential, perhaps one more fronting a railroad track, rusted and disused or polished, well-ballasted, and busy. Now and then emerges a larger town, the "county seat" with its courthouse square a duplicate of some other farther east, a grandiose courthouse, more stores and houses than usual, and a consolidated high school, its giant gymnasium announcing a passion for basketball and other wintertime indoor sports. Contemporary travelers find the vastness of rural America essentially British, certainly white, what Englishman Jonathan Raban, exploring the Mississippi River headwaters in a small boat, discovers as a "vast white ghetto."[9] Secure, quiet, even dull, rural America endures between prosperity and destitution, remarkably crime free, smog free, news free. Only in the rural South, in the territory of the Old Confederacy scarcely touched by the rectilinear survey, does the traveler encounter black families who give cause for wonderment.

Away from the seaboard Southern states, inland from the museum-like plantation houses, rural landscape reflects the subtle infusions of non-Anglo thinking, the continuing longevity of Times Before. Now out-of-favor authors caught in the 1870s—and later—the knowledge of something old, something haunting the landscape. Today, dismissed in their own nation as racist, as crudely local colorist, as second-rate, Southern authors like George Washington Cable stirred the ashes of the Confederacy to find sparks of something deeper. "The original grantee was Count . . . , assume the name to be De Charleu; the old Creoles never forgive a public mention," begins one of his short stories, "Belles Demoiselles Plantation." "He was the French king's commissary. One day, called to France to explain the lucky accident of the commissariat having burned down with his account books inside, he left his wife, a Choctaw Comptesse, behind." Cable understood that the plantation landscape of the western South developed from a culture other than British, even other than African. His stories about New Orleans society, about marriage between ethnic groups, between races, depend in part on their physical and temporal setting, their evocation of African dance on a summer night in the Place Congo, their understanding of Creoles, of a city known as French, Spanish, American, Confederate, and Federal.[10]

William Faulkner's *Absalom, Absalom!* of 1936 rammed home the message of Cable, and others, the message that the western Southern landscape reflects more than the simple westward movement of Anglos and enslaved blacks. The novel is not so much about the era before the Confederacy as it is about Times Before, when a settler named Sutpen arrives from nowhere, buys—using Spanish gold coin—"a hundred square miles of some of the best virgin bottom land in the country" from Chief Ikkemotubbe through the Chickasaw Indian agent, then vanishes, only to return with a covered wagon filled with slaves, and carrying an architect on its one seat. The last, "a small, alertly resigned man with a grim, harried Latin face, in a frock coat and a flowered waistcoat and a hat which would have created no furore on a Paris boulevard," has come "all the way from Martinique" to disappear into the woods for two years to direct Sutpen in building his great house with the help of naked, French-speaking island slaves.[11] Building in the wilderness forms one great theme of the novel, as it does in others Faulkner wrote as he explored the twisted themes so evident in Southern landscape.

Cable, Faulkner, and other Southern writers know what so many east- and west-coast Anglo intellectuals try to hide: the landscapes of Mississippi, Arkansas, Louisiana, even Florida, Missouri, and Michigan still reflect a richer, more shadowed past than that reflected by the rural landscapes of Massachusetts, Pennsylvania, even Virginia, perhaps even by coastal cities like Boston, New York, Seattle, and San Francisco. The first cities of the Mississippi basin attracted the trappers, hunters, watermen of several cultures, the men who knew the savagery and the freedom that repulsed and attracted Anglo historians like Francis Parkman. In the great multicultural stew of the lakes and rivers seaming the archipelago, only the rural regions stood aloof, secure, almost smug in their Anglo-generated agricultural order. But where the field ended and the creek or ravine began, the creek or ravine crowded with rank, luxuriant forest, with roaming predators, escaped slaves, renegade Indians, drifters, and tramps, agricultural order ended and the old order of the *coureurs de bois* obtained.[12] Always at the edge of the field, near the riverbank, up the hillside lurks the forest, lurks something of Times Before.

Many urban intellectuals squirm when the name Faulkner rises in conversation. No local colorist he, but no city dweller either, he of the Nobel Prize. His works linger like landscape, refuse to vanish, always point the way—the channel—back to the last attack on urban intellectuals and manufactured "national culture," the attack from the depression-era rural South. Southern writers knew the legacy of pre–Civil War sectionalism, and the desperation and poverty of postwar Reconstruction. They knew a landscape not only of burned-out plantation houses and grown-over cotton fields, of charred towns and steamboat piers, but a ragged backcountry of pine-board shacks, sharecropper cabins, and gullied roads. But they knew too the South as a specific, identifiable region, one of several such in the nation. "The United States are culturally and economically divided—not like Gaul into three—but into five parts," opined Allen Tate and John Peale Bishop in 1942, casually using "United States" as a plural noun demanding a plural verb. "Each has had its special history; each has a somewhat special way of life. There are New England, the South, the Middle West, the Southwest, and the West Coast." In their thinking, as in the thinking of so many other authors then—and now—dismissed as regionalists or local colorists, New York and its environs are not properly a "part" or region. "New York is the city where books and magazines (but not all of them and not always the best) are published"; it is the city where "writers go to make a living" using energy that "has derived some substance from the sidewalks of New York" but whose "origin is to be sought in the New England village, the Ohio factory town, the Wisconsin farm, the Southern plantation, the dry plains of New Mexico."[13] New York is the manufacturer and wholesaler of a "national culture," a sort of veneer flung over regional identities, something exported overseas. Just as its skyscrapers, wharves, and great avenues are new, without anything remaining from the deep Dutch past, so its broadcast culture is new, divorced from specific pasts, landscapes, and depths.[14] Tate and Bishop suggest that New York–style cul-

THE DEEP PAST AND IMAGES

ture appeals only to Americans who know nothing of the deep pasts of specific regions and landscapes—or else know those pasts so well that they recoil in terror toward something safer.

Others wondered too. The philosopher John Dewey, as early as 1920, mused that the great New York–based magazines "have to eliminate the local" in order to have national audiences, and find in the traveling public their best readers. "They subsist for those who are going from one place and haven't as yet arrived at another," he remarks of magazines sold by the hundreds of thousands in railroad-terminal kiosks. But underlying his argument is a deeper one, one playing on the notion of a traveling readership, a public en route. He implies that the people who absorb the national magazine culture are people not yet in place, people as anxious to be Americanized as any newly landed immigrant. "The country is a spread of localities, while the nation is something that exists in Washington and other seats of government," Dewey decides before remarking that "the defeat of secession diversified the South even more than the North." In using the word *country* in its older sense, in the way Henry James used it in 1886 in *The Bostonians* when he introduces a Southern Civil War veteran as an immigrant in Boston—"He came in fact from Mississippi, and he spoke very perceptibly with the accent of that country"—Dewey slices deeply into the lingering difference between *country* and *nation*.[15]

The difference fascinated dozens of Americans, especially T. S. Eliot, who fourteen years later published "Tradition and Orthodoxy." His willingness to carve the nation into countries jars any contemporary reader, while his remarks about borders and frontiers elicit only smiles. Who now believes that "to cross into Virginia is as definite an experience as to cross from England to Wales, almost as definite as to cross the English Channel?" Who reads, without squirming, his remarks about "the foreign races" invading New York and other cities, and swamping "native culture?" In context, however, precisely bracketed by Dewey and William Faulkner, Eliot becomes seer, a poet gifted with landscape vision. "I had previously been led to wonder, in traveling from Boston to New York, at what point Connecticut ceases to be a New England state and is transformed into a New York suburb," he remarks at the train window, scrutinizing what is so evident aboard Amtrak expresses today. He savors "the sordor of the half-dead mill towns of southern New Hampshire and Massachusetts," the mysteries of abandoned farms grown up in forest. Eliot, like Faulkner and Dewey, sees local landscape as something descried against a national veneer, as something whose past foreshadows future. In another essay, when he remarks that "we have not given enough attention to the ecology of cultures," Eliot makes clear that "if the other cultures of the British Isles were wholly superseded by English culture, English culture would disappear too." In his 1948 "Notes Towards the Definition of Culture," Eliot demonstrates that his earlier likening of the crossing of the Potomac to the crossing of the English-Welsh frontier was not at all frivolous, but critical in any understanding of British or American culture.[16] Without specific regions, without specific local landscape, the veneer of national culture, the skim coat of national, interstate highway landscape can only warp and twist, for *nothing backs it.*

Almost no one listened to Faulkner, Dewey, Eliot, and the others, the last partisans of tradition, of localism, of parochialism, the last measurers of Times Before, the last scrutinizers of local landscape. To be sure, throughout the 1920s and 1930s a handful of intrepid travelers retraced the routes of explorers, finding along the rivers an America already out of the reach of long-distance automobilists. Lewis R. Freeman, for example, took his outboard-motor-powered skiff from Milwaukee to New York City, from Pittsburgh to New Orleans, following the voyageurs, and publishing wonderful books like *By Waterways to Gotham* and *Waterways of Westward Wandering,* books that discover disquieting changes beneath the veneer of radio-broadcast national culture.[17]

After World War II, after television especially, regional culture like regional landscape became essentially local color, something haphazardly preserved—or pickled—in museums, tourist brochures, and fast-food restaurant paper placemats. Airline travel only speeded what the post-Sputnik public-school systems began with the substitution of physics for geography, the gradual discomfort of Americans with maps, the creeping disorientation of Americans confronting long-distance travel. The vast central part of the continent, an expanse encompassing the whole Mississippi watershed, the High Plains, even the eastern slope of the Rocky Mountains, became what airline travelers now dismiss as "Fly-Over Land." A nation anxious to be a world power turned to the world, and so emphasized its coasts, the one fronting an ever-changing Europe, the other facing a transformed Pacific Rim. In the year 2000, predicts the United States Bureau of the Census, over half of the American population will live within fifty miles of the sea, and over three-quarters will live within seventy-five miles.

Forgetting its localities, its regions, its depopulated landscapes whispering of Times Before, above all forgetting that colonization continues, its purveyors of national and world culture ignore the continuing settlement of America. In the great blocks of Anglo-dominated rural landscape, little changes, not even after massive farm mechanization. But

Rivers steal into the national landscape, and the explorer often passes unnoticed by the throngs of motorists racing along interstate highways.

elsewhere, in cities especially, everything changes, as group after group of newly arrived immigrants mark off their turfs, their zones bordered by frontiers as indistinguishable and as important as any between England and Wales; as longtime residents move to suburbs focused on stasis; as gigantic shifts in population stress and overstress extant natural and built ecosystems, infrastructure fabrics, landscapes. Now Cadillac and Joliet are proven right, for twisting among the blocks of Anglo-settled, Anglo-dominated landscape come threads of something different, something of Times Before, something of Times to Come.

Much of the American continent is utterly foreign to most Americans now, not only unvisited, but almost unimaginable. Americans no longer know the immensity of scale—and depth of detail—that transfixed Parkman, that made him sneer at the New England man with his face to the sea, the man surprised at the *chemin du Canada*. Only recently have they begun to imagine the racially mixed populations that entranced Cadillac and Joliet, that terrified Cooper, that fascinated Cable and Faulkner. Americans, especially educated Americans of wealth, influence, and energy, fly over their nation en route to Europe, Asia, or Yucatán, dismissing the immensities the voyageurs so laboriously mapped. But that vast territory, that "great white ghetto" penetrated by Raban in his Mississippi voyaging motorboat, stands now as dense as any African jungle imagined in Joseph Conrad's *Heart of Darkness* (1902). All the ar-

ARCHIPELAGO LANDSCAPE

guments now about racial, religious, ethnic, and class diversity demand some nod, however slight, to the contests of Times Before—and to the great landscape theaters in which they occurred.

Landscape speaks still to anyone thoughtful enough, scrupulous enough to listen, to scrutinize, to realize. Today's artists know and use its power to thrust contemporary Americans into Times Before.

Beyond

So the motorist drives warily to the end of the exit ramp, shifts gears perhaps, or merely glances right and left before joining the local road bordered by local landscape. Geographers merely catalogue the thousands of discrete, named landscapes temporarily corralled by the borders of the United States. Only those who probe those landscapes learn their power, see in them the gulfs and immensities of Times Before, the gulfs and immensities of Times to Come. Only those who leave the interstate highway see.

Notes

1. *Rand McNally Road Atlas* (Chicago: Rand McNally, 1990), 3.
2. Antoine de la Mothe Cadillac, "Memoir," in *The Western Country in the 17th Century,* ed. Milo Milton Quaife (Chicago: Donnelley, 1947), 6–10, 76–77. Still the best for cartographical background, Justin Winsor, *The Mississippi Basin* (Boston: Houghton, 1898), remains a fine narrative history of exploration and settlement.
3. Copy of Joliet's letter in John Carter Brown Library, Brown University, Providence, R. I. Location of original unknown.
4. Original in Archivo General de Indias, Seville, Spain, 61-6-20 (1). On the importance of water in northern New Spain, see Michael C. Meyer, *Water in the Hispanic Southwest: A Social and Legal History* (Tucson: University of Arizona Press, 1984).
5. On Philippe Buache see W. P. Cummings, et al., *The Exploration of North America, 1630–1776* (New York: Putnam, 1974), 181.
6. Nathaniel Hawthorne, "Legends of the Province House," *Twice-Told Tales* (1851; reprinted, Boston: Houghton Mifflin, 1882), 272–342. Francis Parkman, *Works* (Boston: Houghton, 1892).
7. Francis Parkman, *The Old Régime in Canada* (Boston: Little, Brown, 1874), 312, 313, 399, 400.
8. Richard C. Wade, *The Urban Frontier: The Rise of Western Cities, 1790–1830* (Cambridge, Mass.: Harvard University Press, 1959), 1–71. On river commerce, see Robert Capot-Rey, *Geographie de la circulation sur les continents* (Paris: Gallimard, 1946), 192–214.
9. Jonathan Raban, *Old Glory: An American Voyage* (New York: Simon and Schuster, 1981), 152, 153.
10. George Washington Cable, *Old Creole Days: A Story of Creole Life* (1879; reprinted, New York: Scribner's, 1916), 121. See also, Cable, "The Dance in Place Congo," *Century* 31 (February 1886), 517–523, for his understanding of racial energy in New Orleans.

11. William Faulkner, *Absalom, Absalom!* (reprinted, New York: Random House, 1964), 34, 35, passim.

12. Forrest Carter, *The Education of Little Tree* (New York: Delacorte, 1976).

13. Allen Tate and John Peale Bishop, *American Harvest* (Garden City, N.Y.: Garden City Publishers, 1942), 11.

14. Jan Morris, *Manhattan 45* (New York: Oxford, 1987); E. B. White, *Here Is New York* (New York: Harper, 1949).

15. John Dewey, "Americanism and Localism," *The Dial 68* (June 1920), 684–688. Henry James, *The Bostonians* (Boston: Houghton, 1886), 36. See also J. B. Priestly, *Midnight on the Desert: Being an Excursion into Auto-biography during a Winter in America, 1935–1936* (New York: Harper, 1937).

16. T. S. Eliot, "Tradition and Orthodoxy," *American Review* II (March 1934), 513–528, esp. 513–514; and, "Notes Towards the Definition of Culture," *Christianity and Culture* (New York: Harcourt, 1949), 130–131, passim.

17. Lewis R. Freeman, *By Waterways to Gotham* (New York: Dodd, Mead, 1926), see especially his remarks on the voyageurs, 71–75; and *Waterways of Westward Wandering* (New York: Dodd, Mead, 1927).

WALKING SEER

Cole as Pedestrian Spectator

In 1836, Thomas Cole wanted a horse. In June he wrote from Catskill to Asher Durand, again about a horse, thanking him for the trouble he had already taken, and asking him to exert himself further. "I am indeed much in want of a horse," Cole explained before quoting Shakespeare. "'A horse, a horse, my kingdom for a horse!'" Not any horse would satisfy him. "I do not want a tame pony, holding one foot to shake hands with you, but a horse rampant, rearing." And he wanted the horse sent quickly from New York. "If you can obtain one of these animals for me, and can send it by the sloop—the sooner the better—I should certainly be benefitted greatly." But Cole did not want a live horse. He wanted one of statuary, a model one, "plaster, bronze, or wood," and told Durand to inquire with "the Italian plaster man, in William Street."[1] Apparently he needed the model as a visual aid, not as transport. After all, most of the time and in most places, Cole walked.

Everything and nothing of the pedestrian characterizes Cole and his work, but so stunningly obvious is the pedestrian Cole that few who scrutinize the man and the paintings actually realize anything of the significance of the pedestrian. Cole's contemporaries simply accepted his walking and his walking view, and his first biographer, Louis Legrand Noble, offered that acceptance to posterity. *The Life and Works of Thomas Cole* still offers what it offered in 1853, a remarkably straightforward, almost unthinking acceptance of Cole's understanding of looking, of being a spectator.[2] To place Cole and his work in the context of the early-nineteenth-century Republic is to miss something of the importance of that understanding, for Cole lived at the very end of an age-old view, and perhaps he tried to interpret and prolong that view into another age. Just as literary criticism typically concerns itself with the ways individual writers use words while philology concerns itself with the languages of cultures and subcultures, so art criticism focuses on particular painters, and sometimes schools of painters. But for philology the realm of visual

"Walking Seer: Cole as Pedestrian Spectator" appeared in *Thomas Cole: Drawn to Nature,* ed. Christine T. Robinson (Albany: Albany Institute of History and Art, 1993), 17–25, copyright Albany Institute of History and Art.

scholarship has no certain parallel field, and while cultural historians now and then essay interpretations of paintings like Durand's 1849 *Kindred Spirits: Thomas Cole and William Cullen Bryant,* only rarely do they probe commonalities and peculiarities of viewing, of looking. Whatever else this exhibition accomplishes, it makes clear that Cole walked, and walked at the end of a time.

Only two months after writing Durand about a plaster horse, Cole recorded his sense of an ending. "I took a walk, last evening, up the valley of the Catskill, where they are now constructing the railroad," he wrote. "This was once my favourite walk; but now the charm of solitude and quietness is gone. It is, however, still lovely: man cannot remove its craggy hills, nor well destroy all its rock-rooted trees: the rapid stream will also have its course." At the close of the twentieth century, no reader misses the cultural contexts explained by 1960s cultural historians. Certainly Cole is concerned with what has become known as the "machine in the garden," the railroad, the train, even the train whistle that so profoundly disconcerted and enthralled Thoreau, Hawthorne, and other antebellum writers.[3] In August 1836 Cole placed himself squarely in what retrospect identifies as an artistic movement that grew into an artistic tradition. The roadbed scars the forest floor, the locomotive whistles away soft silence as its smoke assaults the eye and the nose. All is changed, but only in the landscape.

Mistake not the significance of Cole's August record. He *walks* up the valley. He does not ride. To be sure, the railroad stands unfinished, so he cannot board a train, take a seat, and look from the window. But neither does he ride horseback. Into the despoiled valley he brings a traditional, pedestrian view. He is the walking spectator so casually forgotten now, or so easily and unthinkingly accepted by so many museum visitors themselves walking among paintings and other important objects from times past. He is like William Cullen Bryant in Durand's painting, *Kindred Spirits,* a man who walks, who carries a walking stick, who wears low boots, who goes places horsemen do not, who sees what horsemen miss. He is indeed the Cole of Durand's painting, the Cole everyone sees in Cole's own paintings and letters and journal entries, the Cole everyone sees but no one notices.

Before the steam locomotive chugged up the Catskill valley or muddied the shores of Walden Pond, observers of landscape had divided into two groups, the horsemen and the walkers. Timothy Dwight, president of Yale College and author of the four-volume *Travels in New England and New York* of 1822, epitomized the horsemen-spectators of the early-nineteenth-century Republic. Astride his horse, sometimes ensconced in a chaise, Dwight rode everywhere in the region he determined to be his theater of observations. But even allowing for his own interests, particularly the shaping of farms from forest and the relative prosperity of towns, Dwight was mightily concerned with the conditions of roads, even when he ventured forth to examine the aesthetics of wilderness scenery. In late September 1815, he and several friends ascended the Catskill Mountains. "The turnpike road, made some years since over these heights from Catskill to Windham, enabled us to gain the summit without any other difficulty except what arises from their elevation," Dwight remarked enthusiastically of an engineering wonder. "Wagons, and at times even chaises, though it must be confessed with many a hard struggle, climb this ascent. We gained it partly on horseback and partly on foot." After admiring the extraordinary views, including a "succession of rainbows" made by a waterfall, Dwight and his party headed back to Catskill and rode into trouble. "We descended from these heights a little before sunset; and after a disagreeable delay occasioned by breaking through a bridge where we had well nigh lost our horses, we reached Catskill a little after ten in the evening."[4] In choosing to ride, in choosing *not* to walk, Dwight chose his angle of vision, and it subtly shaped his magnificent book.

Even as he admired good roads, especially the turnpikes that speeded his travels, Dwight the horseman gave scant thought to their place in the landscape or their role in his thinking. Most unlike Cole, who saw the railroad grade as something spoiling his favorite walk, Dwight unhesitatingly accepted the scar of the turnpike road striking upward into magnificent scenery. The Catskill turnpike made possible a one-day round trip to the mountain summits, even if the last few miles involved night riding and a near catastrophic accident at a frail bridge. However subtly, haste informs all of Dwight's *Travels* from the first page of the first volume, transforming even his view of the weather. "A country changing as rapidly" as his chosen region "must, if truly exhibited, be described in a manner resembling that in which a painter would depict a cloud. The form and colors of the moment must be seized, or the picture will be erroneous." Always riding in haste, always dwelling on his day's destination, Dwight somehow sensed that he rode through a changing scene worthy of a competent painter indeed, not through a simple still life before which a bumbling amateur artist could stand for days, even weeks. A good road meant speedy and indeed almost effortless observation, and the likelihood of an inn or tavern if the weather turned bad. "Behind the mountain rose a black and awful cloud, highly charged with the electric fluid, whence the lightning streamed and the thunder rolled with uncommon grandeur," he remarked of an incident that interrupted a journey to Lake George. "About five o'clock we stopped at an inn," he concluded, "to escape the shower alluded to above."[5]

THE DEEP PAST AND IMAGES

In the first half of the nineteenth century, horsemen-spectators rode everywhere in the Republic, producing a body of literature including not only massive works like Dwight's *Travels* and Frederick Law Olmsted's *Journey in the Back Country,* but far briefer accounts too.[6] Always a peculiar point of view suffuses the accounts, an angle of vision literally steeper than that of walking observers. And nowhere is the angle more noticeable than in the pedestrian perception of weather.

While horsemen took shelter in inns and farmhouses, walkers scrutinized weather, sometimes reveled in it, and certainly endured it. Quite simply, walkers often walked away from turnpikes and other well-traveled roads, and often even away from footpaths. Once off the road or path, they expected to encounter few farmhouses, let alone inns. Rather than merely descrying storm clouds and hurrying on, the walkers accepted the changing weather as another prism through which to view their surroundings, a prism deserving notice in and of itself. "In a journal it is important in a few words to describe the weather, or character of the day, as it affects our feelings," Thoreau confided in his own journal in 1855. "That which was so important at the time cannot be unimportant to remember."[7] More than any other nineteenth-century pedestrian-writer, Thoreau directly confronted the uselessness of walking only on highways. "Roads are made for horses and men of business," he warned in his 1862 essay, "Walking." "I do not travel in them much, comparatively, because I am not in a hurry to get to any tavern or grocery or livery-stable or depot to which they lead."[8] And while walking, Thoreau found what Cole found, what Dwight knew ought to be found but chose to trade away for the speed and comfort of his horse or chaise, a realization of weather, of light, of detailed bounds.

In his own journal, Cole recorded in words what he recorded over and over again in paint. He recorded his pedestrian view. On August 18, 1835, he noted that "it has been a glorious day. A cool and crystal atmosphere is upon the mountains. After work I walked up the valley of the Catskill. The sun was down, and the woods, fields and mountains never looked lovelier." Nothing is extraordinary about the entry. Indeed such entries abound in his journal, and demonstrate beyond measure that Cole could write cogently and gracefully about the most subtle of apparitions. "The weather for a month has been truly delightful; but this day above all," he noted on October 30. "A pure crystal-like atmosphere has floated round the landscape; and the brown of the leafless woods has been tinged with the purest ultramarine. The sky is clear and cloudless, the air is still, but fresh."[9] But however precise and penetrating, such writing is not wholly idiosyncratic, not only the expression of a gifted painter, but the product of sustained pedestrian looking in an age that valued such observation. Somehow walkers glimpsed the light of sun-

In his 1839 painting *The Notch of the White Mountains,* Cole depicted the raw but staggeringly beautiful scenery of landscape being shaped from wilderness. (National Gallery of Art)

down, the indirect light to which words like *dusk* and *twilight* do so little justice. "We had a remarkable sunset one day last November," mused Thoreau about a moment when "the sun at last, just before setting, after a cold gray day, reached a clear stratum in the horizon, and the softest, brightest morning sunlight fell on the dry grass."[10] Sundown-light, acute-angle sunlight, perhaps struck both Cole and Thoreau so strongly not only because both men shared a deep, trained interest in penetrating, sustained scrutiny, but because both had moved far from main-traveled roads, into wooded valleys and frost-hit meadows where such sunlight became part of their destination, part of something vastly more sophisticated than an inn around a bend at sundown.

More Americans than *cognoscenti* like Cole and Thoreau valued sustained scrutiny of light, weather, and other prisms. For a brief time, at least some American school-children learned about the optical effects of weather. In reading John Brocklesby's *Elements of Meteorology,* an 1848 textbook produced by a Connecticut college professor of mathematics and natural philosophy, advanced "academy" students learned not only the science of meteorology, but something of the "beauty and sublimity" of meteorological phenomena which "fill the mind with admiration and awe." In words and illustrations, Brocklesby explored phenomena ranging from ball lightning to rainbows, from mountaintop-hovering

THE DEEP PAST AND IMAGES

clouds to "looming," a sort of terrestrial and marine mirage. Assuming not only a somewhat experienced eye, but a working knowledge of geometry, he attempted to sharpen everyday experience of weather into both an intriguing component of natural philosophy and as something integral to sophisticated aesthetic sensibility. "When the rays of the sun fell upon the fragments of vapor floating in the eastern quarter of the heavens, their jutting heads and broken edges gleamed with a flame-like hue; while, between the masses, the sky appeared of the *deepest indigo*," he writes in a section, "Colors of Clouds," about "a most gorgeous sunset that occurred at Hartford" on July 3, 1844. "As the evening advanced, portions of the western stratum assumed the tints of *lead, lake, pink, green, purple, violet, orange* and *crimson*. About eight o'clock, the vapor in the south-west presented a singularly beautiful appearance; the heavens seemed as if covered with a delicate *lace-work woven of prismatic rays,* and this phenomenon was succeeded by *green, purple,* and *violet* clouds in the west. The last hue of this brilliant pageant was an *intensely vivid crimson,* which was gradually lost in the shades of night." In emphasizing the aesthetic qualities of sunsets, Brocklesby assumes a near-painterly knowledge of light and colors, and at least a passing acquaintance with man-made objects. He describes, for example, an 1845 sunset "resembling *marble paper,* the intermingling colors consisting of *bronze, orange,* a *vivid grass green,* and a *golden yellow*," using the marble paper simile quite casually, but clearly connecting the natural optical phenomena with the realm of artists.[11] While explaining how reflected beams of different colors combine in the "aqueous" strata to produce clouds of particular color, he makes clear that informed scrutiny of meteorological phenomena distinguishes any educated person from the uneducated or the hurried.

While Dwight huddled in an inn, Cole stood out in the storm. In 1826, for example, he records that "in one of my mountain rambles, I was overtaken by a thunder storm," and that he took shelter "beneath an overhanging rock." His long description of the storm demonstrates not only a developed meteorological interest, but a simple acceptance that mountain rambling leads into stunning weather. As the downpour continued, freshets began cascading down the cliff, isolating him in his nook. "Every moment my situation was becoming more comfortless, as well as romantic," he notes, before recording that he had to pile up rocks to sit out of the water. Whether or not Cole embroidered his accounts of such pedestrian adventures, including one detailing his getting almost hopelessly lost in the Catskills in 1827 and wandering for hours in circles, now seems unimportant, for the experiences, however embroidered in prose, shape the paintings exhibited here. In an 1833 letter proposing a series of paintings, Cole explained to Luman Reed that "natural scenery also has its changes,—the hours of the day and the seasons of the year, sunshine and storms: these justly applied will give expression to each picture of the series." What Cole calls "expression" here deserves more than passing comment, for it resembles what Thoreau calls the "character" of the day. Moreover, it suggests, however vaguely, that Cole understood not only the landscape as changing continually, but somehow changing in ways only the elect noticed and depicted. Whatever horsemen and other turnpike travelers of hasty busyness notice, they miss what the elect descry, and what Cole, among the elect a painter, depicts.

In the storm, sheltered under an overhanging rock and "wrapped in the folds of the tempest," Cole begins to imagine. "Then came up a thousand fancies. I fancied anything and everything. I thought myself careering, in a chariot of rock, through airy wastes beyond the reach of gravitation, with no law but my own will." Is such mere fancy only? "Now I rose over mountainous billows of mist, then plunged into the fathomless obscure: light shot athwart the darkness." While in the end he admitted that "no fancy could dissipate the awful reality," somehow the storm not only imprisoned and entranced, but offered him a momentary glimpse of immense power.[12] Of course, in the same year the English balloonist Jolliffe reported that after he discharged ballast, his balloon ascended into "the vapors of the dense mass of cloud," then "at length rose with uncontrollable velocity, and burst, almost suddenly, out of this dark barrier into realms of light and glory."[13] Did Cole the storm-wrapped pedestrian know much of ballooning? Did he imagine himself somehow transported, almost transfigured?

Thoreau suggested that frequent, sustained walking turns pedestrians into a sort of elect. He fancied himself a knight of a new, "or rather an old, order,—not Equestrians or Chevaliers, not Ritters or riders, but Walkers, a still more ancient and honorable class, I trust." Sometimes, disciplined, almost heroic walking makes some walkers special. "The chivalric and heroic spirit which once belonged to the Rider seems now to reside in, or perchance to have subsided into, the Walker,—not the Knight, but Walker Errant. He is a sort of fourth estate, outside of Church and State and People."[14] More than playfulness charges these sentences. *Pridefulness* is too weak a word to properly designate the spirit Thoreau displays, and perhaps *arrogance* is too strong. But whatever the appropriate term, in "Walking" and so many other essays collected in his *Excursions,* and in *Cape Cod, The Maine Woods,* and even in *Walden,* Thoreau distinguishes between the people of the turnpike and the elect walker in woods and fields and mountains. Somehow the walker becomes The Walker, someone special, a sort of noble, someone elect, someone apart, someone answering only to his own will.

In a far more subtle, vastly more gentle way, Cole appears to have fastened too on the ennobling nature of accurate walking. He becomes The Walker too, someone both in deepest touch with his surroundings and someone who bounds them.

Cole emigrated from England when he was eighteen, and he brought with him some trace of faerie, the shadow realm of England so integral in English childhood.[15] Too easily dismissed as "romanticism," something that surfaces in his love of Scott and Irving, Cole's intermittent attention to fairies illuminates his thunderstorm fancies of flying in tempests, of being beyond laws of gravitation, of knowing no law but his own will. Fairies, elves, bogies, hobgoblins, and the other little people of the twilight know no laws but their own, and live as the *genii loci* of rural and wilderness Britain.[16] At dusk walkers encounter them, and at morning leave them, ridiculed, ridden, or rich, bewitched or enlightened. Horsemen on the royal highway pass them by without knowing, for the horsemen ride too quickly over a structure so new, so raw that it wards off the little people of the twilight. In British folklore, only the elect, hapless or otherwise, contact the *genii loci,* for bad or good.[17] At twilight and in storm, in forest and in glade, some walkers encounter the spirits of place.

In July 1835, Cole set out on foot through the New York mountains, starting at nine o'clock at night and heading for an inn. He grew thirsty, and not wanting to awaken any homeowners in the dark houses he passed, he pressed on through Rip Van Winkle's Hollow. Finally, extremely parched, he found a brook. "There was a tin vessel glittering by the rill, placed there for the use of travelers, by some generous soul, perhaps fairy, that expected us at that silent hour." Few American writers peopled any spot in the Republic with fairies, but Cole did, understanding somehow that the elect walker is a sort of nobility indeed, that the *genii loci* contact him, even care for him. Three years later, in a letter to Durand, Cole chose the English motif of the unwary walker trapped by fairies to explain his difficulties in painting a dream of Arcadia, especially an Arcadia of mixed Grecian, British, and American elements.[18] Cole saw himself as Thoreau saw himself, someone to whom revelations might come, but Cole accepted that revelations might come even from fairies, the quintessential *genii loci*.

And Cole saw himself too as the maker and keeper of bounds. Even as Thoreau now and then supported himself as a surveyor, establishing boundaries for legal documents, Cole supported himself by bounding the scenes he created. In the end, his pedestrian observations are paintings, exhibited here in frames. In a very late-eighteenth- and early-nineteenth-century way, they are chests, caskets waiting to be opened, or if open, awaiting scrutiny. Caskets and fairies accompany one another in the old folktales of fairy gold, and in romantic poetry too, say in Keats' "Lamia." "Upon a time, before the faery broods / Drove Nymph and Satyr from the prosperous woods," things happened, some of which remain forever hidden, "unknown to any Muse, / Though Fancy's casket were unlock'd to choose." Once marked, the "airy elves by moonlight shadows seen," as Pope notes in *The Rape of the Lock,* are everywhere in classic and romantic English poetry too, often lugging or guarding mysterious, enticing boxes, chests, and caskets filled with golden coins that vanish, boxes filled with magical delights that permanently enrich. Within the bounds of caskets the elect learn by seeing true, not dimly. Of Cole's American contemporaries, perhaps only Edgar Allan Poe grasped much of this, writing in "Fairyland" of the "dim vales—and shadowy floods— / And cloudy-looking woods, / Whose forms we can't discover." Dwight himself, as he rode into the oak-opening country of western New York, found himself uneasy, then profoundly disturbed by a half-bounded scene. "Yet though the tract around him is seemingly bound everywhere, the boundary is everywhere obscure: being formed by trees thinly dispersed, and retired beyond each other at such distances as that while in many places they actually limit the view, they appear rather to border dim, indistinct openings into other tracts of country."[19] Without natural boundaries, the easternmost edge of the North American prairie proves too much for Dwight, who glimpses something of Poe's boundless, discoverless forms and turns back into familiar scenes. But Cole, out of an English childhood and an American pedestrian view, discovered the drinking cup by the rill and the power to bound his visions, to take the landscape through the prisms of light and weather, and place it in an open casket where only another elect may find his peculiar, pedestrian vision, one touched somehow by the *genius loci* of every spot Cole trod.

Yes, Cole needed a horse. But not a horse to ride. He walked, and saw, and most unlike Dwight and the other hurrying horsemen, became part of the nobility Thoreau describes in words that unsettle turn-of-the-millennium Americans uneasy enough with Brocklesby's verbal rendering of colors and reflected, mixing light, and prey to doubts about their own hurrying busyness, their own careering along Interstate 90. At the end of time, Cole walked, and saw.

Notes

1. Louis Legrand Noble, *The Life and Works of Thomas Cole* (1853), ed. Elliot S. Vesell (Cambridge, Mass.: Harvard University Press, 1964), 162–163.
2. Noble's volume passed through several editions: I use the edition edited by Vesell because it contains a useful introduction.

3. Noble, 164. See Leo Marx, *The Machine in the Garden: Technology and the Pastoral Ideal in America* (New York: Oxford University Press, 1964).

4. Timothy Dwight, *Travels in New England and New York* (1822), ed. Barbara Miller Solomon (Cambridge, Mass.: Harvard University Press, 1969), 4: 122, 124.

5. Dwight, 1: 1; 3: 236–237. Scholarship on Dwight remains sparse. See, however, John F. Sears, "Timothy Dwight and the American Landscape: The Composing Eye in Dwight's *Travels in New England and New York*," *Early American Literature,* 11 (Winter 1976–1977): 311–321; and Timothy B. Spears, "Common Observations: Timothy Dwight's *Travels in New England and New York*," *American Studies* 30 (Spring 1989): 35–52.

6. Frederick Law Olmsted, *Journey in the Back Country* (1860) (New York: Schocken, 1970). See also Stilgoe, *Common Landscape of America, 1580 to 1845* (New Haven: Yale University Press, 1982).

7. Henry David Thoreau, *Writings,* ed. Bradford Torrey (Boston: Houghton, Mifflin, 1906), 7: 171.

8. Henry David Thoreau, *Excursions* (Boston: Houghton, Mifflin, 1863), 172.

9. Noble, 150, 153.

10. Thoreau, *Excursions,* 213.

11. John Brocklesby, *Elements of Meteorology* (New York: Pratt, Woodford, 1853), v, 166–167.

12. Noble, 43–45, 46–51, 129.

13. Brocklesby, 96.

14. Thoreau, *Excursions,* 163.

15. See, for example, Wirt Sikes, *British Goblins: Welsh Folk-Lore, Fairy Mythology, Legends, and Traditions* (London: Low, 1880).

16. For general background, see *A Dictionary of Superstitions,* ed. Iona Opie and Moira Tatem (Oxford: Oxford University Press, 1989); and Peter Burke, *Popular Culture in Early Modern Europe* (New York: Harper & Row, 1978).

17. See, for example, Hugh Miller, *Scenes and Legends of the North of Scotland, or, The Traditional History of Cromarty* (Edinburgh: William P. Nimmo, 1872); and Brian Froud and Alan Lee, *Faeries* (New York: Abrams, 1978).

18. Noble, 147–148, 188.

19. Dwight, 4: 37.

SMILING SCENES

Nine years after his first visit to Lake George, Timothy Dwight returned. The president of Yale College, theologian, and determined observer of landscape found the environs of the lake much improved in 1811, indeed so much so that he did not wait out the stormy weather that prevented his boating about in search of fine views. The most casual glance told him that wilderness magnificence had evolved into moral beauty.

On his earlier trip in 1802 Dwight detailed the spectacular scenery of Lake George, well aware that readers of his projected "Travels in New England and New York" would expect a lengthy description of this scenic wonder about which the young republic might justifiably boast. "Lake George is universally considered as being in itself and in its environs the most beautiful object of the same nature in the United States," he wrote; it was so magnificent that even some European visitors who had seen the "celebrated waters of Switzerland, have given it the preference."[1]

By way of preface to several pages of methodical description, he explained: "The scenery of this spot may be advantageously considered under the following heads, the water, the islands, the shore, and the mountains." The water, of "singular salubrity, sweetness, and elegance," frequently rewards the observer with "a gay, luminous azure," forming a sort of ground on which the islands, "fancifully computed at 365," show "unceasing variety, and with the happiest conceivable relations." Some forested with pine, others with beech, maple, and oak, still others merely naked rocks, the islands in their "exquisite and diversified beauty" complement the shore, where beauty originates in juxtapositions of rock and forest and beaches of "light colored sand." Around water, islands, and shore loom the mountains, sometimes "bald, solemn, and forbidding," sometimes "tufted with lofty trees," now and then "naked, wild, and solitary," always rewarding the observer with a prospect of the "magnificent hand of nature." But more than atomistic cataloguing informs his appreciation; Dwight understood not only the necessity of viewing the lake from several vantage points and of observing the environs from

"Smiling Scenes" appeared in different form in *Views and Visions: American Landscape before 1830,* ed. Edward J. Nygren (Washington, D.C.: Corcoran Gallery of Art, 1986), 213–28.

a boat sailing about the water, but also the absolute need of scrutinizing the play of light across the scene.

"Unceasing variegations of light and shade" entrance him, for on Lake George they are "not only far more diversified, but are much more obvious, intense, and glowing than in smooth, open countries." Clouds, shadows, "the changes of the day" in short engage the eye "with emotions approximating to rapture." On September 30, Dwight remarks, "a little before the setting of the sun, I saw one of the mountains on the east arrayed in the most brilliant purple which can be imagined. Nothing could surpass the luster which overspread this magnificent object, and which was varied through innumerable tints and softenings of that gorgeous color." Surely Europe offered nothing finer.

Suffusing his lengthy description, although so subtly that his geographical and aesthetic terminology frequently overwhelms it, glows the energy of mated religion and patriotism, the energy that illuminated the early national vision of landscape. As Dwight points out, the Lake George region witnessed stirring events in the War of Independence, including the battle of Ticonderoga: in the glorious scenery there occurred glorious events which presaged a glorious future. Implicit in his paragraphs flows an awareness of Lake George as Edenic stage on which a chosen people will shape a light-enlivened landscape. "The road for the three or four last miles passes through a forest, and conceals the lake from the view of the traveler until he arrives at the eminence on which Fort George was built," he muses. "Here is opened at once a prospect, the splendor of which is rarely exceeded." Out of the darkness, out of the forest of bewilderment and struggle, the republican emerges into the promised land ripe for improvement, a land washed in the light of Protestantism, ordered liberty, and the sun.

Sunlight acquires importance, not only in making mountains purple, but in making possible husbandry, the noble occupation of democracy. Lake George, Dwight insists in his description of 1802, is not finished; its shores lack farms. "To complete the scenery of this lake, the efforts of cultivation are obviously wanting," he concludes. "The hand of the husbandman has already begun to clear these grounds, and will, at no great distance of time, adorn them with all the smiling scenes of agriculture." Only then will the promised land become the landscape of promise.

So quickly did the hand move that even Dwight stood surprised nine years later. Perhaps the change confused him a little; in approaching the lake he missed a turn and quickly got lost, but not in dense forest. The wrong road ran "bordered for several miles by a succession of good farms, the appearance of which, and of the houses which were upon them, sufficiently indicated the easy, prosperous state of the inhabitants." The road ended at "a beautiful village, exhibiting, with a brilliancy almost singular," the "neat and even handsome houses" and other "elegancies" of art which so improve the "majesty of nature." Around the improved lake Dwight discovered what he again termed the "smiling scenes of agriculture," the perfect synthesis of farming, village life, and natural grandeur, all washed in the light of divine liberty.

Inclosure

"The hunter, wherever found, is a savage—the herdsman, in every age, a barbarian; but the planter and the farmer are civilized and social beings," William Plumer assured his audience at an 1821 New Hampshire agricultural society assembly.[2] "Permanent wealth, like that in lands, can neither be obtained, nor enjoyed by any people till the habit of regular industry is formed and established among them; and this habit nowhere exists till man begins to cultivate the earth." A decade after Dwight's second visit to Lake George, Plumer told the farm families what they wanted to hear, what they already knew, and what they were just beginning to doubt. Traditional farming lay at the base of all private and public virtue and happiness.

Plumer spent little time on philosophy, however pleasantly his listeners accepted it. Instead he moved immediately to explicating and recommending the latest farming techniques, particularly deep plowing, crop rotation, and, perhaps most important, manuring. Plumer addressed farmers tending long-established farms, and he understood—if they did not—the awesome importance of keeping land "in good heart" by adding to it "the ordinary supplies of the barnyard," along with leaves and other organic material from woodlots and swamps. "Into these neglected nooks, and dark recesses of his farm, the industrious husbandman ought to dig as for mines of gold." The nooks and recesses, "if rightly improved, will furnish him with the means of restoring vigour to his exhausted lands, of preserving those that are still unimpaired, and enable him, by the aid of drains, to convert his useless wastes into fertile fields." A "new era" mandated change; no longer could farmers excuse slovenly agriculture by claiming the exigencies of pioneering.[3]

Everywhere in the eastern portions of the new nation reformers championed the causes of agricultural improvement. "Let us boldly face the fact," announced the Virginian John Taylor. "Our country is nearly ruined. We have certainly drawn out of the earth three-fourths of the vegetable matter it contained, within reach of the plough." In *Arator: Being a Series of Agricultural Essays, Practical and Political,* Taylor fastened on soil exhaustion as a potential, indeed probable, catastrophe for all southern planters. He advocated not only manuring fields but "inclosing" livestock in temporary pens set on impoverished soil and moved to a new location every week or so. Two hundred cattle and sheep "will in this way manure eighteen acres annually, sufficiently to produce fine crops of Indian corn and wheat, and a good growth of red clover after them," Taylor claimed, implicitly acknowledging that Virginia soil lay exhausted indeed.[4]

Plumer, Taylor, and a host of other early-nineteenth-century reformers followed the mid-eighteenth-century precedent set by Jared Eliot, a New England clergyman whose *Essays upon Field Husbandry* used scriptural authority to buttress commonsense pleas for soil improvement.[5] For roughly a century after 1750 reformers urged upon farmers the gospel of stewardship, of perpetually maintaining tilth and fertility; but in the second decade of the nineteenth century their arguments changed, albeit subtly. Westward migration from the ever more barren fields of New England, New Jersey, and the Tidewater South unnerved farmers still committed to eastern soil. The "boundless extent of our unsettled territory," warned Plumer, "tempts the husbandman to cultivate many acres badly, instead of a few well."[6] Revolution brought more than republican government; it and the Louisiana Purchase opened the way to the Ohio Valley, to Kentucky, across the Cumberland River and a thousand unpainted streams to virgin land far more fertile than that two centuries plowed. As young men abandoned farms to aging parents, as aging parents died, as Thomas Birch and others remarked the great Conestoga wagons moving west, slovenliness stole across the eastern landscape, mocking Eliot's gospel of stewardship.

"There is something so pleasing in the appearance of neatness and cleanliness about a dwelling house, that even a stranger, transiently passing by, cannot help being prepossessed with a favorable opinion of those within," argued the editor of *New England Farmer* in 1823 in one of his first issues. "How different the sensation felt on viewing a contrary scene;—a house dismal and dirty, the doors and walls surrounded and bespattered with filth of all denominations, and fragments of broken dishes and dirty dairy utensils scattered in all directions impress on his mind the idea of misery and mismanagement." The newspaper founded to promulgate scientific agricultural practices like those extolled by Plumer and Taylor very quickly focused on praising traditional carefulness only slightly enhanced by modern techniques. "Prosperity and happiness," in the words of its editor, seemed as likely to grow in consistently well-tended soil as in newly manured fields.[7]

In these years agricultural societies began "noticing" efficient farms and awarding prizes or "premiums" for the most productive cows, the plumpest sheep, the swamp most effectively drained, cleared, and planted to wheat. By the mid-1820s, in shows and fairs, reformers displayed the finest specimens of the finest breeds, championing innovative bloodlines and novel experiments. What pleased the societies most, however, was simply the well-managed "thrifty" farm kept by "fore-handed" people conscious of traditional wisdom and contemporary invention, the bountiful, pacific place Washington Irving detailed in his "Legend of Sleepy Hollow" in 1819. Everything about such a thrifty farm bespoke attention to detail, to order; but perhaps the fields spoke most clearly to approaching observers.

Carefully bred horses, cattle, and other livestock standing in pastures of timothy grass, red clover, or other high-quality grass—pastures reflecting in their rich green tint not only a precise monoculture but the perfect evenness of fertility dependent on inclosing and conscientious manuring—caught the eye of Dwight and society judges. Deciduous trees scattered among the pastures and meadows, their lower branches reaching down to the "browse line" of horses and cattle straining upward for leaves, provided shade for the stock and for the haymakers resting momentarily. "I found the upper part of Richmond valley more beautiful than I had thought it before," mused Dwight of upstate New York in 1811. "The fields in their size, figure, surface, and fertility are remarkably fine, and are ornamented with beautiful trees, standing alternately single, in small clumps, and in handsome groves. The cultivation is plainly of a superior cast."[8] Like islands in Lake George, the scattered trees accentuate the smooth green of the fields by introducing vertical shapes into levelness. Elsewhere trees grew in rows along fences and other boundaries, serving as windbreaks and as a regular source of fencing timber and firewood. Interrupting the openness of fields, often on hillsides, farm woodlots further diversified views. Away from Maine and the swamps of the South, the East of 1815 delighted travelers with long stretches of vanquished wilderness, regions where sheep grazed atop treeless hills, where well-tended fences surrounded fields in which no stumps remained to recall the pioneer era.

Next to fields graced with fine livestock and orchards blooming in geometric rigidity, fences advertised the thrifty farm. In all their regional variations from the stone walls of New England and Pennsylvania to the post-and-rail fences of New York to the zigzag snake fences of the Carolinas, fencing separated different sorts of livestock from each other and from corn, wheat, tobacco, and other crops. No structure better advertised a farmer's commitment to order, to what Plumer called "system and economy"; for fences not only made possible the complex internal activity of the thrifty farm but also the larger, even more complicated farm operation of a neighborhood.

THE DEEP PAST AND IMAGES

At their outermost fence, however, even the most virtuous farmers restrained their efforts. Travelers and agricultural-society judges endured wretched roads bordered with fences good and bad, not only because farmers rarely ventured far from their own land, but because American agriculturalists feared good roads as the highways along which tyrannical armies might march. European travelers admired Lake George and its environs, but none enjoyed the rutted, gully-like roads on which Dwight lost his way, which crossed brooks and streams lacking well-marked fords, ferries, and bridges.[9] Well-traveled roads often became extraordinarily wide, as teamsters guiding immense Conestoga wagons pulled by four or six horses swung from side to side around mudholes, living rock, and axle-snapping ruts. Back roads, often roads bordering impeccably fenced farms, wore ever deeper; their three ruts indicated the willingness of way-farers to follow the route of predecessors over rockslides and through mud. "A loose sand below, sufficiently encumbered with stones," the sort of road Dwight followed to Lake George, struck travelers as "middling" good; while not smooth and well-drained gravel, it still offered no threat-ening boulders or mudholes and provided some opportunity for land-scape observation and botanizing.[10] Everywhere along the roadsides grew the wildflowers increasingly absent from thrifty fields, flowers grazed by escaped livestock and collected by lovers enroute to lovers, flowers that recalled the indigenous vegetation of the settlement era.

Wildflowers within the fences, wildflowers breaking the evenness of meadow grass or field crops reminded early-nineteenth-century farm families of the rising threats to their thrifty existence, the forces likely to break through the defenses of system, care, and post-and-rail fences, the forces evidenced in the slovenliness of so many farms. Taylor begins *Arator* with a series of essays investigating the pernicious impact on farmers of tariffs and manufacturing, concluding that a conspiracy leads "agriculture by a bridle made of her virtue and ignorance, towards the worship of an idol, compounded of folly and wickedness."[11] Plumer warns that the "new era" is produced "by the increase of our popula-tion, the diminution of foreign commerce, and the sudden growth of manufactures amongst us."[12] Between 1800 and 1830 the champions of the endangered farm sharpened their arguments, until reformers like Samuel C. Allen, who addressed one assembly of Massachusetts farm-ers in 1830, knew a complete picture of adverse "political economy." Allen understood that his "subject is too dry for entertainment, and too abstruse to be understood without some effort," but since the principles he chose to explicate "contribute more than government, more than morals, more than religion, to make a society what it is in every country," he led his hearers through a complex interpretation of the change overwhelming American farmers, especially those farmers living in long-settled parts of the nation.

"Before manufactures and trade had given rise to much of what is now called capital," Allen argued, "the land with the buildings and improvements upon it, and its annual produce constituted almost all the existing wealth." No longer, however, do farmers control most wealth; instead, they stand ensnared in issues of currency, credit, and "the interest of money," facing "the funds of corporations" and "joint stock companies." Point by point, Allen detailed the changes, until finally he scrutinized "the extent in which real estates among us are passing under mortgages," something "which is bringing the yeomanry of the country into a state of dependence and peril."[13] Along with so many speakers at agricultural exhibitions, Allen understood the immediate, critical need for farmers to improve what they already have, to stay free of the seductions of credit, to manure their fields. Like the icy blasts of winter, the forces of large-scale monopoly and capitalism might strike down the unprepared farmer.

Manured fields became something like the windbreaks that prudent farmers set north of their farmyards and fields. The stands of trees, sometimes evergreen, sometimes deciduous, often served as woodlots too; but chiefly they sheltered house and outbuildings from winter storms. Often nearly embracing one or more sides of the farmstead, the windbreaks epitomized a new concern for firewood conservation and a dawning appreciation of "embellishing" the site of a comfortable, "happy" farmhouse with the trees and shrubs prosperous agriculturists began to equate with beauty. "These rural decorations add more than one would imagine, who had not tried them, to the innocent pleasures of a family," remarked one anonymous essayist in an 1820 issue of *Rural Magazine and Literary Evening Fireside*. "They have no small influence in forming the taste of children; they form a favourite retreat for the birds; and they fling over the whole country an air of peace, and contentment, and innocent enjoyment."[14] Against marked social and economic change the thrifty farm "inclosed" itself, nursing its resources and even essaying a little aesthetic refinement, exemplifying in the eye of its owner—and in that of the traveler—the *traditional* virtue and economy on which rested republican stability.

Village

In villages, in villages growing into towns, and in towns growing into cities pulsed the forces just beginning to unnerve early-nineteenth-century eastern farm families. Southern and northern agriculturalists, not yet sundered by the spectres of slavery extension and disunion, saw villages as very slightly suspect. But before the great mill-village experiments of the early 1840s, farmers and aesthetes joined with craftsmen, "mechanicks," and manufacturers in hoping that agriculture might coexist with manufacturing, that villages might remain the essentially agrarian creatures of the surrounding smiling countryside.

Surely Dwight thought so, and expressed his conviction in a book-length poem of 1794: *Greenfield Hill*. This avowedly nationalistic paean to post-Independence rural life juxtaposes the poverty-stricken English community Oliver Goldsmith described in his 1770 "Deserted Village" with a happy, wholly prosperous place:

> Sweet smiling village! loveliest of the hills!
> How green thy groves! How pure thy glassy rills!
> With what new joy, I walk thy verdant streets!
> How often pause, to breathe thy gale of sweets;
> To mark thy well-built walls! thy budding fields![15]

Of course, Greenfield Hill is an almost wholly agricultural place, a community utterly dependent on the owners of the budding fields around it, a place of distinctly rural crafts like blacksmithing and milling. Greenfield Hill brushes upon Eden, uniting agricultural and domestic economy with the disciplined worship of the Almighty.

Twenty years changed the eastern village almost beyond recognition. Machinery invaded rural space. "Mechanicks" not only worked a wide range of water-driven machinery, they began building new sorts of machines in a thousand villages blessed with waterfalls.[16] Everywhere in the eastern states north of slavery small manufactories attracted farmers into making shoes or cloth or nails or clocks during the slow winter months, and eventually year round. No one noticed the triumph of shop-scale manufacturing more carefully than the publishers of gazetteers. In his *Gazetteer of the State of New York,* a massive 1824 volume presenting villages in the minutest detail, Horatio Gates Spafford described Yankee Street, a village within the township of Florida, near the Erie Canal. Home to 108 mechanics and their families working five grist mills, five saw mills, two fulling mills, two carding machines, and one ashery, Yankee Street is still a fledgling village in 1824, for it depends chiefly on the farmers living around it.[17] Twelve years later Thomas F. Gordon presented his New York gazetteer to a public thirsty for news, and chronicled the maturation of places like Yankee Street. Villages no longer only ground grain and shod horses; in 1836 they manufactured hoes, twine, chemicals, India rubber, carpets, rifle cartridges, flint glass, varnish, needles, lime, files, and a thousand other items in the small wooden structures designated "manufactories" or "shops."[18] No longer did the meeting-house alone exemplify verticality; the new mills announced the elevation, spatial and otherwise, of mechanism.

In the early nineteenth century John Warner Barber, who specialized in describing villages, published a number of illustrated volumes outlining the "history and antiquities" of every town and village in most of the northeastern states, along with up-do-date geographical and statistical information. Barber understood the extraordinary importance of manufacturing villages in the transformation of national culture, and he distinguished among several types. In Connecticut he discovered Colinsville, established in 1826 as a "company village" within the town of Canton. The houses of the workmen, he observes, "which are built precisely of the same form, are compactly set together on the side of a hill" and "are painted white, and when contrasted with the deep green foliage in the immediate vicinity, present a novel and beautiful appearance."[19] The five hundred inhabitants of Colinsville make axes and reside in a new sort of community space—the village of identical houses owned by a corporation. Further south, in New Jersey, Barber found Clinton, one of hundreds of fast-growing villages that comprised another type, one that was ordered about several unrelated industries. Until 1838, when the federal government located a post office there, Clinton existed as a hamlet of three houses and a mill; in 1844 it contained "3 mercantile stores, 2 large merchant-mills, with one of which an oil-mill is connected; 3 public houses, about 15 mechanic shops of various kinds, a brick-yard, a valuable limestone quarry, 3 churches, 62 dwellings, and 520 inhabitants" along with two schools.[20] Colinsville and Clinton represented the future to Barber. Conway, in the Massachusetts hill country, exemplified the third sort of village, that already stranded in the past. While still reasonably prosperous, its "thirty dwelling-houses and other buildings" included no shops worthy of note, but it did have two churches, although one lacked a spire.[21] Conway announced the quiet agrarian prosperity that Plumer and Taylor honored. On the other hand, Colinsville advertised the power of the joint-stock corporation, and Clinton boasted of the prosperity bred of tariffs levied on imported manufactured goods—power and prosperity that Plumer, Taylor, and Allen feared.

Manufacturing villages flaunted the emerging economic order touching every American, even the farmer purchasing a new plow. Company villages sometimes demonstrated in their perfect, often symmetrical arrangements of mills, shops, and houses a military-like understanding of spatial arrangement, but every manufacturing village announced changes from the traditional agricultural order. By 1815 "mill" no longer designated only the low, unpainted, water-driven gristmill or sawmill to which farmers resorted in winter, when snow-covered roads made sledging grain and timber practical. It meant a multistory structure towering over mill-dam and adjacent houses, often painted a distinctive color other than the traditional white. And even the houses, termed "cottages" by occupants and travelers alike, announced in their sameness and their tiny lots a divorce from the agricultural past. The cottages, the two-family "double houses," the houses straggling into connected shops or stores, all boasted of new powers reaching out into agricultural space. Infant industries promised economic independence from Britain, certainly, and many Americans delighted in viewing the manufacturing villages. Like the country's immense new bridges, ever-larger sailing ships flying the new flag, and vast "internal improvements" such as the Erie Canal watering Colinsville, the mills and mechanic shops demonstrated the potential of bearding Britain once again.[22]

Even during the embargo years astute observers like Joshua Rowley Watson watched the slow growth of Boston, Philadelphia, Baltimore, and other coastal cities, remarking the way that mechanics attracted mechanics and shipwrights attracted shipwrights, that the transshipment of farm produce and manufactured goods raised land values and caused property owners to build taller buildings, longer docks, and houses jammed ever more tightly together. Urban growth worried many adherents of the older agrarian philosophy; but for every farmer who worried, another delighted in the ever-increasing range of goods available for sale, in the better newspapers, in the chance to invest in turnpike and toll-bridge companies dependent on urban growth, and best of all, in the new markets cities offered for farm produce. "The streets of New York have unhappily followed, in many instances, its original designation of a fishing and trading village," Dwight decided in 1811. "The streets are generally wider and less crooked than those of Boston, but a great proportion of them are narrow and winding."[23] If New York and Boston grew from villages, what did the future hold for Clinton, or for any village but the stagnating sort like Conway, if not the chance to grow into cityhood?

To stand back, to stand on a hilltop surrounded by fields and woodlots and see far off the manufacturing village or the budding city provided at least the chance to integrate the agrarian vision with the manufacturing, urban one, to see the village and even the city within the broader, reassuring landscape of agriculture, to hope for an equilibrium sometime in the near present. However Taylor and Allen worried, the mechanic shop and the close-packed city represented forces of the future, forces of national economic independence, forces that no right-thinking, patriotic American wholly dismissed in the years before the 1840 tariff and states' rights debates.

Backdrop

Always beyond the most distant fields and woodlots, in the bluish mists inland from coastal cities and above so many valley-bottom villages, the wilderness remained—the unshaped capital beckoning foresters, farmers, and eventually also finely educated observers who were learning something new of scenic beauty. "Up these precipices from the water's edge to their summits, rose a most elegant succession of forest trees, chiefly maple, beech, and evergreens," remarked Dwight in 1799 of the mountainous region near Williamstown in Vermont. "The deciduous foliage had already been changed by the frost to just such a degree as to present every tincture from the deepest verdure of the spring through all its successive shades to the willow green, and thence through a straw color, orange, and crimson to a reddish brown." Even Dwight, scrutinizing and recording the appearance of farms and villages along the Williamstown road, admired the change from "smiling scenery" to "rudeness and grandeur" to "beauty and majesty."[24]

In 1799 Dwight saw grandeur and beauty where other well-educated observers had seen nothing but wildness a decade earlier. In 1789 even the falls of the Niagara River struck Jedidiah Morse as only "curious." His *American Geography* focuses chiefly on the practical uses of wilderness areas and on the delights of productive rural landscape. After briefly noting the "astonishing grandeur" of the drop itself, the noise, and the vapor sometimes illuminated into rainbows, Morse introduces Lake Ontario, a body of water more useful than the falls or Lake Erie. Upstream from Niagara Falls lurks a lake difficult to navigate, dotted with rattlesnake-infested islands and smothered with pond lilies, on the leaves of which in summer basks the "hissing snake," whose "subtile wind," if "drawn in with the breath of the unwary traveler, will infallibly bring on a decline, that in a few months must prove mortal."[25] Morse tried to appreciate the wildnesses of the Blue Ridge and other mountainous places, but *American Geography* reveals how powerfully he felt the love of shaped land.

Appreciation of utter wilderness came slowly, fueled by European aesthetic theory and literary precedent. The agelessness of American wilderness intermittently perplexed Morse and other writers, who missed the reassuring presence of the ruins enlivening European forest and mountain scenery. "At least," argued Dwight in the preface to his *Travels,* the wondrous transformation of forest into farms and villages "may compensate the want of ancient castles, ruined abbeys, and fine pictures."[26] Only the rarest early-nineteenth-century observers of North American wilderness discovered traces of long-abandoned human effort.

Washington Irving succeeded, albeit in a modest way. Near Manhattan Island, for example, he found Hell Gate, the "narrow strait, where the current is violently compressed between shouldering promontories, and horribly irritated and perplexed by rocks and shoals." It was not only a place to study the wild "paroxysms" of nature; near a group of rocks there lay the wreck of a sailing vessel. "There was some wild story about this being the wreck of a pirate, and of some bloody murder, connected with it, which I cannot now recollect," says Irving's narrator in *Tales of a Traveller,* an 1824 collection. "Indeed, the desolate look of this forlorn hulk, and the fearful place where it lay rotting, were sufficient to awaken strange notions concerning it."[27] Much of the book is ordered by strange notions of times past, but the hunting of buried pirate treasure informs the last portion of the *Tales,* along with the "conspicuous part" played by the Devil in most searches. In the first decades of the nineteenth century the seacoast—that wilderness first touched and often first abandoned by the earliest colonists—provided ruins and folktale enough for Irving, Poe, Hawthorne, and other writers grappling with the nearly overwhelming force of trans-Atlantic Gothic and Romantic art,[28] and for painters like Charles Codman vexed by ruinless forest, swamp, and mountain never visited by seventeenth- and early-eighteenth-century pirates.

Sport attracted many visitors to wilderness, although their steps were lightened by the dawning awareness of scenic beauty. "The approach to Sebago Pond is through a rugged hilly land, which opens a communication between the solitude of the waters and busy world around them," remarked an anonymous essayist in an 1829 issue of *Atlantic Monthly Magazine.* A country walk alone pleases him, sparking thoughts concerning prosperous farms and "the manufactories and machinery of a thickly settled country" downstream; but the "clear depths of this beauteous lake" delight him more. Indeed he concludes patriotically that Izaak Walton himself would have abandoned English water for Sebago Pond, so magnificent is its setting and so soothing its "deep hush." Rocked ever so lightly in his rowboat, the fisherman gazes about, discerning here and there the same pioneer fields of grain Dwight noticed around Lake George, and remarking "an immense ridge of gray rocks, standing in bold contrast with the softness of the surrounding waters and landscape like the habitation of the *genius loci.*" Confronting the coming of the smiling rural countryside and the towering "grotesque" rocks, the essayist discovers a few clearings "filled with the charred stumps of the pines, whose blackened surfaces and desolate cheerlessness, were fit emblems of the ancient nobleness, withered and blasted as it now is, of the *rightful* lords of the soil, the American aborigines." From his boatmen he learns something of the "romance" of the environs, a "tradition" involving an Indian love affair ensnared in tribal warfare. On Sebago Pond the essayist finds good fishing and romantic wilderness, and even a ruin—the figures painted by the Indian lovers to commemorate their escape.[29]

No longer is Satan the *genius loci* of the forest wilderness; slowly, tentatively, the vanquished Indian replaces him, then shades of Revolutionary War heroes. As the decades advanced, the love of wilderness grew stronger among educated Americans,[30] but it grew slowly, especially away from places uncharmed by colonial ruins and traditions, or even by the Revolutionary War events so quickly receding into the romance embroidered by Cooper and Simms.[31] As his mid-nineteenth-century *Maine Woods* and *Cape Cod* make clear, even Thoreau distrusted virgin forest and barrier beach.[32]

Balance

> It is questionable whether mankind have ever seen so large a tract changed so suddenly from a wilderness into a well-inhabited and well-cultivated country. A great number of beautiful villages have risen up as by the power of enchantment; and the road for one hundred and twenty miles is in a sense lined by a succession of houses, almost universally neat, and frequently handsome. Throughout most of this extent an excellent soil, covered deep with vegetable mold, rewards every effort of the farmer with a luxuriant produce.[33]

Poised everywhere midway, upstate New York in 1811 pleased Dwight almost beyond measure. Graced by beautiful natural scenery touched by military exploits, improved by precise, inclosed husbandry totally removed from slovenliness, dignified by villages not yet wholly devoted to manufacturing but completely committed to national economic independence, the region epitomized the glories of republican government, of new institutions blooming in a land bathed in divine and celestial light. How long could it want pictures?

Notes

1. Timothy Dwight, *Travels in New England and New York 1769–1815* (1822; reprint, ed. Barbara Miller Solomon, Cambridge, Mass.: Harvard University Press, 1969), Vol. III,

p. 244. The descriptions of the scenery of Lake George that follow are found on pp. 244–252 and 287–289; on the military history of the environs, see pp. 252–272.

2. William Plumer, *Address before the Rockingham Agricultural Society* (Exeter, N.H.: Williams, 1821), p. 1.

3. *Ibid.,* p. 20.

4. John Taylor, *Arator: Being a Series of Agricultural Essays, Practical and Political* (1813; reprint, Petersburg, Va.: Whitworth and Young, 1818), pp. 53, 70.

5. Jared Eliot, *Essays upon Field Husbandry* (1748–1762; reprint, ed. Harry J. Carman and Rexford G. Tugwell, New York: Columbia University Press, 1934), pp. 11–26 and passim.

6. *Ibid.,* p. 19.

7. "On Farms, Farm Houses . . . ," *New England Farmer* 1 (June 7, 1823): 1.

8. Dwight, *Travels,* Vol. III, p. 287.

9. On fences, roads, and farmers' distrust of road networks, see John R. Stilgoe, *Common Landscape of America, 1580 to 1845* (New Haven: Yale University Press, 1982), pp. 188–191, 21–23, 111–115, 128–133.

10. Dwight, *Travels,* Vol. III, p. 288; see also Vol. II, p. 139.

11. Taylor, *Arator,* p. 17.

12. Plumer, *Address,* p. 20.

13. Samuel C. Allen, *Address Delivered at Northampton* (Northampton, Mass.: Shepard, 1830), pp. 5, 18–19, 22, 24, 27, 29, and passim.

14. "The Village Teacher," *Rural Magazine and Literary Evening Fireside* 1 (September 1820): 324.

15. Timothy Dwight, *Greenfield Hill* (New York: Childs and Swain, 1794), pp. 33.

16. "The Mechanick," *Rural Repository* 6 (June 20, 1829): 15.

17. Horatio Gates Spafford, *Gazetteer of the State of New York* (Albany: Packard, 1824), p. 176.

18. Thomas F. Gordon, *Gazetteer of the State of New York* (Philadelphia: Gordon, 1836), pp. 632, 714.

19. John Warner Barber, *Connecticut Historical Collections* (New Haven: Durrie, 1836), pp. 70–71.

20. John Warner Barber, *Historical Collections of New Jersey* (New York: Tuttle, 1846), pp. 244–245.

21. John Warner Barber, *Historical Collections of Massachusetts* (Worcester: Lazell, 1844), pp. 244–245.

22. See Stilgoe, *Common Landscape,* pp. 300–334.

23. Dwight, *Travels,* Vol. III, p. 315.

24. *Ibid.,* pp. 166–167.

25. Jedidiah Morse, *American Geography* (Elizabethtown, N.J.: Shepard Kollock, 1789), pp. 39–40 and passim.

26. Dwight, *Travels,* Vol. I, p. 8.

27. Washington Irving, "Hell Gate," *Tales of a Traveller* (1824; reprint, New York: Bedford, 1891), pp. 206–209.

28. See, e.g., Edgar Allan Poe, "The Gold Bug" [1843], *Best Known Works,* ed. Hervey Allen (New York: Blue Ribbon, 1927), pp. 53–77, and Nathaniel Hawthorne, "Footprints on the Seashore," *Twice-Told Tales* (1851; reprint, Cambridge, Mass.: Houghton Mifflin, 1882), pp. 504–516.

29. "Sebago Pond," *Atlantic Monthly Magazine* 1 (October 1829): 448–452.

30. On the growing love of wilderness, see Cecelia Tichi, *New World, New Earth: Envi-*

ronmental Reform in American Literature from the Puritans through Whitman (New Haven: Yale University Press, 1979).

31. See, e.g., James Fenimore Cooper, *The Spy: A Tale of the Neutral Ground* (New York: Wiley and Halsted, 1822), and William Gilmore Simms, *The Partisan: A Tale of the Revolution* (New York: Harper, 1835).

32. On Thoreau and life-threatening wilderness, see John R. Stilgoe, "A New England Coastal Wilderness," *Geographical Review* 71 (January 1981): 33–50.

33. Dwight, *Travels,* Vol. III, p. 373.

FAIR FIELDS AND BLASTED ROCK
American Land Classification Systems and Landscape Aesthetics

What is good land? Seventeenth-century North American colonists disagreed about its character; land that husbandmen cherished as rich and warm, miners condemned as barren while pioneering agriculturalists scorned it. Agricultural evaluation dominated colonial thinking, and throughout the eighteenth century Americans frequently classified all land unfit for agriculture—especially treeless mountains—as *bad*. Their contempt endured for another hundred years, probably warping national aesthetics and divorcing American notions of landscape beauty from the standards dear to European romantics. "The poet and the painter will seek in vain for those objects which they have been accustomed to behold under the influence of fascination, and to depict with enthusiasm and rapture," wrote Timothy Dwight in 1804 of upstate New York. "The phrase *beautiful country,* as used here, means appropriately and almost only lands suited to the purposes of husbandry, and has scarcely a remote reference to beauty of landscape."[1] Within twenty years, however, American artists had embraced the farmers' equation of rich agricultural land with beautiful country; only a few investigated the mineralogical land classification system and its insignificant aesthetic. The wilderness portrayed in so many paintings and tales reflects the aesthetic of the agricultural land concerns that shaped American thinking until explorers entered the High Plains and Rocky Mountains and learned again the mineralogical classification system. Until the 1870's *beautiful country* defined agricultural land—or land fit for agriculture.

The elaborate agricultural and mineralogical land classification systems comprise a significant part of what Peter Burke calls the "little tradition," the wealth of belief and practice transferred orally and by example from one generation to another.[2] Occasionally, as G. E. Fussell notes in *The Classical Tradition in West European Farming,* husbandmen maintained Roman agricultural practices well into the sixteenth century, weaving into the ancient wisdom an increasingly intricate local lore of soil types and plant indicators.[3] It is clear too, from such studies as Paul Sebillot's

"Fair Fields and Blasted Rock: American Land Classification Systems and Landscape Aesthetics" appeared in *American Studies* 22 (Spring 1981), copyright University of Kansas Press.

Les Trauvaux publics et les mines dans les traditions et les superstitions, Otto Hue's *Die Bergarbeiter,* and more recently, G. Schreiber's *Der Bergbau in Geschichte* and John Ulric Nef's *The Conquest of the Material World,* that early modern European prospectors and miners understood a different traditional but equally complex land classification system that contradicted the one favored by most agriculturists.[4] Much less is known about the North and South American variations of the Old World land classification systems. Archer Butler Hulbert's *Soil: Its Influence on the History of the United States,* though dated, is still valuable, but it has spawned few other studies. Only James T. Lemon's *The Best Poor Man's Country: A Geographical Study of Early Southeastern Pennsylvania* details the usefulness of European soil classification rules in North America.[5] Here I wish only to briefly describe the European systems on the eve of colonization, sketch how they functioned in North America, and suggest that they helped shape American scenery values.

In *A Philosophical Discourse of the Earth,* John Evelyn discusses the Old World agricultural land classification system imported into North America. His treatise of 1678 emphasizes the usefulness of four-element analysis and the power of astrological influence. In ordering soils according to fertility, he describes "black, fat, yet porous, light," surface soil as "the best, and sweetest, being enriched with all that the air, dews, showers, and celestial influences can contribute to it." While he accepts with reservation the Baconian doctrine that the best soil lies wherever rainbows touch the earth, he firmly believes that vegetation indicates soil fertility. Camomile marks "a mould disposed for corn," burnet grows in soil useful as pasture, and mallows indicate soil favorable to root crops. By tasting the soil, a wise husbandman can discover the presence or absence of important salts, and by careful watching he can see "exhalations from minerals and the heat of the sun" as well as true colors. Evelyn insists too on smelling the soil: "Upon the first rain, good and natural mould will emit a most agreeable scent; and in some places (as Alonso Barba, a considerable Spanish author testifies), approaching the most ravishing perfumes." But "if the ground be disposed to any mineral or other ill quality, sending forth arsenical, and very noxious steams," the wise husbandman ought to avoid it. His frequent references to the four elements, often couched in terms like "sweetness," and his faith in celestial influence reveal the power of medieval custom in the early modern era. To be "well read in the alphabet of the earth" required an understanding of traditional wisdom.[6]

Seventeenth-century letters from North American colonists reveal the complexity of soil analysis. "The soil I judge to be lusty and fat in

A Plan of Irasburgh, as surveyed in the years 1792 and 1798 by James Whitelaw.

The Lots in Irasburgh contain 117 acres, strict measure, each. The quality of each Lot is marked in the upper part of it; G stands for good Land, M for middling Land, and B for bad Land.

Copied from the Original, Attest. Herman Allen Rght. Clerk.

In 1792 surveyors of Irasburg in Vermont attempted to classify land according to its value to would-be farmers. (Harvard College Library)

many places, light and hot, in some places sandy-bottomed and in some loamy, reasonably good for all sorts of grain without manuring, but exceeding good with manure, some for wheat, some for rye, etc.," advised one Bay Colony settler in 1638.[7] Dutch colonists delighted in soil that Englishmen dismissed as too cold and wet, noting that low-lying meadows "could be dyked and cultivated," and Germans, Swedes, and other immigrants learned that their national land classification systems made sense of New World wilderness ground.[8] Early colonists understood that every species of tree indicates one or more peculiarities of soil fertility or sterility; each colony quickly produced catalogs of trees to prove the fertility of its soils.[9] As late as 1759, Israel Acrelius described the trees of New Sweden in old-country terms, explaining that while the white oak indicates good soil, the hickory and sassafras mark the richest.[10]

By the middle of the eighteenth century, however, Americans had combined the tree lore of several European nations into one distinctively their own, and land surveyors often casually classified the terrain they measured according to well-understood categories like "good land" or "bad land," as is evident in a 1792 manuscript "Plan of Irasburgh" Vermont and in other surveyors' plats.[11] James Smith's 1799 account of his captivity by the Indians of the Northwest Territory exemplifies the

FAIR FIELDS AND BLASTED ROCK

new national land classification system based on vegetation cover. Smith descried four sorts of land during his wanderings. What he calls "first-rate land" he knew by oak, hickory, walnut, cherry, black ash, elm, beech, and several other species. Second-rate land he recognized by the appearance of spicewood trees among the beech, and third-rate territory by the small size of all trees and the preponderance of species like spicewood. Here and there he crossed land he calls "worse than third-rate," expanses marked by "hurtle berry bushes" or prairie.[12] Americans had forgotten Old World wisdom concerning polder, steppes, and heaths; they perceived all treeless land—even the Illinois country Smith encountered—as barren, even when it produced grasses and shrubs several feet high. They avoided the blueberry barrens of Maine and the pine barrens of New Jersey, North Carolina, and Georgia, and searched for land marked by trees like the hickory, where they stopped and tested the soil as carefully as had their seventeenth-century forebears.

Astute European visitors discerned American modifications of Old World classifications. "The honey locust, which signifies fertile soil, perfumed the crest of the mountain with its flowers," wrote a Frenchman exploring Pennsylvania in 1791. "Hickories and stalwart oaks luxuriously extended their branches."[13] Ferdinand Bayard caught a trace of the emerging synthesis of practicality and aesthetics, but most Europeans learned only the practical significance of trees. A husbandman "may know the quality of the land by the trees, with which it is entirely covered," asserted an English musician traveling through the countryside in the first years of the United States. "The hickory and the walnut are an infallible sign of a rich, and every species of fir, of a barren, sandy, and unprofitable soil."[14] Throughout the first half of the nineteenth century, Americans prized land covered with hickory and walnut trees, and gradually they equated such species with more than good soil. Such trees represented dignity, strength, and courage, characteristics that won for Andrew Jackson the nickname "Old Hickory," and they epitomized national standards of arboreal beauty.[15] Always, however, they first indicated fertile land.

Nineteenth-century agricultural periodicals retained early modern European concepts of land classification in the most up-to-date articles, supporting the suggestion made by Herbert Leventhal in *In the Shadow of the Enlightenment: Occultism and Renaissance Science in Eighteenth-Century America* that much orally-transmitted lore endured as common knowledge long after intellectuals had discarded it.[16] An 1836 *Farmer's Cabinet* editorial, "On the Nature of Soils," for example, echoes Evelyn's theories by asserting that sand, clay, gravel, chalk, loam, and marl have different "degrees of warmth, air, and moisture," and must be carefully identified. "The

The rich soils of Pennsylvania attracted the attention of European and American travelers, who leaned over fences and viewed agricultural value that in time shaped scenery aesthetics.

best loams, and natural earths are of a bright brown, or hazely color," the editorial notes before explaining the various scents and textures of soils.[17] Such thinking biased Dwight and Thoreau as they explored the "sterility" of outer Cape Cod. "In such ground no forest tree can grow either with rapidity or vigor," Dwight remarked of the duneland. "On the driest and most barren of these grounds grows a plant which I have never before seen, known here by the name of beach grass."[18] Fifty years later, Thoreau slogged through the "barren, heath-like plain," wondering at the poverty-grass "despised by many on account of its being associated with barrenness," inquiring, as had Dwight, about the color of the soil, and finding little of beauty anywhere.[19] Both men classified the region according to established but obsolescent standards; farmers in western prairies had learned that grassland might be fertile beyond belief, that a lack of trees might indicate anything but barrenness.

In an 1818 article entitled "On the Prairies and Barrens of the West," Caleb Atwater of Ohio explained to readers of *The American Journal of Science* that *prairie* denotes discrete patches of natural grassland covering

FAIR FIELDS AND BLASTED ROCK

no more than about three by seven miles and producing six- or seven-feet-high grass mixed with "some weeds and plum-bushes." *Barrens* identifies vast, almost limitless low, moist areas covered with grass, although capable of producing a few oaks and hickories in spots marked by low water tables. "From their appellation, 'barrens,' the person unacquainted with them is not to suppose them thus called from their sterility, because most of them are quite the reverse," he asserts before explaining the necessity for ditching. But Atwater knew that such land did not appeal to newcomers: "No pleasant variety of hill and dale, no rapidly running brook delights the eye, and no sound of woodland music strikes the ear; but, in their stead, a dull uniformity of prospect 'spread out immense.'"[20] Even innovators willing to abandon traditional agricultural land classification advice found such land ugly or monotonous. Tradition-minded Americans and most newly-arrived immigrants scorned such regions as sterile, and searched for "good land," the tree-covered ground they identified with fertility and beauty, the land prospectors and miners dismissed immediately.

When the *conquistadores* discovered gold and silver in Mexico and Peru, esoteric sixteenth-century debates concerning quicksilver and mineral gestation, mountains and brimstone, alchemy and infernal heat suddenly involved not only alchemists and theologians, but also merchants, royal counselors, explorers, and colonists.[21] Western Europeans looked to the Alps for expert advice about prospecting techniques and slowly learned a land classification system antithetical to the comfortable one of husbandry.

Richard Eden translated part of Vannuccio Biringuccio's *Pyrotechnia* into English in 1555, only fifteen years after the work appeared in Italian. Biringuccio's mineral-finding advice depends on four-element analysis and painstaking observation, but focuses on land husbandmen called barren. Metals are likely to exist in any mountain, he counsels, "by reason of the great barrenness and roughness thereof," but only wise men understand how to locate the veins. They know that spring water tastes metallic near ore deposits, that mountains "rough, sharp, and savage, without earth or trees" make likely prospecting sites and that wherever mountain herbs or grass grow faint in color "and in manner withered and dried," ores lurk just beneath the surface. Gold "is engendered in divers kinds of stones in great and rough mountains, and such as are utterly bare of earth, trees, grass, or herbs," and announces its presence by the most subtle clues.[22] Biringuccio and his translator cared little for theory; they interested themselves in deciphering the surface signs of subterranean wealth.

THE DEEP PAST AND IMAGES

Seventeenth-century explorers needed works based on New World experience, not Alpine tradition. In response Alvaro Alonso Barba published *The Art of Metals* (1637) while supervising the exceedingly profitable mines at Potosoi in Bolivia, and the book soon appeared in English, German, and French. Barba explains how to follow streams and scrutinize eroded rock, how to use the *cateador* or prospector's pick, and how to identify the lines of plants half-sickened by metallic exhalations from ore veins beneath their roots.[23]

Literate Englishmen slowly acquired such Spanish knowledge through works like Gabriel Plattes' 1639 masterpiece, *A Discovery of Subterraneall Treasure*. After asserting that gold and silver lie almost everywhere in the "burning zone" along the equator, he emphasizes that mountains are the best prospecting sites: "When we come to the rocky and craggy mountains, the first thing we are to observe, is the barrenness of them, for the more barren they are, the greater probability there is that they contain rich mines and minerals." He suggests distilling nearby spring water and noting the residue (a greenish one, for example, indicates copper deposits), and advises his reader "to go to the bare rocks, there to find out the clefts, crooks, and crannies . . . till you find some grass growing right upon the top of said crannies, and then observe diligently the kind of that grass, and how it differs from other grass ordinarily growing in the same mountain." Plattes took much of his information from New World hearsay, but some of it, he insists, derived from experimentation. "About midsummer, in a calm morning," he writes of a successful attempt to discover a vein of lead, "I cut up a rod of hazel, all of the same spring's growth, about a yard long," and wandered about likely sites until the wand bent down. Such divining confused agriculturalists who expected that fertility-indicating trees would indicate precious metals; but hazel twigs sought out silver, ash twigs responded to copper deposits, and not even hickory branches twitched over gold. "Now in the new plantations, as New England, Virginia, Bermudas," he concludes at the end of his book, "where it is likely that few or none have ever tried, that had any skill in these affairs, it is very probable that the orifice of divers mines may be discerned with the eye in the clefts of the rocks . . . and yield more gain in one year than their tobacco and such trifles would yield in their whole lives."[24] More than any other seventeenth-century textbook, *A Discovery of Subterraneall Treasure* illustrates the mineralogical land classification system some Englishmen carried to the New World and applied in frenzied attempts to recreate Spain's wonderful finds.

Repeated failures convinced English prospectors that no gold or silver lay beneath the forested hills of Connecticut and Virginia, but the Spanish-derived fascination with otherwise barren ground still fired imaginations. In New Jersey, asserts Jedidiah Morse in his 1789 *American Geography,* "the *barrens* produce little else but shrub oaks and white and yellow pines," but in Mexico, mines of gold and silver "are always found in the most barren mountainous parts of the country, nature making amends in one respect for defects in another."[25] In schoolbooks, reprinted guidebooks—a Philadelphia printer reissued Plattes' *Discovery* as late as 1784—and in oral tradition, the mineralogical classification system survived, predisposing Americans for the 1849 rush to California's savage mountains.

Prejudice deprived the mineralogical land classification system of a fair chance in the colonies, however, and made suspect its educated adherents. Husbandmen afraid of earthquakes, chemical poisoning, and a swarm of mountain furies distrusted anyone searching out those places likely to host calamity. Anthanasius Kircher explored the infernal entrails of mother earth in *Mundus Subterraneus,* a massive, profusely-illustrated folio that appeared at Amsterdam in 1664. Kircher understood alchemy, subterranean fire, dwarfs, planetary affinities of metals and cave-dwelling dragons; his book appealed only to the very learned, but it analyzes many popularly-held beliefs, and offers first-hand accounts of such terrifying episodes as the swallowing of Euphemia in Calabria during a 1638 earthquake, an event Kircher witnessed.[26] Folk Christianity had long portrayed such incidents as divine retribution, and had long depicted mountain reptiles as monstrous relatives of the primeval serpent.[27]

Mistrust of caves, earthquakes, and lizards arrived in North America with the first colonists, and German, Austrian, and Cornish miners recruited to work the few English diggings embroidered the tapestry of tales defining the subterranean world as the Devil's domain.[28] Earthquakes scented the air with brimstone, and convinced thoughtful colonists that somewhere beneath the sunlit earth, somewhere far below the graveyard sod, burned a great demonic fire, the fire that repeatedly rocked seventeenth-century New England.[29] The 1727 earthquake that shook Massachusetts, New Hampshire, and Maine confirmed American fears dating to the 1692 destruction of Port Royal in Jamaica, and the celebrated "moodus noises" forever rumbling beneath East Haddam, Connecticut, kept alive the belief in underground conflagration.[30] Earthquakes terrified colonists and caused learned men to pore over Kircher's tome; as late as 1883, one geology text cited his remarks concerning Euphemia. They prompted clergymen to preach about punishment and mineral-seeking. "God laid them low," said Samuel Willard of metals in a 1726 sermon directed against "greedy desire" and idolatry, "but man adores them, sets them up in his heart, and worships these, advancing them as high as God, and setting them in His throne."[31] Such sermons

THE DEEP PAST AND IMAGES

emphasize the honesty of agricultural labor and the blessing of fertile soil by condemning the infernal urge to delve into the earth after tainted riches, to chance cave-ins, encounters with supernatural humanoids and serpents and poisoning, all for the sake of quick wealth. Until well into the eighteenth century, *barren land* connoted *blasted land.*

Nineteenth-century periodical writers occasionally described subterranean places, particularly mines like one explored by John Grammer in 1818. "The gloomy blackness, however, of most of the galleries, and the strange dress and appearance of the black miners, would furnish sufficient data to the conception of a poet, for a description of Pluto's kingdom," Grammer remarks before beginning a no-nonsense account. "A strong sulphurous acid ran down the walls of many of the galleries; and I observed one of the drains was filled with a yellowish gelatinous substance, which I ascertained, on a subsequent examination, was a yellow, or rather a reddish, oxide of iron, mechanically suspended in water." In the Virginia coal mines Grammer discovered the chthonic phenomena and perils described centuries earlier by Plattes and Kircher. Not only was coal in a contiguous seam on fire, but also "a strong sulphurous fume" shot steadily "from an irregular hole in the side of the hill of about two feet in diameter," encrusting the nearby soil with crystals of pure sulphur. Explosions of some sort of "damp," probably "carburetted hydrogen gas," had killed several miners a short while before, and Grammer quit the diggings with relief.[32] A few writers intrigued by non-agricultural spaces and activities visited other mines and prospecting sites before publishing similar articles filled with crypto-chemical jargon and tinged with traditional horror.[33] But disastrous earthquakes like those that destroyed several settlements in the Missouri Territory in 1807 reinforced the dominant belief that beneath the earth's surface lies only terror, and that the more barren the place, the more likely an eruption or other catastrophe.[34] Most Americans condemned eroded, rocky land as bad; they deemed it unfit for agriculture and useless for artistic study.

As Cecilia Tichi has shown in *New World, New Earth: Environmental Reform in American Literature from the Puritans through Whitman,* descriptions of wilderness interested chiefly upper-class, well-educated readers able to learn about such places while enjoying urban comforts.[35] Almost always, however, the nineteenth-century wilderness descriptions emphasize wild land with some potential for agriculture, a potential usually announced by forest cover. "There is, perhaps, no part of our mountain regions where so great a variety of trees is presented to the student of landscape art as in the vicinity of the Catskills," remarked one essayist in *The Crayon* in 1857.[36] European-educated painters and critics now and then suggested that rocky places devoid of vegetation deserve scrutiny

FAIR FIELDS AND BLASTED ROCK

too, but the educated public preferred the settings beloved by farmers. Viewers coerced artists, especially those employed as periodical illustrators, into repeatedly depicting rural scenes edged by hickory-, walnut-, and oak-covered wilderness ripe for the axe and the plow.[37] Barren land proved too suspect for art.

Geological theorizing sharpened traditional dislike of barren mountains. Robert Chambers and other scientists scrutinized rock formations and mountain-top fossils, and raised disconcerting questions about the age of the earth and Biblical accuracy.[38] Long essays like Benjamin Silliman's 1833 "The Consistency of Geology with Sacred History" failed to convince educated Americans that mountains did not objectify serious religious uncertainty. Agriculture remained safe and noble, transmitted from father to son; geology and mining grew increasingly suspect, and shrouded in technical terminology.[39] Barren mountains and atypical rock formations are conspicuously absent from much early-nineteenth-century painting, and from much writing too, even from Thoreau's sketches like "A Walk to Wachusett," which concerns his hike to the mountain and the view from its summit, but not the mountain top itself: "The summit consists of a few acres, destitute of trees, covered with bare rocks, interspersed with blueberry bushes, raspberries, gooseberries, strawberries, moss, and a fine wiry grass. The common yellow lily, and dwarf-cornel, grow abundantly in the crevices of the rocks."[40] No transcendental spunk shapes his attitude toward the mountain; his essay almost piously remarks on the mountain as God's handiwork, and studiously avoids geological theorizing. In a subsequent essay, Thoreau remarks that "Ktaadn presented a different aspect from any mountain I have seen, there being a greater proportion of naked rock rising abruptly from the forest," and calls the summit-edges of that mountain "the most treacherous and porous country I ever travelled."[41] Above the timber line Thoreau entered a region that mocked his Concord-woodlot, vernacular knowledge and aesthetic and tested his supposed opposition to traditional theology. Along with most other Americans, he preferred fields and forests.

Did the agricultural and mineralogical land classification systems help mould American painting and literature? An examination of some paintings and literary works suggests that they did. Nineteenth-century American scenery paintings and prose descriptions, as Barbara Novak notes in *American Painting of the Nineteenth Century* and *Nature and Culture: American Landscape and Painting, 1825–1875,* generally emphasize either the rural landscape of farms, pastures, and arable fields analyzed by Leo Marx in *The Machine in the Garden* or the enticing, wonderfully fertile

THE DEEP PAST AND IMAGES

wilderness examined by Henry Nash Smith in *Virgin Land*.[42] Very often, as in Thomas Cole's "Genesee Scenery" (1847), forest abuts farmland.[43] Except in the work of a few painters like John F. Kensett and Martin Johnson Heade, the depicted wilderness, in my opinion, is typical wilderness with an agricultural potential.[44]

Cole and other painters occasionally depicted bad land. "Expulsion from the Garden of Eden" (ca. 1827–1828) illustrates Cole's understanding of the mineralogical land classification system. On the right of the canvas is Eden, a fertile spot shaded by trees resembling those North American species thought to indicate warm, rich soil; opposite Eden stand jagged, rock-strewn mountains dotted by scraggly vegetation.[45] The mountains derive mostly from Cole's imagination, not from his favorite painting location, the tree-covered, fertile Catskills, and they appealed to adherents of the traditional agricultural land classification system and to the educated elite suspicious of modern geology.[46] Rail as he might against injudicious "newspaper praise," Cole found it impossible to escape his patrons' love of farmland and fertile wilderness, and he repeatedly painted scenes that sold, scenes like "Genesee Scenery."[47] Kensett and Heade managed to combine their atypical love of bare rocks with a flair for painting seacoasts, but even their most popular works treat agricultural land.[48] American writers depicted similar settings. Only a handful, often those with some understanding of European gothicism, devoted attention to the land scorned by agriculturists.[49]

Hawthorne, Poe, and especially Melville charged their writing by emphasizing land distrusted by their readers. Hawthorne focuses the action of "Ethan Brand" on a mountain-side lime kiln that "resembled nothing so much as the private entrance to the infernal regions, which the shepherds of the Delectable Mountains were accustomed to show to pilgrims," and sites "The Ambitious Guest" at a mountain house eventually destroyed by a rock slide.[50] Poe heightens the subterranean horror of "The Cask of Amontillado" by choosing a crypto-chemical vocabulary that repulsed readers familiar with old terms like the "sweetness" or "sourness" of soil; the nitre-encrusted vaults derive from the geological vocabulary that marks "The Narrative of A. Gordon Pym," "The Gold Bug," and other tales set in barren places.[51]

But Melville best understood the significance of barren land, and particularly barren mountains; his 1854 "Encantadas, or the Enchanted Isles" juxtaposes the traditional land classification systems and fuels nineteenth-century fears of geological science. "It is to be doubted whether any spot of earth can, in desolateness, furnish a parallel to this group," he writes of the archipelago "cracked by an ever-lasting drought beneath a torrid sky." He mixes a Poesque chemical terminology with traditional mineralogical land classification system information, describing "tangled thickets of wiry bushes, without fruit and without a name, springing up among deep fissures of calcined rock, and treacherously masking them; or a parched growth of distorted cactus trees." But his emphasis is essentially traditional, calculated to summon all his readers' antipathy to barren land. "Little but reptile life is here found:—tortoises, lizards, immense spiders, snakes, and that strangest anomaly of outlandish nature, the *aguano*. No noise, no low, no howl is heard; the chief sound of life here is a hiss." No wonder that he concludes his first chapter by noting that "I can hardly resist the feeling that in my time I have indeed slept upon evilly enchanted ground." He had slept on land as barren as any described in folklore, on land covered with crevices, stunted plants, and rocks, on land prone to earthquake and populated by small-scale dragons as ugly as any found by Kircher two centuries before.[52] Melville's "Encantadas" epitomizes the awesome evocative power of the mineralogical land classification system in a culture wedded to agricultural thinking. "The weapons with which we have gained our most important victories, which should be handed down as heirlooms from father to son," Thoreau remarked in 1862, "are not the sword and the lance, but the bushwhack, the turf-cutter, the spade, and the bog-hoe, rusted with the blood of many a meadow, and begrimed with the dust of many a hard-fought field."[53] No one mentioned the *cateador* or praised the mining of mountains; Whitman and others heard the song of the broad-axe and rejoiced in fair fields and forests marking fertile soil.[54]

No aesthetic tradition aided Americans gazing at the High Plains and the Rocky Mountains; beyond the tall grass prairie broken by stands of hickories and other beautiful trees lay the land beyond the grasp of agricultural land classification systems and the compass of *eastern* spatial aesthetics.[55] "In the mind of an American, frequent forests, and frequent as well as fine groves, are almost necessarily associated with all his ideas of fertility, warmth, agricultural prosperity and beauty of landscape," concluded Timothy Dwight in 1821. "Nor can he easily believe that a country destitute of trees is not destitute of fertility."[56] Not until painters, journalists, and photographers grew intimate with plains and treeless mountains did barrens and blasted rock receive the tender rendering accorded agricultural landscapes and fertile forest wilderness. And even after the conversion of artists, many Americans continued to regard rocky or treeless land as slightly treacherous and very ugly.[57] Much work remains in the deciphering of American land classification techniques and their relation to the scenery values of the "typical" citizen and of the educated elite. Here I have only traced what appear to me to have been two significant land classification techniques that bear indirectly on American painting and letters.

Notes

1. Timothy Dwight, *Travels in New England and New York* [1822], ed. Barbara Miller Solomon (Cambridge, Mass., 1969), IV, 20.
2. Burke, *Popular Culture in Early Modern Europe* (London, 1978), esp. 23–64; see also Carl von Sydow, *Selected Papers on Folklore* (Copenhagen, 1948), 11–19, 44–53 and Robert Mandrou, "Cultures Populaire et Savante: Rapports et Contacts," *Popular Culture in France,* ed. Jacques Beauroy (Saratoga, Calif., 1977), 17–38 for additional analysis of the European "little tradition"; see Henry Glassie, *Pattern in the Material Folk Culture of the Eastern United States* (Philadelphia, 1968), 1–17 for an interpretation of that tradition in America.
3. (Rutherford, New Jersey, 1972), 82–137; on soils and location of farms, see W. G. Hoskins, *The Making of the English Landscape* (1955; rpt. Harmondsworth, 1970), 17–44 and Alan Mayhew, *Rural Settlement and Farming in Germany* (New York, 1973), 118–167.
4. (Paris, 1894), esp. 387–589; (Stuttgart, 1913); (Berlin, 1962); (Chicago, 1964); on Latin American mining, see John Robert Fisher, *Minas y mineros en el Peru colonial, 1776–1824* (Lima, 1977).
5. (New Haven, 1930); (New York, 1976); for additional information on the application of German soil classification rules in Pennsylvania, see Stevenson Whitcomb Fletcher, *Pennsylvania Agriculture and Country Life, 1640–1840* (Harrisburg, 1955), 48–55.
6. (London, 1678), 289, 292, 298.
7. Edmund Browne, "Letter" [September 7, 1638], *Letters from New England: The Massachusetts Bay Colony, 1629–1638,* ed. Everett Emerson (Amherst, Mass., 1976), 226–227.
8. Adriaen Van der Donck, "Description of New Netherlands" [1656], trans. Jeremiah Johnson, New York State Historical Society, (1841), second series, I, 148.
9. See, for example, Thomas Morton, *The New English Canaan* [1637], ed. Charles Francis Adams (Boston, 1883), 182–187.
10. Israel Acrelius, *A History of New Sweden* [1759], trans. William M. Reynolds (Philadelphia, 1876), 182–187.
11. "Plan of Irasburgh," Bailey-Howe Library, University of Vermont, Burlington; for examples of surveyors' land classification vocabulary, see Hildegard Binder Johnson, *Order Upon the Land: The U.S. Rectangular Land Survey and the Upper Mississippi Country* (New York, 1976), 78–80.
12. James Smith, *Remarkable Occurrences* [1799], ed. William M. Darlington (Cincinnati, 1870), esp. 84–90.
13. Ferdinant Bayard, *Voyage dan l'interieur des Etats-Unis dans la Vallee de Shenandoah . . . 1791* (Paris, 1797), 65 (my translation).
14. William Priest, *Travels in the United States* (London, 1802), 35.
15. John William Ward, *Andrew Jackson, Symbol for an Age* (New York, 1955), 54–57.
16. (New York, 1976), esp. 1–10.
17. I (October 1, 1836), 81–82.
18. Dwight, *Travels,* III, 60.
19. Henry David Thoreau, *Cape Cod* (1864; rpt. Boston, 1887), 122, 124, 80, 180–181; for an extended analysis of American evaluations of seashore topography and soil,

see John R. Stilgoe, "A New England Coastal Wilderness," *Geographical Review,* 71 (January, 1981), 33–50.

20. I (1818), 116–125; see also Douglas R. McManis, *The Initial Evaluation and Utilization of the Illinois Prairies, 1815–1840* (Chicago, 1964).

21. For an introduction to the controversies before the discovery of New World precious metal, see Conrad von Megenberg, *Buch der Natur* (Augsburg, 1475).

22. For the *Pyrotechnia* see Richard Eden, *The Decades of the New World* [1555], in *The First Three English Books on America,* ed. Edward Arber (Birmingham, England, 1885), esp. 355, 357, 363–364.

23. Alvaro Alonzo Barba, *El Arte de los Metales* [1640], trans. Ross E. Douglass and E. P. Mathewson (New York, 1923).

24. (London, 1639), 2, 4, 9–10, 12, 13, and passim; for other seventeenth-century attitudes toward mineral-rich land, see John Amos Comenius, *Naturall Philosophie Reformed by Divine Light* (London, 1651), esp. 93–146; Thomas Houghton, *Rara Avis in Terris: or The Compleat Miner* (London, 1681); John Woodward, *An Essay toward a Natural History of the Earth* (London, 1695), all of which derive in part from Georg Agricola, *De re metallica* [1556], trans. Herbert Clark Hoover and Lou Henry Hoover (New York, 1950). An excellent introduction to sixteenth- and seventeenth-century mining is Helmut Wilsdorf, *Georg Agricola und seine Zeit* (Berlin, 1956).

25. (Elizabeth Town, 1789), 286–287, 480.

26. (Amsterdam, 1664), II, 90–103, 184–185, 187, 227, 256, 293, 322, and passim.

27. Johann Jacob Scheuchzer, *Sive Itinera per Helvetiae alpinas regiones* (Leyden, 1723), II, 353–401; "The Two Brothers," *German Folk Tales* [1857], ed. Jacob and Wilhem Grimm, trans. Francis P. Magoun and Alexander H. Krappe (Carbondale, Illinois, 1960), 226–243.

28. George Gershon Korson, *Black Rock: Mining Folklore of the Pennsylvania Dutch* (Baltimore, 1960).

29. John R. Stilgoe, "Folklore and Graveyard Design," *Landscape,* 22 (Summer, 1978), 22–28; Cotton Mather, *The Terror of the Lord: Some Account of the Earthquake that Shook New England* (Boston, 1727).

30. Cotton Mather, *A Short Essay* (Boston, 1727), esp. appendix 46–47; on the moodus noises, see Benjamin Trumbull, *A Complete History of Connecticut* (New Haven, 1818), II, 91–93.

31. The geology text is Robert Bakewell's *An Introduction to Geology* (New Haven, 1833), 251; Samuel Willard, *A Compleat Body of Divinity* (Boston, 1726), 117.

32. "Account of the Coal Mines," *The American Journal of Science,* I (1818), 125–130.

33. "A Description of Bald Eagle Valley," *Columbian Magazine* II (September, 1788), 488–492. On jargon, see Maurice P. Crosland, *Historical Studies in the Language of Chemistry* (1962; rpt. New York, 1978), 65–106.

34. The early-nineteenth-century Missouri earthquakes made an extraordinary impression on the popular mind; see, for example, Timothy Flint, *Recollections of the Last Ten Years* [1826], ed. C. Hartley Gratten (New York, 1932), 212–220.

35. (New Haven, 1979), 173–174; see also Roderick Nash, *Wilderness and the American Mind* (New Haven, 1967), 59–61.

36. "Trees and Rocks at the Catskill Mountains," *The Crayon,* IV (September, 1857), 281–282.

37. "The Relation between Geology and Landscape Painting," *The Crayon,* VI (August, 1859), 255–256. On periodicals, see, for example, "View from Bushongo Tavern," *Columbian Magazine,* II (July, 1788), 354, and the Currier and Ives lithographs like

"Among the Pines: A First Settlement." See also the forthcoming catalog of "New England's Prospect," Dublin Seminar for New England Folklife, Dublin, New Hampshire and the Currier Gallery of Art, Manchester, New Hampshire. The exhibit emphasizes folk and popular landscape sketches, maps, paintings, and other graphic forms.

38. Robert Chambers, *Vestiges of the Natural History of Creation* (New York, 1845).

39. Silliman appended his essay to Bakewell's *Introduction to Geology,* 389–466.

40. [1843] (Boston, 1863), 85.

41. "Ktaadn" [1848], *The Maine Woods* (Boston, 1884), 56, 61.

42. (New York, 1969) and (New York, 1980); (New York, 1964); (Cambridge, Mass., 1950).

43. In the Museum of Art, Rhode Island School of Design.

44. Novak, *American Painting,* 97–101, 125–137. I have compared Novak's conclusions against the works in the Karolik Collection, Museum of Fine Arts, Boston.

45. In the Museum of Fine Arts, Boston.

46. Novak, *Nature and Culture,* 31–56.

47. Louis Legrand Noble, *The Life and World of Thomas Cole* [1853], ed. Elliot S. Vesell (Cambridge, Mass., 1964), 160.

48. Theodore E. Stebbins, Jr., *Martin Johnson Heade* (College Park, Maryland, 1969); see also, Richard B. K. McLanathan, *Fitz Hugh Lane* (Boston, 1956).

49. On the spatial elements of gothicism, see, for example, Maurice Levy, "Edgar Poe et la tradition 'gothique,'" *Caliban: Annales de la Faculte des Lettres de Toulouse,* 4 (1968), 35–51 and Patricia Meyer Spacks, *The Insistence of Horror: Aspects of the Supernatural in Eighteenth-Century Poetry* (Cambridge, Mass., 1962), esp. 67–102.

50. Nathaniel Hawthorne, "Ethan Brand" and "The Ambitious Guest," *Complete Works* (Boston, 1882), III, 477–498 and I, 364–374; for the quotation see III, 478.

51. *Best Known Works,* ed. Hervey Allen (New York, 1927), 205–209, 431–554, 53–77.

52. Salvator R. Tarnmoor [Herman Melville], "The Encantadas, or Enchanted Isles," *Putnam's Monthly Magazine,* III (March, April, May, 1854), 311–319, 345–355, 460–466; for the quotations see 311–313; for an excellent analysis of Melville's land classification perception of the islands, see Donald Worster, *Nature's Economy: The Roots of Ecology* (Garden City, N.Y., 1979), 115–129.

53. "Walking," *Excursions,* 192–193.

54. Walt Whitman, "Song of the Broad Axe" [1856], *Leaves of Grass and Selected Prose,* ed. John Kouwenhoven (New York, 1950), 147–157.

55. On problems in classifying the "barren" regions, see John Wesley Powell, *Report on the Lands of the Arid Region of the United States, with a More Detailed Account of the Lands of Utah* [1878], ed. Wallace Stegner (Cambridge, Mass., 1962); on aesthetic responses of early travelers, see Robert Taft, *Artists and Illustrators of the Old West, 1850–1900* (New York, 1953) and Ronald Rees, "The Scenery Cult: Changing Landscape Tastes over Three Centuries," *Landscape,* 19 (May, 1975), 39–47.

56. Dwight, *Travels,* II, 139.

57. Yi-Fu Tuan, *Landscapes of Fear* (New York, 1979), 79–80, 109, 127, 140, 207.

RURAL LOOKING

Open country endures as the most studied and the most highly valued of all United States landscapes. A gentle mix of farms and woodlots and villages supports not only the house-in-a-suburb dream the world knows as peculiarly American, but inchoate attitudes too. American motorists somehow expect an open road, free of congestion, perhaps even free of police, and American children still expect land over which they can range at will, despite being legally trespassers. Hunters and fishermen share the expectations of children, and all Americans casually accept their right to make paintings and photographs from public ways. Openness, not constriction, endures as a basic American value, but it is fundamentally a rural one.

Such values focused foreign and domestic thinkers early in the eighteenth century. Foreign travelers expressed surprise, and sometimes awe, at the scale and prosperity of farms newly shaped from forest wilderness. Native observers extolled the agricultural landscape in self-congratulatory ways, and explained to European readers that the order and prosperity so evident in the landscape illustrated the devotion to order and free enterprise manifest in American political theory. For decades the Pennsylvania landscape struck many observers as that best exemplifying the entire colonial, then national effort to create a new spatial and social order. Westward from Pennsylvania moved the settlers who brought the spatial framework subsequent observers discovered everywhere in the Mississippi basin.

Envisioning the new nation involved cartographers as well as travel writers, and much cartography fitted into fierce efforts to improve public school education. Wall maps and atlases existed not only to document topographical features and geopolitical entities but to help children think beyond one-room schoolhouses, rural neighborhoods, and small towns. By the time cartographers mapped Indiana and placed it delicately within the spatial order of adjacent states and territories, atlas making depended on informal but powerful rules concerning the coloring of mapped states. But mapping any region, even the environs of Narragansett Bay, thrust cartographers and the educated public into quandaries about the depth of times before and the several ways of reaching toward the future. People debated the keeping of Native American place-names and the bounding of regions simultaneously, producing a rich stew of ideas that nowadays suffuses decisions made by artists, tourism-development authorities, and real estate developers.

Ordinarily cartographers ignore the seasons, and most amateur artists ignore winter especially. Seasons and weather alter landscape, sometimes in stunning ways. Winter transforms ordinary landscape into wilderness as ice makes driving difficult, then dangerous, or as snow blocks vision, covers local paths and roads, and brings down power lines. Proper landscape analysis necessarily requires examining any landscape throughout the year. The bitter cold of winter or the slamming impact of gale-driven snow forces thoughtful observers into wondering how settlers endured the first years in half-shaped landscape. More important, perhaps, winter warns that high-tech gadgetry fails in deep cold, that automobiles slide from highways downhill into woods, that cell-phone batteries weaken as the temperature falls, that too many contemporary houses have no other source of heat than furnaces dependent on electricity. Winter scrapes deeply into the veneer of landscape, sometimes revealing the wilderness beneath.

Before cheap coal, electricity, and fuel oil, prudent Americans designed for climate and weather. Above all, they designed and built against winter cold, not only siting and building houses away from winter winds, but planting windbreaks to lower heating costs. Understanding climate and weather opens on all sorts of architectural and landscape details. For centuries homeowners used vines to shade and cool interiors in summer, knowing that frost would fell leaves and allow sunlight to enter windows. But farmers did vastly more. They understood woodlots to alter microclimates just enough to make raising some crops more profitable, and they arranged barns and barnyards to protect livestock from cold and heat both. What farmers and agricultural engineers learned about temperature modification evolved into moisture control, until by the 1930s agricultural expertise began to transform suburban residential site design.

Designing for energy efficiency and for comfort subtly altered notions of privacy, especially for upper- and middle-class suburban dwellers after 1925. The tall board fences that stopped winter winds, channeled summer breezes, and reflected sunlight in January soon became valued as blocking casual views. As health-conscious families tried to live more outdoors, often in exiguous attire, privacy became increasingly important. The private response to public health issues shaped suburban housing until the 1950s, when real estate developers began ignoring decades of energy-saving, privacy-creating site and structure design. Cheap heating and cooling systems transformed suburban development by 1970, almost exactly in time for homeowners to discover in the 1973 and 1979 energy crises an expensive dependence on purchased energy.

Suburbia endures and spreads simply because most Americans capable of buying real estate value its meaning and financial worth together. The single-family house on a plot of land remains a monument to the farm so fundamental in United States history. The front lawn endures as a meadow, the backyard as pasture for livestock nowadays reduced to dog and cat, while the lone fruit tree recalls the orchard and the vegetable garden recalls the arable fields. Far more important, the house-and-lot concatenation permits and indeed encourages creativity born and matured in rural regions. Equipped with garden and woodworking tools, families plant and transplant shrubs, build decks and garages, and experiment with tree forts and playhouses. No matter how perfectly designed and built the apartment or condominium, such living quarters rarely permit the creativity so many householders treasure. And what is even more significant, the single-family suburban house adapts relatively easily to change from beyond. Homeowners irritated at rising energy costs install wood-pellet-burning stoves or skylights or heat pumps running from solar panels. Others install backyard pools and swim with their dogs, or build workshops or greenhouses next to garages. Hobgoblins still haunt suburbs, making clear the vitality of the ancient attachment so many Americans feel toward a piece of land and a house they shape pretty much as they please, exactly as generations of peasants, then farmers, did before them.

THE MAGIC OF PENNSYLVANIA
TRAVEL NARRATIVES

Pennsylvania is an almost magical land for readers of old travelogues. Foreign observers and its own residents, especially during the century following the year 1750, recorded their impressions of its landscapes in dozens of travel narratives. No other state is richer in evocative memoirs of half-vanished space.

Between 1756 and the close of the eighteenth century, most travelers across Pennsylvania were chiefly interested in the condition of Philadelphia and other towns, and in the state of agriculture. Often they were interested in the natural environment too, but that was never their chief concern. Like Gottlieb Mittelberger, who published his *Journey to Pennsylvania* in 1756 after returning home to Wurttemberg, travelers through the state came to explore and provide firsthand reports to European readers. They traveled about independently, sometimes on foot and sometimes on horseback.

As were most eighteenth-century foreign visitors, Mittelberger was surprised at Philadelphia. "The city is very large and beautiful, and laid out in regular lines, with broad avenues and many cross-streets," he wrote. "All houses are built up to the fourth floor of stone or brick, and are roofed with cedarwood." Mittelberger asserted that it took almost a full day to walk around the city, though perhaps his inquiring into everything from shipbuilding, to the architecture of the new courthouse, to the great outdoor markets slowed him down. His detailed observations suggest that he devoted many days to walking about, visiting churches and courthouses and listening to the peculiar drumming sound made by the rain on the cedarwood rooftops. He was interested in windows made of English plate glass, in fireplaces patterned after the French style, and in the two short benches set perpendicular to the fronts of most houses where every evening people sat and enjoyed the passing scene.

"The streets and houses of this city are so straight," concluded Mittelberger, "that one can look directly ahead for the distance of a half hour's walk." The regularity of Philadelphia is the key to Mittelberger's understanding of the larger landscape of Philadelphia; the traveler passed into Pennsylvania through a gateway of orderliness.

"The Magic of Pennsylvania Travel Narratives" appeared in *Pennsylvania Heritage* 7 (Winter 1981): 9–12, and (Spring 1982): 10–13.

It is that initial impression of the city which allowed Mittelberger to perceive in the rural landscape beyond an order foreign to his own homeland. He wrote, "In the country people live so far apart that many have to walk a quarter or half-hour just to reach their nearest neighbor. The reason for this is that many plantation owners have got fifty or one hundred, even two, three, up to four hundred morgen [from six- to nine-tenths of an acre] of land, laid out in orchards, meadows, fields, and forest."

No settlement pattern could be more different from that of his homeland, but Mittelberger understood that there was as much order in the emerging Pennsylvania landscape of scattered farms as in his native village. In his own language, rural Pennsylvania was an *Einzelhofsiedlung*—an open-country-neighborhood—but it was even more open than the German word suggested. It was a New World landscape indeed, as distinct as the frogs and rattlesnakes and sassafras trees he discovered along the road. The rural areas were prosperous and pious, but not focused on tiny clustered villages. Like Philadelphia, their dominant feature was the road.

While Mittelberger did not engage in much long distance traveling, many of his successors did. Johann David Schoepf, another German, though from the principality of Bayreuth, traveled through Pennsylvania in 1783, just after the end of the Revolutionary War. Schoepf was a learned man, a university-educated physician, botanist, mineralogist, and forester who arrived in America as an army surgeon in 1777. What little of the colonies he saw from vantage points of the British and Hessian armies provoked his curiosity and, with the cessation of hostilities, he set off across New Jersey, through Pennsylvania, and to the southern states into Florida. His *Travels in the Confederation* reveal him to have been a sensitive, untiring observer. Like many other travelers, he devoted a great deal of his time to wandering about Pennsylvania; it was, in his estimation, time well spent.

Schoepf entered Pennsylvania at Bristol, thereby seeing a bit of the country before arriving at Philadelphia. "The nearer one comes to the capital," he wrote, "the freer of woods is the landscape, and there are more people and more farms." Schoepf was continually interested in woods, in their natural state and in their uses to man. In Rocky Hill Township, for example, he paused to study the construction of worm fences and discovered that chestnut wood "is used because of its lightness and because it lasts well, barked." Hedgerows like those in Europe were rare, he learned, because the land was not long settled; some farmers did attempt to make them, however, by interlacing young saplings which grew along the boundaries of their pastures. In another place he discovered two thousand acres deforested to fuel an iron foundry. From time to time he did ride through virgin timber, and near Brinker's Mill crossed Great Swamp, where the road "was nowhere more than six foot wide, and full of everything which can make trouble for the passenger." Forester though he was, Schoepf was unsettled by riding through woods "so thick that the trees almost touch, by their height and their matted branches making a dimness, cold and fearful even at noon of the clearest day." But there was far more to see than forest, and most of his narrative concerns the man-altered environment—since even Great Swamp was pierced by a road, there was less and less wholly untouched wilderness in Pennsylvania to be seen.

Unlike Mittelberger, Schoepf was not wholly pleased with Philadelphia. The city had grown in the twenty-seven years since the Wurttemberg traveler had delighted in its straight streets, and Schoepf thought them too narrow for their traffic. The markets admired by his predecessor, he too criticized for blocking the city's view of the river and skewing Market Street out of alignment. He found the regular architectural style of the houses boring, deciding that the lack of open squares planted with grass or shrubbery detracted from the overall appearance of the place. He thought that privies were well located, however, and commended the city authorities for carefully cleaning the streets. Still, his impression of Philadelphia in summer was negative, and his description is an eerie presentiment of the conditions which sparked the yellow fever epidemic ten summers later. Schoepf was far more familiar with the great cities of Europe than was Mittelberger, and it is possible that Philadelphia suffered in rigorous comparison. It is more likely, however, that he saw it not as a city in the wilderness, but as a city in an established landscape, subject to typical forms of analysis.

Schoepf saw remarkably little untouched wilderness during his travels in eastern Pennsylvania. While he crossed that part of Saint Anthony's Wilderness he called Great Swamp and learned secondhand about a place called The Shades of Death, his wilderness observations were made much further west, near Pittsburgh. Most of the land he saw was somehow altered by man, often so greatly modified that he evaluated the man-altered places against each other, not against the chaos of wilderness. "Bradford is a little town," he remarked in this regard, "but a little town in a great wilderness may easily please without beauty." His travel narrative, then, describes a Pennsylvania no longer remarkable for its wilderness or for its settlements carved from that wilderness, but interesting as a great agricultural landscape focused on Philadelphia. Towns he compared with towns, farms with farms, and houses with houses, setting up such relationships as one concerning chimneys: "From the exterior appearance, especially the plan of the chimneys, it could be pretty certainly guessed whether the house was that of a German or of an

English family if of one chimney only, placed in the middle, the house should be a German's and furnished with stoves . . . if of two chimneys, one at each gable end, there should be fireplaces, after the English plan." A house, then, was no longer worthy of attention simply because it was situated in the midst of a wilderness where houses had never been, but because it told something of its inhabitants or explained attitudes toward farming. Unlike little Bradford, houses and Philadelphia and farms and foundries received from Schoepf a new sort of attention.

Such attention was not peculiar to Schoepf. Five years later, John Penn traveled from Philadelphia to Reading, Harrisburg, Carlisle, and Lancaster and, like Schoepf, compared man-altered places one with another. Penn's *Journal* is filled with descriptions of barns roofed with thatch and houses with tiles, of an irrigated meadow and a patched-up schoolhouse. Between Philadelphia and the township of Roxborough, he wrote, "the soil is not very good, but the country is finely diversified with wood and clear ground." Penn perhaps thought the landscape similar to England's, for between Womelsdorf and Reading, he commented explicitly on the parallel: "There is one spot on this road remarkable for its European appearance, the lands all cultivated, and adorned by some farms, and a very handsome Presbyterian church upon a hill." So struck was Penn by the resemblance that he attached to the scenery aesthetic terms usually reserved for the English countryside; words like *sublime* and *romantic* not only indicate the force of new standards of beauty developed in poetry and painting, but an increasingly "finished" landscape markedly different from that of fifty years before.

Different as their interests were, Mittelberger, Schoepf, and Penn shared something which makes their narratives closer in spirit than they might have been otherwise. All walked or rode horseback on their expeditions. They could go wherever they desired. Sometimes, of course, they became lost; Schoepf, for example, rode miles down a back road without finding an inn and finally sought help from a farmer who took him for a robber. Usually, though, their self-directed and self-paced modes of travel allowed them to stop whenever they wished to question farmers about plowing techniques or the yield of acreage, or to gather wild plants or visit every street in a large town. Roads themselves figure very little in their narratives. If they were rutted or washed out, the travelers clambered around the obstruction and perhaps found something interesting on the detour. They were free to stay overnight with farmers, for as Mittelberger remarked, "It is the custom in this country that when a traveler comes on horseback to a house, he is asked whether he wishes to have anything to eat." Sometimes their lack of mentioning anything of roads and inns is annoying, but the lack is offset by their detailed analyses of the roadside. They and other travelers in late-eighteenth-century Pennsylvania traveled slowly and, by indirection, found all sorts of interesting things in the maturing landscape.

The successors to Mittelberger, Penn, and Schoepf were far more apt to stay on main-traveled roads, and to ride in chaises or coaches rather than walk or ride horseback. The narratives produced by such travelers devote much more space to detailing road conditions and the comforts or discomforts of inns, since roads and inns were of paramount importance to men restricted to wheeled vehicles and established stopping places. Very subtly, too, the new mode of travel altered the perception of the landscape.

Theophile Cazenove, for example, traveled through New Jersey and Pennsylvania in 1794, only six years after John Penn. He rode, however, in a carriage drawn by two horses and accompanied by a servant. His *Journal* is a relation of towns visited and inns endured, and his perception of the landscape is curiously different.

Cazenove delighted in Pennsylvania towns from the moment he arrived in Easton. "This little town is pretty," he remarked, "well laid out for the main square and the rows of streets, partly lined with good houses of blue stone, abundant in the neighborhood." His itinerary led him from one town to the next, and his curiosity about town life led him to investigate everything from the size of house lots (which he studied with the zeal of a real estate speculator), to the occupations of Kutztown craftsmen, to the materials used in house building. His enthusiasm for town life colored his view of agricultural areas too, and on one occasion he remarked that "there ought to be five or six families living close together in these districts; then they would be very happy." Why Cazenove suspected that they were unhappy is difficult to discover, because he seems to have spoken with very few. Most of his information about farm life he derived from tavernkeepers who were not always representative of their farmer neighbors, as Cazenove himself must have realized.

Cazenove did sometimes discriminate among the farms and farmers he passed, but his evaluations lack the clarity of Schoepf's: "No care is taken to keep the entrance to the houses free of stones and mud—not one tree—not one flower. In the vegetable garden, weeds intermingled with cabbages and a few turnips and plants. In brief, with the exception of the size of the barn and a larger cultivated area, you do not distinguish between the rich Pennsylvania farmer and the poor farmer of other states." The remark is based on insufficient observation, because Cazenove was aware that the farmland he passed through was rich. Occasionally he remarked on the beautiful well-kept woodlots planted to chestnut,

PENNSYLVANIA TRAVEL NARRATIVES

locust, walnut, maple, and white oak which broke up the wide pastures, the apple orchards, and the fields planted to corn, wheat, clover, or turnips. Of the farmland near Womelsdorf, which Penn thought looked so much like the agricultural countryside of Europe, Cazenove remarked only that "the neighborhood is remarkably well cultivated, therefore pleasant." Despite the information gleaned from innkeepers then, Cazenove's narrative is based chiefly on fleeting glances from the highway. Like the travelers of early-seventeenth-century England, he was interested in inns, towns, and roads, not in the agricultural landscape behind the fences at the road's edge. His journal suggests that in the span of ten years, Pennsylvanians had shifted from an agricultural lifestyle to one intimately connected with towns.

Cazenove was not alone in his approach to traveling, and others unwittingly imitated his concern for towns. In 1801, John Pearson traveled to Lancaster and Columbia, ignoring the agricultural undertakings beside the road; instead he too focused on towns. He remarked on the paint used on Lancaster houses, the narrow alleys which linked backyards in that town, and the pale brick of Columbia dwellings. He delighted in the fine view from a Lancaster church steeple, where "the town under your feet, distant houses, extensive fields, woods and ridges of mountains many miles remote made it a beautiful prospect." In Pearson's imagination, the state of the landscape reflected perfectly the state of its inhabitants, and indeed his prose often confused the two. Columbia "has not a good prospect," he asserted. "Their fences are ordinary and it appears as if they were extremely careless in respect to planting trees, either for shade or use." The lack of a church building along with poor fences and few trees led him to conclude that "the inhabitants seem to me from appearances to be indolent." Like Cazenove, Pearson trusted the long-distance view. He was content to ride the turnpike and simply glance at the countryside; he was no more distant from his subject in the church steeple than he was on the highway.

Joshua Gilpin traveled in a carriage as did Cazenove, and the view recorded in his *Journal of a Tour From Philadelphia Through the Western Counties of Pennsylvania in the Months of September and October, 1809* shows that turnpike driving produced similar problems and angles of vision. Along the turnpike all signs of wilderness were gone, and Gilpin enjoyed the copses of woods which broke up the vistas of large fields, making the landscape like the "finest park scenery in England." Since Gilpin was interested in farming, his *Journal* is filled with remarks about the excellent soil of the Lancaster region and the use of plaster of Paris as manure, but his view of agriculture was still distant. While he praised "neat farms with portions of irrigated meadow, woodland, and open fields," his information was visual only. Unlike his early predecessors, he rarely stopped to talk with the makers of the landscape he praised.

What intrigued him most was the condition of the road before his carriage. Fascinated with bridges, he described the "Schuylkill permanent bridge" on the Lancaster Turnpike, the "very handsome stone bridge of three arches" over the Brandywine at Downingstown. Such well-made bridges and better maintained roads greatly increased the speed of travel, but they made even more difficult any attempt to observe the back country. Instead, they linked towns closer together and made seeing the spaces between seductively easy. Gilpin seems to have enjoyed covering many miles each day, and perhaps he preferred town inns to those isolated in the country. In any event, he stopped frequently in towns, describing them well; there is a remarkably modern tone to his narrative.

His adventures of September 18 and 19 are a case in point. "Notwithstanding all our exertions we did not reach Chambersburgh till after dark," he remarked, "as we have wished much not to hazard a ride over these roads to which we are strangers and which at best are rough and uneven after sunset." The roads were bad, at least for someone driving a carriage, and Gilpin and his colleagues arrived very fatigued from the effort of trying to make thirty miles a day. Gilpin concluded that an excellent turnpike might be made over the mountain, and that if the day had been a little cooler so that they could have walked instead of jolting about on the carriage seat, the trip would have been far more enjoyable. As it was, they found a good inn at Chambersburgh, slept well enough, and spent the early part of the nineteenth having the carriage repaired and finding a fresh team of horses.

Walking about the town while the carriage was being refitted, Gilpin carefully described the public buildings, the "very neat" street plan, and the dwellings, many of which had courtyards before them. After lunch he and his companion left with a hired driver, and found a road which was "generally a good one, that is, a soft natural road." There is scant trace of Schoepf's casual walking in Gilpin's narrative; unlike his eighteenth-century predecessor, Gilpin was chiefly interested in covering ground, in seeing a great deal, if nothing too closely. To him, a good turnpike was the essential part of every good view.

The Pennsylvania landscape had indeed changed between the 1770s and the end of the first quarter of the nineteenth century, but not nearly so much as the travel narratives indicate. What had changed greatly was the road system; good bridges and turnpikes were everywhere, and traveling over them was pleasant. But away from the main-traveled roads, the Pennsylvania landscape had not greatly changed, although there were fewer and fewer travelers who observed it. Most were seduced into a high-speed, long-distance view from a well-surfaced road.

Philip Houlbrooke Nicklin's travel narrative, *A Pleasant Peregrination through the Prettiest Parts of Pennsylvania,* of 1836 signals a new style of writing. Nicklin traveled only by the swiftest possible conveyances— mail coaches, canal boats, and railroad. Of all forms of transport, he enjoyed the railroad most, even when the cars were drawn by horses or when sparks and soot settled on his clothes. While Gilpin had tried to achieve thirty miles a day, Nicklin was relaxed at ten miles an hour, though such a rapid speed left him time to only glimpse at the passing scene. Even the canal-boat perspective was one of speed and haste, and Nicklin's descriptions matched the view. Phrases like "the scenery for the whole distance is very interesting" derive not from carelessness, but from simple haste. He moved too quickly to talk with farmers, or to collect wild plants, or hear stories at an inn. He stopped only in hotels which catered not to travelers, but to tourists, to the new breed of pleasure seekers enticed away from comfortable homes by the canal packets and railroad trains.

While Mittelberger stopped to eat with farmers, Nicklin rushed by their houses. A rainy week upset his plans tremendously; the streets of Hollidaysburg were ankle-deep in mud when he arrived, forcing him to stay indoors and view the town from windows. The streets, like farmyards, were too sloppy for firsthand observation, so he sat back and generalized from the comfort of hotel veranda or coach.

Nicklin's self-imposed distance from the landscape was encouraged by the railroads, several of which prepared guide books like the *Guide for the Pennsylvania Railroad* published in 1855. The *Guide* is a remarkable document. Passengers are given such extraordinary information as the populations of towns and the dates of stations, but almost no specific information about the land beside the tracks. "Millwood is a small station," remarks the *Guide,* "doing an inconsiderable business," and "Landisville, the next station, is merely a stopping place." Occasionally a trace of aesthetics breaks the factual monotony—"Probably no country in the world can present a finer picture of agricultural prosperity than that through which we have passed from Philadelphia to Lancaster"—but the overall tone is one of narrowness. What is of value to the railroad is mentioned and lovingly described, but structures apart from viaducts and trestles go mostly unnoticed. The *Guide* is a travel narrative, but an anonymous one. Its subject matter and tone, though not linked to any individual, were typical in the 1850s.

In his 1852 *Pictorial Sketch Book of Pennsylvania*, Eli Bowen devoted much attention to the industrial landscape intruding on the agricultural one. As he became especially fascinated with the structures and spaces involved in iron making, Bowen realized that travelers in Pennsylvania would need a new aesthetic to appreciate the evolving landscape.

A year before the *Guide* appeared, Eli Bowen published his *Pictorial Sketch-Book of Pennsylvania*. Like Nicklin, Bowen was satisfied with glimpses, but his glimpses are not always so picturesque. The *Pictorial Sketch-Book* focuses on Pennsylvania industry—on cotton mills, anthracite furnaces, coal trestles, iron foundries, and chemical works—in short, on trackside Pennsylvania. "Between Pottstown and Reading there are several pretty landscape scenes," Bowen remarked, but the chief view is so industrial that Bowen uses the term *landscape* in a pastoral connotation only. Foundries and mills, it seems from his narrative, do not comprise a landscape.

Bowen's angle of vision encompassed such smoke-belching artifacts with difficulty, because they were too near the tracks. A landscape in his mind was a distant panorama; if it had one or two industrial sites within it, so much the better, but it had to be viewed from afar. Otherwise, detail distracted the eye, and the overall effect was lost. Not surprisingly, Bowen saw rather few landscapes from his railroad car. He traveled too quickly to admire all but the widest views, and too near to many industrial sites. In fact, his narrative suggests that in two or three decades all of Pennsylvania had been industrialized.

The railroad traveler was given a far more restricted view than Mittelberger. Commanded to keep his head inside the window, he was forced to look sideways—not ahead or behind. Controlling the train was impossible; it stopped where its conductor wished it to—usually before a station—and went only where the rails before it led. What was over a hill, through a woods, or down a narrow road was almost non-existent. By 1876 the idea of landscape was very vague indeed.

The years between 1756 and 1856 were indeed a century of landscape change, not only in Pennsylvania but across the United States. The change in Pennsylvania was an almost perfect example of what occurred in later years in the South, Midwest, and Far West. What had been an emergent rural landscape, a collection of farms, small villages, and poor roads set against an almost overwhelming backdrop of wilderness evolved into a complex man-altered environment marked by towns and cities, turnpikes and railroads, and factories and furnaces, all interrupted by only a few bits and pieces of romantic wilderness. But the new landscape was not homogeneous. Some areas were far more industrialized than others, and many regions, particularly those removed from good roads and railroads, remained almost wholly agricultural. Towns like Railroad sprang up at transportation junctions, while others like Beulah in Cambria County were abandoned. By 1856 the parts of the larger landscape most familiar to the general public were those alongside main roads and railroads, because it was along such routes that most people traveled, including writers of landscape description.

Today, slightly more than a century later, the landscape of Pennsylvania is infinitely more complex. Great cities and suburbs occupy what was until quite recently farmland; and factories, mines, and oil fields can be discovered surrounded by forest. It is not easy to see any immediate order in the contemporary Pennsylvania landscape, unless one takes an historical view. That view is the great legacy of the old travel narratives. An evening or so devoted to reading descriptions of former landscapes makes present-day landscapes far more intelligible. Old travel narratives are indeed more intriguing than old love letters, because one can still see the shadows of the past and reach out and touch them.

MAPPING INDIANA

Nineteenth-Century School Book Views

Indiana sprawls across two pages of *The New Reference Atlas of the World,* a handsome folio volume published by C. S. Hammond & Company in 1924. The map of Indiana gleams in a rainbow of pastel color; yellow, green, pink, orange, and pale violet designate counties; a faint blue marks Lake Michigan; and a deeper, richer blue identifies English Lake,* the Ohio River, and the lesser lakes of Steuben, Noble, and other counties. Intricate webs of black lines trace the routes of rivers and railroads; dashed lines mark county boundaries; and bolder black lines define the edges of the state, the borders separating the land of pastel counties from the dull, cream-colored states of Michigan, Ohio, Kentucky, and Illinois. And in fine, nearly illegible type appear the names of towns, of rivers and streams and lakes, of railroad companies, and in larger type the names of counties and cities.[1] Indeed the map is a stunning visual construct, an artifact of an age that delighted in atlases accurate and beautiful. Only the size of the map raises questions about the thinking of its publishers.

Why does Indiana enjoy a two-page map, while other states crowd onto single pages? Georgia and Alabama, for example, appear on single pages, as does Florida, whose panhandle appears in an inset placed in the Gulf of Mexico. Vermont and New Hampshire share a single page, as do Maryland and Delaware; the two New England states fit well enough on the cramped page, but the western part of Maryland is depicted in an inset adrift in Virginia. Other states extend across two pages, but only in company with adjacent states; one two-page spread depicts Massachusetts, Connecticut, and Rhode Island, while another illustrates Kentucky and Tennessee. But some states sprawl as Indiana sprawls—Pennsylvania and Illinois extend over two pages. Close examination of *The New Reference Atlas* suggests that area alone means little in the number of pages assigned to a map of a state. North Dakota and Montana each receive single pages despite their large areas, but Texas receives two double-page spreads. Illustration size significantly affects the amount of published detail, as the mileage scales subtly imply. The map of Maryland and

"Mapping Indiana: Nineteenth-Century School Book Views" appeared in *Lectures 1983* (Indianapolis: Indiana Historical Society, 1984), 3–27.

Delaware is printed at "19 miles to the inch"; that of Virginia, "83 miles to the inch," and that of Indiana, at approximately eighteen miles to an inch.[2] The map of Indiana, therefore, presents so much detailed information simply because of its large size. Clearly the publishers determined that Indiana ought to appear in a more detailed format than Virginia, in one almost as detailed as that accorded to New Jersey. Indiana sprawls across two pages in order that the publishers can present very detailed information about it.

In the absence of publishing house records, only the maps and the arrangement of maps in the volume speak. They speak, albeit softly, of subtle value judgments about the importance of some states and the relative unimportance of others. Perhaps population figures, book-buying habits, or other things important to selling atlases determined map size, but larger issues appear to be involved. North Dakota and Montana in 1924 may not have been important in the overall national picture; as newly and thinly settled predominantly agricultural states, their significance appeared to lie in the future, just as the significance of Vermont and New Hampshire appeared to lie in the past. Indiana, thickly settled, marvelously productive in both agriculture and manufacturing, vital in the national railroad network, had entered a golden age of appreciation after more than a century of languishing in geography textbooks and in home, school, and commercial atlases.

Geographies

Old school books are windows on the past. Graded readers offer lessons in morality and the virtue of public men; arithmetic lessons, word problems in particular, reveal the shifting importance of agriculture, land measurement, woodworking, and commercial accounting; history texts speak of the distant past as the recent past wanted children to know it. Geography books chronicle the evolution of the American landscape, and, when hundreds are read together, reveal the curious nature of geographical thinking in the nation's public schools. Unlike the speculators' pamphlets, explorers' maps, and settlers' guides published by adults for adults, school geographies must distill vast amounts of information into a format useful to third graders, or high schoolers, or to all of the students crowded into a one-room schoolhouse on the Indiana frontier in 1815. And from school geography books comes almost all the geography most people ever know.

The father of American geography, Jedidiah Morse, published his *The American Geography* in 1789, advertising on the title page that his book was "illustrated with two sheet maps—one of the southern, the other the northern states, neatly and elegantly engraved, and more correct than any that have hitherto been published." While his announcement reveals his understanding that handsome maps may be as important to the public as accurate ones, it is really less than correct. Both maps illustrate also the "western territory," an immense region Morse defines simply as "all that part of the United States which lies northwest of the Ohio," and "bounded west, by the Mississippi River; north, by the Lakes; east, by Pennsylvania; southeast and south, by the Ohio River." About the region Morse had little definite information, although he reported that "the Wabash is a beautiful river, with high and fertile banks," passable in spring, summer, and autumn with bateaux and opening on a land inhabited by Indians and French colonists. At "Post Vincennes," by order of Congress, the army had erected an outpost armed with "four small brass cannon" and "garrisoned by a major and two companies."[3] Such is the verbal information about the land that eventually became the state of Indiana; the graphic information—little more than a notation that land near the confluence of the Miami and Ohio had been acquired by the "Wabash Company"—is equally vague. Morse intended his *American Geography* for adults, and perhaps adults dealt well with its ambiguities. After all, the westward movement had quickened with peace and independence, and soon better information would be available.

By 1806 it was, and Morse published it in *Geography Made Easy*, an abridgment of his *American Geography* "calculated particularly for the use and improvement of schools and academies in the United States of America." In little more than two pages of fine print, Morse explained that the "Indiana Territory" "has a fine soil, adapted to corn, wheat, rye, oats, cotton, hemp, tobacco, and other articles mentioned in the account of the state of Ohio." He reported the discovery of a silver mine, the condition of navigable rivers, the "fine meadows, which in some places extend as far as the eye can reach," and, under "curiosities," the "Great Cave" on the banks of the Wabash.[4] Certainly the increased detail is significant, but so also is Morse's willingness to define the Indiana Territory in terms of Ohio. Quite clearly, Morse had become accustomed to thinking of both places as parts of the larger region formerly called "the western territories," and in 1806, his textbook suggests, Indiana warranted neither detailed particularization nor description.

In subsequent years other authors produced school book geographies that analyzed the Indiana Territory. Perhaps they borrowed information from Morse's writings—his *Geography Made Easy* passed through many editions; perhaps they borrowed from the same Federal government reports; perhaps they borrowed and reborrowed from each other. H. G. Spafford, for example, published *General Geography . . . Digested on a*

New Plan, and Designed for the Use of Schools in 1809. His book gives slightly different statistics from those presented by Morse and is more detailed about soil types and topography. "The rest of the country, except just on the borders of the rivers, may be called almost uniformly a dead level," he notes. "Of this part, the soil is, in general, a rich loam, or a kind of gravelly and vegetable mold, not deep, and resting on a bed of clay." More than Morse, Spafford recognized the importance of minerals and noted that, in addition to the silver mine, settlers had found deposits of limestone, coal, and copper.[5] A year later Elijah Parish began selling his *A New System of Modern Geography,* which differed only slightly from Spafford's textbook, and in 1813 appeared *Elements of Geography* by Rodolphus Dickinson, which dismissed the Territory in a single paragraph. "In the face of the country, soil, productions, and climate, this territory bears a striking resemblance to the interior and western parts of the state of Ohio," Dickinson remarked, in a passage similar to Morse's.[6] The geographies by Morse, Spafford, Parish, and Dickinson all appear to have been aimed at upper-level school children, perhaps children in the equivalent of today's tenth or eleventh grade. That they do not all present comprehensive information about the Indiana Territory suggests that increasing settlement and prosperity did not necessarily produce more detailed school book descriptions.

· Statehood did. Once Indiana entered the Union as a state, authors devoted much more space to describing its topography, products, and settlements. *The Material Creation,* published in 1818 by Herman Mann (who advertised himself on the title page as "author of several anonymous publications"), devotes only two pages to the new state, but both pages are jammed with specific information and explicitly announce that the pace of settlement is so fast that reliable information is difficult to obtain. "A single example will demonstrate this fact," Mann continues. "In the fall of 1813, the town of *Vevay* was located. In 1814, it was still a forest. In the fore part of 1816, it contained 75 handsome dwelling houses, besides shops, etc., a brick courthouse, jail, schoolhouse, 8 stores, 3 tanneries," and many other amenities including "a public library" and "a neat weekly newspaper." Nevertheless, Mann continues the tradition of describing Indiana in terms of Ohio: "*Aspect and Climate* much resemble those of Ohio. *Soil and Productions.* This state, also, like Ohio, is blessed with a soil which naturally yields every production that the wants and even the luxury of man can claim."[7] *The Material Creation,* therefore, spans the attitudes associated with Indiana as territory resembling Ohio and the understanding of Indiana as a separate state.

Subsequent authors often concentrated on the "basic" description of topography and "productions" before mentioning unique or intriguing

The map of Indiana that appeared in Nathan Hale's 1830 *Epitome of Universal Geography* emphasizes settlement in the southern and central regions of the state: counties are named but not bounded. (Harvard College Library)

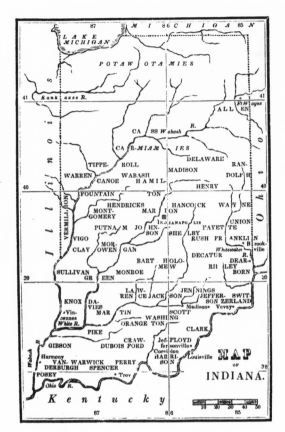

facts. Nathan Hale in *An Epitome of Universal Geography,* a map-illustrated upper-level school geography of 1830, focused his discussion on the making of wine at Vevay and the possibilities of a canal between the Wabash and the Maumee.[8] Daniel Adams devoted only a page to the state in the thirteenth edition of his *Geography; or, A Description of the World,* which appeared in 1831; he thought that soil yielding fifty bushels an acre deserved special mention. But Adams nonetheless emphasized that Indiana was much like Ohio.[9] In his 1833 text, *The School Geography,* John J. Clute catalogued the growing number of expanding settlements, oddities like the cave near Corydon that produced epsom salts and saltpeter, the several steam mills in New Albany, and the exact courses and usefulness of rivers.[10] Unlike Adams, Clute distinguished Indiana from neighboring states, but two years later, when T. G. Bradford published his translated abridgment of Adrian Balbi's *Universal Geography,* Ohio still remained the standard by which Indiana was described. "In the other parts, it does not differ from that of Ohio," he wrote of the climate; "The articles of culture are similar to those of Ohio," he noted of the agri-

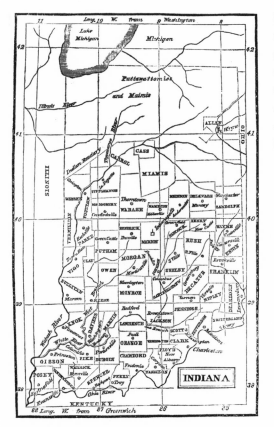

In his 1833 *School Geography* map, John J. Clute bounded and named as many counties as he knew, but he only vaguely depicted lands occupied by Native Americans. (Harvard College Library)

cultural products. Bradford (and Balbi) presented far more information about the state than Hale, Adams, and Clute, however, and the information smacks of firsthand or at least very reliable secondhand information. "Peach trees blossom early in March," they wrote. "The forests are in leaf early in April." They listed the names of all sixty-nine counties, described the principal towns, and commented on the best-growing varieties of grapes.[11] Quite clearly, *Universal Geography* comprehends Indiana as a place similar to Ohio but definitely distinct.

The 1830s marked a turning point. Authors apparently had available much more information about the rising state and no longer felt obligated to define it in terms of Ohio. Edwin Williams, for example, in *A Comprehensive System of Modern Geography and History* catalogued most of the important topographical features and "improvements" in a staccato of numbered paragraphs, all somewhat like number thirteen: "*Jeffersonville* is a small town, on the Ohio, opposite the rapids, with a population of 500. The *State Prison* is located here."[12] Two years later, when Roswell C. Smith's rather more elementary *Geography on the Productive System* appeared, even more details were known to authors. Smith begins his chapter on Indiana by noting explicitly that the state is *not* like Ohio: "Indiana in the southern part, along the Ohio River, is hilly; the other parts are generally level, much more so than Ohio."[13] Sometime in the 1830s either Indiana had developed enough or information about it had spread far enough to require changes in geography textbooks.

In the two decades after 1840 the quality of writing about Indiana rose dramatically, partly because professional geographers-mapmakers produced textbooks for schoolchildren. S. Augustus Mitchell, the creator of many maps intended for adults, produced a sophisticated textbook in 1840 entitled simply *Geographical Reader*. Mitchell provides a detailed synopsis of the role of rivers in Indiana transportation, a pithy paragraph concerning topography, and others tracing the importance of agriculture, industry, and history. "Indiana has expended nearly 4,000,000 dollars in internal improvements," Mitchell records. "The principal work is the Wabash canal, reaching from Manhattan, at the mouth of the Maumee River, to Terra [*sic*] Haute, on the Wabash, 310 miles; thence to Evansville, on the Ohio River."[14] His descriptions of Indianapolis, population increase, important centers of trade, and the educational system, while brief, are factual and up to date. His text appears to have been the model for others, including some intended for younger students. J. Olney's *A Practical System of Modern Geography* (1843) and S. S. Cornell's *High School Geography* (1860) both appear to build on Mitchell's facts and organization of data while adding new information. Cornell, for example, understands the importance of railroads: "Being the terminus of several railroads, it is destined to become a very important city of the West," he writes of Indianapolis. "A [railroad?] bridge spans the river at this point."[15] Within three years, J. H. Colton's *American School Geography* appeared, devoting about one-fifth of its Indiana section to the characteristics— largely commercial—of Indianapolis, New Albany, Evansville, Fort Wayne, and Lafayette.[16] No longer did textbook authors dismiss Indiana as a mere copy of Ohio.

Certainly Indiana by 1860 deserved sustained attention; already a prosperous agricultural state important in the national transportation network, it also showed signs of becoming an industrial power. Its large population undoubtedly purchased thousands of textbooks annually, a fact of some concern to textbook publishers. But perhaps a more subtle reason explains the growing sophistication of geography textbook descriptions. In 1860 Indiana was long past the frontier stage. Easterners, however provincial, had learned of its enormous agricultural production and its massive public works program. They had learned also that Indiana had a *regional* identity. "Indiana is the smallest of the Western

States," wrote S. Augustus Mitchell in 1860 in *A System of Modern Geography,* a geography textbook directed at readers just under high school age.[17] In textbook after textbook, Indiana took its place as one of the "western states," as clearly identified as any one of the New England or middle states.[18] And unlike Vermont or Florida, it lay squarely on the road of national expansion.

All of the geography textbooks cited here have eastern origins. Four were published in Philadelphia, three in New York City and one in Hudson, New York, one in Elizabethtown, New Jersey (although written in Massachusetts), and six in Massachusetts. Place of publication proves nothing about an author's origin, of course, but most of the writers seem to have been easterners, and while Jedidiah Morse's *American Geography* has a compass far beyond the boundaries of Charlestown, Massachusetts, many of the textbooks suggest a genuine provincialism. As late as the Civil War era, Indiana teachers and pupils relied heavily, if not entirely, upon geography books written by easterners accustomed to thinking in terms of the thirteen colonies. For as long as Indiana remained "in the west," many authors gave it little real attention. Only when it became one of the "western states" did they focus accurately. Nowhere is the shift more evident than in schoolroom atlases.

Atlases

Only a handful of geography textbooks published before the Civil War included maps. Printing difficulties and expenses undoubtedly dissuaded most publishers from illustrating their texts with more than one or two maps, if any. Nathan Hale's *Epitome of Universal Geography* and John J. Clute's *School Geography,* however, illustrate Indiana with simple line maps showing rivers, settlement locations, counties, and the large area occupied by the "Puttawattomies." For the most part, such simple but accurate maps remained the exception rather than the rule until after mid-century, even though many high-quality maps intended for adults existed.

Four maps illustrate the breadth of popularly available maps intended for prospective settlers, travelers, and businessmen. H. S. Tanner's handsome *Traveller's Pocket Map of Indiana,* published in Philadelphia in 1831, emphasizes roads and steamboat routes; a "profile of the Wabash and Erie Canal" graces a large blank area to the right of the eastern boundary of the state. The map uses four colors to identify the organized counties and a pale purple to locate two large regions still controlled by Indian tribes.[19] *Indiana,* an 1833 map published in New York by David H. Burr, is remarkably similar; while less handsomely engraved than Tanner's, it employs four colors to designate counties and Indian lands, and it devotes much more attention to river systems and proposed canals.[20] A far more complex and colorful map, S. Augustus Mitchell's *Tourist's Pocket Map of the State of Indiana Exhibiting its Internal Improvements, Roads, Distances, Etc.,* appeared two years later in Philadelphia. Flanked with charts of population statistics and steamboat routes, the four-color map illustrates the rising significance of Indianapolis and the decreasing area inhabited by Indians.[21] In 1846, Mitchell published an updated version, *A New Map of Indiana,* showing not only the profile of the Wabash and Erie Canal and a chart of steamboat routes but also the dramatically more complex road and railroad network and, again in four colors, the multiplication of counties. Aside from rivers, the maps include almost no topographical information; according to them, Indiana is a sort of featureless plain, cut up by rivers and lacking in hills or dales.[22] But the maps clearly indicate the sophisticated information about the state available in the East but frequently lacking in school texts.

One reason that perhaps explains the omission of state maps in so many texts is that contemporaneous atlases proliferated—some the work of the authors of textbooks, others the product of mapmakers or educators aware that many textbooks existed to supplement the bound collection of maps. The atlases are extremely significant, for they reveal subtle biases about Indiana and about the schoolroom view of the nation as a whole.

Modern Atlas Adapted to Morse's School Geography appeared in 1828. Its key map illustrates an extensive and still largely unexplored United States, showing a vast Missouri Territory west of Illinois and a scrawny Lake Michigan washing the eastern boundary of the "Northwest Territory." Indiana is depicted as a near wasteland, scarcely settled even in the south, and embracing the settlement of Chicago. The region controlled by the Potawatomi Indians sweeps far into Illinois, touching the Northwest Territory lands of the Winnebago tribe.[23] Clearly, the anonymous author of the map knew remarkably little about the state but, nevertheless, expected youthful readers of *Geography Made Easy* to make sense of his vague illustration.

J. L. Blake's *American Universal Geography* of 1833 offers little improvement. Its map of the northern half of the nation (excluding New England), while tinted in red and yellow, focuses almost entirely on watersheds. Blake does depict Chicago properly, but he gives the impression that, aside from Fort Wayne, the only settlement north of Indianapolis is "Prophets T.," apparently a reference to the Indian of Tippecanoe fame.[24] The cryptic designation *is* odd indeed, for at least *Modern Atlas Adapted* located the battlefield. "Prophets T." apparently designates the former location of the Indian encampment. Barnum Field's 1837 *Atlas*

Designed to Accompany the American School Geography is nearly as vague, although more colorful. It locates only the Wabash, White, and Ohio rivers and the towns of Indianapolis, Vevay, Vincennes, Harmony, and Madison, totally ignoring the northern half of the state (Fort Wayne is missing) and avoiding any mention of Chicago.[25] The bizarre nature of the atlas maps is not easily explained. Certainly the atlases were designed for upper-level schoolchildren; omission of important details cannot be explained by an intention to simplify. And, as the existence of the adult sheet maps makes evident, high-quality information about Indiana was available.

Whatever the explanation, by 1844 Sidney E. Morse had helped correct the deficiency. His *A System of Geography* presents Indiana and Ohio in a one-page map emphasizing county boundaries, county seats, and communication networks. Beneath the map are paragraphs of questions and other exercises intended to encourage children to scrutinize the visual document.[26] While Morse's high-quality map depicts rivers, it says nothing more about the "face of the country." Perhaps Morse had started a trend; two years later appeared Roswell C. Smith's *A Concise and Practical System of Geography,* one of the first atlases to depict a new grouping of states—"The Western States." The three-color map is not as detailed as Morse's, but it pays more attention to topographical features and to the location of towns smaller than county seats. Perhaps more important, Smith's map places the Indiana transportation network in a regional context, showing the importance of the railroad and canal systems in the westward movement.[27] When Roswell C. Smith published his elementary *Introductory Geography* eight years later, however, he eliminated all designations of transportation routes and allowed only the Wabash River a place; aside from the names of five major cities, his dark green Indiana is blank. But Smith retained the regional designation: Indiana is explicitly one of the western states.[28]

Sectional controversy called more attention to the concept of "western" states, as is clearly evident in S. S. Cornell's 1862 *Companion Atlas,* a volume published as complement to his 1860 *High School Geography.* Cornell located Indiana as one of the "Southern and Western States"; on the red splash of color he identified major rivers and towns and placed the state in relation to the Confederacy.[29] Three years later, J. H. Colton in *American School Quarto Geography* took a different approach, identifying Indiana as part of a four-state region that also included Ohio, Kentucky, and Tennessee and was the crossroads for national east–west routes. In Colton's detailed image, South Bend and Logansport figured as prominently as Indianapolis, apparently because they served as transportation network centers.[30] Colton's map is nearly an equal to the traveler's map produced by Mitchell; it is an attractive, useful complement to Colton's

American School Geography published two years before. By the last years of the 1860s, school atlases began to emphasize the transportation significance of Indiana, although the designation of the region in which the state lay continued to perplex authors.

Theodore Sedgwick Fay, for example, in a lower-level *Atlas* published in 1867 omits transportation routes but notes the new importance of South Bend, Fort Wayne, and Lafayette, along with that of Terre Haute and Evansville in the south.[31] A year later, Francis McNally's *An Improved System of Geography* linked Indiana with the three other states chosen by Colton, depicted county borders in the fashion common in previous decades, and identified transportation routes, showing the recent importance of places like Elkhart. McNally's map is the first to give railroad routes preeminent position; no longer are rivers or county borders the dominant lines. His green-colored Indiana is only a backdrop for marked railroad routes.[32] Late in the decade, S. Augustus Mitchell published several school atlases; in 1868 and 1869, his atlases portrayed Indiana much as McNally's did, emphasizing railroad lines. But Mitchell retained the older designation "Western States," although for his purposes the region so called stretched from West Virginia to Iowa and from Kentucky to Michigan.[33] But in 1870, when he published his *Modern Atlas,* Mitchell made a crucial change; he depicted the same large region but presented Ohio, Indiana, and Illinois as its core, showing Indiana in green, the two flanking states in red, and the rest of the states in a pale yellow. His map emphasizes the railroad network as something that not only reaches beyond state borders but actually comprises new sorts of regions.[34] His depiction of the Ohio, Indiana, and Illinois railroad system seems calculated to diminish the importance of any railroad lines in Kentucky and to show the great barrier still represented by the Mississippi River.

After 1870 even the authors of elementary-level atlases attempted to depict the changed circumstances of the national landscape. Mary Lucy Hall's *Our World No. II,* an 1872 atlas intended for very young children, uses little color indeed but emphasizes the Indiana railroad network as part of the "Northern Central States" system of railroads.[35] No longer was Indiana a frontier state on the edge of wildness, a place known largely for its agricultural produce and booming settlements.

Authors of advanced level texts made explicit the new understanding of Indiana. In his 1873 *Comprehensive Geography,* James Monteith depicted Indiana at the near center of a cluster of states including Minnesota and Missouri, Ohio and Kentucky, but focused on an axis made up of four states: Illinois, Wisconsin, Michigan (including its upper peninsula), and Indiana. Monteith's map eschews almost all topographical features, but

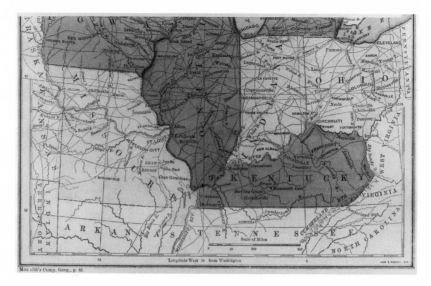

James Monteith's 1873 schoolroom atlas illustrates Indiana crisscrossed by railroad lines in a way that evokes the French view of North America as a massive archipelago. (Harvard College Library)

it emphasizes Indiana rail lines and important junctions like South Bend and Terre Haute along with lesser ones like Crawfordsville.[36] The map makes evident the important role of Indiana in north–south travel as well as travel in east–west directions. His book is a more complex educational device than ones published even fifteen years earlier; it encourages children to scrutinize maps by drawing circles of different radii, by comparing the area of states, and by superimposing state outlines. It shows, for example, that Ohio and Indiana combined are only scarcely larger than Kansas. *Comprehensive Geography* marks a milestone on the long, tortuous path to sophisticated schoolroom geography texts and atlases. Its maps are made to be used over and over again, not merely to be looked at and memorized.

Monteith's excellent textbook quickly acquired competitors, one of the best being *Colton's Common School Geography,* published in 1880 with no information about its author or authors on its title page. The book is illustrated with many maps, and, unlike so many of its predecessors, it provides more than one map of an area. It includes a large map of the United States showing principal rivers and cities; a pale red Indiana is marked by the Wabash River and South Bend, for example, along with other waterways and cities. Another map shows Indiana as part of "Section No. 7" of the nation; the section contains also Ohio, Kentucky, and Tennessee but not Illinois, a state most previously published schoolroom maps included with Indiana. The map is intricate indeed; county boundaries are clearly marked, and county areas are designated in red and yellow. Principal cities and towns and most county seats are named and located, and a railroad network is depicted in great detail along with major waterways.[37] But Indiana also appears in a national railroad map; colored in a pastel yellow, the state seems awash in railroads. The railroad map not only identifies important towns, particularly junctions, but also identifies the name of each company and the mileage between stops. *Comprehensive Geography* and *Colton's Common School Geography* consequently mark the end of a long era. Detailed maps accompanied by complex exercises, multiple maps showing different features of the same state, and refined printing techniques all anticipate twentieth-century atlases.

Indeed Richard Elwood Dodge's *Advanced Geography,* published in Chicago in 1904 by Rand, McNally & Company, is scarcely distinguishable from geography books of the present. In fact, it may be better, for its map locating Wisconsin, Michigan, Illinois, Ohio, and Indiana as "States of the Mississippi Basin, Northeastern Section" is crisply printed, strikingly colored—Indiana appears in a rich yellow flanked by Ohio and Illinois in dark green and Michigan in deep pink—and intimately related to the text that discusses it. Simple features, while not original with *Advanced Geography,* make the map useful; "relative importance of places shown by size of type" reads one part of the key.[38] Dodge's book—and especially its maps—do more than introduce Indiana; they introduce a new, far more sophisticated way of examining states.

Hunches

A century or more after the publication of a school geography text or atlas is indeed a difficult time to ask questions of its author. It is difficult to learn the age or grade for whom the author intended the book and probably impossible to discover how any one student, let alone a group of students, reacted to the prose or graphics. Even contemporary Americans when asked about the schoolbooks of their youth usually recall remarkably little.[39] What, then, can be gleaned from the hundreds of different geography textbooks and schoolroom atlases mouldering in university libraries or in the basements of antique stores or in attics, barns, and schoolhouse book closets? Why *does* Indiana sprawl over two pages of *The New Reference Atlas of the World?*

Of chief importance, perhaps, is the tenuous connection between available information about a territory or state and its publication in school geographies. Long after travelers, settlers, and businessmen had high-quality maps of Indiana, schoolchildren confronted vague and even distorted illustrations. Long after the Indiana state government had made available accurate statistics concerning the state's productivity and public works projects, schoolbook prose descriptions continued to mimic those of earlier books. Whatever explains the lagging behind of school geographies—lazy authors, information unavailable to authors on the eastern seaboard, a warped provincialism on the part of authors—many schoolchildren used books that were outdated or plainly inaccurate on the day they appeared; if a schoolbook remained in use for a decade, by the end of its life it offered badly skewed visions of Indiana and other states. The rapid pace of settlement, of agricultural and industrial development, slowed to a near halt in the schoolroom.

Of almost equal importance to the image of Indiana were the shifting notions of identifying a territory or state as part of a group. Certainly westward expansion made the designation of Indiana difficult. In the beginning it lay clearly in the West, then in the Northwest, then elsewhere, then in the Mississippi Basin. But what explains the need to label, particularly the need to label maps? Colton of *Colton's Common School Geography* circumvented the problem neatly enough by numbering the map illustrating Indiana and neighboring states. Schoolroom geographies and atlases reflect perhaps the continuing and evolving importance of American regional identity, a subject still largely unexplored, at least as it affects the general public.[40] After all, today's schoolchildren learn that the Mississippi River is the armature of the "Midwest," not the western boundary of that region, but few texts, if any, explain the shifting position of "mid-America" or the need to designate such a region at all.

Color is also important. Schoolchildren read maps; they always have. They may look at them, observe them, touch them; but in the end, when teacher or homework presses, the children *read* visual documents. Consequently the significance of color deserves at least passing attention; Indiana is usually depicted in red or green, less often in yellow. Its coloration may depend on the color used to enliven Pennsylvania; if that state is illustrated in red on a national map—and its large area makes that color attractive to illustrators—Ohio must be green, yellow, or some other color. Indiana consequently can be red, and often is, unless illustrated in a map of its "region," in which case it frequently wears green or yellow in order that the larger flanking states of Ohio and Illinois may appear in red. Map coloration remains a largely unstudied issue, but it may be crucial in comprehending how the public, and particularly children, identify a state, region, or country.[41]

Finally, nineteenth-century schoolroom geographies and atlases make clear the stunning importance of a ground-based transportation network, particularly the railroad system.[42] A large, populous state of diversified agriculture and industry received special attention in late-nineteenth-century schoolbooks only if it lay on many routes to other places. Indiana sprawls across two pages of the 1924 *New Reference Atlas* because it was not only important as a place but as a route. Arkansas, confined to a single page, existed less as a route and more as a place and so received proportionately less attention, along with South Dakota, Vermont, and other less-traveled states.

Who knows what a schoolchild half-consciously assimilates when poring over a geography book on a warm day in September or a frigid evening in February? Does it matter that his state is colored in such a way that it fairly leaps from the wall map hanging next to the American flag? Is it important that his state sprawls over two pages while others huddle together on one? In the study of American geographic thinking, such questions are important, for in them lie suggestions about the public perception of important states and insignificant ones, about clearly defined regions and amorphous ones. The appearance of a state in school books may actually reflect national thinking about the value of that state to the union. In the schoolbooks of the twentieth century, some states that once sprawled across two pages now cringe on one. In most instances, however, Indiana still occupies two pages, still announces its importance to schoolchildren in Rhode Island and Hawaii, in Alabama and Idaho.

Notes

  * English Lake began to be drained in 1884 and appears to have disappeared by 1892. See Indiana Academy of Science, *Natural Features of Indiana* (Indianapolis, 1966), p. xv, and *LaPorte County Atlas* (1892).

  1. *The New Reference Atlas of the World* (New York: C. S. Hammond & Co., 1924), pp. 60–61.

  2. *Ibid.,* pp. 44, 45.

  3. Jedidiah Morse, *The American Geography* (Elizabeth Town, N.J.: Shepard Kollock, 1789), pp. 457–66.

  4. Jedidiah Morse, *Geography Made Easy* (10th ed. Boston: Thomas & Andrews, 1806), pp. 208–11.

  5. H. G. Spafford, *General Geography . . . Digested on a New Plan, and Designed for the Use of Schools* (Hudson, N.Y.: Crosswell & Frary, 1809), pp. 293–96.

  6. Elijah Parish, *A New System of Modern Geography* (Newburyport, Mass.: Thomas & Whipple, 1810), pp. 127–28; Rodolphus Dickinson, *Elements of Geography* (Boston: Bradford & Read, 1813), p. 198.

  7. Herman Mann, *The Material Creation* (Dedham, Mass.: H. & W. H. Mann, 1818), pp. 160–62.

  8. Nathan Hale, *An Epitome of Universal Geography* (Boston: Hale, 1830), pp. 91–93.

  9. Daniel Adams, *Geography; or, A Description of the World* (13th ed. Boston: Lincoln & Edmands, 1831), pp. 176–77.

  10. John J. Clute, *The School Geography* (New York: S. Wood & Sons, 1833), pp. 150–54.

11. T. G. Bradford, *An Abridgement of Universal Geography, Modern and Ancient; chiefly compiled from the* Abrége de Géographie *of Adrian Balbi* (New York: F. Hunt & Co., 1835), pp. 126–28.

12. Edwin Williams, *A Comprehensive System of Modern Geography and History* (New York: Bliss & Wadsworth, 1835), pp. 152–54.

13. Roswell C. Smith, *Geography on the Productive System* (Philadelphia: W. Marshall, 1837), pp. 148–49.

14. S. Augustus Mitchell, *Geographical Reader* (Philadelphia: Thomas, Cowperthwaite & Co., 1840), pp. 156–58.

15. S. S. Cornell, *High School Geography* (New York: D. Appleton & Co., 1860), pp. 114–16; J. Olney, *A Practical System of Modern Geography* (39th ed. New York: Robinson, Pratt, 1843), pp. 138–40.

16. J. H. Colton, *American School Geography* (New York: Ivison, Phinney & Co., 1860), pp. 280–82.

17. S. Augustus Mitchell, *A System of Modern Geography* (Philadelphia: E. H. Butler & Co., 1860), pp. 165–66.

18. For a color map placing Indiana among "the western states" see Roswell C. Smith, *Introductory Geography Designed for Children* (23rd ed. Philadelphia: Lippincott, Grambo & Co., 1854), p. 86.

19. H. S. Tanner, *Traveller's Pocket Map of Indiana* (Philadelphia: Tanner, 1831).

20. David H. Burr, *Indiana* (New York: Illman & Pilbrow, 1833).

21. S. Augustus Mitchell, *Tourist's Pocket Map of the State of Indiana Exhibiting its Internal Improvements, Roads, Distances, Etc.* (Philadelphia: S. A. Mitchell, 1835).

22. S. Augustus Mitchell, *A New Map of Indiana* (Philadelphia: Burroughs, 1846). For a superb analysis of the upper states of the Mississippi Basin as they appeared to early observers see John A. Jakle, *Images of the Ohio Valley: A Historical Geography of Travel, 1740 to 1860* (New York: Oxford University Press, 1977); for an examination of the "grid country" landscape before 1845 see John R. Stilgoe, *Common Landscape of America, 1580 to 1845* (New Haven, Conn.: Yale University Press, 1982), pp. 85–134.

23. *Modern Atlas Adapted to Morse's School Geography* (Boston: Richardson & Lord, 1828). Pagination is absent or erratic in many school atlases and geography texts; maps are often unpaged or paged differently from text pages.

24. J. L. Blake, *American Universal Geography* (Boston: Russell Odiorne & Co., 1833).

25. Barnum Field, *Atlas Designed to Accompany the American School Geography* (Boston: Hendee, 1837).

26. Sidney E. Morse, *A System of Geography* (New York: Harper & Brothers, 1844).

27. Roswell C. Smith, "Map of the Western States," in *A Concise and Practical System of Geography* (New York: Paine & Burgess, 1846).

28. Smith, *Introductory Geography Designed for Children.*

29. S. S. Cornell, *Companion Atlas* (New York: D. Appleton & Co., 1862); compare James Monteith, *Youth's Manual of Geography* (3rd ed. New York: A. S. Barnes & Co., 1854), pp. 82–85.

30. J. H. Colton, "Ohio, Indiana, Kentucky, and Tennessee," in *American School Quarto Geography* (New York: Ivison, 1865).

31. Theodore Sedgwick Fay, "Outline," in *Atlas* (New York: Putnam, 1867).

32. Francis McNally, "Ohio, Indiana, Kentucky, and Tennessee," in *An Improved System of Geography* (New York: A. S. Barnes & Co., 1868).

33. S. Augustus Mitchell, *Mitchell's Ancient Atlas* (Philadelphia: E. H. Butler & Co., 1868); "No. 13" in *ibid.* (Philadelphia: E. H. Butler & Co., 1869).

34. S. Augustus Mitchell, *Modern Atlas* (Philadelphia: E. H. Butler & Co., 1870).

35. Mary Lucy Hall, "Northern Central States," in *Our World No. II* (Boston: Ginn Brothers, 1872).

36. James Monteith, *Comprehensive Geography* (New York: A. S. Barnes & Co., 1873).

37. *Colton's Common School Geography* (New York: Sheldon, 1880).

38. Richard Elwood Dodge, *Advanced Geography* (Chicago: Rand, McNally & Co., 1904), p. 153.

39. For an excellent study of history textbooks see, for example, Frances Fitzgerald, *America Revised: History Schoolbooks in the Twentieth Century* (Boston: Little, Brown, 1974), esp. p. 18.

40. On regions see Wilbur Zelinsky, *The Cultural Geography of the United States* (Englewood Cliffs, N.J.: Prentice-Hall, 1973).

41. See, for example, W. H. Nault, "Children's Map Reading Abilities," Geographic Society of Chicago, *Newsletter*, III (January, 1967); Rudolf Arnheim, *Art and Visual Perception: A Psychology of the Creative Eye* (Berkeley: University of California Press, 1969), pp. 322–59; on maps as perceived by children in fiction see Mark Twain, *Tom Sawyer Abroad, Tom Sawyer, Detective, and Other Stories* (New York: Harper & Brothers, 1878; reprinted New York: Harper, 1924), p. 23. (I am indebted to William Harris and Willard Heiss for the information concerning Mark Twain.) On maps as artifacts see Thomas J. Schlereth, *Artifacts and the American Past* (Nashville: American Association for State and Local History, 1980), pp. 66–90.

42. On the turn-of-the-century railroad network see John R. Stilgoe, *Metropolitan Corridor: Railroads and the American Scene* (New Haven, Conn.: Yale University Press, 1983).

NARRAGANSETT BAY

A Particular Landscape

Cuttunnummutta. "Let us launch." The phrase is Narragansett, at least Narragansett as Roger Williams recorded it in his 1643 phraseology, *A Key into the Language of America*. Williams marveled at the Narragansett skill in marine effort, especially in making long passages in small canoes, and his *Key* records his wonder, perhaps because he wrote his book "in a rude lumpe at Sea," in mid-Atlantic, sailing to England.

> I have in Europe's ships, oft been
> In King of terrours band;
> When all have cri'd, Now, now we sinck,
> Yet God brought us safe to land.

But the Narragansetts had frightened Williams equally, by taking him voyaging in *mishittouwands* and *peewasus,* in great and little canoes.

> Alone 'mongst Indians in Canoes,
> Sometime o're-turn'd, I have been
> Half inch from death, in Ocean deepe,
> Gods wonders I have seene.

In Narragansett canoes Williams saw wonders frequently, apparently at least one in every trip. "It is wonderful to see how they will venture in those canoes, and how (being oft overset as I have my self been with them) they will swim a mile, yea two or more safe to land." In his many passages, some in sailing canoes headed for a spot ten or twenty miles downwind, he sometimes "questioned safety," and his hosts told him, "Fear not, if we be overset I will carry you safe to Land." No wonder, then, that Williams' phraseology emphasizes phrases like *Nquawn pshawmen* and *Wussaume pechepausha.* "We overset" and "The sea comes in too fast upon us" he must have heard over and over, along with the shouted *Maumaneeteantaff.* "Be of good courage." One wonders who was teaching whom, how like

"Narragansett Bay: A Particular Landscape" appeared in *What a Difference a Bay Makes* (Providence: Rhode Island Historical Society, 1993), 9–13.

the Atlantic the Narragansetts' own bay seemed to an Englishman afloat in a canoe.

About Narragansett Bay, Williams said little, for soon he took it for granted, beginning the great local tradition of unthinkingly accepting one of the spectacular natural wonders of North America. Indeed even now Rhode Islanders find it perfectly ordinary that they own a bay so vast that it includes magnificences like Greenwich Bay and Mount Hope Bay, or a Providence River larger than bays in states less richly endowed. Perhaps turn-of-the-millennium Rhode Islanders need a key into their own odd local language to discover the wonder that overwhelms tourists.

American bays retain tribal designations. Penobscot Bay, Massachusetts Bay, Delaware Bay, Chesapeake Bay, Apalachee Bay all echo in their names an earlier period, a time when Europeans moved timidly, sounding and feeling their way inshore. To be sure, some bays acquired European names. Cape Cod Bay and Raleigh Bay announce in their names changes in control even as their English-language names spark questions about earlier nomenclature. As bays often open into the land, giving access from ocean into ports and tiny harbors, so the naming of bays remains what Williams might call a key into early Colonial culture. Narragansett Bay was the private sea of the Narragansetts, so intimately a part of tribal life that Williams' educators apparently had no specific name for it, no more than they had a precise name for themselves as a particular tribe or nation. Indeed for the Narragansett people, the Bay might have been designated as simply as the classical Romans called the Mediterranean. *Mare nostrum.* "Our sea." But even then, Williams faced a problem in designation, the tricky use of the English term *bay*.

Bay resists definition. Like so many brief, old words, like the word *if,* *bay* poses immediate challenges. Used in a phrase like "what a difference a bay makes," the word seems utterly straightforward. But under scrutiny it becomes vague, then slippery, defying immediate definition, let alone translation into Narragansett. Scrutiny makes it slippery, but comparison makes it positively eel-like. Implicit in any definition of *bay* lurk definitions of two other terms, *gulf* and *sound.* Tension over definition perhaps suffuses the official self-image of the whole state of Rhode Island and Providence Plantations. What else explains the self-given nickname "Ocean State" but nerve-fraying debate about the definitions of other, perhaps more applicable, terms?

Cartographical analysis offers one potential approach to accuracy. Maps and charts deserve observation, close reading, a finger moved carefully along the blue. Does Rhode Island actually front the ocean? Much of its southeastern shore fronts Block Island Sound, or what newer charts and small-boating magazines call Rhode Island Sound. Where

Block Island Sound begins seems clear enough, at least on some charts. A line running southeast from the midpoint between East Point and Napatree Point to a spot roughly one-third of the distance between Montauk Point and Block Island divides Long Island Sound from Block Island Sound, and incidentally perhaps, separates Rhode Island from New York. But where, exactly, lies the eastern end of Block Island Sound? What separates it from Buzzard's Bay or Vineyard Sound? Does Block Island Sound end at Hen & Chicken shoal, just southeast of Gooseberry Neck and Old & Young Rock, as Eldridge's turn-of-the-century charts suggest, or does it end farther east, at the old Vineyard Sound lightship mooring? Put little faith in library atlases and schoolroom maps, for such are the work of landsmen unconcerned with maritime issues like the boundaries of sounds—or the peace of mind of Rhode Islanders. What else explains the bizarre parabola disgracing the bottom of Plate 150 in the 1949 *Encyclopaedia Britannica World Atlas?* Such an incredible curve, and certainly not the best sea-route between Someplace South and Little Compton. Does it delineate the eastern border— at sea—of Rhode Island and Massachusetts? And if so, why does it curve to the southwest, so wickedly slicing searoom from Rhode Island? Suppose oil or gold lurks beneath the waves near that curving end of Block Island Sound? Then what about cartographical vagueness?

Does etymology offer aid? What about legal definitions? When is a sound a bay, or a gulf a sound? Lexicographers have long struggled with the terms, and abandoned all scholarly effort in the face of gnawing doubts. While a bay is a "road for Ships," according to John Kersey's *New English Dictionary* of 1702, a gulf is "a part of Sea running between two lands, which embrace and almost encompass it" and a sound "any great inlet of Sea, between two headlands, as Plymouth Sound, etc." His definition of *strait,* spelled "straight" in his time, a "narrow arm of the Sea, shut up on both sides by the land; as The Straights of Gibraltar," proves scarcely useful in discriminating among the other three terms. Of course, a road for ships connotes a narrowness, a smallness in scale that makes some sense so long as the Bay of Biscay is overlooked, and perhaps the "two lands" Kersey mentions in his definition of *gulf* are separate nations, although not necessarily. Is a sound indeed a "great inlet" so great as to be bigger than a gulf? Kersey's definitions not only suggest vagueness, they shout it, and their shout is the shout of discovery and colonization, of naming the natural features of coastal New England.

Subsequent generations of Americans learned to live with imprecision, and indeed to use imprecisely named coastal features as prototypes for designating other places. American usage of terms like *bay, sound,* and other topographical terms in part makes American English so decidedly

American. In his first great dictionary, in fact, Noah Webster struggled at length with *bay,* creating what Britons would dismiss as an utterly unworthy, indeed scarcely intelligible definition. A bay, Webster opined in his 1824 *American Dictionary of the English Language,* is "an arm of the sea, extending into the land, not of any definite form, but smaller than a gulf, and larger than a creek. The name, however, is not used with much precision, and is often applied to large tracts of water, around which the land forms a curve, as Hudson's Bay." Moreover, he continued, European precedent confused usage even more: "Nor is the name restricted to tracts of water with a narrow entrance, but used for any recess or inlet between capes or head lands, as the Bay of Biscay." Webster devoted nearly as much attention to defining *sound,* a term that also troubled him: "A narrow passage of water, or a strait between the main land and an isle; or a strait connecting two seas, or connecting a sea or lake with the ocean; as, the *sound* which connects the Baltic with the ocean, between Denmark and Sweden; the *sound* that separates Long Island from the main land of New York and Connecticut." Perhaps his intense concern for Americanizing the English language prompted Webster to lavish attention on terms so commonly used in an era of sea travel, and especially coastwise commerce, but buried within his definitions are terms that merit closer attention, terms that still infuriate Englishmen struggling to translate Rhode Island, never mind Narragansett, into old-world English.

Webster says that a bay is smaller than a gulf and larger than a creek. Apparently, a sound is smaller than a gulf too, but the definition verges on the ridiculous when other bodies of water, say harbors and rivers, enter the analysis, since most bodies of water are larger than creeks. In its definition of *bay,* Webster's *American Dictionary of the English Language* slides willy-nilly into provincial American English, the language of coastal Rhode Island. Almost everywhere in New England people speak of *brooks* when they refer to the small, flowing watercourses generically known as *streams,* except in the American south, where *creek* and *branch* rule watercourse terminology. Long before the Civil War, Americans debated proper versus regional usage, and in 1838, for example, James Fenimore Cooper, in his *American Democrat,* argued determinedly that "*creek,* a word that signifies an *inlet* of the sea, or of a lake, is misapplied to running streams, and frequently to the *outlets* of lakes." Along the coast of Rhode Island the seventeenth-century definition of creek—what Kersey gave as "a little bay"—endures. In a state where *brook,* and in the television era, *stream,* designate small flowing watercourses, Rhode Islanders use *creek* to designate the inlets of the sea that twist through salt marshes. This usage appears in the second sentence of John Casey's 1989 novel, *Spartina,* immediately assuring Rhode Island readers that Casey at least knows the local lingo and that the book has possibilities. Of course, Casey sets *Spartina* on the south coast of Rhode Island, west of Narragansett Bay, and so avoids the problems of definition and designation that beset Webster and subsequent experts. In Rhode Island, after all, *bay* is a special term indeed, maybe, just maybe, a larger creek, a place felt, if not exactly understood, by local alone.

Long ago, in the dimly remembered 1950s, grade-school geography lessons involved defining arcane terms like *peninsula* and *isthmus*— and *bay, sound,* and others of special use to Rhode Islanders riding the Jamestown ferry perhaps, or dodging warships near Newport. Learning geography, and geographical terms in particular, meant much to Americans after independence, not because knowing national topography meant strengthening their right to it, but because westward exploration kept revealing new features, most of which Easterners knew only in print description. By 1831, therefore, when William Channing Woodbridge produced his *System of Universal Geography,* parents, teachers, and schoolchildren knew the importance of defining topographical terms—and defining them systematically, not willy-nilly, as in dictionaries.

While lexicographers worried about terms, Woodbridge defined them, worrying less about etymological roots and European usage than about American patterns of use. "A narrow passage of water into a sea, or between two portions of land, is called a *strait,*" he explained to children roughly twelve years old. "A wider passage is called a *channel.* A *sound* is a channel which may be sounded. When a part of the ocean runs up into the land, with a broad opening, it is called a *gulf* or *bay.*" Finally, he explained two types of anchorages, both critically important in an age of shoal-draft sailing vessels: "A *harbour* is a small bay, where ships may anchor. A *road* is a place of anchorage on an open coast." Nothing of perfection graces his definitions, especially that of *sea:* "When a considerable branch of the ocean is almost surrounded by land, it is called a *sea.* A sea, or portion of the ocean, which contains numerous islands, is called an *archipelago.*" What does "considerable" mean in such a definition? Why does Woodbridge not distinguish more precisely between *bay* and *gulf*? Despite his spelling *harbour* in the British fashion Webster worked so hard to eliminate, his textbook demonstrates a willingness to accept the roughness of existing American speech, and to worry very little about how his definitions might apply to Rhode Island geography.

In 1831, as Woodbridge's textbook appeared in a fourth edition, Joseph Worcester published his *Elements of Geography,* a textbook focused on particulars of places rather than on a more general system. In describing Rhode Island, Worcester makes clear the difference a bay makes. "The most distinguishing natural feature is *Narragansett Bay,* which is a beautiful expanse of water, about 30 miles in length, intersecting the state from north to south. Pawtucket River flows into the north end of this bay." Worcester uses few sophisticated terms, but he makes clear that islands stud the bay, "of which the largest is *Rhode Island,* a beautiful and fertile island, from which the state derives its name." Worcester wrote in the tradition begun in 1789 by Jedidiah Morse in *The American Geography, or a View of the Present Situation of the United States of America.* Children of each state and territory ought to know their geographical situation in order to grow up knowing their place in the world and in the new nation, and in order to prosper. Worcester, Woodbridge, and their successors intended to instill pride too, however, by emphasizing excellences peculiar to particular places. For many late-eighteenth- and early-nineteenth-century geographers, Narragansett Bay constituted the chief excellence of Rhode Island, something remarkably special.

Morse began the decades-long devotion to the Bay by remarking not only that it "makes up from south to north, between the main land on the east and west," but that it "embosoms many fertile islands, the principal of which are Rhode-Island, Canonnicut, Prudence, Patience, Hope, Dyer's and Hog Island." Expressions like "makes up" and "embosoms," however archaic today, imply that the Bay is a sort of psychological organism, somehow developing from the south, seaward end, and nurturing many significant islands, some named after traditional religious virtues. Nothing accidental informs the description. Morse continues by remarking, for example, that the island called Rhode-Island is "exceedingly pleasant and healthful," and that "travellers, with propriety, call it the *Eden* of America." And in this Eden set within this magnificent bay has evolved a race of Eves. The Island "is celebrated for its fine women."

Nineteenth-century geographers assumed that Narragansett Bay shaped Rhode Island character. In an age that agreed with Woodbridge that "the people of colder climates are most distinguished for active and persevering industry, and strong powers of reason and judgment," the remarkable Narragansett Bay climate had to have special effect. Worcester perhaps thought so, for his geography begins its description of Rhode Island with a provocative topic sentence indeed: "Rhode Island is the smallest state in the Union, in extent of territory, but the first, in proportion to its population, with regard to manufactures." Of course, Worcester may have merely echoed Morse's earlier remarks, and those remarks are especially telling. "The summers are delightful, especially on Rhode Island, where the extreme heats, which prevail in other parts of America, are allayed by cool and refreshing breezes from the sea." And the winters, "the air being softened by a sea vapour, which also enriches the soil," are milder, helping to make the region "as healthful a country as any part of

North America." Into the twentieth century, reference book writers asserted the vague but continuing conviction that Narragansett Bay peculiarly enlivened all of Rhode Island. "The climate is milder and more agreeable than in the other New England states," asserted *Lippincott's Complete Pronouncing Gazetteer or Geographical Dictionary* in 1916, and "the island of Aquidneck is for the most part very fertile and has been called 'the Eden of America.'" For all their doubts about definition, geographers knew that Narragansett Bay was special, that it made a difference.

And for as long as people routinely traveled the Bay they understood its unique magnificence, its difference. Only in the late railroad era, then the automobile age, when the New York City boats no longer ran, when the excursion boats no longer steamed forth on picnic expeditions, when the ferries stopped, when travelers drove along its perimeters only, only then did Narragansett Bay slide into an odd obscurity indeed.

The old view-from-the-water has almost vanished now, and can be recovered only in dusty guidebooks like Joseph Banvard's *Guide to Providence River and Narragansett Bay* of 1858, a pocket-size book intended for the thousands of summer passengers aboard the little steamers running back and forth between Providence and Newport. "Narragansett Bay is one of the most magnificent and variegated sheets of water on the American coast," the book begins. "It is gemmed with numerous islands of various sizes and singular forms," and "its shores are indented with many picturesque coves, inlets, and small bays, which with their accompanying peninsulas and cozy villages present many delightful scenes to the eye of the traveler." Filled with precisely used geographic terms and buoyed by a wholly on-the-water point of view, Banvard's book emphasizes the Bay that makes the scenery accessible, remarking always on the depth of water under the steamer keel, the importance of spar buoys and other navigational aids, and the relation of one part of the Bay to another. It deals with the 1772 burning of the revenue schooner *Gaspee* not only as a historic incident, but one depending on close knowledge of particular sandbars, and focuses especially on places where the Bay changes character or identity, say the wharf off Nayatt Point where summer visitors catch sharks and where the Providence River "suddenly enlarges and becomes the bay," or where its beauty masks danger, as at Halfway Rocks, where a "low dark ledge" forms "a point of great danger to unskillful navigators, especially at night." Banvard's book, a sort of complete guide to the spine of Rhode Island, proved the precursor to many others, also now gathering dust in libraries across the state.

In tone and content, the excursion guides to Narragansett Bay evoke a remarkable era, a time of safe, convenient, ten- to fifteen-knot passage by water, a time when excursionists not only delighted in the exquisite scenery around them, but knew enough local geography—and geographical terminology—to see how the scenery worked for fishermen, clammers, shipmasters, and others whose work kept them in it. By 1879, when Frederic Denison published *Narragansett Sea and Shore,* excursion boats ran regularly not only to Block Island and Martha's Vineyard—carrying people through the Bay—but all about the Bay as well, often on circular tours from Providence to Newport by Westward Passage, then north again by the East Passage. "Excursions on the Bay are a part of the life of Rhode Island," Denison asserted. "Perhaps no sheet of water on our New England coast is more alive, through the summer season, with excursionists and pleasure parties." In his final analysis, Narragansett "is a grand thoroughfare of the people." Denison's guidebook speaks eloquently, but always in the Rhode Island idiom, remarking on such vagaries as parts of the Bay that have more than one name, such as Seaconnet Bay, "sometimes styled the East Passage." His book, and others like it, smack of the excursion steamer winding in and around a thousand details of intriguing topography—all known by intriguing names.

"To sail among the islands and explore the arms and tributaries of Narragansett is as fascinating a pastime as any inshore sailor can desire," mused Edgar Mayhew Bacon in his 1904 tome, *Narragansett Bay: Its Historic and Romantic Associations and Picturesque Setting.* The massive volume, profusely illustrated and impeccably researched, marks a departure from the smaller, pocket or handbag-sized guidebooks, and a change in viewpoint, too: "I recall with pleasure many such little voyages, made in all sorts of weather and under all conditions of light and darkness, but with never an hour to regret. The long stretches of open water give ample sea-room for small sailboats, and the winding channels that must be picked out by chart and buoy, by range and beacon, call for the exercise of just those faculties that contribute to the keenest physical enjoyment." No longer is the reader automatically assumed to be a steamboat passenger. In Bacon's book the reader may just as well be a recreational boater, directing his course at will, not simply passing significant historical sites but exploring the bays and creeks that lead to others, and lead to surprises too.

Not all surprises pleased Bacon. He found severe ecological troubles lurking among the history and beauty. On Prudence Island, for example, the wind had scoured some of the thin soil from the rocky base, and farmhands had neglected to cover the spot with a seaweed. "The order was for some reason neglected and the next storm tore out several acres of soil, cutting clean to the bed, and depositing a new bar nearby in the bay." While Bacon admitted that Narragansett gales blow severely indeed, he understood that the failure of farming on the islands really explained the erosion. "For outlook and climate," he determined, Prudence Island "is certainly wonderfully favored, and the application of a little scientific forestry would make it an Eden." His *Narragansett Bay* is perhaps the first book to warn of the fragility of beauty, beauty made fragile by its proximity to marine forces, of course, but also made delicate by human use, misuse, and overuse.

On the whole, however, his massive book is the *tour de force* of Narragansett Bay writing, the first written by a small boatman. "The afternoon light, the real, abundant, vivid, prismatic light that floods sea and land alike in a summer afternoon on Narragansett Bay, is quite sufficient and satisfying for ordinary mortals." That light suffuses his book as it suffuses the Bay, changing everything with its silent luminosity.

And the light endures. As so many other characteristics of Narragansett Bay, the light peculiar to it glows with hard-to-designate character. Rhode Islanders take the light for granted, just as they take for granted what it illuminates. To be sure, it is only moisture that alters the sunlight, but that moisture alters the light across most of Rhode Island and much of Massachusetts. And sometimes, perhaps, the fall of light alone upon a place already special is enough to make that special place magical, as Thoreau often remarked of the light falling on his Walden Pond.

Knowing Narragansett Bay means seeing not only the light Bacon remarked on so long ago, but seeing through that light, to the countless details that together comprise one of the great scenic wonders of North America. Seeing accurately means putting names to details, not just proper names, but general terms as well. Narragansett Bay is more than what the Narragansetts called *wussaum patamoonck,* a prospect; it is an arm of the sea as complex as any ocean. Filled with straits and peninsulas, bays and an archipelago of islands, sounds and estuaries, it is a miniature ocean. Narragansett Bay is the region's *mare nostrum,* its private ocean— a special, indeed, spectacular bay.

DEEP COLD

Winter as Landscape

New England hatched in winter. Sleet, deep cold, northeast gales, and lodging snow withered it, in the formative years. These were the years of the starving at Plymouth, the great blizzards at Boston. Until early in the twentieth century, the grim certainty of winter torment warped both individual character and regional culture. Cast-iron stoves, tar-papered walls, coal-burning furnaces, and eventually down vests and studded snow tires gradually insulated most New Englanders from the older experience of winter. And now an age of home computers, videotext units, and other electronic marvels confronts blue shadows and white silence, and raw winter threatens to congeal the voluptuous warmth of contemporary metropolitan civilization. Old Man Winter now stalks ever more fragile defenses.

What of Cold Friday? The deep cold of Pittsburgh, New Hampshire? Such events, memorialized cryptically in the 1983 *Old Farmer's Almanac,* recall especially grievous visitations of winter. In 1861, the *Almanac* records, February 7 witnessed a temperature drop from forty degrees to minus thirty-two at Hanover, New Hampshire. Of what significance are such entries, set in small type next to this year's monthly weather forecast? And why have they appeared in the *Almanac* for nearly two centuries?

The *Old Farmer's Almanac* stands directly in the mainstream of a little-remarked literary genre, the exegesis of implacable winter. The genre, old as New England settlement, began with William Bradford's *Of Plymouth Plantation,* a history of colonization in a land of winters "sharp and violent." Colonial New Englanders recorded in their diaries the lashings of winters unlike any known in England. "So extremely cold was the weather, that in a warm room, on a great fire, the juices forced out at the end of short billets of wood, by the heat of the flame, on which they were laid, yet froze into ice, at their coming out," marveled Puritan clergyman Cotton Mather in February 1697. Twenty years later he recorded a fall of snow so staggering that it could be only "a rebuke from Heaven upon us"; generations of New Englanders heard tales of the Great Snow of March 7, 1717, when even Puritans could not attend Sabbath-day ser-

"Deep Cold: Winter as Landscape" appeared in *Orion* 3 (Winter 1984), 5–11.

vices. Seventeenth- and eighteenth-century colonists feared the "depth" of winter as a time of frostbite, starvation, spoiled food, and stillborn infants, and learned to accept it as a divinely ordained test of religious faith and worldly endurance. "What can't be cured must be endured," counseled the *Almanac* in a December 1874 echo of past thinking, "so let us make up our minds that it's all for the best." But by the middle of the nineteenth century, many New Englanders no longer feared winter. Indeed, urbanization and industrialization had begun to shield them from its rigors, and had made it a usually comfortable, *indoor* experience.

Thoreau bemoaned the change in attitude, noting in his journals that more and more of his townsmen spent most winter days indoors, snuggled against cast-iron stoves. While others drowsed secure from frostbite, he walked or skated; scrutinizing the "indigo-blue" shadows and "pink light on the snow," he was fascinated by the changes in lighting tone and quality. "A peculiar soft light was diffused around, very unlike the ordinary darkness of the forest, as if you were inside a drift or snow house," he noted on January 19, 1855, the same day he wondered at "various fawn-colored and cinnamon tints" made by dead oak leaves half-covered with snow. Along with many New Englanders of his time, Thoreau continued to see winter as a season when religious truths appeared peculiarly clearly. "My shadow is very blue," he wrote after a walk across frozen Walden Pond. "It suggests that there may be something divine, something celestial, in me." After a heavy snowfall, he remarked that the Concord landscape was "still as at creation," and that the thick, heavy lodging snow created a new construct, one of essentially pure and parabolic form, "a loose-woven downy screen, into which, however, stooping and winding, you ceaselessly advance." But for all that Thoreau castigated his neighbors' unwillingness to enjoy such magnificent aesthetic experiences, he too lived largely oblivious of the rigors of rampant winter. "The Great Snow! How cheerful it is to hear of!" he wrote of the 1717 blizzards that tormented Mather. Not till many years later did the Concord naturalist encounter truly dangerous winter.

Thoreau now and then experienced deep cold, days when, as he wrote, "frostwork keeps its place on the window within three feet of the stove *all day* in my chamber," days, in other words, when even the naturalist stayed home. One evening, the temperature fell so low that his thermometer registered nothing the following morning. His journal entry deserves quotation at length:

> The coldest night for a long, long time was last. Sheets froze stiff about the faces. . . . People dreaded to go to bed. The ground cracked in the night as if a powder-mill had blown up, and the timbers of the

house also. My pail of water was frozen in the morning so that I could not break it. Must leave many buttons unbuttoned, owing to numb fingers. Iron was like fire in the hands. . . . The cold has stopped the clock. . . . Bread, meat, milk, cheese, etc., etc., all frozen. See the inside of your cellar door all covered and sparkling with frost like Golconda. Pity the poor who have not a large wood-pile. The latches are white with frost, and every nail-head in entries, etc., has a white-cap.

Thoreau had heard stories of Cold Friday in 1810, when water froze in pails set on mantelpieces above roaring fires, but the old people told him that even that frigid day had been no colder than the one he experienced. Deep cold had invaded Thoreau's house, freezing his ink, killing his houseplants, making him remember that only a "sturdy innocence, a Puritan toughness" can survive its depredations, making him appreciate a secure house.

Implicit in the New England literature of unfriendly winter is the overwhelming importance of the snug nest, the shelter against snow, wind, and above all, deep cold. Even Thoreau wrote lovingly of the "quiet and serene life" in the chimney corner during the blizzard, the life glorified in 1866 by John Greenleaf Whittier. His long poem "Snow-Bound: A Winter Idyl" juxtaposes a roaring blizzard against a tight farmhouse filled with self-reliant people. A "hard, dull bitterness of cold" presages a fierce storm; the blizzard roars all night, through the next day, and into the succeeding night, making everything "a universe of sky and snow." Within, all is cheerful; the family feasts, tells stories, reads its *Almanac,* and delights in its massive, open-throated chimney, blazing fire, and well-clapboarded walls. "Snow-Bound" remains the quintessential paean to the well-stocked nest prescribed in so many long-ago *Almanac* pages.

"Have you banked up your house, so as to have your cellar safe against frost?" asked the *Almanac* on its November 1839 page. "Have you gone round about your buildings, and seen to the clapboards, the shingles, the knot-holes, the glass, the hinges, the brick work?" Such is the rural wisdom of late autumn, presented year after year, generation after generation, by the *Almanac.* November is always the month of invasion. "Old father Frost begins to run his nose through the cracks," begins a November 1835 entry. "Old cross-grained Winter is on the road, and you may meet him before you are aware of his approach." Failure to secure house and outbuildings against snow and deep cold means no "Snow-Bound" idyl of relaxed cheer, but only destitution and disaster.

Despite Whittier's poetic vision of winter experienced largely from within doors, rural New Englanders continued to fear the invasive character of cold and the mind-deadening effect of prolonged snowstorms. Whittier's farm family is, after all, well-to-do; it can afford to burn log after log in a massive fireplace capped by a damperless chimney. Not all nineteenth- and early-twentieth-century families had wood to spare, and in their attempt to conserve hardwood, and later coal, they closed off rooms of their houses, lived largely in kitchens, and learned to balance the economics of roaring or flickering fires against the psychological effects of deep cold and winter isolation. Robert Frost, perhaps the preeminent dissector of winter and of the need for nests, returned again and again in his poetry to the terrors of winter. In "Storm Fear," "An Old Man's Winter Night," "The Onset," "Desert Places," and other poems, he uses winter as a window on the universe within and beyond the human heart. In particular, he knows the invasive character of cold. In "Storm Fear," for example, he notes "How the cold creeps as the fire dies at length"; in "An Old Man's Winter Night" he remarks the frostwork "that gathers on the pane in empty rooms," and in "There Are Roughly Zones" begins his argument by stating, "We sit indoors and talk of the cold outside./And every gust that gathers strength and heaves/Is a threat to the house." But the storm and cold threaten more than the fabric of the structure; they assault the fabric of the mind.

In "Storm Fear," a poem of 1913, Frost calls the wind-driven snow a "beast" that "whispers with a sort of stifled bark" as it "works against us in the dark." The speaker fears to sleep, and doubts "Whether 'tis in us to arise with day / And save ourselves unaided." Other writers agreed with Frost's perception; in *Northern Farm: A Chronicle of Maine,* Henry Beston explains the onset of a winter gale in terms of a dying coal fire, an old hooked rug shoved against the door, and—importantly—a lantern kept burning all night "for the quiet and reassuring light it keeps for us through the dark." At the beginning of the twentieth century, even magazine writers had begun commenting on the devastating effects of winter isolation on New England farm families. By 1911, when Edith Wharton published her *Ethan Frome,* the cheerfulness of "Snow-Bound" mocked the emerging reality of cabin fever. Even as farmhouses became more secure against storm and cold—tar paper proved a wonderful ally against wind, for example—farm families seemed more and more frail.

Frost's "Storm Fear" concerns power failure, not the failure of electricity and telephone, but the failure of spiritual resolve that enabled earlier generations to surmount winter difficulties like The Great Snow and Cold Friday. What happened in the years between "Snow-Bound" and "Storm Fear"? In the *Almanac* lies one answer. The thin publication, filled with astronomical tables, riddles, and good advice, charged into the void of rural winter evenings. In January 1840 it advised readers to study agricultural periodicals like the *New England Farmer* and the *Farmer's Monthly Visitor*, not only to learn new farming ideas, but also to keep mentally alert. In November 1858 it catalogued books useful on long winter evenings; a month later, it described the cheerful, mentally active farm family enjoying a raging storm from a secure nest. At the heart of *Almanac* preaching lies a delicate understanding of the real meaning of winter. The season of storms and deep cold is essentially the season of death, a season that raises the profoundest philosophical and religious issues. While a secure nest and stacks of good books provide physical security and mental occupation, only faith in the power of God conquers wintertime desperation. But by the early years of the twentieth century, certainties born in the Puritan era and nurtured by regular Bible reading and church attendance had fractured, and the *Almanac* increasingly emphasized the power of intellect to surmount desperation. "The agricultural and scientific press of today is inestimable value," it counseled in 1906. "Encourage the boys to read it." As Frost surmised in "Storm Fear," many farm families no longer faced blizzards and penetrating cold with a certainty of divine help that warmed as it gave confidence. Instead they put their faith in technology, in electricity, and in the scientific press, and when technology failed they had little to counterbalance the fears born in cold and disorientation. They faced winter savagery with vague memories of long-ago determination and with the modern fright Frost describes in "Storm Fear."

Away from the country, twentieth-century New Englanders grew smug about winter. Exactly as Thoreau had worried, they nestled snugly in ever tighter houses. Or they ventured outdoors either to enjoy hiking, ice fishing, skiing, sledding, or skating, or to journey to places of indoor work. In 1866, a blizzard meant holiday-making for Whittier's farm family; after 1930, all it meant for most urban and suburban residents was a harrowing commute to a warm factory or office, a commute made easier every year by new plows, better pavements, snow tires, and copious applications of rock salt. In houses heated by oil or gas to a steady seventy-two degrees, in heated automobiles cruising over plowed, sanded, and salted highways, in express trains racing through snow squalls, New Englanders of the cities and suburbs learned that winter meant only slight inconvenience. In an outdoor world experienced in miracle fabric clothing, in an indoor world experienced in sleeveless blouses and cotton shirts, they forgot Cold Friday. But always the *Almanac* recited the litany, the litany respected by rural families not yet wholly insulated from the beast.

Almost nowhere does the New England periodical press represented by magazines like *Vermont Life* and *Yankee* mention the continuing dan-

For the contemporary rural poor living on farmsteads long bereft of livestock, wintertime becomes eerily empty and isolating.

gers of winter. Now and then, however, a writer captures something of the ever-lurking terror behind the snow clouds. "I went through my pockets for matches, for anything, for a miracle, and found that for my walk in the wilderness I had brought no matches, no knife, no flashlight, no mirror, no compass, no food, nothing of use—a handful of change, my car keys, a wallet with credit cards," recalls Eric Broudy in a January 1976 *Blair and Ketchum's Country Journal* essay, "Lost on My Own Land." His article meticulously documents the onset of a winter storm and its immediate effect on a man wandering through a newly purchased wood-lot. "I was terrified of moving, fearful of stepping even a foot in the wrong direction, and for the first time I began to understand that if I didn't find my way out before dark, I just might freeze to death." The cold, the wind-driven snow that hastens the dusk, the sudden blurring of vision, transform the woodlot into wilderness. Of course, the tourist-oriented magazines rarely address the beast stalking Christmas-card villages, sniffing the trail of the cross-country skier, shaking the trailers surrounded by woodpiles and tanks of propane gas. Until the 1970s, few magazines appreciated the vision of Broudy, of Frost, of Cotton Mather.

And then the flow of oil stopped. If waiting in gasoline station lines profoundly shook the typical New Englander's faith in the national economy, waiting for fuel oil deliveries—and paying for them later—shattered his trust in the snugness of his modern nest. The rich paid their bills, of course, and built active and passive solar-heating units; the

DEEP COLD

middle class bought wood- and coal-burning stoves, installed attic insulation, and learned of chimney fires; the poor got cold and colder, and sometimes died. Now the New England family knows the sinister lessons of high fuel prices, and now the *Almanac* reads as it did in years gone by. "I find the coldest nights make me uneasy," the editor muses of minus twenty-five degree temperatures. His February 1982 "Farmer's Calendar" essay scrutinizes the effects of infiltrating cold. "I imagine the deepest cold as a great bell that is slowly, silently lowered over our house by night, sealing it off, isolating it, while we sleep." He lies awake, wondering, fearing, imagining water freezing in pipes, "frost ferns" growing on window panes. "In the attic the points of the roofing nails are frozen where they come through the roof." In the 1970s, the grown-up children of the 1940s and 1950s saw for the first time frost thick on the inside of double-glazed windows, heard for the first time the sinister hissing of water squirting from cracked pipes, watched ceilings ruined by water creeping inward from gutter ice jams. They learned the horror of finding the gasoline station closed and the cold penetrating their silent cars.

And despite their observations and their fears, they despise the lessons of the rural past, and instead trust in an electronic future. Half-conscious of their danger, they stand now in a portal, armed with electronic contraptions against a grim, implacable enemy. Of course, beyond the portal lies only the sunlit vista of electronic communications, at least according to the articles published in the computer magazines. Mainframe and personal computers, cable television, the longline videotext marvels will produce a new golden age, an age beyond the industrial revolution. New Englanders, indeed all Americans, will work at home, saving commuting energy and time; they will plant their gardens by computer, insuring increased harvests; they will monitor domestic energy consumption, prepare meals, and lock doors according to computer advice; they will shop by computer, date by computer, correspond by computer, and in general learn the joys of escape keys, text processing, videodisks, and bookless studies. Only winter mars the dream.

Computer manufacturers advertise their products against backgrounds of grids, mazes, silver planes, and dark blue curves, against a stylized backdrop unrelated to the "real world." Now and then a firm portrays its home computer product in a firelit den or study, perhaps one paneled in walnut or lined with books, or displays its office equipment in stark, paperless interiors of white desks and green-shaded lamps. What explains the ubiquitous abstract backgrounds, the half-abstract interiors? Do they connote the future, or mask the lessons of the past?

Electronics prove useless in deep cold. The chill that froze Thoreau's ink and killed his house plants, the cold that stopped his clock, most assuredly slays every electronic gadget from flashlights to computers. But most New Englanders trust their new electronic contraptions, which work well enough in all but the winter snowstorms and deep cold. The "electronic cottage" of the future is fragile against the storm; the electronic condominium is already proving dangerous.

Consider the high-rise condominium building, replete with sundecks, large windows, shower massage nozzles, and electric locks. How secure is it against prolonged cold? So long as the heating unit functions, fairly secure, but without the steady warming, its thin exterior walls admit the cold easily. To be sure, the furnace fails rarely, and perhaps the likelihood of a week-long "deep freeze" following a snowstorm that interrupts electric power—and so stills the furnace—is remote. But consider the consequences, the burst pipes, the necessity for draining toilets, the eventual abandonment of the structure, the inability to lock it as the last resident leaves. And what of the suburban house? Its fireplace or cast-iron stove surely makes it more secure against storm, but electric failure nevertheless causes difficulties. The automatic garage door opener, still as a frozen lake, seals in or out the family automobile; the refrigerator and deep freezer thaw, and slowly the cold creeps in, into the cellar, into the bedrooms distant from the hearth. Only a rare stove, and rarer fireplace, heat well enough to protect all house pipes from bursting; only a rare house, and rarer condominium, store food enough for several weeks. Modern kitchens lack the pantries beloved in centuries past, the pantries filled with flour and other staples useful in snowbound cooking. New England storekeepers remember the panic-buying of milk and bread following the four-day Great Blizzard in 1978 as indeed they should; now any radio forecast of heavy snows sends families scurrying to supermarkets and corner groceries, desperate to buy milk and bread enough to last the storm. Late arrivals from condominiums and houses find the shelves bare, and content themselves with purchasing soft drinks and cakes, and perhaps scurry on to hardware stores for containers of solid fuel.

But what of the condominium or free-standing house twenty years from now? Certainly the lodging snow that fells power lines will also collapse telephone and cable television lines too. Powerless, disconnected, the home computer will prove useless in regulating the furnace, let alone in reaching out to neighbors. What of the passengers in the miniature electric car? Will the commuter stuck in the drifts mourn the past era of large cars with trunks stocked with shovels, sand, chains, food, and sleeping bags? Will his CB radio crackle with life, or sit as silently as the car? Will the woman returning from the disco reach into the storage compartment for the down pants, vest, and parka she will use to survive the night in a stalled car, or set off in high heels, nylon dress, and rabbit-fur

Winter coastal storms periodically and ruthlessly rearrange coastal geomorphology and the landscape that sits atop it.

stole for the nearest habitation or gasoline station? Will the wonderfully intricate electronic world predicted by computer advocates experience periodic devastation by heavy snow and deep cold?

A vague doubt, the vestige of rural wisdom, gnaws at the New England expectation of nirvana through the computer looking glass. It explains the popularity of such books as *Gnomes,* an 1977 *tour de force* by Wil Huygen and Rien Poortvliet. The book explicates the natural history of little people who live in close communion with wild plants and animals, who winter in underground, nestlike houses complete with fireplaces and well-stocked larders. Vibrant, four-color illustrations make clear the exquisite comfort of the gnome home, and point accusingly at the contemporary American "residential unit." An adult fairy tale barbed with traditional common-sense thinking about winter, *Gnomes* reminds contemporary Americans that wet and cold remain unvanquished. Winter may be the enduring objective correlative of death, perhaps as the painter Charles Burchfield determined: "Over the rim of the earth—to the North—lies the land of the unknown—it is windy, the ground is frozen, hard, barren—there is no snow—white wind clouds scud over a vast gray sky." Into the winter whiteness, into the deep cold, into the winter of *Gnomes* and Burchfield, marches unthinkingly the transistorized American, the American fond of believing that he threatens wilderness, that it no longer menaces him. Was it colder in colonial New England?

RURAL LOOKING

Did the snow fall more violently, the wind blow more fiercely? Are our present gentle winters the function of a long-term climatic cycle now nearing repetition? Will the world through the computer screen, the winter world of downhill skiing followed by hot rum toddies, of snowmobiling, of reading and dancing and eating in warm rooms, dazzle us so that we forget the beast at our back, the beast that stops clocks and freezes fire? Will the blizzard and deep cold shrivel our hearts with fear and shrink our stomachs with hunger, will the children deprived of videogames grow morose, will the silent computer engender cabin fever? In the ecology of the human psyche, winter deserves a place of honor. After all, winter kills.

SKEWING PRIVATE CLIMATE

What did our ancestors really know about energy-saving, resource-conserving site design? Were they masters of microclimatic manipulation, able to redirect prevailing winds, shift sunlight, and retain moisture? Were they the lore-educated experts remembered now by energy-short Americans? A backward scrutiny of the domestic site design of past generations suggests not only the complexity of such questions, but the near impossibility of arriving at definite conclusions.

Site Selection and Design Heritage

Europeans arrived in the New World carrying with them a sort of baggage of site-design folklore. The typical European peasant had had scant opportunity to colonize virgin territory; for generations, fathers handed sons long-worked farms (Mayhew, 1973). Consequently, many colonists knew little about site-locating, but a great deal about improving existing farmsteads and fields. Nevertheless, agriculturalists had definite ideas about the rudiments of site selection.

Perhaps the finest explication of early-seventeenth-century site locating and site manipulation, Charles Estienne's *Maison rustique or The Countrey Farme,* covers a wealth of western European traditional practice. The massive folio, translated into English in 1616, remains one of the most detailed handbooks of agriculture ever compiled. No other work better describes the thought of American colonists.

Estienne explained site-locating chiefly in regard to prosperous farming and only secondarily in regard to building the complex of farm structures called a farmstead. "You must make choice of a place far from marshes, far from the sea shore, and where neither the southern nor northern winds do ordinarily blow," he began, "and which lies not altogether open to the south sun, nor yet unto the north: but principally see that it be placed near unto some good and honest neighbor." Such directives complicate the understanding of early American site-location prac-

"Skewing Private Climate" appeared as "A History of Microclimate Modification 1600 to 1980" in *Energy-Conserving Site Design,* ed. Gregory McPherson (Washington, D.C.: American Society of Landscape Architects, 1984), 2–16.

tice. Clearly Estienne considered a good neighbor as important as a site sheltered from north winds. He also carefully integrated the design of the structures, and particularly of the farm house and barn, into a larger theory of location. "If there ever be a hill, build upon the edge thereof, making choice to have your lights toward the east; but if you be in a cold country, open your lights also on the south side, and little or nothing towards the north," he counseled in a long passage explaining the different uses of "lights" (permanently set panes of glass designed only to admit sunlight) and "windows" (shuttered openings intended to admit fresh air). A wise builder, according to Estienne, chooses the side of a hill to "recoup the liberty of the air, and a goodly prospect," to "be safe from the annoyances of foggy mists" and to avoid "cold in winter." On such a site, a house should present its chief lights "upon the sun-rising in the months of March and September," but the barn and stables "shall be open toward the sunset, in respect of their greatest lights," and should front their windows on the south. In an age well aware of the expensive luxury of glass and terrified of diseases caused by night air or fog, Estienne emphasized the healthfulness of the perfect hillside site—and did not forget the rewards of a good view.

Of more importance to Estienne, and to most of his contemporaries too, microclimatic manipulation engrossed the attention of husbandmen unable to move to better sites. *Maison rustique* devotes much attention to improving local climates, sometimes assuming that such improvements might take generations to accomplish their work. "Over against the North, you shall procure some row or tuft of trees for to be a mark unto you of your place, and defense also for the same against the northern winds in the winter," Estienne suggested, realizing the equal importance of marking boundary lines and deflecting winds. "But if you be in a hot country, you must set your said tuft of trees on the south side, against such winds and heat of sun as come from there." He warned of the necessity of putting kitchen gardens south of an effective windbreak, and near the farmhouse to save the steps of the housewife. And he noted the usefulness of the garden as a beautiful space, calculated to refresh the eye, and consequently worth locating near the farmyard. His immense, minutely detailed guidebook ranges over hundreds of site-manipulation details, considering the best ways to conserve water resources, ventilate barns, and protect vineyards. Not all of his good advice took root in the colonies, however.

Understanding site-location and site-design practice in the American colonies, including the Spanish colonies, requires an understanding of the practice of shaping entire landscapes (Stilgoe, 1982a). It also requires an understanding of major climatic and resource differences between western Europe and most of North America. Beyond doubt, English colonists found New England winters to be far colder than those of home, just as English people learned that summer in Virginia meant high temperatures and violent thunderstorms unlike anything in their experience. On the other hand, colonists discovered a bountiful supply of firewood. "It may be objected that it is too cold a country for our Englishmen, who have been accustomed to a warmer climate," noted William Wood in 1634 in *New England's Prospect*. "To which it may be answered, there is wood good store and better, cheap to build warm houses and make good fires, which makes the winter less tedious." Such circumstances lessened the authority of tradition and of European experts like Estienne. Old World site-locating theory and site-manipulation practice always implied a scarcity of such resources as firewood. In the colonies, where trees grew so thick that settlers burned huge piles of felled timber simply to make fields, builders cared less about windbreaks and more about effective chimneys. Virginians immersed in raising tobacco and cotton, two plants wholly alien to European tradition, likewise dispensed with much suddenly "old fashioned" practice.

Early Farmsteads and Homes

Almost every North American colonist farmed. From the Spanish settlements in California to the French villages in Louisiana to the British towns in New England, almost all site design revolved around the growing of crops, and often of crops foreign to North America. Farming efficiency also preoccupied the settlers; a few minutes saved from a particular chore, or a chore eliminated from daily or seasonal work freed farmer and farmwife for other, more profitable labors. While colonists quickly abandoned much of their Old World heritage, they retained or invented remarkably efficient site-design practices.

Almost every colonial farmyard reflected male-female job segregation. Men worked in fields and in the farmyard tending large livestock; women worked in the kitchen "ell" and in the kitchen garden. Every structure and space in and around the farmyard reflected the job segregation and the urge toward efficiency. According to several experts, a farmwife ought to be able to see her clothesline from her kitchen window, just as a farmer ought to be able to step from the stall-area of his barn into a harness room (Allen 1852; Stilgoe, 1982a). In cold regions, almost always north of the Mason-Dixon line, the barn typically stood north of the farmhouse, not to shelter the house and reduce its fuel requirements, but to create a sort of court or yard in which outdoor work could be done year round. In northern New England, farmers often connected houses to barns by building a long, shed-like structure that enabled them to move from house to barn without venturing outdoors (Hubka, 1977). Of more importance, however, was the ability of the "connected barn" to act as a vast windscreen for the farmyard; the farmwife could tend chickens and the "family pig" secure from most winter winds. An almost identical arrangement of farm buildings, the *casa-corral,* evolved in present-day New Mexico; the courtyard sheltered by farm buildings and adobe walls provided a sun-trap perfect for outdoor winter work. The farmyard represented the one place on the farm in which both farmer and farmwife shared space, and it materially helped the efficiency of both workers, chiefly by stretching the duration of weather warm enough to perform outdoor activities.

The *typical* American farm had acquired by 1800 very definite characteristics. Wherever possible, the farmstead stood on the side of a south-facing hill, the barn to the north and several sheds making up a screen around the barnyard. The kitchen garden usually stood to the west to obtain some shelter from the structures, and fields stretched away from the farmstead in all directions. Often a woodlot stood at the north end of the holding, acting as a sort of windbreak, and sometimes one or two deciduous trees shaded the farmhouse's south facade. Locating a farm on a hillside meant avoiding the cold air that hangs in valleys, and avoiding too the mists that farmers believed carried disease; of course, slope soil is rarely as rich as bottom-land, so the hillside farmer traded a longer growing season against richer soil. Everywhere in the new Republic, farm families avoided the north slopes of hills, knowing that such exposure produces a much shorter growing season. North-slope farms often failed, and today the astute observer traveling in upstate New York, for example, often finds prosperous farms on south-facing hillsides and only timber on the north-facing slopes.

Landscape historians know that many farms violated many of the typical characteristics. For a multitude of reasons, farm families often abandoned New World practice. Some families feared the health hazard implicit in the odors forever drifting from barns to houses; siting barns to the windward of houses meant living forever with the stench of manure and the possibility of disease. Other families put pure water highest on their list of desires, and located houses and wells on the highest ground. Below that level, they sited barns, stables, and other structures sheltering livestock. In the age before piped-in water, locating the kitchen very near the well saved the farmwife hours of walking. A pure spring, flowing freely even in droughts, proved a powerful attraction to any family looking for farmland; in water-short regions, such a spring made a north-facing hillside seem nearly perfect. In other locations, the children and grandchildren of original settlers, having had the chance to grow intimately familiar with local climate, built farms organized according to winter winds prevailing from the west, for example, or winter storms from the northeast. Deciphering the wisdom of such site-designers is now difficult; in some cases the hills remain and still deflect storms, but often the nineteenth-century woodlots have vanished, and the massive trees that once shaped air flow no longer guide local storms. Much research remains to be done concerning the intentions of uneducated but wise builders; many farmhouses have north-facing lights and/or windows simply because barns stood north of houses and farmwives wanted to watch their husbands, especially when the men did such dangerous work as splitting wood. But where families sited barns to the west or east of their houses, the houses often have only one or two north-facing windows, and often reveal a long roof sloping almost to the ground on the north side. Such roofs, designed to direct winter winds over the structure, nowadays point in directions difficult to understand. It is possible that over two or more centuries weather patterns have changed or else that tree-felling has caused winds to move in new paths.

In the humid South, houses quickly revealed their occupants' awareness of blistering heat and heavy rainfall. The deep porch, sometimes extending totally around the house, not only sheltered the family from rain; it sheltered the interior of the house from sun while providing semi-outdoor space that could be efficiently used. In winter, for example, the low sun fell directly into the south-facing porch sheltered by the house from northern winds; in summer, the north porch provided a shady, often breezy place for the farmwife to work. Partly because of slavery, many southerners worried little about designing houses for coolness; slave cooks, for example, freed planter-class wives from the necessity of working next to wood-fueled stoves in summer. Such simple architectural features as high ceilings, over-hanging porches, balconies, and the free-standing "summer" kitchen did contribute to the coolness of southern houses.

Almost everywhere in North America, at least until the 1950s, builders of "common" houses and farms—those structures not designed by professionally trained architects or by experiment-minded agricultural reformers—toyed with the wisdom of planting deciduous tress just south of their houses. Such trees shaded roofs in summer and, when they lost their leaves, permitted welcome sunlight to warm roofs. Sometimes the trees existed for largely ornamental reasons, but many families feared the effect of prolonged shade on wood-shingled roofs (Stilgoe, 1982a). Beyond that, shading one or more sides of a house sometimes increased insect nuisances; mosquitoes shun sunlight and, in the era before the invention of window screening, sunlight proved more endurable than shady, insect-filled porches and kitchens. Asphalt shingles, tin roofing, and window screens helped popularize the "colonial" notion of using deciduous trees to cool and heat a farmhouse.

If Estienne's *Maison rustique* marks the highpoint of the early-seventeenth-century European site-locating and site-design practice carried to the New World, perhaps S. W. Johnson's *Rural Economy* (1806) marks the epitome of "traditional American" practice. "A farmhouse should be built on the most healthy spot on the farm," Johnson counsels, "open to the south and southwestern breezes, which prevail in the summer; and well sheltered from the northwest and northeast in the winter, by trees either of natural growth, or cultivated on purpose, and set as near the center of the farm as convenient." Johnson summarizes the early American attitude toward pure water, good drainage, prevailing winds, and crop-growing requirements. Within 30 years, however, much of his information had become almost antiquated, and Americans had begun to discard centuries of lore.

Energy Shortages and Architectural Adaptations

In the winter of 1637–38, North American colonists experienced their first fuel crisis. The settlers of Boston, after only seven years of occupancy, had nearly exhausted their supply of firewood. "We at Boston were almost ready to break up for want of wood," wrote Governor John Winthrop of the near catastrophe (Rutman, 1967). Of course, the settlers quickly solved the problem by buying firewood from off-peninsula farmers and by restricting the cutting of trees within the settlement. Nevertheless, a handful of settlers did understand something of the limitations of North American natural resources. Not for more than 150 years did Americans worry about firewood shortages. In the year 1800, a typical New England farm family burned about 15 cords of wood, although 20 made for a more comfortable winter (Brown, 1948). Assuming that a cord of wood is the equivalent of three-fifths of a standing acre, the typical family consumed about 10 acres of woodland annually to cook, process farm produce, and keep warm. The population of Massachusetts consumed approximately 2 million cords, or roughly 2,000 square miles of timber in 1800. The firewood consumption taxed and overtaxed the capacity of farm woodlots and distant forests, already strained by demands for fence and building timber and for charcoal for the new nation's young iron industry (Stilgoe, 1982a).

Several areas of the country encountered severe fuel shortages earlier than most. Cape Cod, for example, had been almost totally deforested by 1800, presenting an almost desert-like appearance to travelers (Stilgoe, 1981). By the middle of the nineteenth century when Thoreau's *Cape Cod* was published (1865), its inhabitants were reduced to purchasing almost all firewood and scavenging for the rest. "Almost all the wood used for fuel is imported by vessels or currents, and of course all the coal," Thoreau remarked. "I was told that probably a quarter of the fuel and a considerable part of the lumber used in North Truro was driftwood. Many get *all* their fuel from the beach." As early as the beginning of the century, however, Cape Codders had begun manipulating microclimates to conserve fuel.

Much of the manipulation involved architectural innovation. The "Cape Cod" house, a one and a half story, compact structure focused on a central chimney, incorporated dozens of energy-saving features. Its low ceilings offered only 6 or 6¼ feet of headroom, but made rooms easy to heat; its small windows, often strategically located to capture sun and avoid prevailing northern winds, reduced infiltration of cold air. Cape Codders experimented with a variety of insulation materials before settling on a mixture of crushed clamshells and dried seaweed, an inflammable but highly efficient barrier against cold. The central chimney warmed the two upper chambers and enabled "zone control" of heating; many Cape Codders closed off the parlor and perhaps one other room during the depths of the winter, and lived in a warm kitchen and "back room." The little houses impressed Thoreau, who eventually determined that "houses near the sea are generally low and broad." He found too that the houses of the typical Cape Codder seemed somehow to fit better into the landscape than those of the well-to-do who could afford to buy firewood and coal. "Generally, the old-fashioned and unpainted houses on the Cape looked more comfortable, as well as picturesque, than the modern and more pretending ones, which were less in harmony with the scenery, and less firmly planted," he wrote in *Cape Cod*. Thoreau devoted little attention to the peculiar siting of Cape Cod houses, but other travelers did.

In the early nineteenth century, Timothy Dwight rode along the sandy Cape and marveled at the small houses, noting in his travels in New England and New York (1821) that "generally, they exhibit a tidy, neat aspect in themselves and in their appendages, and furnish proofs of comfortable living." Dwight noted that almost every such house stood "surrounded by a fence enclosing a small piece of ground," and that in most such enclosures "were orchards of apple trees, defended from the sea winds by a barrier of cherry trees or locusts," which permitted meadow grass to grow in the dry, sandy, but sheltered soil. Such houses, Dwight noted again and again, usually stood in valleys or hollows, where their inhabitants "find a better soil and security from the violence of the winds." Shelter dramatically reduced fuel requirements, provided a microclimate favorable to orchard and garden crops, and shielded cows and other livestock and the family well from windblown sand. Combined with the architectural changes, the Cape Cod house site proved remarkably energy-efficient.

While Cape Codders struggled to adjust to a dramatically diminished firewood supply, pioneers settling the treeless plains confronted life with almost no firewood at all. Women cooked over fires made of grass and dried buffalo dung, and longed for the time when their families could afford a precut house shipped west from Michigan or Chicago. In the meantime, they made do with sod houses.

The dug-out or sod house, sometimes called a "soddie," is a remarkable adaptation to the plains. Homesteaders dug into a south-facing slope and increased the wall height by piling up great blocks of prairie sod around the perimeter. The sod house endured far longer than one or two years (Ise, 1936; Dick, 1937; Henderson 1978). The thick balks of sod resisted wind infiltration; if a family had the luck to find enough cottonwood or other trees to make a log roof, blocks of sod often formed the roof covering too. While not wholly waterproof, in the High Plains where rainfall is limited, the sod-roofed house trapped heat from the fire that often burned on an open hearth and protected its inhabitants against snow, cold, and damp.

Despite its immediate attractions, among which the most favored was its minimal cost, the sod house irritated most inhabitants. Life in a dug-out meant unending toil for the housewife, who fought a losing battle against insects, dust, and dirt (women usually preferred canvas roofs over log-and-sod roofs simply because the more permanent sod roofs forever dropped earth onto food, bedding, and furniture). Lining walls and ceiling with newspaper helped prevent falling dirt, but did little to retard the depredations of insects. Sod houses built wholly above ground lasted only as long as the bottom row of sod balks retained its shape; in a heavy rain, or after days of light rain, the blocks of sod could soften and without warning suddenly collapse the entire dwelling.

Not surprisingly, plains families hoped to prosper after a few years and order a knocked-down house from the many suppliers of such structures. Little is known about the popular reaction to the two-, three-, and four-room houses shipped by rail from major cities, brought by wagon to sites next to the sod houses, and then assembled by farmers or hired carpenters. Certainly their immense popularity suggests the common reaction, but the homesteaders had little other choice, since most lacked timber for fencing, let alone building.

SKEWING PRIVATE CLIMATE

Settlement on the near-arid High Plains circa 1900 involved some of the most stark colonization landscapes imaginable in places suited to ranching, not farming.

The demise of the sod-house occurred, however, in the decades following the Civil War. Farm families obtaining good profits from their massive wheat and corn harvests found it possible to abandon traditional house-siting wisdom, at least for a moment. The sod house—and the Cape Cod house—represent a popular adaptation to energy shortage; what replaced the sod house reflected massive changes in the American way of life.

Modernization

When George G. Hill published *Practical Suggestions for Farm Buildings,* a 1901 United States Department of Agriculture Farmer's Bulletin, most Americans no longer thought much of the farm-siting lore recounted by Estienne. Hill, in fact, only briefly mentions the importance of windbreaks, and then chiefly as a way of improving the comfort of outdoor workers, not as important to household economy. His lack of attention is not at all unique; writers in the *Cyclopedia of American Agriculture* (Bailey, 1907), for example, devote scarcely any more attention. Between about 1850 and 1900, farm families—and the families of storekeepers, physicians, fishermen, and others—had changed their lives.

Iron stoves and, within a few years, coal revolutionized American housekeeping (wood-burning stoves consume far less fuel than open fireplaces). From Benjamin Franklin's prototype to the efficient "air-tight" stoves of the 1890s, the progress of American stove-making drastically decreased the pressure on the nation's timber resources. Stoves altered family habits too, however, and reshaped notions of personal comfort.

Stoves can be moved. Nineteenth-century Americans discovered that a wood stove could be moved from the kitchen onto the back porch or into a free-standing summer kitchen in the backyard. In summer, the housewife found herself cooking amidst breezes that made her chores less onerous, and the rest of the family enjoyed a house free of cookstove heat. In winter, the stove could be moved back into the kitchen, placed against the now sealed-up fireplace, and made to heat large spaces. Well-to-do families sometimes splurged on a second stove, usually located in the "parlor" and lit only on special occasions, but the typical American family living in a single-family house relied on one large cast-iron combination heating- and cooking-appliance often equipped to boil water for bathing and other purposes. A little tinkering enabled the cast-iron monster to heat upstairs rooms; a hole cut in a ceiling or wall improved the flow of hot air. On bitter windy nights, families sat in kitchens, reading, talking, and doing schoolwork not by the fire-light of the 1820s but by the whale-oil (and later kerosene) lamps of the contemporary period.

Coal soon supplanted wood, particularly in the regions deforested or where remaining timber proved more useful for making fence rails. Railroads transported coal everywhere, and eventually even to such poverty-stricken places as Cape Cod. For the housewife, coal meant easier cooking; a coal-stove fire could be more easily and finely regulated than a wood one, and coal was easier to handle. By 1900, suburban families had discovered the usefulness of furnaces carefully placed in basements. In regions where gas enabled housewives to discard coal-burning stoves, furnaces evenly warmed large houses, and families dispersed away from kitchens.

Other inventions helped Americans forget tradition. Tar paper, perhaps the most lowly invention of all, helped prevent wind infiltration. To some writers of the period, only tar paper made possible life in the High Plains (Smalley, 1893). Along with the popularization of cement, cinder block, air-moving fans, and hot-water radiators, tar paper helped convince Americans that comfortable houses could be built anywhere, even atop hills. So long as coal remained plentiful—and very cheap—American house siting departed further from earlier tradition.

Instead of nestling in hollows facing roughly south, late-nineteenth-century American houses usually face roads. Instead of offering only one or two windows to the north, such houses frequently show substantially more north glass area, partly in an attempt to achieve evenness of lighting, partly in an attempt to enjoy good views. Roofs no longer adjusted to prevailing microclimate winds; instead they followed styles dictated by eastern architects. Such houses speak of firm faith in modern industrialism, of a faith in such effective equipment as the gravity-fed furnace. In 1915, a housewife could easily raise the temperature of her house by simply moving a lever on the kitchen wall; below, in the cellar, the elevated hopper dumped coal onto the fire, dampers opened, and valves moved—all with a flick of the wrist. While husbands remained enslaved by the duty to remove ashes and load the coal hopper, housewives and children lived snugly in the clean, draft-free rooms upstairs. Only farmers kept alive the old lore, and then only because their crops needed protection.

Windbreaks and Shelterbelts

Throughout the period of rapid modernization and even more rapid social change, American farmers kept alive time-tested techniques of microclimate manipulation and even invented new ones. Now and then their expertise attracted the scrutiny of landscape architects and other nonagricultural designers, but only rarely. The web of lore, invention, and seat-of-the-pants wisdom is immensely complicated, but the history of windbreaks, while only one small part of the entire web, illustrates the finesse of American agriculturists.

"The face of the country is becoming denuded, and wintry winds and summer storms sweep our farms with more fury than formerly," commented one agricultural editor in 1866 in the *Illustrated Annual Register*. "Young plants of grass and winter grain, after heaving by frost, are beaten about and sometimes torn out by the action of the winds upon them." By the 1850s, American farmers clearly understood the microclimate changes brought about by the diminishing size of farm woodlots (Stilgoe, 1982a). Railroad companies consumed vast quantities of wood for fuel and ties; steamboat firms purchased cordwood for fuel, too. But farmers forced to replace miles of rail or post-and-rail fencing, rebuild barn and house sills, and keep families warm caused most of the timber consumption. A farmer might clear-cut his woodlot for cash or home consumption and suddenly discover his crops "blasted" by storms. Even worse, his neighbors might learn the detrimental effects too, as their own crops suddenly failed. Thus as farmers ceased to rely on homegrown timber and cordwood and began to purchase stovewood shipped by rail or else buy several tons of coal, they embarked on a long struggle to build windbreaks—for the sake of their crops. "Land owners who have planted belts of evergreens have found that the protection they afford has amounted on an average to an increase in the crops raised within the range of their shelter, of about fifty percent more than where fully exposed," continued the editor.

Mid-nineteenth-century windbreaks took two forms. One type derived from careful cutting of forests; farmers left standing mature trees 70 or 80 feet tall. Such "leftover" windbreaks figure in many paintings of American farms, and are sometimes mistaken for vaguely European looking hedgerows. The more common type of windbreak—aside from the strategically located woodlot—began as a row of small saplings. "By selecting thrifty growers, such as the Norway spruce and the Scotch larch, a growth of 25 to 30 feet high will be reached in about ten years, if they are properly cultivated; and 50 feet in twenty-five years," wrote the editor of the *Illustrated Annual Register* in 1866. Agricultural periodicals of the era devote much attention to the proper siting, cultivation, and thinning of such windbreaks. The typical farmer planted twice as many windbreaks as he needed, since young trees protect much less ground than tall ones. After 15 or 20 years, he felled every other windbreak, using the timber for fence repair and fuel, because the maturing trees protected more area.

Experts disagreed about the best trees to plant. Some argued that elms and other trees known for sprawling root systems ought not to be planted near field crops and suggested oaks and black birch instead. Others specified bordering every field on the farm with "shade or timber trees," partly to divert wind, but largely to provide building timber and firewood (*Illustrated Annual Register*, 1880). Other experts counseled farmers to plant evergreen windbreaks, although they realized that such softwood would be of little fuel value. Of chief importance in the literature, however, is the implied assumption that farmers would think about long-term benefits. Again and again, authors speak of 15- or 20-year periods preceding the era of real microclimate improvement. Farmers intending to leave their farms better than they found them, perhaps to sons and daughters, perhaps to unknown purchasers, planted windbreaks for the future, not the present. Between 1800 and 1860, American farmers learned the value of windbreaks and woodlots, and relearned the caution offered by Estienne and other seventeenth-century writers.

Science and pipe dreams furthered the windbreak-planting efforts of thousands of farmers, especially in the plains states. By the middle of the nineteenth century, scientists like George Perkins Marsh had begun studying the climatic effects of trees and forests. Marsh's opus, *Man and Nature: Or, Physical Geography as Modified by Human Action* (1864), investigates windbreaks in two ways. First, it addresses "trees as a shelter to ground to the leeward," noting the local climatic effects of trees. Second, and more important, it analyzes the regional effects of forests. Marsh concluded after studying the large-scale climatic effects of forest removal in western and south-central Europe, "It is evident that the effect of the forest, as a mechanical impediment to the passage of the wind, would extend to a very considerable distance above its own height, and hence protect while standing, or lay open when felled, a much larger surface than might at first thought be supposed." Eventually, he extrapolated from his findings and, while aware of "the slender historical evidence," announced that "almost every treatise on the economy of the forest adduces numerous facts in support of the doctrine that the clearing of the woods tends to diminish the flow of springs and the humidity of the soil." Along with other foresters and ecologists, Marsh unwittingly stimulated a grand American pipe dream.

"Rain follows the plow," a motto that heartened farm families settling the High Plains, derived partly from scientific efforts at understanding rainfall patterns and their relationship to ground cover, and partly from the hope of homesteaders that quasi-arid regions would grow eastern crops like corn. In the first decades of pioneering, the motto seemed true, but gradually the ground water drawn up by continuous plowing— "dry-farming" as it came to be known—began to lessen. Agricultural experts counseled farmers to plant windbreaks to decrease evaporation as well as to divert winds and provide fuel. At least one landscape architect, H. W. S. Cleveland, advocated planting windbreaks to change the regional rainfall of the West. Commenting on the western soil in *Landscape Architecture as Applied to the Wants of the West* (1873), Cleveland indicated that "Where such grasses will grow, trees will grow, and with the growth of trees in sufficient quantity will come the increase of humidity and the modification of the storms, floods, and other excesses of natural phenomena, which are fatal to the success of extended agricultural operations." Cleveland cared little about the varieties of trees planted in the windbreaks he suggested should be set along railroad lines and around farms; he wanted trees set out at once. "Plant those that *will* grow, and in time they will serve as screens for more valuable kinds, as is done on the sea shore, where the worthless silver poplar (abele) will grow luxuriantly and in a few years form a screen behind which more delicate deciduous and evergreen trees will grow as readily as if they were unaware of the vicinity of the ocean." Farmers did encounter difficulty in nursing along the saplings, however, and sporadic years of drought sometimes killed windbreaks just as they withered acres of wheat and other grain. Clearly, rain did not necessarily follow the movement of farming into land previously used only for ranching. Windbreaks did not dramatically increase regional rainfall, and many farms failed.

RURAL LOOKING

By the late 1930s, federal government efforts had produced shelterbelts of trees to deflect wind and calm soil erosion. (Courtesy United States Forest Service)

Marsh, Cleveland, and other experts, while perhaps wrong about the regional effects of mass windbreak planting, unknowingly predicted the dramatic catastrophe of the dust-bowl years of the 1920s and 30s. In response to the blowing dust, the federal government urged farmers to plant windbreaks, partly to control evaporation of ground moisture, partly to stop the dust, and partly to counter the effect of wind sweeping uninterrupted over miles of farms surrounded by barbed wire. Nearly two decades after the first plantings, Joseph H. Stoeckeler and Ross A. Williams in a 1949 *Yearbook of Agriculture* article entitled "Windbreaks and Shelterbelts," summed up the advantages of the maturing belts of trees: Well-maintained windbreaks decreased farmhouse fuel requirements by roughly one-fourth, and in almost every case helped farm families harvest far more produce from vegetable gardens. They made possible growing fruit where winter storms had previously killed orchards. But the results of shelterbelts, windbreaks planted to protect field crops, proved even more cheering. Between the middle of the nineteenth century, when reformers first began urging farmers to plant them, and 1949, some 123,191 miles of shelterbelts had been established. Privately planted shelterbelts frequently consisted of osage orange trees, whose large thorns helped confine wandering livestock. Those planted by the Forest Service, which between 1932 and 1942 set out more than 18,000 miles of trees in farm and ranch country hit by drifting dust, and by farmers following expert advice consisted of such species as Siberian elm, green ash, hackberry, honeylocust, cottonwood, white and golden willow, chokecherry, ponderosa pine, and others (Stoeckeler & Williams, 1949). But the true extent of the actual results of the tree-planting can never be known, for in the dust-bowl years farmers discovered the advantages

SKEWING PRIVATE CLIMATE

of deep-well irrigation, and sometimes dismissed shelterbelts as of secondary value, if that.

Gardeners, on the other hand, had used windbreaks continuously from the time of Estienne to the dust-bowl years. Everywhere in the United States, vegetable and flower growers screened their gardens with plantings of trees. Turn-of-the-century magazines aimed at the ever-growing population of the nation's suburbs directed attention again and again to the many advantages of windbreaks. Some articles explained what famous Americans had done to their grounds; a 1905 *Country Life* (Maynard) article examining the country home of Horace Greeley notes the publisher's effective use of windbreaks: "At the northern end of the plot selected for the garden, he planted a windbreak of evergreens. He planted four rows of them—pines and firs, bought at a nursery, and hemlocks and cedars transplanted from the adjoining woods. Under the shelter of the wind-break he built a good-sized greenhouse, and near by planted strawberries and other small fruits" (Capen, 1905). Perhaps Greeley made such good use of windbreaks because he understood something of High Plains agriculture, but thousands of other suburbanites learned from how-to-do-it essays.

Henry Troth's "Wind-Breaks for Country Homes," another 1905 *Country Life* article, notes that "a wind-break saves coal, makes many a house habitable or comfortable that would otherwise be vacant or cheerless in winter, permits the summer home to be occupied in time for the first spring flowers as well as the last autumn colors, and gives the garden a chance to yield fresh vegetables two weeks or more earlier than unprotected gardens." Troth called the white spruce "the best tree of all for wind-breaks," but he recognized the peculiar difficulties of planting windbreaks along the ocean—for example, where salt spray harmed many species—and in other locations, and advised readers about the planting of Scotch and Austrian pine, black walnut, lindens, and other species. American gardening and suburban-life magazines always devoted some attention to the care of windbreaks, not so much to save home-heating fuel, but to give gardens some protection against late-spring winds and summer dry spells. Of course, the articles shifted focus over the decades. By 1939, for example, *Real Gardening* understood the new notion of backyard privacy; Donald Wyman's "Natural Screens and Windbreaks" includes an analysis of climbing vines that help to screen houses and protect gardeners from neighbors' eyes. In 1961, *Horticulture* published a brief article detailing the fuel-saving advantages of windbreaks adjacent to suburban houses and emphasizing their ability to control drifting snow (Plimpton, 1961). The many articles concerning siting or maintaining gardens often mention windbreaks, but by the 1960s, most advice concerned only their use in lengthening growing seasons.

Not all microclimatic manipulation focused on reducing cold winds; indeed farmers worried as much about controlling evaporation, or did until engine-driven deep-well pumps seemingly freed them from rainfall and evaporation worries. Too, Americans tried to retain coolness throughout the summer, and sometimes wondered about the summertime effect of windbreaks that might cut off soothing breezes.

Natural Cooling

Planting for cooling and moisture retention never preoccupied Americans. Other factors than the worry about roofing deterioration caused farmers to keep trees away from their houses. Nurturing saplings in or near barnyards proved immensely difficult; manure and urine frequently killed those saplings that survived attacks by hungry livestock. In 1864, *The Country Gentleman* advised planting apple trees instead of cherry trees, only because "apple trees will bear a much larger amount of manure." Many farm families planted an apple tree on the site of a disused privy, but did so largely for the crop value (Stilgoe, 1982a). Only the advent of synthetic roofing, primarily tar paper and "combination" shingles, encouraged householders to plant trees designed to shade houses.

Moisture retention received even less effort. The popularization of the windmill made possible vegetable gardening in the High Plains, and windmills often pumped enough water to fill troughs for cattle stricken by drought (Webb, 1931). A windmill-powered well pump is at least somewhat ecologically sound, since it pumps only when the wind, which hastens evaporation, blows. Self-regulating windmills, designed to pump steadily even as wind speeds increased, freed housewives from the nerve-wracking chore of adjusting the ever-squeaking blades, and provided an even flow of water intended first for household use, then for livestock watering, then finally for garden—but not field—irrigation. Irrigation ditches encouraged volunteer plants, including trees, to grow along them, and provided cool places to sit or swim, but nineteenth-century Americans devoted little time to relaxing. The windmill remains a little-known factor in microclimatic manipulation, largely because contemporary agricultural periodicals analyzed the machines, not their uses.

If Americans embraced any one technique intended to retain moisture and provide coolness, they embraced the planting of vines, and particularly of grapevines. Wisteria and other ornamental vines frequently shaded front and back porches, dooryards, and summerhouses, tea houses, and gazebos. Grapevines proved more popular, simply because they produced an edible crop, not one fit only for wild birds. "The grapevine is an ideal covering for the pergola near the house, for it gives shade in summer and light in winter," noted Mary P. Cunningham in a 1922 *House Beautiful* article. "It has more stability and flatness as a top covering than the rampant bittersweet or actinidia, and is darker and better in color than the yellow-green wisteria." By 1922, of course, many suburbanites no longer cared to make their own wine or jelly, and the grapevine became an ornamental plant used chiefly for shading patios and other places intended for relaxation. The grape arbors that decorated farmhouses existed for a more "useful" purpose, of course, and the fact that they provided shady bowers for the family to enjoy in rare moments of leisure struck most agricultural experts as a pleasant but scarcely important consideration.

Why did Americans not make better use of moisture-retaining, air-cooling planting? The answer lies partly in the national preoccupation with agriculture. Farming required long hours of arduous work, and the isolation of farms prompted many families to devote Sundays to visiting. Everywhere in agricultural America, from the panhandle of Florida to the plains of Montana, summer meant a time of hard work, and coolness arrived, if it came at all, at sundown. A vine-shaded, west- or east-facing porch, its floor freshly "washed" with several buckets of water flung hastily over it, seemed as cool as it might be. To sit beneath the several fully-grown maples before the house, to enjoy a Fourth of July picnic by the creek lined with cottonwoods—such was the search for coolness in rural America.

In suburban America, particularly in the East, well- and municipal-water enabled suburbanites to maintain green lawns in all but the worst droughts, and soon electricity powered fans. Until the 1930s non-farming Americans remained an essentially indoor people, at least at home; only gradually, as new sports like swimming changed living habits around the home, did suburban Americans begin a new epoch in microclimatic manipulation. That epoch emphasized planting for outdoor enjoyment, and prompted a reevaluation of time-tested climate controls and the discovery of new ones.

The Era of Abundant Energy

Cheap energy fueled the transformation of the American built environment, including the form of new houses and yards (Fitch, 1972). Air cooling, called "air conditioning" in advertisements and eventually in popular American speech, seemingly solved the problem of cooling interior space; no longer did ivy-shaded walls seem vital. Oil-fueled furnaces, particularly those forcing hot air throughout houses, encouraged householders to fell windbreaks and to install massive "picture win-

Windmills became the machines that made gardens, and orchards and meadows, possible, and farm families invested in them before buying much else. For children (*above*), windmills provided something to climb, to get a view, to escape a ground in which all trees were too young for climbing.

dows" facing in any direction. Water struck most Americans as an inexhaustible resource, and enabled the making of ever greener lawns, even in the arid Southwest. Cheap energy saved energy. The husband, who formerly devoted hours to shifting coal, discovered how much human energy an oil-free furnace conserved; the housewife using an electric clothes dryer discovered long hours freed from the chore of hanging laundry on outdoor clotheslines. Children no longer pumped well water or stacked cordwood or carried kindling from woodshed to kitchen. Americans discovered enormous amounts of "free time," something their grandparents had never had, and devoted themselves to working a second job, working outside the home, going to night school, and relaxing. And relaxation led to much microclimatic manipulation.

The transformation of American domestic space by the "recreational mood" that swept the nation in the years following 1945 is a little-studied, often condemned one, but in its time it struck most observers as entirely laudable. A nation tired of economic depression, world war, and political tension hoped to relax outdoors.

No series of articles better explains the transformation than those published by *House Beautiful* in 1949 and 1950. In October 1949, the magazine began its "Climate Control" series, "a continuing project to show you how to manipulate the design and materials of old or new houses to reduce the stresses and strains of climate on Man and Materials." The lengthy series of articles began partly as an attempt to familiarize readers with "scores of new techniques and materials" developed in the 20 years preceding the issue, and also to help readers design more comfortable houses. The last concept is immensely important for our own era as well. The editor, Elizabeth Gordon, intended the project as something much more than a how-to-save-money series emphasizing ways to conserve fuel, build more cheaply, and rehabilitate obsolescent houses. Emphasizing "better living and better health" and focusing on climate understanding and climate modification, the *House Beautiful* series remains one of the finest collaborations ever undertaken by climatologists, ecologists, architects, and landscape architects.

The exceptionally well-illustrated, well-researched series included a number of articles emphasizing microclimatic manipulation by careful siting and planting. Articles such as "Good Site Planning Can Double Your Outdoor Living," "How to Pick Your Private Climate," "How to Fix Your Private Climate," and "Here, Climate Control Began with a Tree" emphasize the overall nature of microclimate control. Wolfgang Langewiesche (1950) and other authors asserted that families should plan grounds for sunshine to extend the season of outdoor living, should erect fences to screen views and modify air circulation, and should make use of every sort of plant to improve their "private" climates. "You can doctor your climate. (You can also spoil it.) Country people have always known that," wrote Langewiesche (1949) in an article about improving microclimates. "They have always used windbreaks, shade trees, hedges, garden walls, L-shaped houses, houses built around a court." His comments are the beginning of the "wise countryman" theme, which asserts that agricultural people know the most about climate modification. "But we city people have forgotten such things," he continued in a description of a sun-pocket. He stressed the usefulness of converting rural knowledge into suburban practice, giving as examples the wonders worked by white-painted garages and fences on dark rooms needing reflected light, the way a gate at the bottom of a walled garden releases cold air down hill, and the different temperature-keeping qualities of different colored paving. One *House Beautiful* 1949 "Pace-Setter House," a sort of ideal house designed for Orange, N.J., developed most of the general themes outlined in the first part of the series. A scarcely more energy-efficient, well-planted house and site cannot be found in design periodicals today, if one excludes solar-heating attachments.

Other articles in the series detailed specific modifications. "How to Control the Sun," "Good Lawns Keep You Cool," "Vines: Climate Control Device for Summer Coolness," "How to Manipulate Sun and Shade" all focus on the need for well-designed spaces for outdoor recreation. "Climate Control is no *substitute* for good architecture and good engineering, but it is the most significant *supplement* to them made during the Twentieth Century," announced James Marston Fitch in a 1949 article entitled "How You Can Use *House Beautiful's* Climate Control Project." Fitch lamented the spread of Cape Cod houses "all over the U.S.A." "This is a good climate-control design for the long winters and short cool summers of New England," he noted. "But it has no business in Alabama or Kansas." So much spectator-built housing struck experts as poorly designed and sited that *House Beautiful* hoped to improve buyers' ability to recognize good and bad sites and to improve the bad. Written by experts but addressed to laymen, often to laymen newly arrived in suburbs from cities, the articles remain a wonderfully useful tool.

A third type of article in the series focused on climate problems in particular parts of the country. Buford L. Pickens' "How to Live at Peace with the Gulf Coast Climate" (1950), exemplifies this type. Well-illustrated with climate maps, carefully researched, and accompanied by a companion article detailing a model home, the article represents an attempt to end standardized house-building by showing prospective buyers wonderfully more pleasant houses available at similar costs. The integration of architecture and landscape architecture at every level, from site selection to patio design, produced "model regional houses" of grace and—perhaps more important—of usefulness to a generation anxious to live outdoors.

Interpreting the *House Beautiful* series and its model homes by today's standards proves difficult, but it is clear that the message so well defined and illustrated went largely unheeded. Overall, typical house and garden design varied little from an increasingly energy-dependent path. Suburbanites in the 1950s and 1960s indeed enjoyed cheap electricity, oil, gas, and gasoline prices, along with plentiful water supplies, and they certainly wasted them, keeping houses exceptionally warm in winter, for example. They also enjoyed energy-saving inventions of a type other than that analyzed by *House Beautiful*—a type little studied today, involving new social inventions, which continue to haunt Americans.

Until the 1940s, for example, upper-class people prized pale skin; farmers worked in the fields, and became deeply tanned, but the American "leisure class" carried parasols, wore straw hats, and showed its freedom from manual, outdoor work by its paleness. Industrialism changed the social rules: factory workers laboring indoors 10 or more hours each day exhibited a genuine pallor, and gradually the upper class began to prefer a suntan, even to the point of going south for wintertime vacations. In the years between 1900 and 1950, consequently, shady places, particularly the vine-covered gazebo, lost much of their prestige. Space for sunbathing became vastly more important, and gradually outdoor coolness came to mean either a leafy tree under which a child might read or fix his bicycle, or some sort of swimming pool. Perhaps the most common replacement of the "arbor" or "tea-house," the "sun deck" came to symbolize the new social attitudes. The whole social adaptation to what *House Beautiful* called "outdoor living" remains uninvestigated but important, for it emphasized sunlight, warmth, and leisure, things seemingly lacking in the "energy-short" 1980s.

The Future

Americans have indeed manipulated their microclimates, but always with differences from one generation to another. Essentially, the guiding rule seems to have been this: manipulate for one or two dominant reasons. The Cape Codder and the High Plains settler manipulated to save fuel; the established High Plains farmer manipulated to lengthen his growing season. A single manipulation undertaken for one reason had expected secondary effects—the High Plains farmer lengthened his growing season and realized some saving in fuel for heating his house. In the 1980s and 1990s, two needs will dominate microclimatic manipulation by site modification.

First, Americans will strive to conserve "purchased" mechanical energy, particularly energy used for heating. Site design that lowers winter fuel bills—and perhaps lengthens gardening time—will prove particularly important (Stilgoe, 1982b). Windbreaks especially will return in popularity, and perhaps ivy, grapevines, and other plant screening in the humid South. Proper placement of shade trees will accompany a growing increase in use of solar energy features in new homes.

Second, Americans will continue to desire outdoor living. Landscape architects must recognize that the creation of *enjoyable* outdoor places, places to be used as long and as much as possible every year, will attract clients in every part of the nation. So many "energy-efficient" houses are simply unimaginative—but superbly engineered—overinsulated boxes surrounded by uninspired, ugly, *useless* grounds. Their inhabitants save on fuel bills, but often lament their lack of "old-fashioned" luxuries like patios, sun decks, and shady places. The continuing desire for healthful, gracious outdoor spaces makes the 1949–50 *House Beautiful* point of view as historically important as anything written by Estienne, Dwight, or Thoreau. Climatically effective grounds can be beautiful and useful, even as they conserve water, deflect fuel-wasting winds, and stop drifting snow.

The past holds no secret microclimatic manipulation keys. Americans have manipulated climate for important reasons, and they have always understood the reasons before beginning replanting and other tasks. New materials like tar paper and new machines like electric air coolers have altered national goals, but the connection between reason and design change has always been misunderstood. In the decades ahead, fuel and water conservation will be of equal value with pleasant, useful outdoor recreational spaces.

The energy crisis has only begun. Predictions of severe gasoline shortages and drastic price increases suggest to any thoughtful individual that the decades ahead will witness a new appreciation of stay-at-home living. It will be too expensive to drive far, too expensive to go to restaurants, movie theaters, or covered shopping malls to escape the heat or cold. The efficient design of homes and surrounding grounds will acquire greater and greater significance as energy prices rise (Stilgoe, 1982b). Now is the time to learn from the past, and plan for the energy-short future.

References

Allen, L. F. (1852). *Rural architecture*. New York: Moore.
Bailey, L. H. (Ed.). (1907–1909). *Cyclopedia of American agriculture* (4 vols.). New York: Macmillan.
Brown, R. H. (1948). *Historical geography of the United States*. New York: Harcourt.
Capen, O. B. (1905). Country homes. *Country Life, 8,* 58–61.

Cleveland, H. W. S. (1873). *Landscape architecture as applied to the wants of the west.* Chicago: Jansen.

Cunningham, M. P. (1922, January). The use of the grapevine. *House Beautiful, 51,* 30–31.

Dick, E. (1937). *The sod house frontier.* New York: Harper.

Dwight, T. (1821/1969). *Travels in New England and New York.* Cambridge, MA: Harvard University Press.

Estienne, C. (1616). *Maison rustique, or, the countrey farme.* London: Joslip.

Fitch, A. M. (1949, October). How you can use House Beautiful's climate control project. *House Beautiful, 91,* 141–143.

Gordon, E. (1949, October). What climate does to you and what you can do to climate. *House Beautiful, 91,* 31.

Henderson, A. (1978). *Architecture in Oklahoma.* Norman, OK: Point Riders Press.

Hill, G. G. (1901). *Practical suggestions for farm buildings.* Washington, D.C.: U.S. Government Printing Office.

Hubka, T. C. (1977, December). The connected farm buildings of southwestern Maine. *Pioneer America, 9,* 143–178.

Illustrated Annual Register. (1866). Woodland and timber crop, *4,* 256–265.

Illustrated Annual Register. (1880). Wind power, *8,* 126–129.

Ise, J. (1936). *Sod and stubble: The story of a Kansas homestead.* New York: Harcourt.

Johnson, S. W. (1806). *Rural economy.* New York: Riley.

Langewiesche, W. (1949, October). How to pick your private climate. *House Beautiful, 91,* 146–150.

Langewiesche, W. (1950, July). How to manipulate sun and shade. *House Beautiful, 92,* 42–45, 91–94.

Marsh, G. P. (1864/1965). *Man and nature: Or, physical geography as modified by human action.* Cambridge, MA: Harvard University Press.

Mayhew, A. (1973). *Rural settlement and farming in Germany.* New York: Harper & Row.

Maynard, S. T. (1905, September). Laying out the grounds of a country home. *Country Life, 9,* 13–14.

Pickens, B. L. (1950, July). How to live at peace with the Gulf Coast climate. *House Beautiful, 92,* 102–106.

Plimpton, F. T. P., Jr. (1961, September). Plant a windbreak. *Horticulture, 39,* 456.

Rutman, D. B. (1967). *Winthrop's Boston: A portrait of a puritan town, 1630–1649.* Boston: Beacon.

Smalley, E. V. (1893, September). Isolation of life on prairie farms. *Atlantic, 72,* 378–382.

Stilgoe, J. R. (1981, January). New England coastal wilderness. *Geographics Review, 71,* 33–50.

Stilgoe, J. R. (1982a). *Common landscape of America, 1580 to 1845.* New Haven, CT: Yale University Press.

Stilgoe, J. R. (1982b). Suburbanites forever: The American dream endures. *Landscape Architecture, 72,* 88–93.

Stoeckeler, J. H., & Williams, R. A. (1949). Windbreaks and shelterbelts. *Trees: Yearbook of agriculture, 1949.* Washington, D.C.: U.S. Government Printing Office.

The Country Gentleman. (1864, September). Shade trees for barnyards, *24,* 144.

Thoreau, H. D. (1865/1961). *Cape Cod.* Boston, MA: Crowell-Appollo.

Troth, H. (1905, February). Windbreaks for country homes. *Country Life, 7,* 363–366.

Webb, W. P. (1931). *The great plains.* New York: Ginn.

Wood, W. (1634). *New England's prospect.* London: Bellamie.

Wyman, D. (1939, February). Natural screens and windbreaks. *Real Gardening, 1,* 78–85.

CAMOUFLAGED AND SAVING ENERGY

A windbreak of white pine, a barn situated northwest of the farmhouse, a birch planted south of the solar room—such are the landscape details that now speak so strongly to an energy-hungry nation. In ten years, Americans have relearned the siting and construction wisdom so well known to past generations of farmers, carpenters, and other common builders; an outpouring of popular books and magazine articles has reeducated the homeowner, and a similar flood of technical reports has reoriented the professional designer. The rich history of energy-conscious building encompasses details like skylights and porches, philosophies like "rain follows the plow," and mistakes and misadventures by the score; I have written at length on the complex history of energy-efficient site selection and site development, and only recently have begun to view my efforts, and those of other historians, with some unease. The success of an energy-efficient design may in the end depend less on technical expertise than on a near-perfect congruence with prevailing cultural concerns. Twentieth-century American notions of privacy, for example, explain much about energy-efficient residential design—and may explain more in the years ahead.

Not every previous generation venerated energy-efficient siting and design. The most casual drive through America reveals thousands of houses and other structures, most dating from the 1880 to 1920 period, located and designed with no apparent thought for fuel economy. Certainly, one can argue that the perfecting of coal-fired central heating, hot-water transmission devices, and even now-ignored inventions like tar paper contributed to a developing abandonment of eighteenth- and early-nineteenth-century principles. Plentiful, cheap coal burning in an effective firebox heated water or air well enough to keep the most exposed houses comfortably warmed and ventilated; sleeping porches, and soon thereafter, electric fans, made hot summer nights more bearable. But Americans sacrificed energy-efficient siting and design by choice, as well as by accident. "Our gardens have generally been too much open to

"Camouflaged and Saving Energy" appeared as "Privacy and Energy-Efficient Residential Site Design: An Example of Context" in *Journal of Architectural Education* 37, nos. 3 and 4 (Spring and Summer 1984): 20–25.

Sheds often connect northern New England farmhouses with barns, offering indoor passage in cold weather and providing a windbreak and sun trap that protects the outdoor workplace called the dooryard.

the public and to the wind," cautioned landscape architect Frank A. Waugh in his 1930 book *Everybody's Garden*. "There has been too little sun and too little friendly company. Especially has there been in our gardens too little of the domestic home life." In 1930 Waugh designed and wrote for a nation slowly rebelling against earlier notions of public and private living; twenty years later, *House Beautiful* devoted a series of issues to addressing the three design concerns of 1950: the "American Style," climate control, and privacy. At the start of the 1950s, at the beginning of the decade many designers condemn as the moment when energy-wasting became a national pastime, the *House Beautiful* editors had joined other experts in condemning an earlier era, the era berated by Waugh. What happened in American design thinking between 1880 and the mid 1920s?

Perhaps Edward Payson Powell knew the answer as early as 1900, when he published his *Hedges, Windbreaks, Shelters, and Live Fences.* "The twentieth century will open with a vastly increasing country population, all bound together with telephones and trolley roads," he remarked after noting that the great move to the city had begun to end around 1890. "A large share of business will be done by telephone. Merchants will sit in their houses one hundred miles from their stores, yet within speaking distance of their employees." Powell predicted vast metropolitan areas neither wholly suburban nor totally rural, regions occupied by people *from the city,* but searching for something new. He intended his book for

RURAL LOOKING

the newcomers, and for their landscape architects; today it is a guide-book to the age that abandoned energy-conserving site design.

Powell argued against "exclusivity," the nasty idea that the public should be excluded from private grounds. Of course, he understood that the public would not wantonly trespass on lawns and into gardens; in the new suburbs resided people far too polite for that. Instead, he argued that every passerby had the right to look at the entire house site, includ-ing the backyard. The passage of "herd laws" in the years following the Civil War precipitated the drive against exclusivity; the new laws forbade livestock owners to let cattle, pigs, and other animals roam freely. Almost overnight, rural and small town families began uprooting costly, high main-tenance fences intended to fence out straying livestock.

Down came the board fences recalled by Mark Twain in *Tom Sawyer;* down came the white, rose-covered picket fences that lined most small town residential streets. The new love of openness originated in a long-time dislike of fence maintenance perhaps, but it quickly expressed itself in lawns running between houses and streets, and flowing into the green-sward of next-door neighbors. Mass-marketing of lawn mowers accel-erated the lawn-making craze, and successful lawn-making encouraged the playing of croquet and lawn sports—and the creating of front porches intended for street watching and lawn-sport watching. No cap-sule history does justice to the intensity with which Americans destroyed fences and embraced open views.

Into the newly fenceless countryside moved the post-1890 city people in search of rural happiness. As city people, they had lived with remark-ably little outdoor privacy, if any; in the suburbs, they quickly suspected any family residing behind high walls or hedges. Not only did such walls or hedges—or fences—block the view of neighboring families, they un-doubtedly hid scandalous behavior. In the socially homogeneous suburbs, the families lived openly outdoors, and landscape architects, horticul-turists, and other designers commended such open behavior. "My own opinion of hedge fences is that they do not add to the attractiveness of the country," wrote one horticulturist to Powell. "If allowed to grow high they hide the landscape, and give an air of exclusiveness that is un-American." Over and over again, designers emphasized the fierce at-tachment to public living on private sites. One architect, writing in a 1902 issue of *Architectural Record,* insisted that the attachment had gone too far: "The American suburban resident of the present day not only likes to expose himself and his family to public view, but he has a much less commendable want of reticence about some of his domestic arrange-ments—such, for instance, as the drying of his laundry—which are not either interesting or seemly objects of public inspection." The author of

CAMOUFLAGED AND SAVING ENERGY

"The Contemporary Suburban Residence" nevertheless accepted the overall dislike of privacy and resultant openness of design. Along with so many other turn-of-the-century designers, he knew that privacy was out of fashion.

The many causes for the late-nineteenth-century turning away from privacy remain lost in the echoes of a very complex era, an era that witnessed technological change, social disruption, and economic dislocation of a magnitude much like that of our own. But the spatial consequences are evident. Fences, walls, and hedges disappeared, opening views and altering microclimates. Indeed microclimate degradation not only increased fuel consumption and made hotter hot summer days and nights— it may actually have limited the range of ornamental plants grown about houses. In the years between 1890 and 1920, American ornamental gardening seems to have fallen on hard times.

Now and then a particularly astute observer questioned the wisdom of privacy-free living and spatial openness. "There is not a little to be said for the confidence and friendliness which carry life forward so sociably in the open," remarked H. G. Dwight in "Gardens and Gardens," a 1912 *Atlantic Monthly* article that juxtaposed Italian gardens against American suburban residential streets. "Yet I never admire one of these thoroughfares without amazement at the householders who can freely throw away half of their land and all their privacy in order to make a boulevard of an indifferent highway." Dwight continued by arguing that he would sacrifice the front lawn "on the altar of public opinion," and grow "a hedge so thick and so high that my neighbors would have to go to some trouble in order to take observations of my affairs." Within the hedged land would not only flourish privacy, but a magnificent garden, something that would boggle the typical American suburbanite enamored of wide lawns. Dwight lambasted the "actual hostility toward gardens" in "a people devoted to the cult of fresh air," and "given to piazzas and 'sleeping porches'," ridiculed the common reason given for avoiding ornamental gardens (mosquitoes) and "the altruism of those who protest against walls because they prevent outsiders from enjoying one's own grounds," and finally focused on the "fear lest the rocker on the piazza be cut off from the spectacle of the street and of neighboring rockers." In one concise, hard-hitting article, Dwight scorned the existing suburban landscape and posited a better one.

Only in context does his article acquire genuine power, however, and reveal the courage of its author. In 1912, suburban Americans lived remarkably homogenized lives, trapped in a secure web of Victorian morality and behavior that endured until the chaos of the Great War and roaring twenties. Moreover, they delighted in displaying wealth in ways one economist, Thorstein Veblen, designated in 1899 as "conspicuous consumption." Veblen's *Theory of the Leisure Class* explained high-heeled shoes and front lawns in terms of wealth-advertising; the woman in heels advertised herself as too wealthy to walk far—the suburbanite mowing his lawn and discarding the clippings advertised his financial ability to pay for water, fertilizer, and machinery—and perhaps labor—to maintain something other than a vegetable garden. Suburban Americans displayed wealth in public, behaved respectably in public, and watched in public the public activities of other suburban families, all the while in supposedly private space. In such circumstances, hedges rarely flourished.

Foundation planting offers a clue to the essence of the era. American farm families traditionally planted nothing around the foundations of their houses; as late as 1940, many farmers continued the age-old custom. Foundation plants not only bred dampness, but more important, interfered with "banking the house" in autumn. Banking foundation walls with cornstalks, leaves, brush, and other material helped keep cellar and floors warm; since farmwives stored food in the unheated cellars, banking received considerable care. After 1880, suburban families began planting ornamental shrubs along foundation walls, not only to hide the high walls necessary to elevate the house above ground-level germs identified by public health authorities worried about the disease-breeding propensity of indoor plumbing, but because cellar walls stayed warm all winter. Not only did the great coal-burning furnaces make banking unnecessary, they warmed foundation walls enough to permit the growing of imported shrubs susceptible to freezing. Exotic shrubs perished when planted at the corners of wide-open lawns, but flourished when warmed by coal fires. And such low-growing shrubs blocked no views whatsoever.

In destroying walls, windbreaks, hedges, and other impediments to the open suburban lifestyle, Americans constricted their gardening capabilities. But as Dwight, Powell, and other mavericks argued, the suburbanites also harmed their recreational capabilities. Dwight suggested that the popularity of country clubs and mountain or sea-shore vacations might originate in the uselessness of suburban houselots for summer recreation. Powell went even further, stating bluntly that women needed to rest more frequently, and ought to have outdoor places adapted to relaxation. "Woman has a right to such retreats, sheltered from the sun, and peculiarly her own," he emphasized. "She does the hardest work— fretting, nerve-wearing work." He described one such retreat, "a circle of arbor-vitae, fifteen or twenty feet in diameter, and grown together overhead," with the inner branches cut out up to a height of fifteen feet. Furnished with a writing desk, a few chairs, and a hammock, the nook adapts to many purposes—a place to relax while watching a baby, a place for a tea party, a place to read or sleep. "Woman needs her particular flower nook, where she can work a little, rest a little, think a little, and sleep in a hammock if she likes," he concluded.

In an age of incipient feminism, in a period before Virginia Woolf argued that every woman needs a room of her own in order to acquire true independence of thought, Powell had deciphered one frightening meaning implicit in the open suburban landscape. Women continuously on view lacked a hundred options—including dozing on wash day. The open suburban landscape sapped human individuality and human potential as surely as it altered the consumption of fuel energy.

In the 1920s a number of forces combined to reorient American thinking. As early as 1902, the anonymous *Architectural Record* writer knew that "the great need of the average suburb is something more of the atmosphere and flavor of rural life, a more intelligent attempt to individualize each separate house and grounds," and while he feared that "it is improbable that American neighborliness will ever consent to the complete separation both from the passers-by and each other which the foreign suburban resident likes," he nevertheless hoped that "screens, both of brick and foliage, will be much more freely used than at present." Ever smaller lot sizes simply made suburbs almost too public, so long as residents eschewed fences and hedges. But new activities prompted the creation of screens—of brick and of plants.

A host of changes conspired to destroy the old openness of suburban life simply by increasing its publicity to the breaking point. The automobile brought strangers onto suburban streets, and produced enough noise and fumes to drive many front-porch observers into backyard chairs. Telephones and, later, radios, changed notions of conversation and audio-privacy. But the impact of such devices, great as it seems in retrospect, pales beside the impact of behavorial change. By the mid-1920s, Victorian sensibility no longer ruled urban or suburban America; housewives no longer carelessly displayed their laundry to the world, for they worried about the effect of revealing risqué lingerie. Americans slowly discovered the healthfulness of sunbathing, too; by the 1930s houses had not only sprouted "solariums" for wintertime enjoyment of sunny days, but suburbanites, and particularly women, were lying in backyards in ever more revealing bathing suits. Almost imperceptibly, suburban life shifted from front porch to backyard, from openness to semi-privacy. No longer was "the yard" open to casual view from the street now filled with strangers, although it remained semi-open to neighbor's eyes. And equally imperceptibly, the microclimate changed.

The Great Depression quickened the suburban reorientation to

A new porch planted with grapevines admits sunlight in spring and fall, warming the outdoor relaxation and work area.

private living, largely by making suburbanites anxious to hide their relative wealth from the unemployed and poverty-stricken. Until the early 1930s, the American rich and middle class proudly displayed its finery; indeed until the great financial panic of 1893, the typical wealthy manufacturer or speculator built on a hilltop overlooking his factory or on a well-frequented urban boulevard or suburban road. Only after the massive financial smash of the early 1890s did the rich begin to relocate away from angry workingmen, moving to Newport in Rhode Island, to the new coastal resorts of Florida and California, and to other secluded places. And the rich began to live behind walls and gates, to travel less ostentatiously, to appear less flamboyantly in public. After 1932, the era of the flamboyant rich ended, as F. Scott Fitzgerald, the author of *The Great Gatsby* and other novels, understood. But the typical suburban family withdrew as well, knowing that the vast number of American families could not afford detached houses on large lots of land. Depression-era deprivation lies behind the GI Bill of Rights, of course; veterans of World War II knew that they would be able to realize their wildest dreams and build or buy new houses in the automobile suburbs. Between 1945 and 1955, it seemed to many experts that the veterans and their families were turning away from the private living and private spatial design that characterized the Depression, but the experts soon understood their mistake.

All sorts of domestic gardening prospered in the Depression. Families unable to afford much travel and other away-from-home recreation settled down to eke out food budgets by growing vegetables in larger and larger gardens, and by enjoying ornamental gardening too. Perhaps some of the fencing and hedging evolved from a desire to protect vegetable plots from thieves, but more likely, the improved microclimate stimulated the gardening efforts. The backyard surrounded by hedges or fences proved a veritable Eden, a place free from devastating winds, a place with sunny nooks enjoyable in spring and autumn, a place with shade for humid summer days. In such yards many children grew up, and the men—and sometimes the women—who fought in World War II recalled the yards when they moved to the much satirized suburbs of "ticky-tacky" houses on scarcely graded lots.

In hindsight, the speculator-built suburbs indeed reflected an age of cheap energy. Houses oriented only toward streets, no windbreaks, no insulation, no awnings or porches, the list of energy-efficient details forgotten; scarcely one speculator appears to have oriented houses according to sunlight patterns or prevailing winds. At first, the brand-new suburban "developments" boasted vast open areas; yards flowed one into another, lawns stretched along whole streets. But once the newcomers overcame the financial difficulties of furnishing their houses, perhaps buying a second car, the landscape improvements began. *House Beautiful* responded to the needs of a new generation of suburbanites beset by vexing difficulties. How does a porchless house respond to summer sun? Where does one locate the barbecue pit for early spring enjoyment? What can be done to provide immediate shade for summer days? In the many 1949 and 1950 issues devoted to matters of microclimate modification, *House Beautiful* published one of the finest series of technical articles ever presented to clients and designers, a series as useful now as then, a series including articles on energy-efficient houses *and* sites for all parts of the country. By the early 1960s the typical suburban street still reflected the love of public front lawns Dwight derided in 1912, but the new backyards, all closely surrounded by cedar screen fences, hedges, or other defenses against wind and prying eyes, demonstrated a genuine change in attitude.

The large-lot American suburb of the middle 1960s fascinated every sort of expert; indeed it fascinated the American public, for news media emphasized it as the American dream come true. The landscape historian who scrutinizes the documents of the era—*Look* devoted almost all of its May 16, 1967, issue to "A Report on Suburbia: The Good Life in Our Exploding Utopia," for example—sees in the photographs not only the blossoming outdoor life of cookouts and pool parties, but a proliferation of fences and other privacy devices. To be sure, the fences and hedges derive from the urge to control microclimate; even the advent of cheap window air conditioners did not stop the rush to summer outdoor coolness. But clearly the suburbanites had quickly abandoned the openness of their pioneering years and begun walling off their backyards.

The walling-off continues, along with an ever faster retreat from the street. Indeed the 1950s suburban house often featured a picture window facing the street; through the plate glass the family gazed at a homogenized social environment while passersby gazed at family life perfected. By the middle 1960s the window had been curtained, and on new houses faced the backyard filled with ever newer recreational devices like sundecks and gasgrills, screenhouses and pool cabanas. Exactly as the *House Beautiful* editors predicted, microclimate modification for fuel efficiency triumphed only when designers proved to clients that the microclimate modification furthered recreational use of outdoor space while increasing family privacy. In January of 1950 alone, *House Beautiful* published *six* articles on the combination of microclimate modification and privacy: "Fences That Stop the Eye—But Not the Breeze"; "How Privacy Can Increase Your Living Space and Improve Your Climate"; "Do the Neighbors Know Your Business?"; "How to Make the Neighbors Disappear"; "Your Own House can be Your Best Privacy Device If It's Arranged Right"; and "Good Living Is *Not* Public Living." The articles speak clearly to the homeowner—and the architect and landscape architect—of the 1980s.

Energy conservation cannot by itself create good design. As any successful professional designer knows, good design addresses scores of issues; focusing on one concern leads eventually to catastrophe. But consider the plight of the American homeowner today, or even more pointedly, the client about to commission a house and site design. What information guides the client in relating energy issues to issues of recreational use of space—particularly gardening—and privacy, for example? Assume that the client's house faces south, directly onto a busy street. Where does the client install a solar room, a greenhouse, even a glass wall if he or she chooses privacy above energy concerns? It is here that the architect and landscape architect supersede the engineer, for the question involves knowing vastly more than purely technical information about sun inclinations. Since the 1920s, Americans have been following a path toward ever more private living, a path rarely studied by scholars—including historians—but one of immense significance for the design professions. A growing urge for privacy may be one of the most significant issues in understanding the decay of the nation's cities as well as in implementing successful urban design. A growing urge for privacy may explain the proliferation of backyard swimming pools and the simultaneous abandonment of public pools. A growing urge for privacy may bedevil most condominium developments, most high-rise apartment developments, most public housing developments. Indeed, if the American public is silently but decisively opting for more privacy, especially more outdoor privacy, then the large-lot suburban house may beckon ever more strongly. Energy scarcity may combine with the urge for privacy to create the wonderfully delightful, Italian-like garden spaces Dwight predicted decades ago. Perhaps Powell understood the sensuous pleasure of the walled yard better than most designers writing at the turn of the century, but there is no doubt that he speaks for our time as well.

Energy-efficient design—from the design of a house site to the design of a condominium unit to the design of a low-rise office complex—exists in an ever more intricate context of aesthetic and behavioral change. Privacy is only one element in the context, but a powerful one indeed; if present patterns endure, American designers will increasingly encounter privacy as a crucial element in the success of energy-efficient design.

RURAL LOOKING

HOBGOBLIN IN SUBURBIA

Origins of Contemporary Place Consciousness

What *is* the spirit of the place, the *genius loci* landscape architects honor by creating "sensitive" site designs? Is it the mood of a locale, the feel of a particular spot, something quantified by visual assessment specialists? Is it a figure of speech only, or is the spirit real, but masked by time and language? "An old house," writes Gaston Bachelard in *The Poetics of Space,* "is a geometry of echoes." Is the old copse, the old garden, the old landscape the haunt of shadowy figures still shaping design? Why *do* we knock on wood?

Pan's Progeny

Bits and pieces of answers lie nearly two millennia back, shrouded in vaguely sinister mystery. Christianity clashed successfully with the major Greek and Roman deities and later with the gods of northern Europe; Zeus and Thor vanished into perpetual limbo. "Great Pan is dead," Plutarch recorded in *De defectu oraculorum* near the end of the first Christian century, but the tens of thousands of *genii loci* lived on. These were the spirits of particular places who once had served their great overlord Pan, in part by translating the language of inhuman things into human speech. Translation is significant; unlike the American Indians, who understood the voice of a cedar, a swamp, or a hilltop, the European peasants encountered ethereal creatures who spoke for trees, groves, fields, and streams. All over Europe, *shellygoat, fear dearg, fachan,* and a whole legion of similar creatures lived—snugly attached to specific locales, sometimes demanding obeisance from neighboring humans, sometimes enjoying the obscurity of wilderness.

Slowly, inexorably, the Church converted the spirits into imps, helpers of the new devil that lurked in forests and mountains, waiting to overrun Christian villages. Pan died, indeed, but he returned to Europe as Satan, leader of the Wild Hunt that coursed through forests on May Day Eve. Peasants and travelers instructed by parish priests to shun the spir-

"Hobgoblin in Suburbia: Origins of Contemporary Place Consciousness" appeared in *Landscape Architecture* 73 (November/December 1983): 54–61.

its learned to hate them; the spirits themselves, angered by the shift of allegiance, grew silent.

Pan's death and subsequent transmutation altered the European view of the natural environment. "No river contains a spirit, no tree is the life principle of a man, no snake the embodiment of wisdom, no mountain cave the home of a great demon," muses the psychologist Carl Gustav Jung in *Man and His Symbols*. "No voices now speak to man from stones, plants and animals, nor does he speak to them believing they can hear. His contact with nature has gone, and with it the profound emotional energy that this symbolic connection supplied." Artists, too, recognize the importance of the death of Pan. Most recently, Janet Bleicken has scrutinized the transmutation; her painting, "The Adversary," emphasizes the impoverishment of music that accompanied the change.

Not everyone scorned the spirits of the other realm, the denizens of faerie. What in pre-Christian times had been proper religious behavior, what in the late middle ages had been blasphemous, immoral activity, by the eighteenth and nineteenth centuries became more or less superstitious practice. On Sunday, the European peasant worshipped properly; during the workweek he acknowledged the spirits of the Old Religion. He tossed a coin into a ford before crossing, or into a well before wishing; he placed tiny wheat breads in the first furrow of newly plowed fields. On All Hallow's Eve he made a crude lantern from a gourd or squash, lit a candle in it, and placed it outdoors, honoring Jack-of-the-Lantern, a spirit inclined to uproot boundary markers. The more pious individuals feared the rejected local spirits and attempted to ward off the uninvited by placing iron, especially horseshoes, outside their houses, by decorating with crosses and crucifixes and by keeping handy a sprig of St. Johns-wort.

The *hobgoblin,* alone, maintained his central importance in the early, modern pantheon of lingering Old Religion spirits. He kept alive householding traditions from both the classical world and from pagan northern Europe.

Ancient Greeks and Romans invested the house with intense religious meaning, for the house shielded the family altar, the hearth stone on which a sacrificial fire burned continuously. "What is there more holy, what is there more carefully fenced round with every description of religious respect, than the house of each individual citizen?" asked Cicero. "Here is his altar, here is his hearth, here are his household gods; here all his sacred rights, all his religious ceremonies, are preserved." In Roman tradition, according to Ovid, the household gods kept away burglars; in Roman law, they shunned other household gods. A Roman act forbade houses to touch each other; the walls of houses could be no less than two feet apart, and the ribbonlike zone stood consecrated to the "god of the enclosure." Within the house lot, and particularly within the house itself, a family worshipped gods wholly private, wholly unique.

Far north of Greece and Rome, the so-called barbarians evolved a parallel belief structure focused on the single-family house. Since few barbarians left written records, documents compiled by missionaries who were determined to erase the Old Religion offer the only clues to the existence of house spirits, now called *kobold* by Germans, *puck* or hobgoblin by the British. Belief in kobold and hobgoblin endured into the eighteenth century, perhaps later, and struck some educated inquirers as the vestige of an older, more intimate understanding of nature. Typically defined as small, shaggy male creatures clothed in ragged garments, most hobgoblins moved about houses at night, unseen. They nibbled at cooked food, sipped milk or beer, and occasionally appropriated a fragment of cloth. They performed useful tasks too, often aiding poor or elderly people or lonely, distressed maidens; contemporary Americans may dimly recall a nursery tale centered on three helpful elves aiding a poverty-stricken shoemaker. If insulted, however, the creatures could work all sorts of minor mischief, from souring milk to stymying churning. Clearly, the house spirit of Germany and the British Isles lacked the predominance accorded to Greek and Roman family gods, but hobgoblin, nevertheless, had a defined position in household life as a half-human, half-spirit creature whose presence reminded family members of other realms.

Peasants firmly believed that spirits could take on animal form. Dogs and cats, kept as watchdogs and mousers, often sensed the presence of hobgoblins. Sometimes, however, the animals themselves were spirits, and the strange dog or cat which walked indoors unbidden attracted penetrating scrutiny. Witchcraft focused the whole issue of animals-as-disguise. The witch, having renounced Christianity, gained some of the ancient ability to see and converse with spirits. The witch's "familiar," usually a black cat or crow, might be a disguised spirit; more frequently, the familiar acted as messenger and translator. Clerics called the spirits devils, of course, and judges burned or hanged the witches; black cats, crows, bats, toads, and other hapless creatures became suspect in the eyes of pious peasants. Other peasants respected such animals rather than feared them; a cricket chirping indoors in winter meant nothing but good luck. Such folk shirked from killing a bat or spider; it might be a spirit visiting the hobgoblin of the house, or it might be hobgoblin himself.

Around 1650, therefore, two distinct attitudes characterized European belief in spirits. On the one hand was the attitude expressed in Shakespeare's *A Midsummer Night's Dream,* in which one character says, "Those that Hobgoblin call you, and sweet Puck, / You do their work, and they shall have good luck." On the other was that expressed in John Bunyan's Puritan tract of 1678, *Of Pilgrim's Progress:* "Now he saw the Hobgoblins, and Satyrs, and the Dragons of the Pit." One attitude was casual, almost relaxed; the other, strained, the product of fervent, nearly fanatic fear of all spirits. Believers in hobgoblin believed also in God, of course, and certainly renounced the Devil and many lesser spirits of wilderness and field; they put iron above doorways to keep out such spirits, secure in the knowledge that a friendly, *familiar* spirit lived within, a spirit *of the family.*

New World Spirits

No leprechauns crossed the Atlantic and few hobgoblins. The "little people," say aged Irish-Americans, feared the ocean passage; genii loci from other lands proved no more courageous. Scant evidence exits of migrating German or French place spirits, and while Swedes and Finns in Delaware read incantations before felling trees—on the chance that protective place spirits might reside among the roots—colonial diarists and other contemporaneous recorders of popular usage make no mention of immigrant spirits. But something lived in New World forests, something Puritans and other colonists loathed.

Not all conflict between settlers and Indians involved military activity. Within a few years of colonization, Indian medicine men worked magic against the white newcomers, and by the mid-seventeenth century, the power of sorcerers terrified all colonists. "Upon the arrival of the English in these parts," related Cotton Mather in 1702 in his *Magnalia Christi Americana,* "the Indians employed their sorcerers, whom they call powaws, like Balaam, to curse them, and let loose their demons upon them, to shipwreck them, to distract them, to poison them, or in any way ruin them." The late-seventeenth-century witchcraft hysteria at Salem and lesser incidents elsewhere often involved native place spirits leagued with Indian sorcerers or with the Devil himself. As tribe after tribe of Indians withered, the colonists began to consider the place spirits as the angry ghosts of the former occupants of the land—exterminated both accidentally and deliberately.

Everywhere in the colonies, although particularly in New England and in western areas settled by New Englanders, the house became a fortification against supernatural creatures as well as against Indians. Worried colonists were aware that unknown, angry place spirits still haunted the forest. No colonial family enjoyed the protection of a friendly hobgoblin who watched over the homestead.

Protecting the house against violation by supernatural spirits preoccupied few colonists, however, simply because wolves, Indians, French soldiers, and many other more palpable dangers required immediate attention, and because the typical American colonist looked to the future, not to the past. Colonists had deserted their village heritage, risked a dangerous ocean passage, and lived in a dangerous land that rewarded only hard, continuous work. A nation of immigrants rarely honors place and place spirits; after all, such a nation is composed of people who honored place and spirit very little in the old country.

Nevertheless, the vestigial belief in place spirits, and particularly in hobgoblins, proved powerful enough to shape American culture. Even today, Americans knock on wood to inform the listening spirits that everything attempted by humans requires the help, or at least the nonintervention, of hobgoblins, elves, or other creatures. "We'll make a fortune with this idea, touch wood," is an expression charged with medieval belief. But in a land without house spirits or friendly place spirits, knocking on wood may be a way of placating every angry spirit of another race, another time. Those who think otherwise should examine the fierce attachment of Americans to their homes and particularly to freestanding suburban houses sited on large lots.

The Suburban Shrine

"The language of a ruder age has given to common law the maxim that every man's house is his castle," mused Emerson in the middle of the nineteenth century. "The progress of truth will make every house a shrine." His essay entitled "Domestic Life" emphasized that the shrine would honor beauty, a privately nurtured, privately enjoyed beauty. Emerson spoke for his age; writer after writer emphasized that the home should be a bulwark against all of the evils of the outer world. No longer, of course, did authors speak about the angry spirits of trees or marshes; the new evils, largely urban and industrial, ranged from alcoholism to prostitution to atheism. What is of great significance is this: almost all of the reformers were clergymen or closely associated with religious movements, and they feared that traditional Christianity could not successfully confront modern evils—unless it had in every home a sort of shrine.

In much of the literature, and perhaps in daily life, religion became a household affair. While the farmer might pray as he walked behind his plow, the factory hand surrounded by madly spinning belts, wheels, and levers could not. Thus, the house became a shrine, a place of rest, meditation, and prayer. The literature of home life was complex indeed; whole volumes focused on the role of wife and mother, the angel who kept the house beautiful and pure; other works emphasized home prayer or proper child-rearing practices or correct diet. And much of it—surprisingly much of it—concerned the physical design of the house and yard.

Privacy was the key concept in the literature of home life. "The home ought not to be open to the casual eye, or the secrets of it liable to the prying or the propinquity of neighbors," asserted John Ware, a New York Protestant clergyman-reformer. "Every family should be brought up distinct from every other family. The house should be within an enclosure sacred to it." His *Home Life—What It Is and What It Needs* emphasized the necessity of a freestanding house: "To the well ordering of a family, privacy is absolutely essential. What chance is there for that, where houses stand so near that, through the open windows, inevitably, you hear much that is said, or through a thin partition comes the thrumming of a piano, the scolding of a mother, the crying of the child, the entrance and exit of every guest?" Ware coined the term "home-spirit" to designate the correct sort of family living; while he had not the slightest desire to conjure up hobgoblin or kobold, he understood that a happy home indeed exudes or possesses a sort of spirit and that, as in ancient Rome, that spirit must not be scarred by touching another.

Certainly the insistence on the freestanding house was derived, in part, from the American agricultural experience, but the literature of home life suggests that reformers valued privacy for another reason. In the freestanding house and yard, the family might create not only a moral order, but a place of beauty. This equation of morality and beauty was fundamentally important, because the nineteenth-century American housewife—not farmwife—had increasingly less to do. Labor-saving machines enabled the housewife to enjoy more and more leisure time, and home life reformers counseled her to devote the hours to creating a home that would soothe her husband, wearied by industrial and commercial sordidness, and would mold her children's view of the outside world.

The old-fashioned parlor best exemplifies the equation of morality and religion. The parlor, made beautiful by horse-hair-stuffed furniture, a carpet tacked down over fresh straw, one or two tinted lithographs, and a patent lamp and stove—existed for such religious events as funerals and weddings and visits by the minister. Only gradually did the love of beauty as a reinforcement of morality begin to spill into the kitchen and into the yard, as home life reformers advised families to "beautify" every part of the home.

A few reformers turned their attention first to farm families. In an 1876 agricultural fair address, landscape architect Donald G. Mitchell told his audience to add porches, install window boxes for flowers, and furnish parlors for "good, honest, every-day enjoyment." These and other beautifications would create a "cheery, comely air which educates the young, and which contents the old." But farmwives, already burdened by massive housekeeping and produce-processing tasks, proved slow to make such improvements; instead, suburban wives championed home beautification as a way of saving husbands and children from the evils of urban industrialism. Between 1880 and 1925, an outpouring of garden philosophy books stressed the morality implicit in the beautiful suburban "estate"; perhaps Mabel Wright's *The Garden of a Commuter's Wife* best represents the literature. The book details the building of a suburban garden, but emphasizes the almost spiritual nature of the "uplift" the garden provides to the harried, commuting husband. Wright speaks frequently of the "Familiar Spirit," which whispers in her ear guidance concerning her attitude toward city and garden. Certainly the spirit is no hobgoblin, but rather a sort of invisible genius loci anxious to make suburban life a success. And the commuter's wife does succeed in creating a garden that soothes, even after nightfall: "It is quite dark now when he comes home, so we carry a flash lantern when he takes his after-dinner cigar walk, that we may neither run into trees nor fall into the new violet frame while we tell of the day's work." By 1914, children's magazines were advertising not just doll houses, but doll houses with gardens—little girls were being taught the importance of shaping the entire home space.

Wright's book of 1901, J. P. Mowbray's *A Journey to Nature* of the same year, the anonymously published *Garden in the Wilderness* of 1909, Julia H. Cummin's *My Garden Comes of Age* of 1926, and scores of others emphasize a powerful attachment to small, three-acres-and-under suburban home-places. The literature is important not only because it explains the origin of so many still-admired suburban home gardens, but because it explicates the pro-suburban feeling that made possible planned suburbs like Forest Hills Gardens and Shaker Heights, developments intended by landscape architects—and speculators—to fulfill the new desire to create home-places free of urban evil. Running through the literature of home-place as shrine of moral beauty are two lesser themes, however, both of which illuminate the enduring nature of hobgoblin.

In the 1880s, in the suburbs, dogs entered the American family heart. Mabel Wright spoke joyously of dogs assisting her in her garden work, of having a "dog's soft nose" at her elbow in the dining room, of dogs accompanying her on long autumn walks. Dog mania developed partly from a new love of all animals—*The Garden in the Wilderness* devoted some attention to the garden turtle—but largely from a new love of a distinctly suburbanized nature. Not rural, not wild, decidedly not urban,

Despite the drudgery of laundry day, many newly arrived suburban women loved walking outdoors on a sunny day to tend drying lines rigged inside an attractive backyard.

suburban nature existed as a semi-controlled, semi-formal ecosystem in which cows, foxes, and pigeons played little part. No longer was the dog a cowherd or watchdog; it existed to warm its owner's heart, to play with children freed from agricultural chores. "The owning of my first dog made me into a conscious sentient person, fiercely possessive, anxiously watchful, and woke in me that long ache of pity for animals, and for all inarticulate beings, which nothing has ever stilled," remarked Edith Wharton in *A Backward Glance,* her 1949 autobiography of a late-1860s, upperclass childhood experience that was common within two decades. The same age that produced so many books devoted to ways in which the home-place could be made a shrine to moral beauty also produced an extensive literature of dog stories. From Jack London's *Call of the Wild* and *White Fang* to Thomas C. Hinkle's *Tawny,* the novels and short stories depicted thinking, feeling dogs, dogs with near human personalities. In the suburbs, such dogs enjoyed lives of ease, wandering aimlessly over clipped lawns and through backyard gardens, and napping in winter before roaring fires.

Open fire is the second of the lesser themes that unifies so much turn-of-the-century home-place literature. In the suburbs, stressed writers, the freestanding house offered the joys of fireplaces; despite the era's devotion to central heating, the open fire remained a powerful amenity, one that became more important as the decades passed. "The open fire lights the open book with a glow of peculiar cheer and friendliness," remarked Hamilton Wright Mabie in 1896. "It seems to search out whatever of human warmth lies at the root of a man's thought, and to kindle it with a kindred heat." Mabie's *My Study Fire* explored the psychological advantages of a fireplace fire as the focal point for family life. Filled with digressions on driftwood as fuel, the building of an enlarged hearth, and the sound of the flame on windy days, it epitomized the suburbanite's joy in a roaring fire. Mabel Wright, along with other home-place writers of the period, described the pleasures of reading seed and bulb catalogs next to a crackling blaze. In an age suddenly aware that central heat dispersed family members to many rooms, nostalgia for the open fire of pre–cast iron stove days prompted dozens of writers to emphasize the moral beauty of a well-laid fire. The blaze created in winter the "cheery, comely air" produced in summer by the blossoming garden. Fireplace and garden, both morally beautiful, soothed the nerves of commuting husbands and instructed children in the ideals of home life—and both were the delights of the well-behaved dog.

Out of John Ware's insistence that privacy was the key to a proper home life evolved an entire philosophy of the home-place and its attendant "spirit." Compounded of residential segregation, space to create delightful interiors and gardens, space for a dog and a fireplace, the new philosophy prospered in an age of urban and industrial complexity, and it "elevated" American women from housewife to homemaker. The clean, orderly, beautiful house and yard became an island around which swirled the dangerous currents of twentieth-century life.

Creativity's Last Resort

After World War II, the philosophy changed subtly but significantly. Urban dwellers fled decaying cities for now well-known reasons, including a federal mortgage program that made single-family houses especially attractive to newly married veterans. The urge for privacy, for a secure refuge from an increasingly turbulent world, grew stronger and gathered force from changing habits of American work.

How many families deserted cities out of fear of the atomic bomb will never be accurately known, but buried in the popular lore, half-hidden in *Saturday Evening Post* articles, is enough information to suggest that many adults realized that cities had become ground zero. Escaping to the suburbs meant fleeing back in time to the pre-war security of

Main Street. Living in the suburbs meant living in a *privacy,* for centuries ago, the word denoted not a state of being, i.e., aloneness, but the *place* of aloneness. Given the rudimentary public understanding of atomic horror, parents sincerely believed that being twenty miles from target might well protect themselves, their children, and their property from a force as satanic as any that charged through the medieval night.

At the same time, fewer and fewer Americans worked at jobs in which they shaped space. The bank teller might place a vase or tiny statue at his or her window, but repainting the counter was beyond imagination; the secretary could no more rebuild a desk than the assembly-line worker could design a pneumatic wrench. The suburban house became not only a refuge from newly discovered horror, therefore, but the last resort of creativity. Painting a room—or the whole house exterior—or adding a window or transplanting yews meant the exercising of the fundamental human need to shape space, to make beautiful the space around them. As A. C. Spectorsky pointed out in his 1955 *The Exurbanites,* not all new-comers to suburbia, even far-out suburbia, did such work themselves; indeed, according to William H. Whyte's *The Organization Man* of a year later, not all newcomers chose to live in single-family houses. But Holly-wood thought otherwise, and as early as 1948, when Cary Grant and Myrna Loy starred in *Mr. Blandings Builds His Dream House,* the American public learned that life in the post-war suburbs meant a grand adventure into do-it-yourself land, a land much different from air-cooled offices in glass-skinned towers or from windowless factories.

And what of hobgoblin, the ancient genius loci, or even the turn-of-the-century "spirit of home"? What of horseshoes and St. Johns-wort, flower gardens and dogs? Both ancient tradition and modern philos-ophy converged in the post-war suburb.

American suburbanites invested house and yard with extraordinary emotional significance. The family real estate represented the only gen-uine financial investment; in an age of installment buying, a new car every year, and credit cards, only the house and land appreciated in value. Then, too, the house displayed the family love of order, of beauty, of morality, of the suburban good life; the well-mowed lawn, the clipped hedges, the stranger-guiding lamppost, the backyard barbecue grill, pool, and swingset spoke volumes about their family owners.

Throughout the '50s and '60s, professional designers often laughed at the imitation antique furniture, the rigidly rectilinear planting, the plastic elves and flamingos that characterized so many suburban homes of all social classes. Only rarely did they attempt to understand the vital philosophical and psychological forces that produced the objects scat-tered about lawns and gardens. They ignored the continuing significance

RURAL LOOKING

of the family dog, the creature that links humans with wild animals; the notion that suburban living is incomplete without a close relationship with an intelligent animal presaged the environmental awakening of the 1960s and '70s. Designers ignored the importance of the barbecue grill and the complex customs surrounding its use; but the fire of charcoal briquets, the splashing of steak sauce, the smell of hickory smoke reflected a renewed desire to enjoy a traditional hearth. The suburban house and yard provided an illusionary retreat from urban and international crisis and a genuine laboratory for spatial manipulation.

The '50s and '60s house and yard also provided an enduring habitat for the reincarnated hobgoblin, the gnome or elf or dwarf that suddenly appeared everywhere in suburbia. The plastic lawn ornaments, descended from the rare carved stone or cast iron garden sculpture of the late nineteenth century, continue to sell well in a variety of styles. In some neighborhoods, the inquiring observer finds plastic gnomes lurking beside plastic birdbaths; in others, one discovers a bronze dwarf and frog nestled in a viewing garden. What explains the resurgence of pagan statuary?

Love of personal space, of family plants and structure, grew deeper in the post–atomic bomb years, perhaps as the planet seemed suddenly so fragile. The long estrangement of occidental people from the spirits of the earth, as remarked by Jung, began to end with the deepening fear of nuclear holocaust. For the pious, particularly for Catholics, a statue of a saint in the garden protected the home-place. For the less formally devout, the dwarf or gnome played a similar role, becoming a sort of protector of tranquility, a bringer of magic.

All these gnomes, elves, dwarfs, and similar creatures are descended from the ancient classical god Priapus, the god of gardens worshipped by Greeks and Romans. The ithyphallic god long ago defended gardens everywhere in the Empire; gardeners set statues of him to warn trespassers of threatened rape. Priapus was indeed a major deity, a sort of overarching genius loci close in power to Pan himself; he guarded well the classical garden and the Roman notion of the sanctity of *private* space which reinforced family identity. Hobgoblin is perhaps his near contemporary; certainly the scarecrow is his most common descendant, although harvest figures made of pumpkins and clothes stuffed with cornstalks are related to him as well. But the plastic, bronze, cast iron, and— far more rare—antique cast plaster gnomes are part of his lineage too, and deserve the scrutiny of landscape architects.

Four centuries after occupation by transplanted Europeans, it seems that the little people have begun colonizing the New World. Perhaps the Indian spirits have finally departed, perhaps the gentle philosophy espoused by Ware, Wright, Mabie, and others has made hobgoblin welcome. Perhaps the fierce love of suburbanites for their island paradises has attracted the genii loci from another continent, another time. Out of the cryptic mix of barbecues, dogs, hedges, fireplaces, fences, and free-standing houses and gardens is evolving a new understanding of the place or house spirit, the contemporary genius loci that suggests the possibility of a new golden age of small, private gardens. Landscape architects might ponder the maturing American love of small-scale outdoor space, a love every bit as strong as the much noticed love of vast forests and mountain ranges. They might think less about open space and more about privacies. Indeed, they might think very deeply about the relation of individuals and families to small pieces of handcrafted land. If landscape architects fail to hear the geometry of echoes, they may at least glimpse the fleeting shadow of hobgoblins.

Selected References

Jacob and Wilhelm Grimm, *German Folk Tales* (1857), trans. by Francis P. Magoun and Alexander H. Krappe (Carbondale, 1960).
C. G. Jung, *Alchemical Studies,* trans. by R. F. C. Hull (Princeton, 1967).
John R. Stilgoe, *Common Landscape of America, 1580 to 1845* (New Haven, 1982).
Jan Vries, *Altgermanische Religions-geschichte* (Berlin, 1956).
Eurwyn Williams, "The Protection of the House: Some Iconographic Evidence from Wales," *Folklore,* 89 (1978) 148–153.

CONTEMPORARY SPACE

Contemporary landscape defies casual interpretation. In all but the most isolated, often poverty-stricken, rural places, landscape exists as maddeningly complex. Components as seemingly innocuous as up-to-date electric lines or newly asphalted roads transform landscapes that hitherto seemed set pieces from another era. But the pace of living frustrates observation too. Just looking around, absorbing details of landscape in half-conscious ways, becomes difficult when speeding vehicles or beeping cell phones interrupt. In the end, expectation often mars interpretation.

Landscapes strike many observers as disjointed, muddled, or worse simply because observers want landscapes to be otherwise. Defining wants precisely often involves analyzing what theorists call the vehicle of landscape analysis. For theorists, the vehicle might be semiotics, literary theory, or something far more arcane, but a simpler approach frequently proves more useful. A vehicle might be an Amtrak first-class car towering above High Plains rails, an intercity bus stalled in ring-road traffic, or an automobile negotiating city streets on Saturday night. Mass-transportation vehicles, and subsequently the automobile, transformed the ways observers of landscape move through landscape, and often prevent observers from meeting each other in serendipitous ways.

Vehicles punctuate most landscapes. Sometimes moving, sometimes parked, automobiles, trucks, and, to a lesser extent, trains dot and scribble industrial color and design into landscapes dominated by plants. In rural areas, especially ones beset by poverty or frugality, many vehicles stand immobile, useful for nothing more than spare parts or as shelter for sheep, ducks, and other small livestock. Abandoned automobiles become the vehicle by which observers classify other machines, especially farm and construction equipment. At some point, machines become so massive that they morph into structures of a sort defying easy analysis. Glass-lined farm silos, winter-wheat elevators, and gravel conveyors acquire traits urban observers see in vertical-lift, bascule draw, and other moveable bridges. Machine or structure, such devices often annoy observers who seek the reassurance of traditional landscape but find solar panels atop traditional farmhouses and electricity-generating windmills adjacent to traditional barns. Far too rarely do landscape observers realize that machines make the rural landscape, and that without tractors, combines, bulldozers, bicycles, automobiles, and trucks, even snowmobiles, much landscape would remain wilderness or revert to wilderness.

Ordinary or common landscape, especially everyday rural landscape, deceives in part because city-based experts see urban sprawl devouring it. But large-scale landscape, rural or mining or managed forest, has brutally powerful ways of altering the urban fabric reaching across it. What results proves neither metropolitan nor suburban, but something resembling both traditional small towns surrounded by large-scale farming landscapes and the edges of small, mid-twentieth-century cities. As is not surprising, many devotees of landscape interpretation prefer to examine locations already densely developed. Such places prove easier to study, at least in some ways, chiefly because they lack the spatial potential for vast and sudden change. But complex weather happens when fronts collide, and finding the edges of different landscapes often draws the observer into the most intricate spatial and structural confusions imaginable.

LANDSCAPE JELLIES, LANDSCAPE JAMS

Landscape preservationists might profit from reading old cookbooks. Consider the designations applied to put-up food, and particularly the distinction between preserves and conserves. By *preserve,* the housewives understood large pieces of fruit canned in thick syrup, sometimes slightly jellied; by *conserve,* they understood a fancy jam made from a mixture of fruits, usually including some citrus ones, especially orange or lemon. A preserve topped ice cream and other confections; a conserve, being far more runny, topped cakes, perhaps.

Landscape is not some delicate jelly graced with suspended bits of citrus fruits. It is jam, made from ground or crushed fruits and seeds, unable to hold its shape, forever dripping from cake or bread. And the richest of landscapes are the conserves of landscape, jam still, but jam made seductive with a mixture of fruits, including the pieces of citrus hidden in the sweet murk. Mistake not the metaphor. Contemporary landscape preservationists delight in rare jellies, savoring the Olmsted and Jenney Parks, the Steele and Farrand gardens, the Monticellos. Certainly the educated public evidences a growing intrigue with such jellies, an interest already not without crises. But *jam* no longer delights the ear. In American English the word connotes clogged highways, not put-up sweetness.

If the landscape preservation movement continues on its present course of finding and savoring jellies, it will slowly but surely collapse. It is the jam of landscape, not the jelly, that deserves attention, and the conserves of landscape that demand it. Consider South Park in Buffalo. Olmsted-designed and now somewhat changed—it presently hosts a golf course—its circuit drive survives, as does much of its original planting. It is a jelly, not very clear perhaps, but a jelly. It holds its shape, is of roughly one chronological consistency (excepting the golf course), and indeed deserves the attention it receives from Buffalo's preservation-minded groups working to fulfill Olmsted's dream of an arboretum of indigenous North American trees. Assuming the millions are raised and properly spent—under the direction of properly trained landscape preservation-

"Landscape Jellies, Landscape Jams" appeared in the Society of Architectural Historians *Forum* 18 (April 1989).

ists, one supposes—South Park might be restored to perfect jelly and be put up on the shelf along with other permanently preserved sites.

To visit South Park without marvelling at its context, however, is unimaginable. The park lies in an industrial ruin, a perfect set-piece of the "rust bowl" athwart the old New York Central tracks between New York and Chicago. Surrounded by decay and depopulation, flanked on one side by Lackawanna, a tiny municipality of abandoned factories and a gigantic dead steel mill, South Park typifies the fundamental weaknesses of the landscape-as-jelly view. It is the streets of rundown, ex-steelworker houses and the concatenation of space and structure comprising the abandoned Bethlehem Steel Works that cry for scrutiny. It is the larger landscape, the jam, that must have the attention of preservationists as well.

If preservationists focus only on the jellies, the rare bits of incredible if dilapidated beauty in the jam, more broadminded gourmands will appropriate the jam. Consider for example, the fast-growing, as-yet-undesignated movement reaching across rural America, that vast, relatively unpopulated region frequently ignored by preservationists trained in urban things. Intimately allied with two other movements, farmland stabilization and rural regional planning, what might be called countryside conservation—the term derives as much from the 1950s wilderness conservation effort—emphasizes the identification and preservation of locally significant historical and aesthetic landscape elements.

Unlike so many landscape-as-jelly preservationists, the countryside conservationists plunge wholeheartedly into vexing issues ranging from soil erosion to family-farm bankruptcy to tourism- and retirement-related growth to powerline siting. Bit by bit they create a sophisticated, forceful literature focused on whole counties, watersheds, and larger regions. Sometimes the literature originates in historical and visual concerns. Other literature is produced by townspeople struggling not to preserve their entire home landscape against all change, but to conserve it in specific ways peculiarly meaningful. While still relatively rare, these documents originate from rural and other suburban places inhabited by well-educated, politically savvy individuals deeply concerned about the degradation of conserve-like landscapes. Perfectly aware that they live in comfortable, attractive landscapes of no national historic or scenic value, and wholly cognizant that growth and change cannot be escaped, they choose to control, often very strictly, how change will occur.

To be sure, many preservationists involve themselves in large-scale planning issues, but as yet the preservation effort has dealt poorly with large-scale landscape, and especially with landscapes in which constituents run together jam-like. Such landscapes often disturb not only the educated general public—defined here (momentarily) as readers of

Sunday morning is a good time to examine the jam-like mix of commercial, industrial, and residential structures that often perplexes planners and other authorities attempting to design perfect landscapes.

preservation-oriented periodicals—but nearly everyone else too. Areas of massive rapid change like that surrounding Princeton, New Jersey, or Tysons Corner, Virginia, trouble all sorts of people. But all too often the preservationists caught up in such change urge fellow citizens to "save the best" elements, the jellies, and let the rest be transformed. It is here that the trouble comes. Not only does the preservationist all too often fail to explain how "the best" is defined and identified, he deftly slices it from its context, lifting the South Parks out of their neighborhoods. No wonder that preserved landscapes so often strike visitors as skewed, almost fake. Everywhere around them exist landscapes in process, even if only slow deterioration, which make the jellies somewhat suspect.

The Republic needs inventories of the jellies, but it needs far, far more penetrating analysis of landscape jam, crushed seeds and all. As the era of heavy industry slips away, for instance, a whole range of landscape types—including dead steel mills like that in Lackawanna—grows rusty, then mysterious, then fascinating to a new generation of young, well-educated people to whom gantry cranes and back shops prove as alien as an Olmsted plant list. Questions of adaptive reuse or large-scale development of regional economies likely to stagnate for a foreseeable future, all require the input of preservationists anxious to dirty their hands not only with the loam of Olmsted parks, but the rusty, greasy, cinders of Lackawanna factories.

Once upon a time architects argued about how facades might best turn corners. Now the preservationist movement must not only turn the corner figuratively, evolving a conceptual framework able to address jellies and jams, but literally, from the jelly-like landscapes everyone immediately recognizes as significant to the jam-like ones nearly everyone overlooks, if they do not look, shudder, and look away. Not every landscape can be put up on the shelf. Not every landscape should be. But the pantry shelves ought to contain a mix, a mix of preserves and conserves, of jellies *and* jams.

RENDEZVOUS BY DESIGN

The Automobile City and the Loss of Serendipity

"So how did you two meet?" Couples meeting couples still ask the same question. And anyone interested in urban structure and space must pay close attention to the answer, for the urban fabric no longer facilitates serendipitous encounter. A plethora of communication devices now masks the fundamental meaning of "city." A city is a communication device itself. But the device works only when people meet each other in a way fundamental to human happiness.

Until the 1880s, unmarried women stayed at home and met eligible bachelors at orchestrated social events like cotillions and barn dances or through personal introduction—and by serendipitous accident. The cumbersome process of meeting and courtship preoccupied whole generations of novelists, but nowadays romances like Jane Austen's 1816 *Persuasion* mystify men and women growing accustomed to personal ads and electronic chat rooms. But does some vague and unfortunate change in urban life drive the unhappiness and depression Robert E. Lane brilliantly describes in his new book, *The Loss of Happiness in Market Democracies?* Do electronic media subvert not only personal happiness, but the urban fabric, too?

Architects easily forget the era before 1890, when department-store windows finally and suddenly gave women a moral reason for standing on sidewalks, when "street-walker" began to disappear as a euphemism for "prostitute," when city people blossomed free of rural tradition. They forget, too, the yeasty urbanity of the brief era that followed, the era novelist Stephen Crane detailed in his 1896 *Maggie: A Girl of the Streets* and that Theodore Dreiser explicated so forcefully in his 1900 novel *Sister Carrie* that his publisher refused to distribute the book. Yet in that brief, far too easily forgotten urban era lie clues to revitalizing an urban fabric that facilitates psyche-strengthening personal encounters in ways far beyond any virtual-reality facsimile.

Armored inside the glass-and-steel automobile carapace, protected by automatic locks and cellular phones, contemporary city motorists pose a stunning riddle to historians unraveling the mysteries of urban ar-

"Rendezvous by Design: The Automobile City and the Loss of Serendipity" appeared in *Architecture Boston* 3 (Fall 2000): 24–25.

chitecture and urban design between 1890 and 1920. Cars did more than jam boulevards and intersections. They dimmed the startling, utterly modern excitement of the sidewalk, the tall-building lobby, and the department-store café, an excitement grounded in meeting friends, acquaintances, and above all, strangers in new sorts of spaces designed for people who knew themselves as modern. In the first years of the twentieth century, Margaret Penrose and Laura Dent Crane each produced a series of young-adult-reader novels called *The Motor Girls* and *The Automobile Girls,* in which teenage girls temporarily freed from parental control roar into all sorts of adventure best exemplified in *The Automobile Girls at Washington: Checkmating the Plots of Foreign Spies.* The girl-focused driving novels predate the Nancy Drew and Hardy Boys detective series by twenty years, and nowadays offer a spectacular view not only of fast-changing female roles in urban life, but the sudden wrenching of the urban fabric itself as men and women alike begin cruising in relative isolation. Urban politeness—what "urbanity" essentially designates—decayed as both men and women discovered that the automobile insulated them from other urban travelers, that it made them anonymous. No longer did city people expect "boulevard manners" everywhere; instead they quickly focused on motor-vehicle traffic control.

Put simply, the urban automobile squelched serendipity, especially the serendipity of meeting the perfect man or woman or an old acquaintance or the friend from two blocks away. As the automobile became something more than a trendy technological toy, the arbiters of manners confronted a genuine challenge.

Etiquette books published between about 1890 and 1915 emphasize the continuous accidental meetings of strangers, often male and female strangers, in new sorts of spaces like Pullman-car sleeping accommodations, tall-building elevators, and railroad terminals. The books accepted the ordinariness of all social classes mixing on the street, on the subway, in libraries. But by the 1920s, etiquette authorities knew that automobile ownership had essentially divided urban populations into motorists and everyone else. Such division proves incredibly tricky to trace, but by the 1930s, when Dashiell Hammett published *The Maltese Falcon* and *Red Harvest* and *The Thin Man,* all urban-set mystery novels building on his 1920s short stories involving blundering into the wrong part of town, Americans knew the distinction between people with cars and people who took the trolley. Hollywood only furthered the distinction throughout the 1930s, making clear the perils and rewards of chance encounters like that exemplified in the 1934 film *It Happened One Night,* in which a society girl finally travels by bus. After 1930, etiquette-book writers ignored the street and sidewalk, the subway platform, and the grocery store,

By 1928 women magazine readers had seen a decade of advertisements depicting groups of women driving not only within cities but from cities to suburbs and small towns.

and left the growing split in urban living to writers of detective stories, Hollywood scripts, and romantic novels. Boulevard manners skidded into defensive driving.

Architects need to study the buildings and spaces shaped between about 1890 and 1915, in the magic moment when city people enjoyed a stimulating modernity but were not yet imprisoned in and by the automobile. Most cities still retain sumptuous puzzles like the intersection of Boylston Street and the Fenway in Boston where stately apartment houses with names like "Fenmore" face curvilinear streets and a linear, waterfront park, but offer only token automobile parking. The old bridges over the Muddy River suggest what historians know, that turn-of-the-century Bostonians enjoyed canoeing and that they loved walking on weekends, following the Fenway and the Jamaica Way all the miles to Franklin Park. But how else did the apartment occupants get around before the motor car? Did they use the trolley system? Did they know the trolley system in a sophisticated way almost impossible to recover today? How did the urban fabric work when everyone walked the streets freely but before the automobile made pedestrians the organized prisoners of traffic engineering?

Envisioning a city without automobiles means paying attention to the city just before the automobile era, but after the arrival of the telephone and electricity. That is the magic moment of the 1910 guidebook *Everywhere in Boston and How to Get There,* a thick, fine-printed pocket-sized book that not only lists every streetcar, subway, and elevated railway route in Boston and contiguous cities and towns, but also sorts every park, railroad station, wharf, hospital, and other popular destination, and every street alphabetically within a framework of rapid-transit route numbers. *Everywhere in Boston* remains a masterpiece of systems theory, for its judicious display of options reveals how the long-vanished transit system functioned as a series of optional routes between addresses—not as colored lines on a map. Indeed, the book provides no maps at all but instead creates a skein of numbers that connect addresses. Just before the automobile wrenched urban society into a chaotic, exhaust-choked epoch still remembered as the "Roaring Twenties," everyone moved swiftly on an electrified, number-based net, and delighted in accidental encounters—not accidents.

Such encounters strengthened social cohesion, of course, but they deepened personal happiness, too. Certainly they enlarged the mind with all sorts of new information. But perhaps more important, they expanded the psyche. "What's new?"—the common greeting phrase of the city in 1905—meant more than new information. It meant the fundamental magic of the city just before the automobile. A new encounter in real space.

HARD TIMES AND THE EVOLVING
VERNACULAR LANDSCAPE

Hard times mock traditional understandings of landscape evolution, significance, and perception. Continued economic inflation and fuel shortages exacerbate unnerving social change; old lifestyles and values alter, often subtly, often suddenly. Already the vernacular landscape reflects trends unimagined a decade ago, and as economic and social problems multiply, landscape architects will confront a rapidly evolving vernacular landscape vastly different from its predecessor.

Travel patterns began changing after the 1973 gasoline shortages, and the roadside landscape immediately reflected the shifts. Independently owned gasoline stations failed, and many secondary highways now wind past deserted and decaying wooden filling stations. Marginal fast-food establishments also failed in the next few years, especially in rural areas with low traffic volume. But now the impact of decreased automobile traffic is reflected in the interstate highway landscape; in parts of Illinois, for example, every other chain-operated fast-food outlet is abandoned, and some clover-leaf intersections are almost devoid of active businesses. Commercial shopping strips are no longer brightly illuminated long after sundown, and many are punctuated now by abandoned businesses. Throughout the 1960s, the roadside vernacular landscape epitomized the continuously rebuilding, repainting, optimistic American businessman intent on attracting ever-larger numbers of motorists. Now the roadside offers appalling challenges to designers. How does one "reuse" a failed gasoline station, dry cleaning store, or hamburger stand when the volume of automobile-riding shoppers decreases further each year? How does one reuse structures and spaces originally built to last ten to twenty years and to serve a single purpose? Surely the roadside offers glimpses of the difficult problems in store for an energy-short society.

While people drive less often, more and more frequently they choose to ride buses and trains on long and short trips. Speculators quickly realized the value of abandoned railroad stations and parking lots, and retailers have learned to locate new stores near commuter rail stations. But the overall spatial effect is not yet clear. Industrial real estate agents now

"Hard Times and the Evolving Vernacular Landscape" appeared in the Council of Educators in Landscape Architecture *Forum* 1 (Spring 1981): 13–15.

find manufacturers and warehousers intent on buying, building, or leasing structures with railroad sidings; industrial park structures located far from railroad lines prove less saleable every year. Old, multi-story brick buildings adjacent to any railroad track, and particularly to high-speed rail routes, now undergo better maintenance, refurbishing, and enlargement. Hotels near Amtrak's major urban terminals are suddenly worth much more each year, and the country store owner hopes to become a Trailways or Greyhound ticket agent.

Much analysis of the vernacular landscape has traditionally been accomplished from automobiles; the "view from the road" distorted larger perspectives of the entire national landscape. Express-train passengers see a totally different vernacular landscape than do motorists, and their vision is increasingly important to advertisers. New billboards appear alongside railroad rights-of-way, restaurants reorient their signs to entice train passengers at nearby stations, and trackside factory walls receive new coats of paint. Growing rail and bus traffic means that cities will have new "gateways," that passengers will expect hotel and other services adjacent to stations, and that "Pullman touring" will be fashionable again. Any community with a slovenly railroad-station-area is courting disaster by presenting to strangers the worst possible image of itself.

Of more significance, however, is the maturing landscape perception that increased rail and bus riding will encourage. Dramatic costs for airplane and automobile travel will put individuals in vehicles that reward landscape observation; airliners fly too high for landscape scrutiny, and motoring allows little time for observing anything but the road ahead. Train and bus travel, on the other hand, encourage scrutiny, and permit the reading of guidebooks to the landscape beyond the window. The well-known sensitivity to landscape that characterizes Britain is partly a result of excellent rail and bus networks, and of simple and complex guidebooks that interest passengers in the passing architecture, tree cover, topography, and crops. Amtrak understands the pleasure given by "informed observation," and is experimenting with free guidebooks; riders of the "Lake Shore Limited" receive a small guide to places of historic and visual interest, and the passengers enjoy it.

Landscape appreciation derived from the popularity of comfortable train and bus travel will likely produce a renaissance of travel-writing. The success of recent travel books like Paul Theroux's *The Old Patagonian Express* is stimulating many authors to travel around the country, often to out-of-the-way places, and record their impressions of the landscape. Until the 1950s, when Americans began driving enormous distances on vacation, such travel books enticed readers to travel by train to see specific sights, to linger for a week or two at Niagara Falls, Yellowstone, or San Francisco, and to "tour" such places with a guidebook in hand. Americans are now learning the lessons long known by Europeans. They are learning that high-quality trains make getting to a place "half the fun" by encouraging relaxed landscape viewing: Berton Roueche's lengthy essay in the September 15, 1980, *New Yorker* about seeing the High Plains in winter from a new, high-level Amtrak express emphasizes the rediscovered perception. They are learning too that travel by train and bus often means spending at least several days in a city or national park, and touring on foot. Tourists willing to spend several days in a place may well demand not only better places, but places with well-designed tourist paths and well-written guidebooks. A new age of landscape appreciation is dawning—now.

Rising travel and entertainment costs already reshape the vernacular American landscape by encouraging people to stay home. Certainly the home will become more important in the coming decades, and the designer will confront new difficulties in understanding changing structures and lifestyles.

On the one hand, the traditional rural and suburban detached single-family house will probably become more popular for many reasons. High heating costs temporarily frightened many individuals in the late 1970s: people decided to buy condominiums, return to urban apartments, or purchase small houses. As families have fewer children, the market for large, many-bedroom houses will shrink, and the prices asked for energy-efficient, small houses will rise. But the terror of the late 1970s is over, and suburbanites are learning the enormous advantages of their vernacular houses. The typical American house, built of wood according to well-known methods, is easily modified to conserve energy; observant travelers realize that across the nation, homeowners are insulating attics, installing sun spaces, and experimenting with wood, and more recently, coal stoves and furnaces, or else affixing solar water heaters to south-facing roofs. Much of the "retrofitting" is done with the aid of do-it-yourself manuals, or with the assistance of a professional technician. Such modification of existing dwellings is, psychologists report, immensely calming to the nerves; moreover, it is creative, and an investment. Rising food prices have already just begun to encourage the same homeowners to plant vegetable gardens, or enlarge existing gardens. Housewives angry at the exorbitant cost of raspberries or cabbage learn that with a small start-up cost and a little care, a vegetable garden will produce a great deal of food at a very low cost. Suburban lots are beginning to show the increased emphasis on vegetable gardens; not only are gardens larger and better cultivated, but flower gardens and lawns are often smaller, and sometimes half-neglected, or else better maintained

The rural poor often enjoy a high level of do-it-yourself response to change: in this view, a young New Mexico couple connect an adobe addition to their trailer.

than ever by people devoting their leisure time to manipulating their houses and yards, and saving money not only by not driving, but by growing their own food. Europe may once again offer an instructive example; for decades, Europeans have traveled wisely, and devoted much of their leisure energy to improving their gardens, to learning about trees, soils, and crops. Americans will continue to invest in such backyard recreational items as swimming pools, but they will devote increased attention to gardening. Their greater interest in home-ground plants and layout bodes well for landscape architects, who will find in future years the popular support the profession has long known in Europe.

On the other hand, millions of Americans cannot afford such detached, large-lot houses, and will live either in mobile homes or in apartments—or in some less popular habitation like condominiums or town-houses. The burgeoning popularity of mobile homes requires design solutions now, not twenty years from now, but little is known about mobile-home siting. How does one design for a temporary habitation perceived by its occupants as an interim housing solution? How does one design for a structure that is, after all, mobile? Do mobile-home occupants still enjoy the 1950s closely packed "trailer park," or do they desire more privacy? How do the problems perplexing the designer of mobile home sites illuminate the difficulties of designing and siting urban and suburban apartment structures? The so-called boom in apartment living is the result of the high cost of single-family suburban houses

CONTEMPORARY SPACE

coupled with a high rate of divorce. What sort of apartment is required for a young couple saving for a house? Is it different than that needed by a divorced mother with two young children, and can such different units be accommodated in a single place? Designers will learn the complexities of these and other housing questions as the "typical" nuclear family becomes less typical, as young singles compete with senior citizens for very small, low-cost apartments, as garden-apartment owners learn the problems of small children dashing about swimming pools built for adults. At the core of the difficulties is the innate human need to manipulate individual space, and the growing reluctance of apartment-building owners to permit occupants to paint, wallpaper, or otherwise modify the units. The office worker who is forbidden to manipulate his work environment needs some creative outlet; if he lives in an apartment, he is unlikely to find it, unless he has a hobby. One can sit only so long by the pool, or in the game room. How does the designer resolve such issues?

Economic trends suggest that the need for individual self-expression will become increasingly expensive and difficult. The clothing industry hopes that as automobiles become less of a status symbol, people will turn to dressing more flamboyantly, and a close check of contemporary fashions, particularly in women's clothes, confirms a subtle, post-1970s shift. The health-and-exercise industry hopes that Americans pressed for cash will invest a little in running shoes and begin jogging, and the bicycle industry hopes that Americans will buy fancy, expensive touring and racing bicycles. The vernacular landscape already illustrates the power of such new movements, not only in the growing numbers of clothing stores and health "spas" and gymnasia across the nation, but in the changing uses of public space. Joggers and bicyclists use park space differently than the strolling pedestrian, of course, but they also demand access lanes on public roads. Designers now address such issues, but they must be aware that changes in attitudes toward clothing represent a more significant trend already emerging. Europeans unable to afford automobiles enjoy the promenading that makes street life so colorful and sidewalk cafes so profitable. If Americans, and particularly poorer Americans, begin to emphasize such display of themselves and their clothes, designing for urban streets will be as complex as designing a park for joggers and dog walkers. Self-expression will undoubtedly change the public vernacular landscape; how many Americans now go to shopping malls so that they can promenade along the concourses, enjoying the passing show of other individuals, sheltered from inclement weather, and choosing from one small fancy-food stand after another—but buying very little? In Houston, San Francisco, Chicago, and Boston, the use of the shopping mall as promenade ground will increase in popularity as inflation makes other forms of self-expression impossible for many Americans. In ten years, many urban Americans may demand redesigned urban parks useful for promenading, jogging, and eating; if inflation makes impossible the owning of single-family homes, the need for self-expression will surely have an impact on park and public garden design.

Apartment living may well require some outlet for the need to manipulate space too, however, and many new complexes may have to be designed with rooftop gardens apportioned among the tenants, or with easily modified interior walls. Designing multi-family housing complexes will be one of the most difficult tasks for professionals, and will become nearly impossible for the amateur builders who erected in the 1960s so much of the now-seedy multi-family housing that comprises a large portion of the inner-suburb vernacular landscape. No longer is there a "typical" apartment dweller, and no longer do rents easily pay off building mortgages. Owners of existing complexes install swimming pools and other amenities to placate tenants unable to afford houses and increasingly upset at restrictive apartment living.

Advertising already illustrates the changing landscapes of travel and home as manufacturers and advertising agencies grapple with a quickly changing economic and social situation. Advertisements directed at upper-income buyers appear far more frequently in magazines than on television; indeed, some evidence suggests that wealthy people are turning away from television viewing to more active recreations or to reading. Thus traditional automobile commercials showing luxury cars in suburban settings—and implicitly associating quality and luxury with suburbs, not cities—appear infrequently on television now, but remain in exclusive magazines. Much television and newspaper advertising directed to lower-income individuals either emphasizes inexpensive products devoid of any landscape background—soap, for example—or displays products in environments that viewers can perceive as suburban, rural, or even urban. Advertisers perhaps fear that once-popular images from the vernacular landscape—the open road, the mountain wilderness, the suburban house—may now alienate viewers and readers who cannot afford to visit or own them. But undoubtedly advertising images of the vernacular landscape, and particularly the vernacular landscapes of travel and home, have changed dramatically, and no longer reinforce simple beliefs about suburbs, main-street small towns, and rural areas.

Remarkably little is known about the evolution of the American vernacular landscape, about public perceptions of it, about its use as a symbol in advertising, about its present physical and economic condition. Much of it is old and in need of repair, particularly that part along roads, in cities, and in rural areas; gasoline stations, urban street pavement, and barns often show signs of advanced deterioration. Much of it is unstudied; the role of food stores in an urban neighborhood or rural county traffic pattern, the effect of public-school location on residential development, the significance of new building materials like vinyl siding receive little attention from the designers who must deal with them. Much of it is part of a perceptual scheme unconsciously formulated by Americans who turn out to be attracted to mansard-roofed stoves, "natural" colors, and well-lit parking lots. When businessmen learn of some fragment of the scheme, carpenters attach mansard-roof fronts to stores and painters soften the gaudy 1960 colors of the commercial-strip restaurants. Much of it is condemned by professional designers as ugly, and thereafter ignored despite the lessons it teaches about design in a democracy, about social change, about economic and energy disruption. And until designers and scholars direct their attention at the vernacular landscape and the forces that shape it, much professional design will be slightly out of touch with client wishes.

During the next two or three decades the American vernacular landscape will change and change again, ceaselessly reflecting the unprecedented complexity and rate of economic, technical, and social change. Hard times compounded of inflation and energy shortages will make crucial the study of the vernacular American landscape, and especially the landscapes of travel and home, because the vernacular landscape is often the first to indicate changes in lifestyle and attitude, and because it is the built form that shapes the lives of most Americans.

PARTS CARS, GREEN ROOFS, AND RURAL LANDSCAPE PRESERVATION

Landscape preservation stands now not at a fork in the road, but beyond the fork, in the scrubby, nondescript ground that lies between most diverging paths. No longer is the "historic landscape preservation movement" so weak that it must beg help from other movements; indeed, the "movement" is now so powerful that all sorts of groups ask for alliances. Water-supply advocates, wildlife conservationists, limited-growth alliances, condominium developers, rural poverty reformers, state tourism boards, and others come courting, interested not so much in landscape preservation, but in the spinoff effects of preservation. And the courtship, while exciting, may lead preservationists astray, far distant from their own narrow path, the one so difficult to discern, let alone follow.

What differentiates landscape preservation from its ancestor, "historic preservation"? Essentially, landscape preservation confronts not only the preservation of large-scale spaces, but incidentally the preservation of artifacts still unrecognized by traditional preservationists. Who cares to preserve back-road potholes, the loathsome, growing things that sprawl spiderlike across springtime asphalt? Like quicksand, potholes attract the favor of almost no one, not truckers, not bicyclists, not tourists, but the landscape preservationist understands the pothole-strewn road as an important item in a larger landscape deemed worth preserving. And not only is the pitted road of visual value, the sort of road travelers expect to find in "the real countryside," the rough road slows traffic, making tourists more likely to enjoy the landscape through which they pass, and constricts the building of houses, businesses, and other structures announcing "growth." Herein lies the distinguishing facet of landscape preservation. Everything in a landscape comes in for attention, and once made, the decision to preserve the landscape involves preserving things other preservationists ignore.

Yet implementation problems—perhaps conceptual problems, too— remain and must be addressed soon. Vehicles and other machines pose potential difficulties in the landscape preservation movement, for ex-

"Parts Cars, Green Roofs, and Rural Landscape Preservation" appeared as "Parts Cars, Green Roofs, and 1990s Landscape Preservation" in the University of Massachusetts Landscape Preservation Seminar *Proceedings* (March 1988): 7–10.

ample. Since the mid-1980s, magazine and television advertisers have emphasized old pickup trucks and tractors in advertisements for products from jeans to cereal to cosmetics. Part of the popularity originates in the burgeoning sales of pickup trucks to noncommercial users, but much arises in a nostalgia detected and nourished by advertising agencies. The old pickup truck, the red Ford with flaring fenders, the Studebaker with its running boards, and the old red tractor with high rear wheels and absolutely no rollover-protection structure speak of rural days gone by, hard work outdoors, and the virtues of farming, ruggedness, and leaded gasoline. Moreover, such vehicles are identifiably old, not restored. Aged pickup trucks and older tractors rumble everywhere in the rural New England landscape: rusted, scraped, modified in a dozen ways, the vehicles advertise a sort of Yankee cussedness, a determination to make a machine endure. Magazine photographers working since the mid-'80s have begun using such vehicles for center-piece spreads. *Vermont Life* and *Yankee* among others publish nonadvertising, full-color photographs of rural landscapes in which old machines, sometimes as old as Model T Ford pickups, sometimes as new as Farmall 460 tractors, dignify some tiny corner. Rosamond Orford's spectacularly beautiful landscape photograph postcards demonstrate the cohesiveness of the rural-landscape-with-machines image, and the purchasers of the cards in such tourist havens as Woodstock apparently see nothing discordant in landscapes like her "Winter Sunlight," which links a red barn and silo with an old yellow bulldozer, red tractor, and two battered pickup trucks, all surrounded not by stone walls, but barbed-wire fence.[1]

Nevertheless, examining the place of old vehicles in the frame of the landscape preservation movement poses genuine problems. Old cars, say from the '60s and '70s, are noticeably lacking in advertisements and noncommercial magazine photographs. Such cars call to mind gasoline shortages and near-catastrophic inflation even as they spark memories of roomy, comfortable vehicles intended to cross and recross the Republic in a two-week vacation. Yet in the rural landscape, such cars are everywhere, not only roaring over dirt and ill-paved roads, but parked everywhere behind, beside, and in front of structures "worth saving." Such cars are either completely abandoned or else serve their rural owners as incredibly valuable "parts cars," vehicles of the same make and year as operating ones, vehicles to be cannibalized for spare parts. Old cars and parts cars clutter the rural landscape from Maine to Arkansas to Idaho, and speak not only of the fierce need for motor vehicle transportation in the rural places, but of the enduring trying-to-make-ends-meet way of life in rural America.

Rural landscape interests, intrigues, and even charms because it often announces older ways of doing things, older ways of thinking. Only rarely do its tourist-devourers realize that poverty slows change in rural America, and that a beautiful rural landscape is often a very poor one. Everywhere, of course, one sees the signs of failed agriculture: no longer do we weep at the stone wall in the woods, at the hillside grown up in trees. But the old tractor with no contemporary safety devices, the rickety nineteenth-century farmhouse with plastic nailed about its sills and over its windows, the carefully patched wooden barn all testify to a poverty, sometimes grinding, sometimes not, that forbids the purchase of safe tractors, snug mobile homes and other manufactured housing, and prefabricated metal agricultural sheds. The dirt road pleases the tourist except when rain makes driving difficult, but always it worries the parents consigning children to old schoolbuses; always it worries the volunteer firemen wondering if their 1946 pumper is good for another mud season; always it worries the oil-delivery man who sees covered bridges and ill-graded roads as potential traps.[2]

Of course such poverty curtails change, and rural people often love it, or at least tolerate it for the gifts curtailed change brings. No tourist speeds along the dirt road, and the railroad-company-owned timber highway bridge labeled "8 Ton Limit" keeps trailer trucks on state highways. Poverty often enhances scenery, and the locals, for all that intellectuals sometimes demean their understanding of local scenery, know the value of scenery—and the quiet that permits enjoyment of it.

But must rural people live always in a poor but beautiful trap? What does landscape preservation mean to them? Does it mean not replacing a leaking cedar-shingle roof with corrugated metal sheets, does it mean never knocking down the old homestead and moving into a trailer? Does it mean never replacing galvanized metal sapbuckets with polyethelene tubing and tubs? Does it mean never widening and paving the road along which the schoolbus feels its way? For whom must the landscape be preserved?

The most cursory look at rural landscape reveals the complexity of things often photographed but unrealized. Asphalt roll-siding and roll-roofing offer good examples. Much rural New England architecture remains sided with 1920s- or 1930s-era roll covering, much of it embossed to resemble brick and much colored a tannish brown. Such siding remains in urban places too—many Rhode Island mill towns still boast three-story houses covered with it—but city people, especially landlords, often replaced it with asbestos, aluminum, or vinyl siding after the late 1950s. In the rural landscape, the old pseudo-brick still covers farm outbuildings—particularly the great abandoned poultry houses in which thousands of hens needed protection from winter winds—and sometimes frame buildings. Its rooftop relation, black and green roll-roofing, covers farmhouses everywhere people have been unable to afford newer asphalt shingles or metal sheeting. Yet wall and roof siding remain curiously un-studied by landscape preservationists, for all their importance, and for all the stunning "official" examples, like the apparently indestructible 1920s asbestos shingle roof on Calvin Coolidge's birthplace in Vermont. Roof-ing and siding materials *must* concern landscape preservationists as they, sometimes, intrigue preservationists interested in structures only.[3] A brown-sided, green-roofed structure blends into the surrounding topog-raphy and foliage in ways a white-vinyl-sided, aluminum-roofed build-ing does not. As the century advances, will coverings manufactured in the 1920s and 1930s become almost as antique, and almost as worth pre-serving, as wooden ones? Is the old barn graced by a brand-new, copper-colored, new-penny-shiny roof an eyesore or delightful proof of the resurgence of farming? Who tells the aging widow, the young parents starting a family, the recently retired professional couple that their drafty, drab wall covering is historically significant—and must be retained or duplicated?

Landscape preservationists must ask and answer such questions for themselves, lest their new suitors shape dialogue for selfish ends. Above all, landscape preservationists must scrutinize existing landscapes. They must not only see, but realize, *make real,* the rusting farm machinery, the abandoned pickup trucks and parts cars, the rutted dirt road down which the schoolbus skids, the 1960s mobile homes from which stovepipes jut, the narrow bridges, the green-roofed houses wrapped in plastic. Land-scape preservationists must beware the seductions of those who would have them create a rural dreamscape, a landscape mimicking the bits and pieces of landscape long portrayed in tourist advertising and regional New England magazine centerspreads. They must somehow make sense *for themselves* of the concatenation of space, structure, machinery, and rusty junk that characterizes American, and especially New England, rural land-scape. Right now the landscape preservationists, so long accustomed to asking for help, must learn the dangers and rewards of being asked for help—and must learn to distinguish those suitors with honorable in-tentions from those intending trickery.

Notes

1. Rosamond Orford's cards are published by Upcountry Cards, East Thetford, Ver-mont. I have watched tourists purchasing the cards in Woodstock, Vermont, and inquired about their preferences.
2. On the relation between rural poverty and rural landscape little has been written, but see Cynthia M. Duncan and Ann R. Tickamyer, "Poverty Research and Policy

for Rural America," Rural Economic Policy Program, Aspen Institute, 1333 New Hampshire Avenue, N.W., Suite 1070, Washington D.C., and Cynthia M. Duncan, "A Preliminary Look at Developmental Progress in Rural Kentucky, 1960 to 1980," *Kentucky Economy: Review and Perspective,* 8 (Summer 1984). See also Carol Stumbo, "Married to the Land: Farming in Appalachia," *Appalachian Heritage,* 14 (Winter 1986). Everyone intrigued with rural landscape, landscape preservation, and rural poverty might well read Gaston Roupnel, *Histoire de la campagne française* (Paris: Bernard Grasset, 1932), *Australian Historic Landscapes,* ed. D.N. Jeans (Sydney: Allen & Unwin, 1984), and Carolyn Chute, *The Beans of Egypt, Maine* (New York: Ticknor & Fields, 1985).

3. These comments on siding and roofing, and on old and abandoned vehicles, derive from research done for a book-in-progress on the rural New England landscape between 1900 and 1939. For information on abandoned machinery as monument, see David P. Hill, "Notes Concerning Ruins of Motion Machinery in the Appalachian Landscape," *Blue Ridge Parkway: Agent of Transition,* ed. Barry M. Buxton and Steven M. Beatty (Boone, North Carolina: Appalachian Consortium Press, 1986), pp. 245–257. On the relation between urban and rural landscape artifacts, see Frederick Rice, "Urbanizing Rural New England," *New England Magazine,* 33 (January 1906). I discuss the views of Rice and others in my *Metropolitan Corridor: Railroads and the American Scene* (New Haven: Yale University Press, 1983). For an analysis of reactions of the educated elite to nineteenth-century rural slovenliness, see my *Borderland: Origins of the American Suburb* (New Haven: Yale University Press, 1988). In *From the Land and Back* (New York: Scribner's, 1972), Curtis K. Stadtfield traces the impact of farm machinery on rural landscape and life in the decades surrounding World War II.

EVERYDAY RURAL LANDSCAPE AND
THOREAU'S WILD APPLES

Whatever else the New England rural landscape is, it is for sale. Everywhere in the region, even along "class five" New Hampshire roads impassable to all but four-wheel-drive pickups, the signs of change loom over abandoned pastures or stare out from second-growth oak and pine woods. The rural landscape is, as Emerson put it so long ago, a commodity. But of course it always was, even in colonial days when whole provinces fell into the hands of speculators who surveyed the woods and sold them wholesale and retail.

Yet something is different now, something difficult to define, to designate, but something important all the same. The land is for sale to consumers of landscape, not to makers. Eighteenth-century farmers intended to shape wilderness into landscape, to make new clearings produce crops, to maintain man-made spaces in the face of powerful natural forces. They paid speculators a fair price, a price based on what they hoped they might earn from decades of working pieces of land. Now the situation is different: prices spiral upward, out of touch with any productive value of the land, driven not by the fertility of the soil but by national economic indicators. To sell a cornfield to a speculator-developer in the Connecticut River Valley today rivals hitting the state lottery grand prize.

And the *landscape* is for sale too. Thoreau argued long ago in *Walden* that the landscape belongs to the wise observer, to the walker who sees farms not as individual economic units, but as constituents in a larger visual order. "I have frequently seen a poet withdraw, having enjoyed the most valuable part of a farm," he wrote of his excursions in landscape appreciation, "while the crusty farmer supposed that he had got a few wild apples only." But by the 1930s tourist boards, railroads, and hotels had succeeded in packaging a handful of rural New England landscape images as easily as Thoreau's farmer boxed apples for market. In the years following World War II, regional magazines, especially *Vermont Life* and *Yankee,* publicized the images, the white-painted church building, the town green, the forested hills interrupted by pasture, the stone walls, the crossroads valley hamlet complete with one-room school, general store/post office/hardware store

"Everyday Rural Landscape and Thoreau's Wild Apples" appeared in *New England Landscape* 1 (1989): 5–10.

with front porch, the covered bridges splicing fall-foliage hills, the Christmas trees sliding downhill behind Belgian horses, the temporaneous poetry, fiction, travel writing, and visual imagery. No longer did old fields growing up in juniper, sumac, and white pine unnerve New Englanders worried about the decline of agriculture. In the early years of the new century most New Englanders lived separately from farming, and saw the maturing pines not only as beautiful, but as evidence of a simpler, more livable era sliding past. As Spring pointed out, the phenomenon spread across the region, and soon the white pine became a regional image, something linking Vermont with Rhode Island. As writers sought to make "the real New England" clear to New Englanders and to readers in other regions, the white pine proved a perfect motif for mass-circulation publication.

Today the white pine remains an important constituent element of the landscape of nostalgia, of difference. But no longer can one element define the rural New England landscape. No longer can a sort of pop-phenomenology approach be expected to work. The rural New England landscape cannot be defined as something between "what is out there" and what is on the cover of *Yankee Magazine*. Something so vague could scarcely be for sale. Instead we might look to the example of the white pine, and the long-ago recognition that the "real" rural landscape is essentially an anti-type, a sort of opponent of everything the metropolitan public loathes or fears in its everyday landscape.

To proceed in that manner means sifting the New England rural landscape for its essential general characteristics, for many of its small-scale components are not unique. White-painted churches dignify crossroads in Kentucky, covered truss bridges carry cars across Oregon rivers, and pit-silos sprout everywhere in Iowa. For far too long, the components have focused the attention of tourists, natives, preservationists, and scholars, even though it is their concatenations that comprise the larger characteristics of rural New England landscape.

Diminutiveness

Diminutiveness is the first characteristic. Everything about the New England rural landscape is small, compact, narrow, almost shrunken. Turn off the main Cape Cod roads, wander into a cluster of low-roofed Cape Cod houses, and suddenly automobiles seem large. Automobiles loom large at Vermont intersections designed long ago for horse-drawn vehicles; they move in ungainly fashion over one-lane Maine bridges. Diminutiveness shows up in high-tension power lines carried on wooden poles, not steel towers; it appears in narrow roads bordered not with midwestern grassy berms but with stone walls perilously near pavement; it appears most often, and perhaps most frighteningly, in curves of too-sharp radii, curves encountered on sleety evenings by skiers in BMWs. But diminutiveness is *not* quaintness. Much that is diminutive in the rural New England land-scape is not old: the new John Deere 900HC tractor at which Nebraska farmers can only laugh, the resurfaced two-lane bridge that still makes encountering oncoming trailer trucks thrilling, the prefabricated metal farm building not much bigger than a hay wagon. But much is simply aged, not old, and certainly not antique. Indeed the most casual look at the rural New England landscape suggests that much of it—exclusive of houses and perhaps barns—dates to the 1950s, to the post-war opti-mism about dairying and other specialized farming enterprises.

It is diminutive in two other ways as well. Narrow, twisting roads en-courage slow driving—often they enforce it for drivers of pickups, old sta-tion wagons, and heavy trucks. Unlike eastern Colorado or northeastern New Mexico, rural roads in New England defy—and punish—sixty-mile-an-hour drivers. The actual rate of travel *is* slower on secondary and nar-rower roads; the pace of life not only seems slower, it is. Moreover, the rural landscape exists as a vestige of horse-drawn transport. Not only do most back roads follow assignments intended for horses, or even for oxen, the whole web of distances between town centers tends to originate in facts of pedestrian and equestrian travel. Native rural New Englanders know this in their hearts, half-consciously perhaps, but deeply. They expect either town centers or lesser commercial foci—"villages" in regional usage—at re-markably regular intervals, although they voice their understanding only at sundown when gas gauges read one-eighth. But unlike the great grid land-scape stretching west from the Pennsylvania-Ohio border, the skein of vil-lages bears no immediately recognizable pattern. Only when one knows the speed of a team and wagon—in flat and in hilly terrain—does it begin to make sense, and then only faintly at first. Contemporary motorists in Wyoming and Texas drive in space ordered about railroads and automo-biles; little of the horse-and-buggy era endured to define distances between wheat ranches and county seats, and Texas "farm-to-market" roads—back roads that resemble New England state highways—announce the 1920s and 1930s primacy of the car. To drive in rural New England means to drive slowly over the roads of another age, to expect crossroads and com-mercialization "every now and then," to meander in diminutive space.

Dilapidation

While rural New England is not quaint, it is *dilapidated*. Despite the best efforts of state tourist authorities and regional magazines, the detritus of the late nineteenth and early twentieth centuries lies everywhere away

Abandoned lanes snake everywhere in rural places: often known as cart paths or bar ways, they remain as created, private ways ordinarily closed by bars or gates.

from the newness of the interstate cloverleaf and the studied pickling of the tourist-focused hilltown center. Much of rural New England is abandoned; indeed much of the so-called agricultural view is a view of barns, silos, and ells waiting to fall. But a vast amount of other space and structure awaits one heavy snowfall, one vandal's match. The New England railroad right-of-way lies littered with steam-engine-era wreckage and near wreckage, not simply weeds nearly obscuring the rails. Rivers and large brooks sweep past mill buildings abandoned in the 1950s, buildings equipped with electric hoists and other gadgets announcing post-war enthusiasm, and sweep over dams perhaps most safely photographed from up-stream locations. Gravel roads in New Hampshire and Maine skirt the material for a massive museum of the mobile home; indeed the landscape historian in search of post-war trailers need only drive into any one of several "lake districts" to be overwhelmed with examples. Of course many travelers see right past the semi-ruins, see past the three-story chicken house to the eighteenth-century mansion, and fail to recognize the passing of the twentieth century. Much that is dilapidated is on the verge of becoming antique, of being respectably ruinous.

Afforestation

Trees both mask and emphasize the dilapidation. The rural New England landscape is "frosted" with trees, and as any first-rate pastry cook knows, frosting does much to hide the appearance—but not the taste—of the cake beneath. The wildering of New England after the Civil War, and especially after World War I, is well documented, of course, but the significance of the trees in defining the rural New England landscape for natives and for newcomers remains little studied. In some cases at least, farmers from Iowa and other cornbelt states find much of rural New England—Vermont tends to be the exception—"scruffy" or "let go," and really rather sad. New England may be "treed" or "wooded," but away from northern Maine it is scarcely forested, afforested, or re-forested—it just has an incredible diversity of warped, twisted, stunted, crowded, trees. Yet New Englanders native to the rural landscape accept the second-growth woods not only as forest, but as inevitable forest, and frequently fail to grasp the incredulity, humor, or sadness with which Pacific Northwest lumbermen greet the spectacle of diminutive, dilapidated "logging equipment"—what New Englanders call "doodlebugs" and "skidders"—working away at scruffy woods. Rural New England landscape is landscape shrieking of accidental re-wooding, of pronounced nonmanagement of timber resources, of twenty-acre logging enterprises, late 1950s logging rigs, and period-piece sawmills. Modern forests and lumbering enterprises remain the exception, as do long vistas of clear-cut acreage, stands of managed forest, and large mills. As Spring noted in 1905, the old-field succession beginning with white pine identified the regional rural landscape. In the waning years of the same century, after major wars, economic depression and recession, farm failures, and fuel shortages, the New England woods remain, and remain almost exactly as Spring and other foresters feared they would remain.

Of course the woods entice tourists, hunters, skiers, and other recreating folk more inclined to think about foliage or ground cover or snow quality than about the soundness of the timber. And give locals enough white oak to cut and split and burn, and they think little of ash and hickory and other species difficult to find. The scruffy woods close in the narrow road, making it even more diminutive of course, and they make views shorter by the year. Dairying keeps Vermont open, and used Brush-Hogs show up on more failing pastures than they did ten years ago, but the tall trees, some a century old now, dignify otherwise undistinguished structures. Like frosting on a tilted or fallen cake, they mask all sorts of error.

And the trees do cut views—and create illusions. Rural landscape in New England is not only diminutive, it is confined, and the confinement emphasizes nodality. Until the 1950s, except in a handful of near-suburban regions in the lower three states, rural New Englanders understood only commercial and manufacturing nodes—not commercial strips running miles along secondary roads. Near the beaches of Cape Cod and New

Hampshire such strips were growing more obvious as more trees fell each year to make way for lobster shops, bait stores, and motels, but elsewhere the nineteenth-century pattern of villages held sway. Removing trees today would mean changing views dramatically. In some instances improvement would result as hillsides reverted to pasture, and as bottom land produced alfalfa. But clear-cutting would surely cause alarm elsewhere as homeowners learned that downhill lay the junkyard behind the gas station and—more important—that winding through much of the landscape are commercialized country highways choking on traffic. And the illusion of privacy, of distance between town centers, would fade into a wholly new—and potentially unpleasant—reality.

Accretion

Trees and shrubs mask another characteristic of contemporary rural New England landscape, however, one instantly noticed by observant outsiders. The landscape is *accretionary*. Growth occurs in thin layers, in continual additions to existing form—or at least it used to do so. Everything in the "old" rural landscape announces such change—the barbed wire fencing twisted along rusted wire fencing draped atop fallen stone walls, the barn thrusting additions in every direction away from the original structure, the farm-equipment dealership stretching away in a series of wood, cement block, and pre-fab steel additions from the original frame blacksmith shop. Layers of growth mingle and flow together, announcing the prosperity of the 1880s and 1920s, the rough years of the 1930s and early 1970s. Elsewhere in the Republic such accretion is rare. Wyoming wheat country seems essentially the same shapes and views as it did in 1950; eastern New Mexico cattle country is little changed from the 1920s; much of the rural old Confederacy is scarcely changed since 1865. But like the layers of growth which mark the development of a tree—layers only noticed after the tree is felled—the layers of change and growth and shrinkage that characterize the New England rural landscape today do little to alter the shape of the landscape. Only the felling of the tree, or the blunt, brutal erasing of landscape form and its replacement with wholly new structures and spaces—say a Freeport, Maine-like shopping zone—makes natives aware of the loss of layers and the coming of a wholly new, immediately new, form.

Apples

These characteristics are not easily studied. Certainly they are subjective. Certainly they hark back to older questions about "real Yankees," questions now slightly off-color in a discrimination-fixated society. Does the landscape reflect ignorance, stubbornness, determination, or even arrogance? Is it the maintained symbol of a continuing quasi-rejection of values, lifestyles, and attitudes advertised on television and for sale in shopping malls?

Consider the pickup truck. Somewhere in rural New England must be a new pickup truck. But visual analysis suggests that every rural New England pickup is used, frequently rusted out along rocker panels and tailgate, and littered in its cab with an array of equipment, paper, and stale food. This truck is picturesque when parked in farmyards and in front of general stores, and somehow even more picturesque loaded with cordwood or hay and rumbling along a back road. Only rarely is it condemned as evidence of poverty. Usually outsiders consider it clear evidence of the "Yankee make-do" attitude that long-ago defined the heart of New England culture. But locals know the trucks as something else. They know them as vehicles not only of the road, but of personal expression. Long after they can afford to finance new trucks, they hang onto their present ones, taking quiet pride in keeping contrary, almost possessed vehicles running in deep cold and deeper mud. The rusted trucks derive from what remains of the New England character—a sort of half-organized opposition to anything, and especially anything from out of town, from flat country, from New York, from away.

The rural New England landscape is the landscape which throws us back on examining the landscape that is in—but not of—New England, the landscape that daily eats into home. In his own time, Thoreau wondered about the long-term social and spatial impact of the railroad, and concluded that the great invention of his age had mixed results. At the close of the twentieth century, rural New Englanders, even those who have never heard of Thoreau, know something of his philosophy of landscape appreciation, know that the common treasure is fragmented, despoiled, and vanishing, know that without some sort of concerted, determined effort the everyday landscape of rural New England will be nothing special, nothing peculiarly Yankee, nothing but cheap profit and quick loss, nothing but a smear of sprawl. The rural New England landscape will not only lack its defining characteristics, it will lack even its stunted apple trees. Its visual feast will be reduced not to a few wild apples, but to nothing, to nothing at all. What Thoreau knew as the most valuable part of a farm, its place in a larger landscape of dignity, will be gone.

References

Arr, E. H. [pseud.: Ellen Chapman Hobbs Rollins]. 1880. *New England Bygones*. Philadelphia: Lippincott.

Johnson, Clifton. 1894. *The Farmer's Boy*. New York: Appleton.

Johnson, Clifton. 1915. *Highways and Byways of New England*. New York: Macmillan.

Nutting, Wallace. 1922. *New Hampshire Beautiful*. Framingham, Massachusetts: Old America.

Spring, S. N. 1905. *The Natural Replacement of White Pine on Old Fields in New England*. Washington, D.C.: Bureau of Forestry.

Thoreau, Henry D. 1899. *Walden*. New York: T.Y. Crowell.

Wharton, Edith. 1911. *Ethan Frome*. New York: Scribner's.

SMALL TOWN AND URBAN EDGES

Contemporary Americans abuse the word *city*. Everywhere in the outer suburbs stand businesses named Car Wash City, Ford City, or Tile City, and shopping centers like the gigantic Park City Mall outside Lancaster, Pennsylvania. The names of such establishments mock the traditional meanings of *city*, and hint at complex perceptual difficulties that will vex urban design in the years ahead.

Originally, *city* denoted the people of a densely settled place. The Latin root word, *civitas*, designated people living in a sophisticated political order; the word gives English the terms *civil, civilized,* and *city,* all of which connote a refined way of life focused on frequent, close human contact. Another Latin word, *urbs,* designated the physical fabric inhabited by *civilians;* today the word lies behind *urbane* and *urban.* Until well into the modern era, the words remained distinct; *city* continued to designate the people and their political and cultural order, in the way Shakespeare used the word in *Coriolanus:* "The city is its people." *Urban* remained rare until the nineteenth century; as cities grew very large, however, the word began to appear in print more frequently, usually meaning "of the city" in phrases like "an urban neighborhood," and slowly became, unfortunately perhaps, a synonym of *city*.

What explains the conflation of terms? One reason lies in the unprecedented scale of late-nineteenth-century urban expansion. Neither *city* nor *urban* adequately addressed the metropolitan-size forms rapidly spreading across hitherto rural land, and the word *suburb,* haphazardly applied to commuter villages, residential neighborhoods, and outlying industrial zones, soon became nearly meaningless. *City* and *urban* are words that date from the era of walled, clearly demarcated "great towns," not the age of amorphous places like turn-of-the-century New York or Chicago. Underlying both words is an unstated emphasis on *edge* as the most important characteristic of city life and urban form.

Many turn-of-the-century writers scrutinized the disturbing character of the American urban fringe. "Everything is rough, unfinished, rushed up and apparently on the point of falling down in a ruin," remarked Arthur Shadwell in his *Industrial Efficiency* (1909) of the outskirts

"Small Town and Urban Edges" appeared in *UD Review* 6 (Spring/Summer 1983): 5–7.

of Pittsburgh. Speculators built poorly in the fringe because they expected changes that would eliminate much of their work; apartment houses would replace flimsy single family houses, great factories would supplant stockyards. Almost continuously in flux, the fringe zone contained urban and rural elements simultaneously, along with structures and spaces not so easily categorized, and its pace of life struck many visitors as anything but civilized. *City* began to define "downtown," not the outskirts, and *urban* soon connoted verticality and finished, permanent structures and spaces, not the horizontal, impermanent forms of the fringe. If Americans had examined the fringe from a citified, urbane point of view, they might have understood and controlled the sprawl in ways European urban designers successfully advocated. Instead, Americans studied the fringe through the prism of the small-town edge.

In American small-town culture, "edge of town" means a very specific place, a place defined only in part by the "legal limits" sign that marks the political boundary. In the minds of the townspeople, the edge of town is a distinct, physical edge defined by structures. Sometimes the structures house retail businesses like motels or gasoline stations or wholesale enterprises like grain storage; sometimes they are houses or mobile homes. In both cases, they are served by town utilities—sewer and water mains, fire department, garbage collection. Beyond them, even between them and the legal limits sign, is only agricultural land no different from that stretching across the county, or forest or mountain. Traditionally, working or living on the edge meant enduring a slightly marginal existence slightly distrusted by people more closely tied to the center of the building cluster. American novelists have long understood that the edge zone is lacking in a precise behavioral code. In *Winesburg, Ohio* (1919) and *Main Street* (1920), for example, Sherwood Anderson and Sinclair Lewis use the edge of the land just beyond as the habitation of social misfits and the theater for marital infidelity, for neither town manners nor rural virtue controls behavior along the edge. Life on the small-town edge used to be balanced between town and rural codes, and consequently uncomfortable; most people chose to live on one side of the edge or the other.

Most small towns attempt to expand their sphere of influence over the surrounding countryside, however, and by erecting signs hope to entice travellers to stop. Today the typical small town has two sorts of edges, therefore, one the distinct physical boundary best understood by townspeople, and one the concentric set of edges discerned by the observant traveller following secondary highways and back roads. The first edge is the overnight accommodation advertising edge, the place where the first motel billboards appear. Such billboards appear 65 miles from

On back roads in Oklahoma and neighboring states, the explorer still stumbles on simple signs that encouraged buggy-driving farm families to shop at stores an hour or two away.

Amarillo, for example, but the size of the town bears little relation to the location of the edge; the little Colorado town of Eads places its outer-most billboard 100 miles away. The second edge is the food advertising edge; the simple signs advertising Murphy's Cafe stand 60 miles outside Colby, Kansas, about 75 minutes away. Signs in the first two edges are suggestive only, not insistent, for the businessman relies more heavily on the signs comprising the third edge, the reminder edge. Usually about 25 miles from town, the reminder signs are stark, but effective: "Sand Hills Cafe—Merriman, Nebraska, About 30 Miles" announces a typical one in the High Plains. The reminder edge is also the old-time advertising edge, the place where retailers erected their outmost signs in days of slower driving. The old-time signs, many long rusted or vandalized or stolen by antique hunters, are small, intended to be noticed by motorists driving no more than 30 miles an hour. "Tipton's Bargain Store," a two-by-four-foot blue enameled sign, still swings from a barbed wire fence outside Hennessey, Oklahoma; old signs flake from silos outside Man-assa, Colorado. Within the third edge, sometimes mingled with it, lies the fourth, that of the highway department signs, "Spring Green 24 Miles" is typical of the signs placed everywhere in the United States by highway departments trying to announce towns about a half hour before the mo-torist arrives in them. The fifth edge lies closer, in a vaguely defined zone running from 8 to 3 miles from town; it advertises the local churches, and is perhaps placed to keep church advertising separate from com-

SMALL TOWN AND URBAN EDGES

Many small-town booster committees erect signs that encourage travellers to give communities a second look, especially if they are planning on locating a business.

mercial signage. Everywhere in rural America the traveller discovers signs like two in North Dakota, "Salem Covenant Church, 3 Miles" and "Pleasant Prairie Church of God." By the time he has passed the church advertising, he has driven through all five of the edges that mark the outer edge zone of the typical small town.

The inner edge zone consists of concentric edges much more closely spaced, usually beginning about three miles from the actual places of business. There, at least on secondary highways and many back roads, the traveller passes through an edge jammed with signs for motels, gas stations, restaurants, and other businesses, an edge that moves slowly outward from Main Street each year as businessmen strive to erect the outermost sign in the grouping. The jumble of signs standing in wheat or corn fields or placed carefully on the shoulder abutting forest can distract the motorist from the most significant edge of all.

About two miles from town, the traveller encounters the seventh edge, the welcoming edge. Here are signs erected by the town government to advertise either the town's uniqueness or its sameness. Most of the signs, painted on large sheets of plywood, rarely show professional skill, but their messages are vital to understanding how small towns imagine themselves. For example, Inkstar, North Dakota, is "Home of Miss North Dakota of 1967"; Dove Creek, Colorado, is "Pinto Bean Capital of the World"; Miami, Texas, hosts the "National Cow-Calling Contest"; and Lewis, Kansas, is "Home of the Spartans, State Basketball Champs in 1971." The signs remain for years, sometimes growing faded, sometimes repainted and varnished against the weather; each expresses a matter of great importance in the small community ahead. Other towns, not lucky enough to achieve distinction in beauty contests or sporting events, boast of their sameness, of their friendliness. "Greeley, Kansas: County Seat: 580 Friendly People and a Few Old Sore Heads" reads one such sign; "Howard, Colorado: The Home of 150 Nice People and a Few Old Sore

Heads" reads another. Along with such signs stand others, usually metal frames carrying the shields of fraternal organizations like the Lions, the Kiwanis, the Odd Fellows. The welcoming edge, therefore, advertises both the uniqueness and the unassuming friendliness and sameness of the town; like the advertising slogans, the welcoming signs entice the traveller to stop.

Beyond the welcoming edge are others, less easily defined. The visible edge, unless topography interferes, stands perhaps a mile from the structures of the town; often it coincides with the railroad sign edge, the place where railroad companies erect town-name signs for locomotive engineers. Just beyond is the legal edge, the limit of incorporated political power, almost always marked by a sign erected by the state highway department, and sometimes by other legal notices prohibiting door-to-door peddling. Beyond the "town limits" sign usually lies the actual physical edge of houses and commercial buildings, and the motorist has arrived "in town."

Not long ago, being "in" a small town meant being anywhere within the structures that comprise it. Certainly Main Street or the courthouse square was the center of activity, but the gas station on the site of the long-demolished livery stable was part of the town too, just as were the grain elevator and railroad yard. Indeed, until very recently, the vast region defined by the various advertising edges existed as some place else for the townspeople, "the county" or "down the road." While town businessmen might occasionally boast that the whole area lay within the town's commercial influence, the signage edges existed for travellers, and especially for tourists. "Going to town" meant something specific for the farm family driving in for Saturday shopping and visiting, just as being "in town" meant something equally specific for the town residents. The building of new single-family houses on farmland began to change matters in the 1950s, however, and soon many small towns had "suburbs" of fifteen or fifty houses beyond the legal limit of fire and police protection, beyond the range of walking postmen. Small towns still struggle with the legal issues of adjacent "developments" of houses and mobile homes, and they struggle too with reinterpreting the significance of *edge,* as the concentric signage rings make clear, but most still have quite distinct physical edges understood by townspeople, farm families, and visitors.

Concepts like the "edge of town" and "being in town" are significant beyond rural and small-town America, for the rural bias of the nation has always affected the national view of cities, and the national language. Until the years following the Civil War, most Americans understood city edges in ways akin to town edges, and into the 1930s, motorists approaching smaller cities encountered the same sort of advertising rings as circled small towns. What complicated national thinking, then confused it, seems to have been the hop-scotch type of land development that characterized suburban real estate operations after World War II.

Speculators bought land cheaply, and developed it for housing or retail business or, more rarely, for industry. In their haste to accommodate a public made mobile by the automobile and a massive road-building campaign, they simply passed by the farmer or other land owner unwilling to sell for a seemingly too-low price. Suburban development, as Shadwell noted in 1909, had long progressed by fits and starts, but in the 1950s and later, the scale expanded tremendously. Coupled with different zoning patterns, the change in scale created vast regions of no immediately identifiable character. Not urban, not rural, not suburban if *suburban* meant residential, the new regions lacked a name and lacked distinct edges. Who knew where country ended and the new regions began, who knew where urban form began?

Old edges vanished, swept away by bulldozers and housing developments, and no distinct edges replaced them. The national love of small-town physical and signage edges endured the sweeping spatial transformation, however, sparking debates about greenbelts and parkbelts, unsettling residents of housing suburbs that stretched undifferentiated for miles, and warping American English.

Businessmen captured the word *city* for themselves sometime in the 1960s, and for two decades they have refined their use of the term until its prior usage has withered. What is the significance of a store name like "Furniture City" or "Computer City," of a mall name like "Garden City"? Essentially, the meaning is this. First, the structure has a clearly defined edge zone consisting of a parking lot and front door; Furniture City is an absolutely identified place. Second, within the doors all is civilized; certainly the interior is well lit, air cooled or gently heated, smoothly paved, and nicely painted, but more significantly, behavior inside is civil. At Computer City salespeople and customers speak politely, sharing common concerns, and appreciating the goods displayed throughout the store. No wonder that retailers have captured the word *city*. They use it not only to connote the civilized behavior once associated with cities, but in a way that harks back to the era when cities had edges, when going to a city meant leaving the rural space, passing through a wall or other distinct edge, and entering into a world of refined behavior and exciting activity.

Americans have always understood the essential characteristics of city life and urban form, and small towns hoping to grow into cities grandiosely added the word *city* to their names. But now the word *city* is undergoing a sort of adaptive reuse, one perilous to the health of the nation's metropolises. If *city* comes to define not only the people inside a store or shopping mall, but their behavior and the environmental conditions they enjoy, what word will define New York, Los Angeles, Atlanta, or Indianapolis? The massive force of advertising uses the word *city* to imply that only privately controlled structures and conglomerations have the distinct edge through which people pass into civilized life. If words like *city* and *urbanity* are to be rescued from the clutches of retailers and advertising agencies, then urban designers must study carefully the deep cultural significance implicit in the physical and signage edges encircling rural American towns, for the small-town edges still shape the national perception of the sprawling, amorphous regions that ring "cities." It is not only the center or inner city that needs attention from urban designers, it is the edge zone of the city.

PHOTOGRAPHED LANDSCAPE

These pages reflect light. After 1900 landscape became the subject or backdrop in a variety of media manipulating light. Cinema projected images onto screens that tricked the human eye into seeing motion. Despite the projectors whirring behind the audience, the cinema view is essentially one of reflected light regularly interrupted by blackness in a sequence that produces quasi-hypnogenesis. But television, video, and computer monitors all emit light, the blue light observers of nighttime landscape seen glimmering from behind so many darkened windows. The present fascination with emitted-light imagery exists almost free of any knowledge of the human eye, brain function, or high-tech manipulation of images. It deflects attention from reflected light, not only that reflected from book pages but from daguerreotype and photographic images.

Despite the surfeit of images, the public school system still teaches little about analyzing any image. Television commercials flash past almost as fast as magazine readers flip pages. Images that arrest individual attention receive little sustained analysis, and images that slow attention time after time receive even less. But period daguerreotypes and photographs of landscape prove evocative portals to anyone who devotes sustained scrutiny to analyzing visual images that shape attention and thought. In some instances, period images suggest that written history is at best incomplete.

In the early modern era, sustained looking involved scrying. Part intense observation, part fortune-telling, part art, scrying rewards scholarly attention today simply because it suggests that at least some people learn differently than most. Scryers see not only details others miss but larger patterns and frames others miss too. In a nation bedeviled by standardized tests that focus on verbal and quantitative aptitude and acuteness, visual acuity gets little reward in most classrooms. But scryers who struggle against the dictates of schoolteachers and state boards of education sometimes discover others like themselves. Together they not only see things in landscape others miss, but envision landscapes not yet constructed.

Until very recently, scholars ignored daguerreotypy as unimportant. Now experts realize it not as proto photography, but as a different medium that transformed the vision of the educated elite. Before the Civil War it became something considered almost magical and sometimes demonic: the daguerreotypist might see shades of landscapes past, or evil lurking behind the human eye. Late-nineteenth-century historians, and perhaps the educated general public too, so connected daguerreotypy with disunion that they omitted the medium from history texts. Making daguerreotypes seemed somehow dangerous in the extreme, and thinking about it in the era of photography seemed tempting the devil.

Making photographs struck many contemporaneous observers as only slightly less dangerous. Amateur photographers used George Eastman's Kodak box cameras to make the snapshots that compared so poorly with the view-camera images professional photographers made. But between the amateurs and the professionals moved a new cadre of image makers equipped with sophisticated cameras and masses of detailed instruction. The popular photographers not only followed landscape aesthetics dictated by self-appointed experts but created an aesthetic of landscape grounded in how well any landscape appeared in a photograph. Out of popular photography emerged contemporary scenery values and much of contemporary landscape aesthetics, for popular photography shaped advertising imagery. Only now does digital photography enter the popular-photography enterprise.

Popular photographers merged specific landscapes with the human form in the late 1920s, and by the 1950s the welding of landscape and portrait formats had been accomplished. As the daguerreotype dovetailed with disunion, so the popular photograph merged with the fear of atomic warfare and the radioactive fallout that fogged film. The beach became the epitome of healthful landscape, and the bikinied woman the apotheosis of good health, sexual freedom, mental alertness, and above all, self-confident risk taking. Photographers and models understood the beach as background as well as theater, and Hollywood followed their lead.

Beach became studio. Contemporary Americans now assume a beach to face the setting sun, to be the marge not just of ocean but of social correctness and futurity alike. Beaches face the evening, then night, and always tomorrow, at least in most print-media and Hollywood imagery. East Coast beaches that so shaped popular landscape photography between 1895 and 1940 have far less power now. The observer of landscape must be up at dawn to see the sunrise, and behind the beach lies today, not tomorrow.

Advertisers and markets shaped the popular photography image of the beach empty of people into a tourist-attracting trope. Nowadays the best beach is a lonely one, perfect for the solitary wanderer or the romance-entangled couple. Crowded beaches seem unphotogenic. Only on them do Americans remove most of their clothes and fall asleep next to total strangers, although lately such behavior seems almost down-scale. In advertisements for lawn furniture, paint, boats, and always but always clothing, the empty or sparsely populated beach is the chief icon and most powerful motivator of people almost wholly unclothed and enjoying the sunlight that frightens the timid.

But the sparsely settled American West, especially the High Plains, attracts far less favorable attention when it attracts attention at all. It is as lonely, sun drenched, and often as sandy as beaches, but it strikes advertisers as not nearly as romantic. After the demise of television westerns in the early 1970s, the windswept West began to defy all but the most intrepid landscape observers and photographers. In a nation in which most intellectuals live in densely settled landscape, the sparsely settled regions unsettle. For many visitors and travelers, photography proves too difficult, and flukes in the wind prove too easy to hear.

Only the hardiest of photographers ventured to ocean beaches in 1885, and nowadays only the most courageous work north of eastern New Mexico toward the Arctic.

REFLECTED LIGHT

Books reflect light. From the open page bounces the illumination of sun, candle, lantern, and incandescent bulb, light that suits the reader best when it bounces perfectly. Let light grow dim, let it flicker or glare, and the reader squirms slightly, reorienting the open book or adjusting the lamp. So obvious is it all that few readers consider reflected light any more than the rustle of turned pages. But reflected light insures the survival of the book, the primacy of print on paper.

Computer, television, and video monitors all *emit* light. Fundamentally different from the cinema, in which imagery basks in projected light reflected from a screen, video-screen imagery snares the eye. Once only fire emitted eye-snaring light, and lovers, old farmers, wayfarers, and others often sat rapt, gazing into the flames. Open fire, usually a controlled wood fire confined to a fireplace, meant more than hearth, good cooking, and home; it meant the special light that encouraged mental states once called fantasy or reverie—not imagination. Firelight proved slightly hypnotic, but hypnotic without particular message or directive. Its ceaseless movement, continuous change of color, and varying intensity not only intrigued Hawthorne and other romantics mourning the coming of cast-iron stoves, but thoughtful individuals of any period intrigued with its peculiar mental effects. Self-disciplined intellectuals valued imagination over reverie not only because imagination is volitional, but because fire-induced reverie could become addictive, and often choked imagination. The natural world—excluding fire—and the world of art, books especially, take visible form in reflected light, they argued, and reflection, and its illuminating counterpart, imagination, are beyond the reverie of fire-watching. Television, of course, changed things in the 1950s, for its emitted light had definite message, definite directive.

Video screens snare the eye as fire snares gnats. Television essentially destroyed cinema, at least Hollywood cinema, not because television programming seemed free or convenient or somehow better, but because the emitted light snared individuals, even whole families, transfixing them in their homes. Any department-store video display demonstrates the snaring. People, especially children, walk past the single or multiple

"Reflected Light" appeared in *Boston Review* 16 (December 1991).

monitors and lose volition, their eyes snared by the images, their legs slowed to a stop. But unlike fire, video imagery directs the mind, keeping it even from reverie, keeping it from much except passive receptivity. Programming, be it Desert Storm news or Nintendo games or word-processing menus, receives far too much attention. It is the emitted light that deserves scrutiny in these multi-cultural times.

A division deeper than anything racial or ethnic or economic now splits the Republic, but the division slices so sharply and so deeply that few mark its crucial importance. For the vast majority of American adults, and for almost all children, electronic media dominate information flow, shaping everything from speech patterns to attention spans. But a minority, a very smug minority, understands the raw profit in eschewing the screens, in engaging in imaginative, self-disciplined, *self-directed* inquiry, in reading hard-copy only, in reading books. Wallace Stevens hit it best in his brief poem "The House Was Quiet and the World Was Calm," fitfully tracing the brutal, silent effort culminating when "the reader became the book." Those who know only light-emitting screens know only tawdry entertainment, cheap exactitude. Their imaginative potential shrivels before flickering bluish light or yellow letters glimmering against a black ground. Others, slightly wiser at the start, or guided by sages learning the power accruing to the wired-out, read in reflected light, figure in pencil, doodle as they think, as they imagine. To those few come understanding and appreciation of ambiguity and estimation, of echoes and innuendo, of personality and meter, but above all comes self-directed imaginative inquiry. They, not the manipulators of music videos or spreadsheets or paintbrush programs, understand reflection, imagination, even serendipity, types of mental effort scarcely mentioned by the champions of VDTs. They know how rarely a fireplace fire co-exists with a video screen, how the fall of light on a printed page works its own imaginative magic.

SCRUTINIZING PHOTOGRAPHS,
TRACING PORTALS

Is Locomotive No. 45 haunted? Does the little girl with ringlets know it? Is something seriously amiss? Or do I hold one more flea-market photograph, a glimpse of life down by the depot a century ago?

Period photographs deserve scrutiny. After George Eastman popularized the snapshot camera with his "You push the button, we do the rest" motto in 1888, photography degenerated into snap-shooting. Susan Sontag argues accurately, and most probably correctly, in *On Photography* when she catalogues the hunting vocabulary of high-quality photography. Not only does the photographer *load,* then *aim* his camera, he also *shoots* his subject.[1] But Sontag says little about the snapshooter, and yet the snapshooter is the typical American photographer. The snapshooter shoots differently. Indeed, he gets his name from a sort of fast, offhand type of gunplay in which the gunman appears to take no aim. When photography was part art, part technical wizardry, the photographer agonized over choice of subject, lighting, and angle; glass-plate negatives cost too much for carelessness. Wholly involved with his operation from mixing chemicals to coating negatives to developing to printing, he understood the actual releasing of the shutter as only one event in a chain of equally important ones. To be sure, the choice of subject required care, but care by someone accustomed to caution in every photographic step. Comparing the turn-of-the-century photographer with the 1920s snapshooter resembles comparing the Kentucky rifleman to a hunter armed with a repeating shotgun. The one makes a single effort with a difficult weapon, risking all on one shot. The other fires rapidly at his target, and may not even know which round winged the goose or downed the duck. In a world of snapshot photography the photographic image loses value. Viewers assume a fine photograph to be a lucky image, or worse, a casual product of a nearly automatic precision instrument.

Yet, even in our contemporary technological society, Americans prove amazingly reluctant to destroy photographs. Ask lovers to photograph each other with instant cameras and then exchange the images. Next hand each an icepick and tell them to poke out the eyes on each scrap of

"Scrutinizing Photographs, Tracing Portals" appeared in different form in *Hayes Historical Journal* 7 (Fall 1987): 36–40.

cardboard. Almost invariably revulsion stays their hands. The images are left whole. The icepick might be a voodoo needle, the American citizens Haitian peasants. However casually made, the snapshots acquire awesome potency as instantaneously as they slide from the camera.

Period photographs share this double character. On the one hand, historians, archivists, and the interested general public handle them with care, and greet their presence in museums and journals with pleasure. On the other, almost no one scrutinizes them. Americans look at old images; they do not read them. Almost never do they realize them, make them real. Every period photograph is, to borrow a line from Wallace Stevens's 1915 poem "Peter Quince at the Clavier," a "fitful tracing of a portal."[2] Through the portal flickering still on the faded, sepia cardboard is a past, a past deserving more than a glance from the snapshot age, a past nearly touchable, a past the reader can almost enter.

Regard another, of an interurban car, for example. The archivist tells us that it belongs to the Lakeshore Electric Company, that it is running on State Street in Fremont, Ohio, around 1900, and that behind it is the opera house. What else does scrutiny reveal?

To begin, consider the season and speed. The trees appear in full leaf, or nearly so, and the store has its awnings set, seemingly over a potted palm. But clearly it is not summer. The men lounging on the observation platform wear derbies and dark coats, not the straw hats and light jackets of summer. So it is late spring, sometime in May perhaps. And the car is cruising slowly, for the men are relaxed, and scarcely holding the railings.

What do they see on their ride? Their postures suggest an easy familiarity with each other, and with Fremont; only one looks away from the platform. But certainly Fremont is modern enough. For one thing, the street is lined with utility poles. Not only do the crossarms suggest sophisticated electric service, but the four-armed pole just ahead of the car suggests that Fremont has more than one telephone company, and that wires crisscrossed downtown. On the street and the rear of the car, just about on the second window from the platform, is the shadow of another utility pole—one with at least two arms. Yet aside from the trolley wire and its supports, few wires hang directly over the street. Fremont appears to have been wired in parallel lines.

In the late afternoon sunshine, the big car—about three times the size of a city trolley—coasts downgrade, providing its now nearly forgotten service. Interurban lines connected centers of small towns with centers of cities, running along both private rights of way and public thoroughfares, now and then frightening horses, but usually ghosting past in near silence. Electric motors only hum; the car in the picture makes some noise, particularly air-compressor-pump clatter—the cylinder slung beneath it probably contains compressed air—and the clickety-clack of steel wheels on steel rails, but compared to the jarring racket of steel-tired wagons moving over brick streets, its sounds are muffled—and quickly past. No smoke, no fumes, no manure left behind, the big car proceeds, caught forever in late-spring quietude.

Only slightly more noisy is another photographed conveyance, appropriately named *Frolic* and carrying a group of young women on an outing. The women seem content enough, to judge by their postures—one is half-sitting, half-reclining over the wheelhouse beside the name-board—and not at all concerned about smoke.

Indeed no smoke mars their view. The little vessel is churning along sprightly—note the modest bow and side waves—but its engineer is minding his fire well. Not only does a clean fire mean no waste of coal, it pleases the young women topside, some of whom have removed their jackets and exposed white blouses, "shirtwaists" in their terms, and other early spring finery to sun and fresh air. Smoke is *not* blowing away somehow. The American flag suspended over the stern and the smooth water away from the hull—and the random facing of the women—combine to show how slightly the wind is blowing.

This image demonstrates the cleanliness of coal-fired engines, something often forgotten now. Perhaps the forgetting began in the late 1940s and early 1950s, when railroad buffs grew suddenly and painfully aware that diesel locomotives meant the end of steam. By the thousands they rushed to photograph the vanishing coal-fired machines, and often sought out those making smoke, since the smoke struck them not only as spectacular against the sky, but as the clearest evidence that steam moved the aging engines. Certainly external-combustion engines make visible smoke and soot, usually mixed with steam; the very cleanliness of the interurban car attracted many passengers anxious to open windows and enjoy fresh air.

But in the decade after World War II railroad locomotives made far more smoke than in earlier times. Abused almost beyond belief in the herculean war effort and then given only minimal maintenance by owners investing in diesels, the engines poured forth smoke despite the best efforts of firemen and engineers vainly trying to meet company fuel-burning regulations (some railroads even sent out spotters to enforce rules) and smoke-abatement ordinances. And the railroad buffs waited for the most glorious blasts, and photographed them. In time Americans knew mostly the photographs, and forgot the cleanliness of professionally fired coal. Today at railroad museums they wonder why the restored locomotive hissing along at the head of their train smokes so little, if at all.

Sherlock Holmes offers sound advice applicable to photograph reading. In a short story entitled "Silver Blaze," Arthur Conan Doyle demonstrates the reverse side of close observation. Holmes calls to Doctor Watson's attention the curious activity of a watchdog in the night; when Watson replies that "the dog did nothing in the night-time," Holmes pounces: "That was the curious incident."[3] Almost invariably, scrutinizers of period photographs try to find everything in the image; but part of the task is to see what is not there. Nowhere in this image is there smoke. Nowhere, expect for the shadow in the wheelhouse, is there a man.

The young women aboard the *Frolic* cruise along two parallel transportation routes, railroad and road. Implicit in the photograph is the whole history of aligning American transportation routes. In a new nation, vast and still poor, men and women traveled along water, taking always the low road. Much of the time they gazed uphill, toward a forest skyline in pioneer years, then toward open fields interspersed with trees, as here.

On what time does the photograph-portal open? The passenger cars suggest the last two decades of the nineteenth century. As John H. White points out in his monumental *The American Railroad Passenger Car,* open-platform cars decreased sharply in popularity once the vestibule became common.[4] All of the cars beyond the *Frolic* lack vestibules, but all are in immaculate condition; clearly this is no photograph of sidetracked second-rate cars. And the second car from the right is no ordinary car; unlike the others, it rides on six-wheel trucks. Maybe it is a "varnish," a first-class car, a Pullman perhaps, made of wood so fine its owner varnished rather than painted it. The cars appear to be a train—the second car from the left is a combination coach-baggage car usually placed at the head of a passenger train—awaiting a locomotive, perhaps a locomotive backing the left-most car into the train.

The cars sit on a busy track, or on a sidetrack paralleling a busy main line, for not only is the right of way lined with poles boasting nine cross-arms each—a sure sign of heavy telegraph traffic—but uphill is a large advertising sign, alas difficult to read. The sign faces the track and river, as well as the road above both. A sort of early billboard, it addresses travelers, not residents. Riders weary of reading or card playing might look from their windows and read its message—from the few decipherable letters probably a real estate offering—and stop in the next town to inquire further.

Not every stop was scheduled. The photograph of the wrecked locomotive and cars pictured here demonstrates beyond words the hideousness of late-nineteenth-century railroad calamities. Immediately apparent is the devastation, of course, but perhaps the shattered locomotive speaks most clearly of colliding forces. The big passenger car trumpets the im-

A serious train wreck in Lindsey, Ohio, attracted not only repair personnel and the photographer but onlookers too. (Courtesy Rutherford B. Hayes Presidential Center)

portance of the train, however. It is a "varnish," a vestibule sleeper—note the lack of an open platform—intended for first-class riders. Its vestibule allows its passengers to pass to the next vestibule-equipped car without venturing into the open air. And sleepers rolled only in first-class, high-speed trains.

In this photograph of collision aftermath, onlookers appear relaxed, and generally intrigued with the wrecking derrick in the background. Track-clearing operations appear to have been slow enough; men—and even two women, one with parasol—stand or walk about in the midst of the wreckage. Of course the wreckage lies strewn over a road crossing—note the diamond-shaped warning sign just next to the boom of the wrecker—in a small town, so many of the pedestrians may have simply stopped for a moment while on other errands.

With this photograph the archivist connected a news story in the *Fremont Daily News* of August 7, 1893. At least three people died in the crash, and of the nine critically injured, the reporter heard two more would most probably die. No lengthy investigation determined the cause of the wreck. Employees on the scene learned that the night passenger train thundering through the little Ohio village of Lindsey at 45 or 50 miles an hour—the train was ten minutes late and "running at a high rate of speed"—began to pass a freight train stopped on a parallel sidetrack. The freight-train crew, sitting on the ground next to its stopped locomotive, had no time to jump as the second half of the eleven-car express

SCRUTINIZING PHOTOGRAPHS

sheared sideways, sideswiping the engine and cars. "The engine was almost completely turned around, lifted off its tracks, stripped of pilot, smoke-stack, and trimmings and thrown over on its side," the reporter learned. "The tender was thrown into a car loaded with flour." The big wooden sleeping cars disintegrated into splinters as they struck the mass of steel, scattered their passengers over the ground, and came to rest in the midst of freight. Only the last sleeper, the one in the photograph, survived intact. "Bolts holding the plates securing the first joint of the rails together were broken," the employees concluded, allowing the track to move beneath the speeding train almost as if a switch had been turned.[5] Fortunately the overturned steam locomotive did not ignite the wreckage.

Horrible as it was, such an accident was not uncommon in the 1890s. Railroad companies balanced safety against public demands for high-speed service, and technology frequently failed at critical moments. Metal fatigue, not the more common human error of the time, struck death into the warm night in Lindsey. By morning, as the wrecking crew struggled to open the route, bicyclists and other onlookers had arrived to survey the failure of technology, to wonder at the speed, not of the night express, but of disaster.

Watching and wondering at technology and its failings entranced late-nineteenth-century Americans. The little girl so prettily dressed staring at locomotive No. 45 is doing nothing out of the ordinary. As Cecelia Tichi so convincingly demonstrates in *Changing Gears: Technology, Literature, Culture in Modernist America,* the little girl lived in an age fascinated with gears, steam, speed, horsepower.[6] After all, her adult contemporaries thought that machinery had helped to produce national greatness, progress, and "a better life"; often viewing these things seemed startlingly wonderful.

Consider the railway mail car. Standing in its center door is a clerk with a mailbag; just beyond, a mailbag crane. Equipped with a hook, the clerk could snatch a full mailbag from the crane as the train sped by, and almost simultaneously toss out a mailbag onto the station platform. The railway post office, as the Post Office officially designated such cars in the Railway Mail Service, provided high-speed, regular, reliable mail service to the smallest of towns crossed by rails. The midnight express might never stop, but it picked up and discharged mail as it roared through. Overnight delivery of mail between large cities served by airliners is possible today, but no patron of the modern postal service believes in over-night delivery between distant small towns—at least not without the premium paid for express mail service. But at the turn of the century railroads stitched together distant small towns like beads on a string, and the Post Office trumpeted the triumph of trains called "The Fast Mail."

Perhaps no other object made eternal in four stark photographs speaks more poignantly of the role of the railroad in American life during the years of Rutherford B. Hayes than the railway mail car. Nationwide, utterly reliable (except for wrecks and blizzards), incredibly inexpensive (almost all first-class mail moved by train and the Post Office charged no premium for sending mail via crane, hook, and mail car), the Railway Mail Service linked small towns with great cities of course, but more important, linked small towns with each other. Small-town residents *expected* overnight, on-time delivery, and took the mail crane for granted, except when they grew thoughtful, and momentarily realized its role in business and social life.

And what of the girl? Almost certainly, the photographer was an amateur, perhaps a father struck by the unexpected stopping of a fast express and able to coax his daughter into posing. The photographer lacked professional finesse. Consider the great side rods on the locomotive. They are up, near the top of their revolution. Professional photographers, in a sort of professional conceit that became custom, chose to photograph locomotives only with rods down, in the opposite position than those on No. 45. Of course, the photographer confronted with a stopped locomotive accepted the rods as he found them, but rods up suggests that the little girl, not the train, was the center of attention.

Indeed she was. Only scrutiny reveals the bell, and makes the contemporary observer wonder. No one stands in the cab of the locomotive, no one grasps the bell rope visible through the open door. So who rings the bell? For surely someone pulls the rope so carefully strung down through a guide atop the boiler. The bell rings. And the little girl looks, with reason. Now we can only wonder, and look more closely, trying to discern the fitful tracing of the portal into—not "the past" exactly, but into a past, into a moment in a specific place.

Notes

1. Susan Sontag, *On Photography* (New York, 1977), 10–16.
2. *Poems,* ed. Samuel French Morse (New York, 1959), 4–6.
3. *The Complete Sherlock Holmes,* ed. Christopher Morley (Garden City, New York, n.d.), 347.
4. John H. White, *The American Railroad Passenger Car* (Baltimore, 1978), 447–451 and passim.
5. *Fremont (Ohio) Daily News,* 7 August, 1893, 1.
6. Cecelia Tichi, *Changing Gears: Technology, Literature, Culture in Modernist America* (Chapel Hill, 1987), 17–40 and passim.

SCRYING XANADU

Nowadays *scrying* floats free of all but the densest dictionaries, the word itself drifted into near-oblivion. Like crystalomancy and catoptromancy, like daguerreotypy and photography too, scrying is fundamentally optic, something accomplished with the eyes. No dictionary definition catches its nuances, no dictionary definition monumentalizes its long-ago importance. Words do scrying only the slightest honor. But scrying demands scrutiny in these millennial, image-saturated years, for it opens on the shadowy iridescence that is the deep-past but ever-present optic context of photography, and especially the optic context of genuine landscape photography, the photography of *scryed place*. And scrying rewards scrutiny, for scrying is sibling to scrutiny itself.

Only the word *descry* hints at the old importance of scrying. At the beginning of the great age of exploration, Elizabethans used the term to designate especially acute seeing of islands, headlands, and other seamarks. "Some travellers shall the Contreyes far escrye, / Beyond small Thule, knowen furthest at this daye," John Studley translated Seneca's *Medea* in 1566, rhying *escrye* with *survaye,* a word far closer to contemporaneous French, a word meaning literally "over look." Exploration and navigation "requireth a particular Register of certaine Landmarkes (where markes may be had) from the sea, well able to be skried, in what point of the Seacumpass they appeare, and what apparent forme, Situation, and bigness they have," insisted John Dee in his 1570 preface to Euclid's *Elements of Geometry.* Adventuring mariners routinely used *descry* or some variant of it, and Captain Thomas Wyatt, the soldier-author of the 1595 narrative *The Voyage of Robert Dudley to the West Indes,* understood scrying as the accomplishment peculiar to the experienced mariner who "beinge on the quarter deck in lookinge abroade was the first that scryed a sayle." Even Spenser, in his 1596 opus *The Faerie Queen,* knew descrying as a very special kind of looking: at the end of the fifth book of the great poem, he describes two witches rushing at a knight "As it had bene two shepheards curres, had scryde / A ravenous Wolfe amongst the scattered

"Scrying Xanadu" appeared in *21st: The Journal of Contemporary Photography, Culture, and Criticism* 1 (1998): 67–73.

flockes." Explorers and mariners, witches and watchdogs might descry, then, and see differently, might know their place in near-formless sea or heath or other wilderness.

Apheresis eventually reduced *ascry, escry,* and *descry* to *scry,* but even as Elizabethan and subsequent generations of English-speakers abbreviated the words, meanings endured, sometimes obviously, sometimes not. Into the twentieth century, rural Englishmen knew *scry* as a noun, a word designating sorts of sieves, even sieves big enough to sort manure, sieves through which some things passed and not others. While that use of *scry* only hints at the discrimination writers understood when using the word in a visual sense, the root meaning of *descry* involves not only the "tracing out" glimmering in the deep past of the word *describe,* but the exclamation that follows tracing out. *Scry* of course is a form of *cry,* perhaps especially the "crying out" that makes the Latin root meaning of *ex-plore,* but *scry* also meant, especially in Elizabethan times, a military attack or reconnaissance, a *force* coming at one. Together, *scry, descry,* and *scrying* bound a juicy concatenation of ideas ranging from a *thing* that discriminates to a way of seeing to a type of voiced message to a sort of attack or reconnoiter. Why, then, did the words disappear so abruptly from learned English at the beginning of the seventeenth century? Why did *scry* survive as a noun among rural, unlettered Englishmen, but *scrying* as a noun almost vanish?

Scrying is esotery. Glimpsing anything of the sudden disappearance of *scrying* and related terms means glimpsing something not only of the limitations of dictionaries but of all print media, especially of books. Indeed any glimpse explains the continuing menace certain photography poses to people who read but cannot scry.

"The ancients, delivering their lectures by word of mouth, could adapt their subjects to their audience, reserving their esoteries for adepts, and dealing out exoteries only to the vulgar," argued Abraham Tucker in his 1763 treatise, *Freewill, Foreknowledge, and Fate.* "Whereas we moderns having no other channel of communication than the press, must throw out both sorts to the mercy of every man that can raise the pence to buy a copy, or has a friend of whom he can borrow one." In distinguishing between esotery and exotery, Tucker says nothing particularly devastating: what the vulgar know often differs from anything known by the cognoscenti. But in lamenting the end of oral transmission of knowledge, he raises the issue so rarely raised after the late-sixteenth-century triumph of printing. How does the possessor of knowledge disseminate it differentially? After all, *anyone* may read the book, may bring charges ranging from heresy to perversion to necromancy.

One solution to the dilemma Tucker poses is to write in code, something that fascinated a handful of learned Europeans in the years just before the Spanish Armada sailed to slay Protestantism. Even a printed book might carry two messages, one the obvious text for the vulgar reader, the other hidden, accessible only to the chosen, the adept. But Elizabethans in the secret service of their monarch understood secret messaging in ways that far transcended mere cipher or some message laid between lines. They knew the usefulness of drawings, even doodles, and one of Elizabeth's most trusted agents emphasized not just the secret looking designated by *spying,* but the necessity for hooded eyes. He signed his messages with a device that emphasized eyes hooded, two circles followed by the numeral seven with its top bar extended above the circles. John Dee worked as the first agent 007.

Mathematician, astronomer, linguist, espionage agent, and occultist John Dee never achieved the lasting renown he nearly grasped. Literally a renaissance man, a genius deeply intrigued with the problems of celestial navigation confronted by sixteenth-century mariners, he insisted that England must become a great imperialist power or succumb to Spanish and French might. He argued in his *Atlanticall Discources* for expeditions to find the Northwest Passage to China, and he prepared plans to deal with potential invasions by Spain with as much flair and precision as he invented a system of pulleys to move heavy weights. Sometimes disappearing for months or years on secret missions, sometimes appearing at Court, he knew everyone from explorer Martin Frobisher, to whom he gave instruction in cosmography, to Shakespeare, to whom he provided information about Bermuda for use in *The Tempest.* But more than a lifelong espionage effort put Dee on the margins of respectability. Dee devoted years to scrying.

Mirrors fascinated Dee. At first, he conceived of mirrors as long-distance signaling devices, and composed a code by which mirrors might send messages across the Thames estuary. Then he began studying how mirrors might make ordinary handwriting esoteric. Unlike Leonardo da Vinci, who merely wrote reversed in his journals, Dee seems to have struggled with mirrors altered for espionage purposes, staring at the page reflected in the undulated mirror as he wrote, and producing on paper what seemed mere scribbles to all but someone equipped with an identical mirror before which the mysterious page might lie. Elizabeth grew intrigued by his mirror research, perhaps witnessed one of his cross-Thames demonstrations, and after one of his visits to court urging the creation of a coast guard service, paid Dee a surprise visit. In March, 1575, Dee brought outdoors from his house the "magic glass of which she had heard so much," and within minutes Elizabeth and her courtiers were laughing uproariously as they saw themselves reflected in what seems to have been a concave or undulating mirror. Whatever its usual use, the Queen of England found it comic.

Not everyone else did, at least not later. Twenty-one years after, Spenser depicted the incident utterly differently in his *Faerie Queen,* casting Elizabeth as the female warrior Britomart anxious to scry her future lover. "By straunge occasion she did him behold, / And much more straungely gan to love his sight, / As in bookes hath written beene of old," the passage begins. Out of the deep past comes an object, some sort of speculum, Merlin's "looking-glasse," a globe Spenser describes as "Frothy it round and hollow shaped was, / Like to the World itselfe, and seemed a world of glas." Britomart dabbles for a moment in catoptromancy or crystalomancy, maybe both. At any rate, she scries.

By 1596 Spenser knew the rumors that swirled around Dee, that he served as Elizabeth's astrologer, that he skirted the black arts in searching for treasure trove. Certainly the espionage agent had continued his study of mirrors, but while Dee had conceived plans for great mirrors to be used as "burning glasses" that might incinerate advancing armies, he had begun to muse on the philosophic components underlying mirror optics. His interest in measuring the speed of light led him to conclude that a mirror moving through space faster than the speed of light must necessarily reflect the past, and might demonstrate the truth of one of his hunches, that the light emitted by stars was at least fifty earth-years old. Moreover, Dee decided, mirrors might be used to capture reflections of other planes of existence, a concept he had more or less approached as early as 1557, when he published his *Zographie,* a treatise on radiation, color, and light. But by 1581, when he was fifty-four years old, he shifted his attention from mirrors to crystals, and devoted his energies to scrying, something that troubled his wife, his friends, and his enemies.

In the Middle Ages, scrying remained an art form with ancient roots, a past Spenser alludes to in his line about ancient books. Typically, scrying required the help of a young boy or girl, for most savants intrigued by it learned that they had no gift for it, or if they had such a gift, learning to read and write had eradicated it. The child, and sometimes the adult, focused on either the mirror or the sphere until his or her subconscious opened itself to ideas or images not ordinarily discovered by the usual senses. The mirror or sphere and the child together became a medium through which the learned adult might gather fragments of knowledge, but not necessarily knowledge about the future. Dee acquired appropriate spheres, which he described in his diaries as "the great Christaline Globe," the "Shew-Stone," and "as big as an egg, most bryght, clere and glorious," but he most unfortunately had very bad luck finding a child to help him. Instead, he encountered a criminal who for years seems to

SCRYING XANADU

have sometimes tricked Dee, trading his scrying efforts for introductions to European heads of state and struggling always to convert base metals to gold, but at other times performing stunning feats of telepathy.

Dee devoted years to what he called "angelic conversations." Whether or not his assistant tricked him constantly, or even if his assistant proved an honest medium and correctly translated the complex messages from a number of spirits, especially a young girl angel called Madimi, Dee found himself captivated by the potential for espionage and earth-shattering discovery. Caught up in a mix of cryptographic information the angels spoke in Enochian—a language Dee had to translate from his medium one letter at a time plucked from a chart of forty-nine horizontal letters and forty-nine vertical ones—and the likelihood of mental telepathy with higher beings, Dee abandoned much of his other work, and in time lived in Poland and elsewhere in Central Europe as advisor to Emperor Rudolph and King Stephen. Historians make no coherent sense of Dee's scrying in these years, except that somehow he knew in advance that the year 1588 would be marked by terrible gales that would do more damage to the Spanish Armada than English warships. Was Dee spreading misinformation, knowing that Rudolph, a firm believer in astrology, relayed his dire predictions to both the Spanish ambassador and to the Vatican? Or was Dee merely recounting what he scryed through assistant and crystal, and sometimes through the crystal without help? Or was he toying with the portals to other planes of existence?

At least once, Dee thrust beyond such questions to something more complex and more immediately potent. A man can be "curstly affrayed of his owne shadow: yea, so much to fear, that if you, being alone nere a certaine glass, and proffer with dagger or sword, to foyne at the glasse, you shall suddenly be moved to give back (in manner) by reason of an image appearing in the ayre between you and the glasse with like hand, sword or dagger, and with like quicknes." Dee knew that words alone did little to advance his argument. "Straunge this is to heare of, but more mervailous to behold than these my wordes can signifie; and nevertheless by demonstration opticall the order and cause thereof is certified; even so, as the effect is consequent." Make people participate in the "demonstration opticall" and they would begin to believe something of the power of visual images, begin to understand the limitations of words, and begin to accept the potentials implicit in scrying.

But all turned black early in 1603, with the death of Elizabeth and the accession of James VI of Scotland, a man who not only perceived himself the victim of witchcraft but had studied enough about his persecutors to write *Three Books on Demonology*. Almost overnight, the intellectual climate changed. By June, 1604, James had rammed through Parliament

PHOTOGRAPHED LANDSCAPE

an Act to "uproot the monstrous evils of enchanters," and overnight Dee petitioned James for a trial to prove he was neither conjuror nor "invocator of divels." Perhaps in admiration for the old man's secret service, James ignored the request, and left Dee in a peace others even remotely associated with "natural magic" no longer knew as James began a nationwide hunt for enchanters. Catoptromancy, crystalmancy, scrying, even fortune-telling with cards quickly became too much enmeshed in witchcraft and the other black arts.

No mirror today reflects accurately the centuries-long significance of the Jamesian reaction to Elizabethan neo-Platonism and Renaissance magic. At the cusp of the twenty-first century, the shift away from Spenser's masques and visual-image-laced poetry and Shakespeare's brilliant theater to a culture dominated by words, especially by what James VI designated as the *authorized* version of the Bible, then by Puritanism and regicide, seems unaccountably high-paced, almost frenetic, and its permutations defy summary, sometimes even the most dogged analysis. And no matter how brightly polished the mirror, it reflects almost nothing of what vanished, especially the vanished magic and mysticism that had not long before invested the ways of seeing connoted by *scrying*. Nowadays even well-educated visualists scarcely know words like *catoptromancy* and *crystalmancy,* in part because to publish such words *in print* meant investigation, perhaps punishment. Only adepts know the esotery of visualizations before King James VI.

Jamesian attitude and Parliamentary act combined to change British ways of seeing, even of knowing, not for a decade or so, but for centuries. However Protestant, British anti-conjuring work dovetailed nearly perfectly with the witchcraft-routing efforts of the Catholic Inquisition, and by the early seventeenth century had spread across Europe and into the New World. Seeing differently, seeing as Dee had tried to see, almost immediately became sin worse than heresy, and regimes punished the sinners as ruthlessly as the Colony of Massachusetts eradicated the witchcraft at Salem, witchcraft that began with girls trying to see into the future, to scry a bit with regard to future husbands. So powerfully swept the hand of punishment that even Newton himself succumbed to fear. Every modern schoolchild playing with a prism hears teacher say that light shatters into seven colors, one of them indigo. And every obedient schoolchild struggles to see seven colors, to discern indigo. Almost never does teacher explain that Newton watched light shatter into six colors, and determined to see indigo between blue and violet lest his experiment be linked with Satan. After all, six is the number of Satan, seven the number of the Almighty. And a prism is, in the final—and what might have been for Newton the fatal—analysis, merely a triangle-shaped crystal that does such stunning things to ordinary light that Newton argued for years about his discovery. Whatever his interest in optics, mathematics, and physics, Newton devoted much of his later life to writing on theology, seeming motivated at least in part by a powerful desire to demonstrate that his research does nothing to diminish the Almighty, that it is perfectly godly, perfectly respectable, not at all demonic.

Innovation further diminished the old art of scrying. Technological advances like the telescope and microscope, and the prism too, convinced many inquirers that twisted mirrors and polished crystals had been supplanted by easy-to-use devices of immediate practical value. Then too, exploration delivered to Europeans all sorts of physiological novelties, certainly tea and coffee, then tobacco, then opium and other drugs that mingled in the romantic era in ways still frequently ignored. The caffeine rush, the nicotine hit, then the sustained effects of opium, laudanum, hashish, and other less popular drugs altered sensory perception and mental states both, becoming in the eighteenth century the shadowy context of Locke's philosophy and Berkeley's theories on vision, then the stuff of books like Thomas De Quincey's 1822 *Confessions of an English Opium Eater*. Drug-taking and drug addiction became esotery, as more than one early-nineteenth-century author suggested. "The ordinary language of a Philosopher in conversation or popular writings, compared with the language he uses in strict reasoning, is as his Watch compared with the Chronometer in his Observatory," wrote Coleridge in 1825 in *Aids to Reflection*. "He sets the former by Town-clock, or even, perhaps, by the Dutch clock in his kitchen, not because he believes it right, but because his neighbour's and his Cook go by it." What philosophers and poets envisioned at the very end of the eighteenth century, then, depended in part on technological innovation, in part on a range of drugs, and in part—a very small part—on scrying as John Dee knew it.

When Coleridge published "Kubla Khan" in 1816, for example, he understood—and expected some of his readers to understand—the meanings implicit in lines like "A damsel with a dulcimer / In a vision once I saw." Visions came by then from more than tiredness, more than seasickness, more than religious ecstasy. Visions came from opium, and Coleridge well knew it. But visions might come too from the Xanadu construct itself, for after all, what Kubla Khan built might have made sense to Dee two centuries earlier. "It was a miracle of rare device, / A sunny pleasure-dome with caves of ice!" For adepts, Coleridge imagines a gigantic seeing stone, a crystal into which Khan and Alph, the sacred river, both move and flow and tarry. What Coleridge accomplishes in the poem is essentially the scrying of a vision, something he approaches in other, much less well-known poems like "The Destiny of Nations: A Vision," in which he imagines what follows "if the Greenland Wizard in strange trance / Pierces the untravelled realms of Ocean's bed." Does the wizard have an opium stash? Coleridge does not say. But Coleridge and his contemporaries often emphasize the romantic-era esotery of drug-induced envisioning that obscured the old art of scrying and accentuated the technical illusions that from the first invented daguerreotypy and photography.

Now an abyss of time separates inquirers from the earliest years of daguerreotypy and photography. By the time of Daguerre's birth in 1789, Scheele and Senebier knew that violet rays darkened silver chloride faster than red, and Rumford had presented his paper on the chemical properties attributable to light. Two decades before Daguerre became a serious student of photo-chemistry, Wedgwood had demonstrated how to copy profiles onto silver-nitrate-coated paper, and as early as 1810 Seebeck explained how to produce natural colors through photographic action. When Daguerre and Niepce created their own process, they understood only the longest of exposures. "The time required to procure a photographic copy of a landscape is from seven to eight hours, but single monuments, when strongly lighted by the sun, or which are themselves very bright, can be taken in about three hours," Daguerre explained. Only the antiquary nowadays struggles through the masses of chemical esotery gathering dust in university libraries to learn how much daguerreotypy depended on polished silver plates, on almost painfully long exposures, on near trance-like exposures. Daguerreotypy descends directly from catoptromancy, and in 1839, the year the educated world learned of it and Talbot's photographic process, mirrormaking still puzzled many people accustomed to looking-glasses made of well-rubbed tin. Daguerre accomplished something almost magical, something Dee would have honored. He froze or fixed or imprisoned the fleeting looking-glass image his contemporaries usually accepted without thinking.

Our contemporary fascination with daguerreotypy springs in part from the deepest of mirror memory, from our enduring inability to separate daguerreotypy from the mysteries of the looking glass we glimpse every now and then when shaving or applying makeup or plucking eyebrows, just often enough to make mirrors ever so slightly suspect, just often enough to spark reflection on reflection. Catoptromancy still separates daguerreotypy from photography. The art forms are different. But new light, cheap light, skewed vision at the turn of the twentieth century, and produced a moment of scrying every bit as important as the moment of Daguerre, a moment whose power infuses the photography of Michael Kenna and other contemporary masters of the landscape.

"Singly, and in small companies of two or three, they emerged from the dull colourless, sunless distances ahead as if the supply of rather roughly finished mechanical toys were inexhaustible in some mysterious cheap store away there, below the grey curve of the earth," mused Joseph Conrad of steamships in his 1919 memoir, *The North Sea on the Edge of War*. "When they switched on (each of these unlovely cargo tanks carried tame lightning within its slab-sided body), when they switched on their lamps they spangled the night with the cheap, electric, shop-glitter, here, there, and everywhere, as of some High Street broken up and washed out to sea." Nowadays honored for books like *Heart of Darkness*, Conrad deserves to be read and reread for his magisterial understanding of light, and especially for his precise chronicling of what visually acute people lost with the coming of electric illumination, even at sea. What began as a technological marvel quickly became a nuisance that fractured night and dark, an illumination that became cheap glare.

Around the year 1900, the crystal globe suddenly glowed, became incandescent, became the light bulb impossible to scrutinize when charged.

Scrying reemerged largely as a response to cheap images and cheap illumination, the High Street advertising and glare Conrad condemned. Between 1890 and 1930, crystalmancy attracted thousands of educated people revolted by the illusions of superiority bred by technological accomplishment. Moreover, imperialism brought home to educated Europeans and Americans something of the scrying traditions of Africa, New Zealand, and southeast Asia that reminded the classics-trained cognoscenti of Egyptian, Greek, and Roman scrying too. And the spiritualist movement infused scrying with purposes far higher than the utilitarian one of fortune-telling. Here and there scholars began testing Dee's multi-plane universe against the theories promulgated by Einstein and other physicists. Scrying offered a way from the sudden surfeit of tawdry images and glaring light toward something unknown but now and then glimpsed, almost by accident.

Most modern scryers, opined Andrew Lang in his 1894 *Cock Lane and Common-Sense*, "are no more hypnotized by crystal-gazing than teadrinking, or gardening, or reading a book, and who can still enjoy visions as beautiful as those of the opium eater, without any of the reaction." Lang summarily dismissed fortune-telling and most of spiritualism, and laughed off side effects ranging from superstition to headaches. "A ball of glass serves just as well as a ball of crystal, and is much less expensive," he argued, and about the only danger of either is that in bright sunlight the spheres may set tablecloths afire. The magic of the sphere lies not in its ability to link scryers with other planes of existence, but in its ability to make people see differently. "A crystal-seer seems to be a person who can see, in a glass, while awake and with open eyes, visions akin

PHOTOGRAPHED LANDSCAPE

to those which perhaps the majority of people see with shut eyes, between sleeping and waking," Lang concluded. "It seems probable that people who, when they think, see a mental picture of the subject of their thoughts, people who are good 'visualizers,' are likely to succeed best with the crystal, and that some of them can visualize purposefully in the crystal, while others cannot." In other books, say his 1897 *Book of Dreams and Ghosts,* Lang explored ways in which people "see things," and explained away crystalmancy-based fortune-telling as coincidence. What intrigued him so about scrying is simple. Done intently and honestly, scrying often produced short-term psychological effects and visions remarkably akin to drug-induced ones and to ones Europeans and Americans had begun to learn originated in Far Eastern techniques of meditation, but far more important, a permanent broadening and deepening of visual acuteness.

Knowing anything of the arguments of Lang and others explains the subtle genius of painters like H. Siddons Mowbray, whose 1895 "Iridescence" depicts two upper-class young women gazing at a sunlit glass ball, perhaps a blown-glass fishing-net float ball, perhaps a sphere produced for scrying. Mowbray painted an avant-garde activity that once complemented the work of the painter, something that by 1925 had been reduced to the glancing admiration of crystal spheres mounted on fluted columns at the center of gardens. For a brief moment, say the thirty years following 1880, educated Europeans and Americans enjoyed a visual feast beyond surfeit. Perhaps bounded by the light bulb of Swan and Edison and by the introduction of sound-track cinema, the era remains astonishingly rich, provocatively puzzling to anyone intrigued by visual exploration, visual adventure, visual nuance. Did Mowbray's astute young women learn something from the glass ball that prepared them for Braque, Picasso, Mondrian? Did scrying prepare them for Einstein physics?

World War I terminated the spiritualist movement that reinforced scrying, and what wartime devastation and disillusionment failed to accomplish, cinema did. Folklorists and physicists, painters and photographers, chemists and conjurers, all abandoned crystalmancy, dismissed catoptromancy and daguerreotypy, and eschewed what Lang and Mowbray scrutinized. Almost everyone went to the cinema, seduced first by *moving pictures,* then by *talkies.* Cheapened by tawdry reproduction in newspaper Sunday-supplements, magazines, and in package advertisements, photographs of any sort received less and less close attention. Roll-film and factory processing devalued the photographic skills of the 1890s, jerked amateur, then professional photographers from making custom emulsions to accepting any films and papers sealed inside black pasteboard boxes, and soon most photographers worked only with so-called standard cameras, lenses, films, and papers. In a culture pronounced "more visual" by the decade, the old art of scrying nearly disappeared. For every child, every scientist, every college undergraduate studying painting or photography or art history who actually looked into a crystal sphere, who tried to scry as Mowbray's thoughtful young women scry in "Iridescence," fifty thousand jeered at "crystal-ball fortune telling" when they condescended to notice at all. Yet scrying endured, snug inside an alchemy of its own.

"The crystals observed in the photographic emulsion generally belong to the octahedral class of the regular system, although cubic forms are found," Kenneth Mees explained in his 1942 *Theory of the Photographic Process*. "The actual shape of the crystal can vary enormously, depending upon whether growth takes place equally in three dimensions or is restricted to two or even one dimension." Mees knew vastly more than Rumford, Daguerre, and Talbot, of course, but much of what he knew he learned from investigators like W. deW. Abney, whose 1889 *Journal of the Camera Club* article entitled "Photography and the Law of Error" explicated the relationship between length of exposure and transparency of negatives. Well into the beginning of the cinema era, a handful of photographers still knew the esotery of their art, and puzzled not only about the ways light behaved as it passed through Newton's triangular prism and through camera and enlarger lenses, but about how light acted on the crystals suspended in negative gelatin, on the grains coating paper, on the chemicals of processes invented in the years of Daguerre and Talbot and then supplanted, perhaps too hastily. For photographers deeply, indeed passionately intrigued by every aspect of photography, light seemed anything but cheap. Light connected photography with every sort of ancient visual magic, with catoptromancy, crystalmancy, even alchemy, for after all, photography inveigled light into making opaque film more or less transparent, made film become something akin to Dee's "shew-stone."

At the turn of the twenty-first century, then, scrying means two things. It designates the work of rare photographers like Michael Kenna who use photography as a medium to see beyond the ordinary, to descry in the colorless, sunless distance Conrad delineated some fitful tracing of Xanadu. Only a handful of great photographers can say, and perhaps even then not for certain, if their finished prints approach the visions of their minds' eyes that screen space and object, light and weather through personal visual and aesthetic sieves, but certainly the photographers choose the place and the moment to direct light through lens onto crystal. But scrying means something else, the gift of elevated vision the photographs provide to some who use them as sixteenth-century savants used mirrors or crystals. To scry Kenna's landscape images is to move first into the images, then *through* them to something else, to somewhere else, to discrete if different Xanadus.

Scrying a photograph induces or produces a venture, then, a voyage, a passage, a trip. The 1960s drug culture co-opted the word *trip* in a way that cheapened the envisioning Lang understood as the possible if not guaranteed product of scrying. Lang, and Dee and Spenser too, knew that scrying produced something transporting and transforming, something Daguerre and Talbot perhaps understood through their long landscape exposure times as ever so slightly akin to the romantic-era opium dream of Coleridge, something so powerful that James VI and later authorities have sometimes forbidden it. Scrying in the crystal or glass sphere means penetrating the shifting images to something else, the else that rewards any scryer of the scryed images produced by truly great photographers. Dee could only describe in words what his scyer scried. Here in these pages, landscape photographs leave open the portals into landscapes as stunning and free of time as Xanadu.

LANDSCAPE IN LIMBO

Landscape in daguerreotype is landscape in limbo. Not some mere frozen moment, some space captured with a sunbeam, the daguerreotype landscape hovers in something, beneath the glass. Daguerreotypes put to rest forever the casual charge that no daguerreotypist made a good landscape image, made even one worth more than a hasty glance. But the images raise questions beyond those asked of paintings, lithographs, and photographs. Especially they force the question of visual limbo, the skewed uses of landscape daguerreotypes at the turn of the twenty-first century.

In the halcyon years of the daguerreotype, *limbo* underwent a metamorphosis, changing in meaning rapidly, if vaguely, yet always shifting further from the taut definitions of medieval churchmen. What scholastic theologians once meant by *limbus,* as in *limbus infantium* (the limbo of the unbaptized infants), had begun changing even in Shakespeare's time. The "O, what a sympathy of woe is this, / As far from help as Limbo is from bliss" of *Titus Andronicus* keeps most of the old connotation of limbo as an other-worldly region, a borderland of Hell, as does Milton's use of the word in *Paradise Lost:* "A limbo large and broad, since call'd / The Paradise of Fools."[1] Both uses depart from the strict theological definition of *limbus,* however, and point toward the romantic use of the term, perhaps best exemplified in Coleridge's poem "Limbo":

> 'Tis a strange place, this Limbo!—not a Place
> Yet name it so;—where Time and weary Space
> Fettered from flight, with night-mare sense of fleeing
> Strive for their last crepuscular half-being . . .

By 1817, when Coleridge published his poetic view of "a spirit-jail secure," *limbo* already flourished as a slang synonym for prison or other sort of confinement.[2] The romantics only hastened—and dignified—its transformation into a supratheological term.

The secularized word crossed the Atlantic easily. In 1828 Webster de-

---

"Landscape in Limbo" appeared in *America and the Daguerreotype,* ed. John Wood (Iowa City: Univ. of Iowa Press, 1998), 58–66, copyright University of Iowa Press.

fined it as a place of general restraint and confinement, and in 1859 Worcester defined it as "*any* place of restraint and confinement." Within a few years, certainly by the time of the 1864 unabridged *Webster's Dictionary,* it had acquired a solid nontheological denotation: "Any real or imaginary place of restraint or confinement; a prison; as, to put a man in *limbo*."[3] About the word still lingered a trace of mystery, as though it designated a zone confining unexplained phenomena, the "limbo of curious evidence" about which Oliver Wendell Holmes ruminated in the 1883 preface to his 1859 novel *Elsie Venner.*[4]

Holmes may well have understood more of the subtle complexities of limbo than his remark indicates. His mid-nineteenth-century *Atlantic Monthly* articles on early photography and stereography, now so often quoted and reprinted, reveal a more-than-passing interest in the spiritual element implicit in the techniques and contain a near-cryptic remark about the daguerreotype. "The Stereoscope and the Stereograph," an 1859 piece, begins with a lengthy analysis of classical thinking on perception, moving from the ideas of Democritus through those of Epicurus to Lucretius, emphasizing the continuity of a concept of seeing. Essentially, Holmes argues that the classical philosophers posit "effluences" given off by all objects and continuously striking the eye: "Forms, effigies, membranes, or *films,* are the nearest representatives of the terms applied to these effluences." According to Worcester's 1859 *Dictionary,* a more likely synonym, *aura,* referred only to flows of air, and Holmes struggles to translate satisfactorily, hitting on *films* to open his analysis of photography. The prefatory comments are of critical importance in two ways— both, however, easily missed. First, they introduce his statement about the daguerreotype, and second, they open his lengthy remarks about the three-dimensional nature of the stereograph viewed in the stereoscope.

"This is just what the Daguerreotype has done," Holmes asserts of the power to transfix images. "It has fixed the most fleeting of our illusions, that which the apostle and the philosopher and the poet have alike used as the type of instability and unreality." While Holmes immediately remarks that the photograph "has completed the triumph, by making a sheet of paper reflect images like a mirror and hold them as a picture," the bulk of his essay suggests that the stereograph has restored something of the miraculous to the "everyday nature" of the paper-based photograph. Implicit in his argument is an understanding of the daguerreotype and the *viewed* stereograph image as different from the everyday photograph.

Holmes emphasizes repeatedly the fragility of the daguerreotype, speaking of its granular deposits "like a very thin fall of snow, drifted by the wind," the thinly sprinkled silver "as the earth shows with a few scattered snow-flakes on its surface," and the unfixed plate from which "a touch wipes off the picture as it does the bloom from a plum." Equally important, however, is the palpable three-dimensionality of the daguerreo-type, something visible to the discerning eye, and to the discerning eye aided by a "microscope magnifying fifty diameters or even less."[5] The daguerreotype is less fragile than the stereograph, whose illusionary power lasts only as long as a viewer sees it through the stereoscope, but both are vastly more magical than the photograph, which appears in the article as mundane, even pedestrian.

More than novelty made the daguerreotype entrancing to educated Americans. The daguerreotype fitted perfectly into the delicate world of the American romantics, and particularly into arresting questions fo-cused on the usefulness of American landscape and history for the pur-poses of art.[6] Indeed the daguerreotype made palpable the visual concerns of romantics like Nathaniel Hawthorne, whose fiction juxta-posing historical and contemporaneous events insisted on new ways of seeing, of seeing into limbo.

Hawthorne asserts the prime necessity of seeing things slightly differ-ently, of comparing things seen in "the white sunshine of actual life" with things seen by moonlight.[7] Moonlight makes everyday things different, makes a limbo of mundane places. "Moonlight, in a familiar room, falling so white upon the carpet, and showing all its figures so distinctly,—mak-ing every object so minutely visible, yet so unlike a morning or noontide visibility,—is a medium the most suitable for a romance-writer to get ac-quainted with his illusive guests," he argues at the beginning of *The Scarlet Letter*, remarking how "all these details, so completely seen, are so spiritu-alized by the unusual light, that they seem to lose their actual substance, and become things of the intellect. Nothing is too small or too trifling to undergo this change, and acquire dignity thereby." In the white light "the floor of our familiar room has become a neutral territory, somewhere be-tween the real world and fairy-land, where the Actual and the Imaginary may meet, and each imbue itself with the nature of the other. Ghosts might enter here, without affrighting us." Perhaps, he concludes, the ghosts might not need to enter. They might be always there, having never stirred from the fireside, but noticeable only in the "streak of magic moon-shine" that illuminates the limbo coexisting in ordinary space.[8]

Hawthorne continually toyed with the possibility of fixing the images glimmering in moonlight. In "The Hall of Fantasy" he created a man who "had a scheme for fixing the reflections of objects in a pool of wa-ter, and thus taking the most lifelike portraits imaginable," and in "The Prophetic Pictures" he pried into the human love of portrait-making. "The looking-glass, the polished globes of the andirons, the mirror-like

Daguerreotypists often placed people in the foreground to give scale to scenic wonders like Niagara Falls, producing images strikingly like the woodcuts illustrating so many early-nineteenth-century gazetteers and travel narratives. (Collection of Matthew Isenburg)

water, and all other reflecting surfaces, continually present us with portraits, or rather ghosts, of ourselves, which we glance at, and straightway forget them. But we forget them only because they vanish. It is the idea of duration—of earthly immortality—that gives such a mysterious interest to our own portraits." Yet sometimes Hawthorne rejoiced that the glimmerings of the familiar moonlit chamber could not be fixed, could not be plucked from limbo. "God be praised," he asserted in "The Old Apple Dealer," "that the present shapes of human existence are not cast in iron nor hewn in everlasting adamant, but moulded of the vapors that vanish away while the essence flits upward to the Infinite."[9] Fixing images, fixing the Holmesian "films," might unbalance things, might wrench the powers of art and skewer the white sunshine with a shaft of limbo.

Hawthorne honored the visual arts—including the art of seeing—as the "image of the Creator's own," and in "The Prophetic Pictures" he probed deeply into the awesome significance of picture-making. "The innumerable forms, that wander in nothingness, start into being at thy beck," he wrote, speaking in the guise of a portrait painter. "The dead live again. Thou recallest them to their old scenes, and givest their gray shadows the lustre of a better life, at once earthly and immortal. Thou snatchest back the fleeting moments of History." But arrogance propels the portraitist. "O potent Art! as thou bringest the faintly revealed Past to stand in that narrow strip of sunlight, which we call Now, canst thou summon the shrouded Future to meet her there?"[10] Such is the extrapolation of seeing in the moonlight, of seeing not only ghosts but presentiments.

Hawthorne wrote in the daguerreotype heyday, and in *The House of the Seven Gables* created a daguerreotypist, making him a mysterious descendant of ancestors rumored to be wizards. But Holgrave, the austere daguerreotypist associated with mesmerists and curious ideas, serves mostly to point up Hawthorne's concern with new ways of seeing, say, the fleeting views of landscape outside the windows of a speeding train.

Ordinary pioneer landscape shimmers in the luminosity peculiar to daguerreotypes, subtly nudging viewers toward a reexamination of landscape newly shaped from wilderness. (Collection of Matthew Isenburg)

It is he who sees not only into the secrets of the human heart and into the crankiness of American society but into the secrets of the old house and its decaying garden. Holgrave sees the value implicit in built form, and in the end he literally plucks a secret—the long-lost deed to vast acreage in Maine—from a recess hidden behind a picture.[11] Simply put, Holgrave sees more deeply into ordinary things, perhaps because he uses different slants of light and shadow to steer his inquiries.

In the years before the Civil War, American daguerreotypists moved through utterly ordinary landscape, a national landscape new, almost raw, almost always lacking the legends and traditions of the ancient castles and villages of Europe, much to the despair of American writers. "Europe held forth the charms of storied and poetical association," reflected Washington Irving in his 1820 *Sketch Book*. "Her very ruins told the history of times gone by, and every mouldering stone was a chronicle. I longed to wander over the scenes of renowned achievement,—to tread, as it were, in the footsteps of antiquity,—to loiter about the ruined castle,—to meditate on the falling tower,—to escape, in short, from the commonplace realities of the present, and lose myself among the shadowy grandeurs of the past."[12] Irving wanted to walk in a landscape of shadows, of ever-present moonlight, but he found some traces of a usable past in the bits and pieces of colonial Dutch landscape enduring in New York. And slowly other Americans argued that the contemporary landscape, acutely viewed, might provide the stuff of art too. America, asserted William Cullen Bryant in the *North American Review* in 1825, "is at least the country of enterprise; and nowhere are the great objects that worthily interest the passions and call forth the exertions of men pursued with more devotion and perseverance."[13] The poet, the painter, the novelist might find in the raw, bustling landscape something of genuine artistic value, if only they would scrutinize it deeply enough.

In 1841 Ralph Waldo Emerson glimpsed the significance of that raw

PHOTOGRAPHED LANDSCAPE

landscape in the hearts of his compatriots and, perhaps, suggested that it meant more to some than the visages of loved ones. "And so why not draw for these times a portrait gallery?" he asked in his "Lecture on the Times." "Let us paint the painters." He argued that verbal descriptions of the congressmen, professors, editors, contemplative girls, reformers, and others would be documents of great historical value. But why the need of verbal description? Perhaps because contemporaneous daguerreotypists concentrated on landscape features, not portraits. "Whilst the Daguerreotypist, with camera-obscura and silver plate, begins now to traverse the land, let us set up our Camera also, and let the sun paint the people."[14] However puzzling the remark, it suggests that a landscape shaped from wilderness by enterprising Americans had a larger value than might be supposed, at least for the farmers, house-builders, and others who actually created fields and buildings, who took enormous pride in their work.

In many daguerreotypes nothing stands out more clearly than the importance of enterprise. The portraits reveal it, of course, the druggist with his mortar, pestle, and balance, the miners with sluice box and pans, the piano tuner with tuning fork, the farmer with hoe, the bandsmen with instruments. And beyond the portraits shimmer the action shots, the painter priming the scraped clapboards, the steeplejacks high on their scaffolding. As Bryant so aptly pointed out, Americans lived to work, to build a strong, prosperous nation even as they advanced themselves. But so many of the other views demonstrate with equal strength the importance of structure, the forms erected from enterprise.

Consider the most ordinary of daguerreotype landscapes, that of the stable and daguerreotype studio. Outside the stable stand the hands and horses and a water wagon. Nailed to a porch upright glistens a sort of advertisement, presumably daguerreotypes in frames, shielded only a little from the sun. What visual magic thrives in the scent of manure, the sound of champing horses? Were daguerreotypes often made in frame structures surrounded by litter? But it is this utter ordinariness that makes the view so potent. Something of genuine importance, and probably not the men or the horseflesh, stands built in the clearing. Two businesses, two enterprises.

So many of the views depict immensely scruffy landscapes, landscapes seemingly beyond the power of moonlight, landscapes lit by whitest sunlight. The unpainted frame structures jammed together in a sea of loose boards scream something of the rawness, the tenuousness of so much American space in the 1850s, just as the winter street scene screeches with frigid starkness. Barrenness rules the New Hampshire Valley despite the flourishing orchard. The rocky hills loom over the farmstead, and few trees shade the road the traveler must follow. Against the sky and the leafless trees, the church building floats almost free of the bare ground, gigantic somehow, and detached from the nearby house. Where indeed is the magic of moonlight?

Thoreau found the magic in the very *depth* of the daguerreotype. "Nature is readily made to repeat herself in a thousand forms, and in the daguerreotype her own light is amanuensis, and the picture too has more than a surface significance,—a depth equal to the prospect,—so that the microscope may be applied to the one as the spy-glass to the other," he mused in a February 2, 1841, journal entry.[15] Here pulses the same energy of vision as that discerned years later by Holmes, an awareness that the daguerreotype rewards close scrutiny, almost begging for microscopic examination.

It is that vision which rewards, in spite of the fact that nowadays most daguerreotype landscapes are reproduced only photographically and cannot be held in our palms. After the 1860s, photographers caught only the surface of American landscape and often sought any but ordinary landscape to photograph. The photograph paled in importance, offering no magic at all, only accurate rendering. To be sure, the stereograph and stereoscope restored something of the magic of the daguerreotype to a public rapidly yawning over photographs, but the clumsiness of the stereoscope, even the hand-held one Holmes invented, failed to arrest the boredom.

Even reproduced images remind us that the peculiar visual construct of the daguerreotype caught up landscapes every bit as uncannily as it caught visages, penetrating deeply into ordinary scenes and revealing the moonlit wonder of them. What the landscape images offer is landscape in limbo, the stunning realization at the beginning of the twenty-first century that in the middle of the nineteenth century photography became so ordinary that photographers avoided ordinary landscape. The photographic process blinded photographers to the moonlit limbo only the daguerreotypist perceived and, perhaps more frequently than we might ever have guessed, recorded.

Notes

1. *Titus Andronicus,* III, 1, 149; *Paradise Lost,* III, 495.
2. Coleridge, "Limbo," *Poetical Works,* ed. James Dykes Campbell (London: Macmillan, 1898), pp. 189–90. *Dictionary of Buckish Slang . . . Eloquence* (London: Chappel, 1811).
3. Noah Webster, *American Dictionary* (Springfield, Mass.: Merriam, 1852), and Joseph E. Worcester, *Dictionary of the English Language* (1859; rpt. Boston: Brewer & Tileson, 1874) (italics added).
4. *Elsie Venner: A Romance of Destiny* (1859; rpt. Boston: Houghton Mifflin, 1891), p. ix.

5. "The Stereoscope and the Stereograph," *Atlantic Monthly,* June 1859, pp. 738–48.

6. This issue has received such extended treatment that only a mention suffices here. But see F. O. Matthiessen, *American Renaissance: Art and Expression in the Age of Emerson and Whitman* (New York: Oxford University Press, 1941).

7. "The Hall of Fantasy," *Works* (Boston: Houghton Mifflin, 1882), 2: 204.

8. *Works,* 5:54–56. See Darrel Abel, *The Moral Picturesque: Studies in Hawthorne's Fiction* (West Lafayette, Ind.: Purdue University Press, 1988), for a superb analysis of Hawthorne's understanding of the powers of light. See also Carol Shloss, *In Visible Light: Photography and the American Writer, 1840–1940* (New York: Oxford University Press, 1987), pp. 25–50, for an exceptionally cogent overview of Hawthorne's understanding of daguerreotypy.

9. *Works,* 2: 202; 1: 199; 2: 503.

10. *Works,* 1: 207.

11. *Works,* 3: 304, 374.

12. 1820; rpt. New York: Belford, Clarke. pp. 10–11. See also William Gilmore Simms, *Views and Reviews in American Literature, History, and Fiction,* ed. C. Hugh Holman (1845; rpt. Cambridge, Mass.: Harvard University Press. 1962), especially pp. 48–55.

13. William Cullen Bryant, "Review of Catherine Sedgwick's *Redwood,*" *North American Review* 20 (April 1825): 245–72, especially 251–52. See also Emerson, "The Poet," *Essays: Second Series* (Philadelphia: McKay, 1892), pp. 23–24, 43–44, for another assertion of the usefulness of ordinary society and landscape for the poet.

14. Ralph Waldo Emerson, *Complete Works* (Boston: Houghton Mifflin, 1884), 1: 252.

15. Henry David Thoreau, *Journal,* ed. Bradford Torrey (Boston: Houghton Mifflin, 1906), 1: 189.

DISJUNCTION, DISUNION, DAGUERREOTYPE

Retrospect welds daguerreotypy and disunion. Antebellum experimenters with the new image-fixing process quickly discovered that it seemed as fitfully out of control as national politics. Within a year or two, the daguerreotype image stood as something other than it appeared to its first admirers. "We have seen the views taken by the Daguerreotype, and have no hesitation in avowing, that they are the most remarkable objects of curiosity and admiration, in the arts, that we ever beheld," proclaimed a *Knickerbocker* essayist in 1839. "Their exquisite perfection almost transcends the bounds of sober belief."[1] Eight years after William Lloyd Garrison founded his abolitionist newspaper *The Liberator,* four years after an angry anti-abolitionist Boston mob nearly killed him, six years after furious sectional debates in Congress concerning not abolition but tariff, the *Knickerbocker* writer understood daguerreotypy in words of hope, of transcendence, words that mocked the deterioration of the Republic, the fraying of "the more perfect union" articulated in the Constitution. Imported from France at the end of the 1830s, daguerreotype technology entered the United States under tariff provisions, especially the provisions of the 1828 Tariff Act, what the South and West called "the tariff of abominations" in a controversy that led to the 1832 compromise act and the nullification explosion that followed a year later. Between 1828 and 1860, importers of European technology confronted the whipsawing of tariff provisions enacted and revoked as northern protectionists intermittently lost control of Congress to southern free traders. After 1840, as national politics became the series of compromises schoolchildren still memorize but rarely understand in cultural context, the daguerreotype became a favorite way of achieving personal permanence in an era wracked by upheavals remembered now in terms of failures like the Tariff of 1842, the Missouri Compromise, the Kansas-Nebraska Act. As the Republic blundered toward fragmentation, daguerreotypy offered a portal opening on personal, sometimes family stability increasingly unlike the chaos riving the nation. But the portal opened too on a division between illustration and art that confounded

"Disjunction, Disunion, Daguerreotype" appeared in *Harvard Library Bulletin* n.s. 14 (Spring 2003): 47–56, copyright by the President and Fellows of Harvard University.

contemporaneous observers weighing the half-controlled success or failure of the personal daguerreotype against out-of-control national politics. Nowadays Americans remember the Civil War through the prism of
photography, and shun the daguerreotype as the cryptic medium me-
morializing the years leading to war.[2] Only a handful muse on the larger
context of the early daguerreotype, let alone the meaning of daguerreotypy in our own era.

Daguerreotypy haunts the academy still. As daguerreotype collectors
know so well, the glass-imprisoned images turn up at the back of escri-
toire drawers, at the bottom of blanket chests, on the upper-most shelves
of bedroom closets. Surprise struck no collector when Harvard announced the 1976 discovery of daguerreotypes of slaves in a cabinet in
the disused attic of the Peabody Museum. By then collectors knew what
a handful of young American Studies scholars had begun to understand,
that the daguerreotypes had been put away, not so much for safe keeping, but because they represented a window on an era too painful for
twentieth-century Americans to remember.[3] In subject, the put-away daguerreotype is frequently a young man in a rudimentary militia uniform
but armed in idiosyncratic fashion, sometimes with a musket or hunting
rifle, in the South often with a Bowie knife and horse pistol. Family Bibles
and faint pencil markings on the back of the daguerreotype itself often
indicate that the soldier died in service. In format, however, the daguerreotype remains always a daguerreotype, the glass-and-mat-and-image
whole that by 1870 represented something other than curiosity and admiration, something different from classical notions of portraiture by in-
control artists. Daguerreotypes by then screamed of wholesale failure and
wholesale death even as they whispered of image-fixing processes gone
awry. While Civil War veterans, especially Grand Army of the Republic
members, immediately accepted post-Appomatox personal and group
photographs, especially "mustering-out" photographs, the bereaved often looked only to one-of-a-kind daguerreotypes for images of the dead
who lay in windrows for tariff, abolition, slavery, free trade, states' rights,
and union. The quarter-century prologue to civil war became a bad dream
best forgotten, then something else, the ever-unsettling prologue to a
new nationhood, the prologue as unnerving as its peculiar visual artifact,
the prologue with which academics still grapple.

Daguerreotypy resurfaced in American Studies writing in the years
leading to World War II, in ways that now deserve extended analysis. A
few scholars understood the gathering darkness in Europe through the
murky prism of uncontrollable darkness swirling over the Union in the
1830s and '40s. "Concerned as he was with every possibility of seeing,
Emerson was fascinated with the developing art of photography from

the time of the invention of the daguerreotype in the late eighteen-thirties," wrote F. O. Matthiessen in his 1941 *American Renaissance: Art and Expression in the Age of Emerson and Whitman*. "He conceived of the camera as a powerful symbol for his age's scrutiny of character, just as Hawthorne was to do in making his hero in *The House of the Seven Gables* a practitioner in the new technique, and thus a searcher in the traits and motives behind men's faces." Along with many of his contemporaries, Matthiessen blended daguerreotypy and photography, but he reproduced an 1854 portrait of clipper-ship-builder Donald McKay, what he called "the finest daguerreotype I have ever seen," rather than well-known daguerreotypes of American authors.[4] However much he prized its subject as representative of his period, Matthiessen glimpsed something about the daguerreotype portrait by the Boston artists Southworth and Hawes, something so powerful that he used it as the frontispiece to his volume. In the 1940s, mature scholars knew their great-grandparents, especially those who died in the Civil War, largely through daguerreotypes, of course, and it is not surprising that many Americanists understood the daguerreotype not only in the context of disunion, but as a unique art form of immense period power. In her posthumously published *The Roots of American Culture*, which appeared a year after Matthiessen's book, Constance Rourke condemned the painting of Grant Wood. "This painter many times used superficial and transient elements of the American subject without touching its core," she argued in a paragraph about painting imitating crewel work and other folk art. "To give a portrait in oils the style of a daguerreotype even to the shine of the copper base, presumably because the daguerreotype has played a large part among us, is an extreme sentimentalism that has nothing to do with the art of painting."[5] But what large part? Why the charge of extreme sentimentalism? What lies behind the writing of Matthiessen, Rourke, and other eve-of-World War II scholars who imply that the daguerreotype is not only special, but especially something, something gone, something no longer done?

"Were you ever Daguerrotyped, O immortal man? And did you look with all vigor at the lens of the camera or rather by the direction of the operator at the brass peg a little below it to give the picture the full benefit of your expanded & flashing eye?" asked Emerson in an 1841 journal entry. "And in your zeal not to blur the image did you keep every finger in its place with such energy that your hands became clenched as for fight or despair, & in your resolution to keep your face still, did you feel every muscle becoming every moment more rigid: the brows contracted into a Tartarean frown, and the eyes fixed as they are fixed in madness, or in death; and when at last you are relieved of your dismal duties, did you find the curtain drawn perfectly, and the coat perfectly, &

PHOTOGRAPHED LANDSCAPE

and the hands true, clenched for combat, and the shape of the face & head? but unhappily the total expression escaped from the face and you held the portrait of a mask instead of a man. Could you not by grasping it very tight hold the stream of a river or of a small brook and prevent it from flowing?"[6] Emerson thus recorded not only his understanding of the daguerreotype, but the peculiarity of being daguerreotyped, of entering into an image-making process that seemed out of control, that made eyes mad or dead or worse.

His fascination with light focuses his October, 1841, journal musings, but his thinking immediately bifurcates. On the one hand, he writes about types of light in what even undergraduates nowadays recognize as the Transcendental way. "I see that the lights of the common day as they fall on every face & figure of animal or plant are more excellent & speaking than any of those lights which painters like better, twilight, deep shade, moonlight or torchlight; yet what avails my cold knowledge that they are better if I find them unaffecting." On the other, a single sentence removed, he writes about fixing light: "In writing, the casting moment is of greatest importance, just as it avails not in Daguerre portraits that you have the very man before you, if his expression has escaped."[7] By 1841, Emerson had begun to understand not only that painters no longer controlled the fixing of light, but that the daguerreotypists had begun to produce images in a process the daguerreotypists themselves only partially and fitfully controlled. Moreover, the daguerreotype process frequently penetrated beyond the ordinary visage and permanently recorded attributes sitters usually kept hidden from view. Sometimes the daguerreotypists recorded mere masks, but sometimes they looked behind the masks to something else.

Interpreting Emerson's journal entries concerning daguerreotypy proves difficult, in part because many are extremely brief, and often juxtaposed against remarks on light, seeing, and subjects less immediately connected with imported image-fixing. At least three times, for example, Emerson used the word grim to define the essence of daguerreotypy, noting that "the first Daguerres are grim things yet show that a great engine has been invented," and once used the term asinizing. "Daguerreotype gives the sculpture of the face, but omits the expression, the painter aims at the expression & comes far short of Daguerre in the form & organism. But we must have sea and shore, the flowing & the fixed, in every work of art. On the sitter the effect of the Daguerrotypist is asinizing." Whatever daguerreotypy did to his thinking, it seems to have reshaped his language. "People are glass, I see the whole thing through them," he wrote a few lines after noting that the first daguerreotypes are grim things, but by then he perhaps understood the implications of sending daguerreotype images of himself to friends.[8] People might not be glass, after all, but some substance so plastic that daguerreotypy might change them.

In the spring of 1846 Emerson struggled to obtain a daguerreotype likeness to send to his friend Thomas Carlyle. In one letter, Emerson explained his difficulties in getting an image that pleased him enough to send. "I was in Boston the other day & went to the best reputed Daguerrotypist, but though I brought home three transcripts of my face, the housemates voted them rueful, supremely ridiculous, I must sit again, or, as true Elizabeth Hoar said, I must not sit again, not being of the right complexion which Daguerre & iodine delight in," he wrote on 14 May to Carlyle, before concluding that he had in mind hiring "a good crayon sketcher." On 31 May he wrote again, explaining that on his forty-third birthday "I went to a new Daguerrotypist, who took much pains to make his picture right. I brought home three shadows not agreeable to my own eyes. The machine has a bad effect on me. My wife protests against the imprints as slanderous. My friends say, they look ten years older, and, as I think, with the air of a decayed gentleman touched with his first paralysis." But Emerson sent one of the three, and on 17 July, Carlyle wrote bluntly that the "image is altogether unsatisfactory, illusive, and even in some measure tragical to me! First of all, it is a bad Photograph; no eyes discernible, at least one of the eyes not, except in rare favourable lights: then, alas, Time itself and Oblivion must have been busy." Carlyle asked for "some living pictorial sketch, chalk-drawing, or the like, from a trustworthy hand."[9] For Carlyle, whose own daguerreotype, made in consultation with a painter, had not only pleased himself but Emerson too, what Emerson had sent was an abomination having none of the exquisite perfection that so excited the *Knickerbocker* essayist. And Emerson knew it. Somehow, the grim engine of Daguerre not only made poor likenesses of Emerson, it had a bad effect on him.

Other things had bad effects on Emerson, however, and anyone probing his journal entries about daguerreotypy, and about light and shadow, and for that matter, about painting, discovers the eerie contiguity of daguerreotype entries and entries about abolitionism. "I rode to town with some insane people: the worst of such company is that they always bite you, and then you run mad also," he remarked in 1841 of a trip to Boston. Emerson worried about casual conversation with strangers, because all too often the conversation swung instantly to abolition, and the anti-slavery advocates struck him as dangerous, insane, almost loathsome. "But the Garrisons & fanatics,—forgive me, if when I come near to them & sit in the same stage coach, I seem to see nothing but management, tactics, boys' play & philisterei. Unreal, spectral, masks." Emerson linked the daguerreotype image with the faces—or masks—of abolitionists, seeing the abolitionists by the light of common day as utterly incomplete, as mere spectral shadows, as men and women almost entirely consumed by the reforms they urged beyond reason. Occasionally he wrote about their consumption at length, and now and then recorded his realization that they were consuming national energy, spirit, and health too. "The times, the times. Forgive me. I told Garrison that I thought he must be a very young man or his time hang very heavy on his hands who can afford to think much & talk much about the foibles of his neighbors, or 'denounce' and play 'the son of thunder' as he called it," he noted immediately after comparing the abolitionists to masks. Reformers advocating everything from pacifism to temperance struck him as avoiding any sustained scrutiny of the larger impacts of their reforms, and in the final analysis acting incredibly immaturely by refusing to accept responsibility for what evils their reforms might create. Those "who prolong their privilege of childhood in this wise—of doing nothing but making immense demands on all the gladiators," might be likable on rare occasions, but far more often they became incomplete, troubling to the stagecoach passenger, far more troubling to the Republic.[10]

Sixteen years later Emerson retained his worries about abolitionists, but by then he had begun to support their cause with far less caution, overlooking the appalling violence in Kansas, listening with approval to John Brown speak in Concord, confiding only in his journal the lingering lesson of the daguerreotype. "And I learn from the photograph & daguerre men, that almost all faces & forms which come to their shops to be copied, are irregular & unsymmetrical, have one eye blue & one grey, one the nose is not straight, & one shoulder is higher than the other," he wrote in 1857. "The man is physically as well as metaphysically a thing of shreds & patches, borrowed unequally from his good & bad ancestors,— a misfit from the start." The daguerreotype now and then caught a spectral something that caused him momentary worry about Brown, that caused him to speculate that "most men are insolvent, or, promise much more by their countenance, & conversation, & by their early endeavor, much more than they ever perform," to wonder that "men's conscience . . . is local in spots & veins, here and there, & not in healthy circulation through their system." Was it the lesson of the daguerreotype that caused Emerson to wonder if Brown lied about bleeding Kansas, if abolitionists might not precipitate a civil war that would forever change, perhaps even destroy the Republic? "But 'tis of no use to tell me, as Brown & others do, that the Southern is not a better fighter than the Northerner,—when I see, that uniformly a Southern minority prevails, & gives the law. Why, but because the Southerner is a fighting man & the Northerner is not." By 1857 Emerson saw the irregular and asymmetrical arguments of the North failing before the magisterial constitutional logic of Calhoun and other southerners who repeatedly honored the Constitution, who saw not only in Kansas, but everywhere in the North, a massive flouting of the rule of law that would surely lead to war.[11]

In allegiance to a "higher moral law," northern abolitionists gradually abandoned their respect for civil and criminal law, even for Constitutional rights. After the enactment of the Fugitive Slave Act in 1850, abolitionists redoubled their efforts to hurry escaping slaves to Canada, to block the efforts of southern slave-hunters, and to rescue escaped slaves held for rendition. Violence escalated in ways United States schoolbooks still hide. Local law enforcement officers arrested United States marshals on trivial charges and otherwise interfered with their duties, and rarely stopped abolitionist mobs that injured and even killed Federal officers obeying Federal statutes. In 1851, Federal marshals and two hundred policemen armed with cutlasses defended a Boston courtroom against attack during a rendition trial that culminated in an escaped slave being marched under guard at three in the morning to a schooner waiting to take him south. By May, 1854, however, authorities could no longer maintain order in Boston. A group of Massachusetts abolitionists, among them Theodore Parker and Thomas Wentworth Higginson, organized a slave-rescue riot to occur after a tumultuous meeting in Faneuil Hall, a riot that culminated not in rescue but in a stormed courthouse, a dead deputy marshal, and Higginson fleeing into the night, bleeding from a saber cut across his face. Not long after, Parker, Higginson, and four other well-to-do abolitionists began financing the violence of John Brown, and in time funded his abortive assault on the Federal armory at Harpers Ferry. In the grueling aftermath of the Harpers Ferry catastrophe, the United States Senate voted to arrest one of Brown's Massachusetts backers, Franklin Sanborn, as a contumacious witness in its inquiry proceedings, and Sanborn instantly fled Concord to Canada. When he returned, thinking the Senate had forgotten the complicity his letters found with Brown indicated, Federal marshals arrived with a warrant. The night of 3 April 1860 devolved into nightmare, as boys from Sanborn's private school surrounded the marshals, as his sister ran for help screaming "murder," as citizens turned out, as Sanborn's sister struck the coach horses with a board and made them start, throwing Sanborn and the marshals to the ground. With church bells ringing as they had in 1775, Emerson and a local judge arrived, and the marshals found themselves enmeshed in a crowd and the technicalities of habeas corpus. The next day the writ of habeas corpus was upheld in the Massachusetts Supreme Judicial Court, Sarah Sanborn was presented with a revolver, and a few days later the Commonwealth indicted the United States marshals on charges of felonious assault. No wonder the Senate report on the Harpers Ferry murders is so sharp in its condemnation of northern behavior. Issued on 15 June 1860, it makes clear that liberty had devolved into license across most of the northern states.[12]

What Emerson saw that April night on a Concord street no one could daguerreotype. It was action best recorded not by a landscape or a portrait painter, but by another genre painter, the painter of histories. But no history painter ever recorded the interference with Federal marshals, let alone the handing down of state indictments. By then things moved too fast for painting, for daguerreotypy, even for the new successor to Daguerre's engine, photography.

In 1851, the lone slave marched at three in the morning to the Boston docks marched through the darkened streets of a city boasting many daguerreotypists, four on Washington Street alone. Whipple's Extensive Daguerreotype Establishment at 96 Washington Street advertised "all likenesses warranted perfectly satisfactory to friends, if not so at the first trial, repeated without charge, it being his aim not only to produce the best thing the art is capable of, but pleasing likenesses to those for whom they are intended." Moreover, Whipple's boasted a small viewing gallery too. "The public are invited to call and examine a large collection of Daguerreotypes of some of our MOST DISTINGUISHED CITIZENS; also, those of JENNY LIND, Benedict, Belletti, Barnum, Amin Bey, the Turkish Ambassador, and THE MOON, taken through the large Cambridge Telescope; Microscopic objects, too small to be seen by the naked eye, etc., etc."[13] In short, a number of the images now collected in Harvard libraries may well have been on view at Whipple's, although not to the slave marched past in the dark, a dark that still swirls around the juxtaposition of the daguerreotype and what came to be called "the higher moral law."

As Theodore Parker explained it (in a letter he emphasized was "for your private eye, and, it may be, for the ear of the Fraternity") the higher moral law that superseded the Constitution included as its fourth commandment, "It may be a natural duty for the freeman to help the slaves to the enjoyment of their liberty, and as a means to that end, to aid them in killing all such as oppose their natural freedom."[14] Whatever else Emerson knew of the abolitionist higher moral law, he knew it as something other than Transcendentalism. And from the beginning he seems to have known what so many manuscript documents filed among daguerreotypes imply, that the abolitionists owned not only an appalling moral law but an agenda they hid from all but "the Fraternity." Carefully filed in the Wendell Phillips papers in Houghton Library is a 13 December 1863 confidential letter from Albert G. Brown, a Treasury Department (4th Special Agency) official writing from Beaufort, South Carolina. "It has come to my knowledge today that a force of colored troops will be dispatched for to take possession of Florida and organize a state Government, with universal suffrage, bringing it in as a free state. I say this understandingly," Brown wrote, urging Phillips to form a real estate investment company of his friends and look forward to a ten-fold profit "in six months." Land would appreciate beyond imagination "once peace is declared," and the rebels will make "scarcely any resistance" to the real-estate investment scheme. "Heretofore all such chances have been in the hands of outside barbarians," Brown determined. "I look upon this chance as perfectly legitimate and honorable."[15] In the framework of "the Fraternity," perhaps it was. And perhaps a daguerreotype of Brown might reveal some of the emptiness or nastiness or spectral madness Emerson saw now and then on the faces of abolitionists he encountered in the light of common day, but could not descry after dark, when his neighbors, including a judge, stopped warrant-carrying United States marshals about their lawful work.

What is it exactly that made Emerson so aware that the daguerreotype process was likely to go off on its own in the casting moment, was nothing at all what the *Knickerbocker* essayist found, was something not noble, not transcendent at all? What did he mean, that the daguerreotype process had a bad effect on him? Did he mean what his journal entries hint at, that daguerreotypy made him aware of things whose flickerings he now and then glimpsed in the faces, in the eyes of men and women he respected, especially in the eyes of abolitionists caught up in their version of a law higher than that of the Constitution? Did he mean that daguerreotypy made him see something in his own eyes? "The daguerreotype is good for its authenticity," he wrote in his journal in 1841. "No man quarrels with his shadow, nor will he with his miniature when the sun was the painter. Here is no interference and the distortions are not the blunderings of an artist, but only those of motion, imperfect light, & the like."[16] But did Emerson grasp the significance of his repeated entries? In almost every entry, he examines daguerreotypy as a process always at least slightly out of the control of the daguerreotypist.

No answer comes immediately to hand. But a snatch of dialogue in Hawthorne's 1851 *The House of the Seven Gables* suggests that Hawthorne for one saw more in the daguerreotype than his contemporaries. "I don't much like pictures of that sort,—they are so hard and stern; besides dodging away from the eye, and trying to escape altogether," says Phoebe, a young woman fresh from the country. "They are conscious of looking very unamiable, I suppose, and therefore hate to be seen." To her straightforward remark, Holgrave the daguerreotypist replies, "Most of my likenesses do look unamiable; but the very sufficient reason, I fancy, is, because the originals are so. There is a wonderful insight in Heaven's broad and simple sunshine. While we give it credit only for depicting the merest surface, it actually brings out the secret character with a truth that no painter would ever venture upon, even could he detect it." Then Holgrave takes from his pocket a daguerreotype miniature, a likeness he has made repeatedly, shows it to Phoebe, and notes that while the world respects its subject, the daguerreotype shows the man as "sly, subtle, hard, imperious, and, withal, cold as ice." In the romance, the daguerreotype image resembles the seventeenth-century oil painting inside the old house, a painting with "a look which an artist (if he have anything like the complacency of artists nowadays) would never dream of presenting to a patron as his own characteristic expression, but which, nevertheless, we at once recognize as reflecting the unlovely truth of a human soul." At the heart of *The House of the Seven Gables* lies some insight into the bad effect daguerreotypes worked on Emerson. Hawthorne's fictional daguerreotypist, surrounded by "reformers, temperance-lecturers, and all manner of cross-looking philanthropists," the man about whom a journalist writes of "making a speech, full of wild and disorganizing matter, at a meeting of his banditti-like associates," in time sees his colleagues as clearly as he sees the evil in Judge Pynchon's daguerreotyped image, and abandons them before they drag him into the sump of reform.[17]

Daguerreotypes are perhaps more than images of an art form routinely ignored, but are an art form—once a large part of American culture—abandoned overnight for photography, then put away. Whatever darkness lies in the daguerreotype itself was last glimpsed by scholars like Matthiessen and Rourke in the late 1930s, but it is a darkness now just descried again by scholars aware that while Emerson lived across the Civil War he did no great work afterward, that few abolitionists rose to lasting post-war fame in the arts or politics, that no scholar has traced fully abolitionist ties to Reconstruction real estate scandals, that while an occasional artist works still in the daguerreotype genre, the genre died in a civil war that shattered the early ideals of the Republic, that ended forever popular faith in the Constitution as the fundamental guarantee of a free people, that cemented the higher moral law firmly and permanently in place as the final arbiter of right and wrong in the United States of America. What was it that Emerson saw in the daguerreotypes of the 1840s and the 1850s? Could we see it in the faces of our contemporaries, if daguerreotypists worked among us once again? Who talks easily to strangers in the airliner, the express-train club car of issues like abortion, same-sex marriage, legal suicide? Could the contemporary daguerreotypist fix images of the militia in the Midwest the way a daguerreotypist fixed forever the image of John Brown, the image no schoolchild sees? What is the art form that made photography a relief, that had a bad effect on Emerson?

Notes

1. "The 'Daguerreotype,'" *Knickerbocker* 14 (1839): 560–61.
2. For an example of the continuing ambivalence about antebellum daguerreotypes, see Edwards Park, "John Brown's Picture," *Smithsonian* 28 (August, 1997): 18–19. Only recently have scholars begun to explore the artistic undercurrents of the antebellum era and the ways those currents moved events. See, for example, David S. Reynolds, *Beneath the American Renaissance: The Subversive Imagination in the Age of Emerson and Melville* (New York: Knopf, 1988).
3. Two books that illuminate the 1960s rediscovery of the put-away daguerreotypes are Beaumont Newhall, *The Daguerreotype in America* (New York: Dover, 1964) and Floyd Rinhart and Marion Rinhart, *American Daguerrean Art* (New York: Dover, 1964). See, for example, John Wood, *The Scenic Daguerreotype: Romanticism & Early Photography* (Iowa City: University of Iowa Press, 1995) and, with Merry A. Foresta, *Secrets of the Dark Chamber: The Art of the American Daguerreotype* (Washington, D.C.: National Museum of Art, 1995). See also *America and the Daguerreotype*, ed. John Wood (Iowa City: University of Iowa Press, 1991) and *The Daguerreotype: A Sesquicentennial Celebration,* ed. John Wood (Iowa City: University of Iowa Press, 1989). See also the essay by Alan Trachtenberg in *American Daguerreotypes from the Matthew R. Isenburg Collection* (New Haven: Yale University Art Gallery, 1989).
4. F. O. Matthiessen, *American Renaissance: Art and Expression in the Age of Emerson and Whitman* (New York: Oxford Univ. Press, 1941), xxvi.
5. Constance Rourke, *The Roots of American Culture and Other Essays,* ed. Van Wyck Brooks (New York: Harcourt, Brace, 1942), 288–289.
6. Ralph Waldo Emerson, *The Journals and Miscellaneous Notebooks,* eds. William H. Gilman, J. E. Parsons, Susan Sutton Smith, Harrison Hayford, et al. (Cambridge, Mass.: Harvard University Press, 1966–1978), 8: 115–116.
7. 8: 113–114.
8. 9: 13–14, 382, 15.
9. *The Correspondence of Emerson and Carlyle,* ed. Joseph Slater (New York: Columbia University Press, 1964), 398–405.
10. 8: 112, 116.
11. 14: 126, 127.
12. For general background on this period, see Edward J. Renehan, Jr., *The Secret Six: The True Tale of the Men Who Conspired with John Brown* (New York: Crown, 1995), esp. pp. 60–68, 73, 83, 222–262. For an analysis of the sort of abolitionist who made Emerson dislike stagecoach trips, see Stacey M. Robertson, "'A Hard, Cold, Stern Life': Parker Pillsbury and Grassroots Abolitionism, 1840–1865," *New England Quarterly,* 70 (June, 1997), 177–210. As early as 1831, Alexis de Tocqueville understood the potential splintering of the new Union: see his *Journey to America,* ed. J. P. Mayer, trans. George Lawrence (New Haven: Yale University Press, 1959), esp. pp. 245–49. The Senate report is best read against contemporary Federal reports concerning events at Ruby Ridge, Idaho, and Waco, Texas.
13. *Boston City Directory* (Boston: Adams, 1851), n.p.
14. "Letter to Francis Adams," *Life and Correspondence of Theodore Parker,* ed. John Weiss (New York: Appleton, 1864), II, 173. Such letters make more intelligible the post-

war remarks of writers like James Russell Lowell. See his 1881 essay, "Democracy," *Democracy and Other Essays* (Boston: Houghton, Mifflin, 1887), esp. pp. 25–26.

15. Quoted in L. G. Williams, *A Place for Theodore: The Murder of Dr. Theodore Parkman* (Greenville, North Carolina: Holly Two Leaves, 1997), 160. This monograph is particularly insightful concerning the relations of abolitionists and non-abolitionists in the Union Army.

16. 8: 106.

17. Nathaniel Hawthorne, *The House of the Seven Gables* [1851] (Boston: Houghton, Mifflin, 1883), 115–17, 108, 210–13, 217, 259–60, 363, 79.

POPULAR PHOTOGRAPHY, SCENERY VALUES, AND VISUAL ASSESSMENT

Photography skews most visual assessment studies. Armed with a sophisticated camera to record firsthand impressions, the researcher moves through space making images for subsequent use in comparison testing perhaps, or in a finished lecture or book. But what of the craft of photography itself? What of the American traditions of landscape photography? Has the camera helped shape American notions of scenic beauty? A close scrutiny of popular photography and rural landscape attitudes suggests that photography has indeed helped mold the attitude of the general public toward rural space.

Definitions

Terminology devised by art historians to designate nuances of scenery painting has little bearing on the American language of spatial description. In *The Personality of American Cities,* for example, Edward Hungerford in 1913 described the railroad view of Chicago by detailing "long vistas with the ungainly, picturesque outlines of steel mills with upturned rows of smoking stacks." A year later, in *Abroad at Home,* Julian Street wrote about the constituent elements of the Kansas City industrial zone, "which, reduced by distance, and seen through a softening haze of smoke, resembles a relief map—strange, vast, and pictorial."[1] In such writing, words like *picturesque* and *pictorial* appear at first reading almost meaningless, and certainly much detached from their use in such eighteenth-century works as William Gilpin's *Observations, Relative Chiefly to Picturesque Beauty, on the Highlands of Scotland* or Uvedale Price's *An Essay on the Picturesque, as Compared with the Sublime and the Beautiful,* or Richard Payne Knight's long poem, *The Landscape.*[2] Undeniably, the terminology of such aestheticians, and of subsequent generations of art historians, goes far toward explaining the creations of William Kent, Capability Brown, and Humphrey Repton, as well as those painters.[3] *Picturesque* changed meaning subtly in the romantic era, at first identifying scenery features having a roughness that stimulates the senses, then defining scenery having marked texture, then identifying

"Popular Photography, Scenery Values, and Visual Assessment" appeared in *Landscape Journal* 3, no. 2 (Autumn 1984): 111–22, copyright University of Wisconsin Press.

countryside of "intricate" lighting and coloring.[4] But by the middle of the nineteenth century, it and *pictorial* appealed to all manner of landscape observers, including many untrained in the formal definition of the terms. By *picturesque* and *pictorial,* Hungerford and Street appear to have meant nothing more than "deserving of scrutiny" or "worthy of a photograph." Exploring the impact of popular photography on scenery values means not only defining terms carefully, but realizing that many early-twentieth-century writers habitually used terms in ways utterly alien to contemporary art historians. As used here, *popular photography* designates photography by persons equipped with cameras of variable aperture, focus, and shutter. Such people had the technical capacity to make images far superior to those made by *snapshot photographers* equipped with much simpler cameras, but they rarely made images as fine as those produced by *serious photographers.* A serious photographer might have the same sort of camera owned by a popular photographer, but frequently made several exposures in order to produce a high-quality image; often the serious photographer used a tripod-mounted, large-format camera fitted for plates or sheet film. Such definitions are important. On the one hand, terms like *amateur* and *professional* say remarkably little about the equipment and expertise possessed by any one photographer; on the other, differentiating between popular and serious photographers refines discussion by emphasizing that one group is more interested in a good photograph of an important subject while the other is chiefly interested in an excellent photograph whatever the subject.[5] Between 1880 and 1940, a number of American photography magazines addressed a mixed audience of popular and serious photographers more or less familiar with a variety of illustration traditions ranging from "high art" painting to Currier and Ives lithographs to cigar box sketches. If the terminology of magazines like *Photo-Era* is any indication, few popular photographers cared much about exact definitions of *picturesque* and other terms.

Camera here designates only hand-held equipment, not tripod-mounted view cameras. Camera technology evolved rapidly after 1895, allowing photographers to make images under conditions previously impossible. Consider a typical Eastman Kodak Company advertisement from 1926. The upper-class young woman riding in a Pullman car glimpses through the plate-glass window a winding, tree-lined river flowing through open countryside, the sort of scene long beloved by landscape painters. But as so many early-twentieth-century landscape observers remarked, the scene is almost instantly gone as the train rushes on. How, then, does one "capture" the fleeting glimpse? As early as 1910, in *Motoring with a Kodak,* the Eastman Kodak Company had advertised cameras and films fast enough to be used from moving automobiles. "Every motorist feels the fascination of speed whether he indulges in it with his own car or not," its catalogue says of "The No. 1A Speed Kodak." "And when he becomes a devotee of Kodak, as he surely will, he will have an intense desire to obtain pictures of the exciting events in cup races, or to picture the scenes and events from his car when in motion."[6] As a survey of the company advertising makes clear, Kodak engineers struggled to create cameras usable from moving bicycles, trains, and motorcars, and in time they succeeded in producing small, easily portable cameras capable of making fine exposures in either high-speed or low-light situations. No longer was photography a mystery, or even remarkably difficult; roll film allowed easy and inexpensive bracketing of exposures, fine lenses permitted precise focusing, and fast shutter speeds made possible the capturing of views from trains or automobiles.

At the same time, however, image quality declined, if only slightly. Negative size decreased, and the higher speed films proved more grainy than the older, far slower ones (many nineteenth-century large-format cameras used films with speeds approximately ASA 3). The hand-held cameras lacked both swings and tilts, making corrections for parallax impossible except on the printing easel. For a vast number of people, therefore, photography meant using a hand-held camera fitted with high-speed roll film, the perfect camera for recording scenes along a vacation route or for documenting a Sunday afternoon drive, but not for producing a magnificent, crisp photograph.

As David M. Steele remarked in *Going Abroad Overland* in 1917, the effects of the hand-held camera were many. Here and there along the new automobile roads in the Rocky Mountain national parks, "chiefly paper covers torn from rolls of Kodak films bestrew the spots where parties have paused and dismounted and where interest has focused cameras."[7] The litter marked places of stunning prospect indeed, for the park visitors had not only stopped their cars to enjoy the views, but had actually gotten out to observe and make photographs. For most popular photographers, a good image could be made from the car, sometimes without even stopping. All they needed to do was follow the directions of magazine experts.

Composition

Readers of photography magazines like *Photo-Era, Photo-Miniature,* and other early-twentieth-century periodicals learned an immense amount about the proper composition of a landscape photograph. Much of the advice given by magazine writers derived, of course, from the maxims of generations of landscape painters.[8] But more than tradition governed the advice; technological difficulties and innovations subtly altered the composition guidelines. Filling more than half the viewfinder with bright sky, for example, meant not only contradicting traditional aesthetic theory, it meant over-exposing negatives and making dark objects nearly black. Articles addressing the composition of scenes including close-ups of tall trees, church steeples, and other tall objects confronted not only the issue of over-exposure, but the intricate problems of parallax correction by easel tilting. The hand-held camera, however, presented the greatest of composition difficulties; its rectangular format taxed the ingenuity of magazine experts who realized the overwhelming power of the view-finder in shaping potential shots. As popular photographers quickly out-numbered serious photographers after the turn of the century, more and more articles addressed the general issue of landscape photography composition by combining discussion of composition and subject matter.

The bulk of the articles addressing the landscape photograph emphasized the rural landscape. The editor of *Photo-Miniature,* himself a "landscape gardener," published in the April, 1901, issue a long article entitled "Landscape Photography," in which he argued that designing "real live landscapes of fences, trees, and blue grass" taught him a great deal about photogenic landscapes and scenery photography. John Tennant suggested that "a road, a bridge, a stone fence, a flock of sheep, a hill, some trees and a flourish of clouds may make six or seven good pictures, but they can't all be put into one." His article mentions some tried-and-true guidelines from painting—"As a general rule, almost without exception, the skyline should not bisect the plate"—but emphasizes techniques peculiar to photography. He worried about getting foreground objects into exact focus, a depth-of-field problem besetting many popular photographers anxious to "capture" distant mountains and foreground objects on the same negative, and counseled readers about the sorts of clouds most likely to appear well on slow-speed film.[9] Other experts shared his concerns, and added others, some scarcely related to either the aesthetics of painting or the brief history of serious photography. Elizabeth B. Richardson cautioned her readers that "modern houses seldom appear artistic in rural surroundings, and the same principle holds in the introduction of the human figure," and warned against including "an unsightly stump or telegraph pole."[10] Turn-of-the-century critics believed that British landscape photographers did a far better job of selecting and photographing rural landscapes than American, and gradually introduced into American magazines standards especially well suited to England. "The most obvious elements of excellence in the English landscapes are these," wrote one photography magazine critic, "primarily, a broad, broken, expressive foreground, as in paintings, an unimportant middle space, and abundance of appropriate, well-defined clouds filling in the

ROAD SCENE, DOUGLAS HILL, ME. PP.

sky."[11] Undoubtedly, the long and rich history of British landscape painting informs such arguments, but so does an awareness that such topography and weather work well for most hand-held cameras using the more popular film speeds. British landscape became the standard of popular photographers not only because of aesthetics, therefore, but because it photographed well, without difficulty.

Photography magazines emphasized subject selection as an important element in good composition. In "Tree-Studies," a 1912 *Photo-Era* essay by William S. Davis, popular photographers learned that "trees in full foliage are best photographed in early morning or late afternoon, and in a diffused light," that "the presence of water often adds to the charm of the scene," and that "to avoid sharp reflections the surface of the water may be agitated slightly" with a stick or pebble. The photographs accompanying the text make clear that Davis worked most successfully in "old fields" growing up in young trees but still brightly lit by meadow-like sunshine. Forest photography remained almost undiscussed; instead experts concentrated on advising readers about photo-

PHOTOGRAPHED LANDSCAPE

graphing isolated clumps of trees set off from others by water or fields.[12] Specific-oriented articles like "Tree-Studies" reinforced the theories of such experts as Tennant and Richardson, and provided the framework for a combined photography-landscape aesthetic.

As early as 1900, photography magazines had begun pointing out ugly spatial features that had no place in proper photographs. "A wretched old shack," according to one 1904 writer, deserved no picture at all.[13] Some writers suggested that factories, railroads, and smoke-belching chimneys, the components of the early-twentieth-century industrial zone, deserved as much attention from photographers as any rural landscape.[14] But by the 1930s a definite principle had evolved from such suggestions. Readers learned from photography magazines that while beautiful photographs could be made of industrial zones or rural landscapes, a correct photograph of a rural landscape—and by extension, a beautiful rural landscape—ought to contain nothing hinting of industry. The problem of industrial products, including machines, derived from the strong rural bias that shaped the work of most artists until after the Armory Show, and it made difficult the photographing of much of rural America, which by the early twentieth century exhibited the effects of agricultural mechanization.[15]

Almost everywhere in the High Plains, for example, photographers discovered nothing of English-like landscapes. In a handsomely illustrated 1930 *Photo-Era* article, "Photography in West Texas," Helen and Roland Beers described the tribulations of landscape photography in a region nearly devoid of trees. "Because of the general lack of trees and vegetation—and for many other reasons, no doubt—pictorial landscapes have eluded us," they wrote in a passage suggesting that for them the word *pictorial* designated landscapes represented in traditional scenery painting. But they had discovered the windmill, not only by extrapolating from the beauty they saw in oil rigs, but because they had determined that windmills made good substitutes for trees. As vertical elements in open short-grass prairie, the windmills proved excellent, but the Beerses, well aware of the dictum that machinery spoiled rural landscape perfection *a la* photography magazine dictates, worried about including them in photographs entitled "a prairie home" and "sunset on the prairie."[16] If the photographs published in the magazines indicate anything about habits of popular photographers, very, very few had the courage of the Beerses. Most eschewed industrial subjects, and rarely ventured into West Texas and other regions unlike the British and eastern North American rural landscapes preferred by the magazine writers.

"Motoring" also shaped public perceptions. On Sunday afternoons and on vacations, urban and suburban Americans drove into rural regions,

POPULAR PHOTOGRAPHY, SCENERY VALUES

searched for "picturesque" views, and stopped to photograph them. The Kodak Company quickly perceived the potential of the new market; as early as 1897 it had introduced the "Bicycle Kodak" designed to be operated from handlebars.[17] By 1910 it had published a lavishly illustrated booklet entitled *Motoring with a Kodak.* Part guidebook, part catalogue, *Motoring* extolled the delights of bringing along a camera: "Of what shall you make pictures? What shall you take? Rather, what shall you not take! In an automobile tour, what do you see most of? Scenery. Very well, take pictures of scenery."[18] Its illustrations suggested what many Kodak magazine advertisements suggest—photographing rural scenery was a woman's job. Husbands drove the motor cars; wives watched for perfect rural landscapes, commanded husbands to halt, then aimed and "snapped" the cameras.[19] According to several magazine experts, using a camera improved one's ability to see; by extrapolation, carrying a camera while automobiling sharpened one's notice of beautiful rural landscapes.[20]

Motoring and popular photography combined to restore the old stereograph scenery aesthetic.[21] While magazines like *Outlook* and *Suburban Life* published articles explaining vacation photography, many motorists half-consciously imitated stereograph views.[22] They framed pictures to include a foreground object, usually a tree or fence, and a distant object; about the vague middle distance they worried little, content to have a lake, pond, or field in the center of their composition. What prompted the return to the stereograph aesthetic? Tradition exerted some power, of course, but the larger force appears to have been the "view from the road" experienced by most motorists. Early-twentieth-century rural roads remained lined with trees and fences; beyond the bordering, vertical edge lay open fields. Popular photographers looked through the screens lining the roads, discovered picturesque views, and stopped to make photographs using the screening trees and fences as foreground objects. Only rarely did they insert human figures, but they did favor herds of livestock, particularly cows; by the 1930s, photogenic rural landscapes usually included herds of cows or a few mid-pasture trees "browsed" by cattle.[23] And more important, despite the advice of photography magazines, the motorists had incorporated roads into their rural landscape photographs.

More than any other figure, Wallace Nutting understood and reinforced the popular photographer-motorist roadside view. His "States Beautiful Series," a collection of illustrated travel volumes produced in the first three decades of the twentieth century, proved enormously popular. *Connecticut Beautiful, Pennsylvania Beautiful,* and many other companion volumes display hundreds of photographs, most of which fall into one of two categories.[24] Many are literally "views from the road," taken either from motor cars or from the ground beside stopped cars.

Throughout the first decades of the twentieth century, the Eastman Kodak Company advertised photography as something women might do during weekend automobile trips.

Take a KODAK *with you.*

Beautifully illustrated booklet, "Motoring with a Kodak," free at the dealers or by mail.
EASTMAN KODAK CO., Rochester, N. Y., *The Kodak City.*

Many others are views of rural landscapes in which tree-lined, dirt roads are prominent elements in the compositions. Nowhere in any of the photographs are telephone poles, steel-frame windmills, or other products of twentieth-century industry. In 1927, Nutting published *Photographic Art Secrets,* a massive explanation of how he made photographs. The book explains much about his vision of the rural landscape. "The retouching of landscape negatives is another department. The most usual requirement is to get rid of the telegraph pole," he wrote. "Just now they are the bane of country road work and spoil more compositions than all other obstructions whatsoever." Nutting catalogued the best scenic features, noting that "noble elms, road bordered, suggest charm," that "nothing gives a more opulent sense than the clean side of a wheat field where the reaper has just passed," and that "Pennsylvania is the most attractive farming country, because the good farms are often in a rolling country." So convinced was he of his aesthetic standards that he advised his readers to travel prepared to improve landscapes before photographing them: "The writer always travels with a hand axe. In a wild or abandoned country a stub or sapling may spoil the scene and may be removed without trouble."[25] His dislike of abandoned rural landscapes, not uncommon in the first part of the twentieth century, is evident in his many photographs, almost none of which portray run-down fields.[26] The "States Beautiful Series" is an extraordinary milepost in the history of American landscape appreciation, for it is the work of an immensely talented professional photographer who understood that popular photographers would appreciate his work, buy more, and try to imitate it.

By the late 1930s, the motorist-photographer had won. Landscape aesthetics revolved around the view from the road, through a screen of trees (not utility poles) into well-kept open fields, and across toward an object of interest, an old house, a stand of deciduous trees, or perhaps a winding dirt road. In 1936, the Kodak Company, well aware of its customers, published *How to Make Good Pictures: A Book for the Every-Day Photographer;* its "landscape" section echoes in brief format much of Nutting's advice.[27] The invention of reliable color film in the 1930s sent even more photographers into the countryside, intent on capturing autumn foliage, spring wildflowers, and red barns. The motorists drove through the rural landscape searching for perfect vistas; they ignored "industrial" items like guardrails and "incongruous" items like new houses and straight, paved roads. By the 1950s they frequently made color slides, and in the 1960s and 1970s they experimented with "instant" films. But they adhered to popular standards of rural landscape beauty.

Today the mass media cater to their wishes. The typical photo-postcard is contrived according to Nutting's guidelines; almost never does it show power lines or new structures, but frequently it depicts watering cattle or autumn foliage. Newspaper and magazine photographs reinforce the postcard view, and still exhibit a trace of the stereograph composition. The calendars distributed by pizza parlors, gasoline stations, and funeral homes likewise emphasize the popular aesthetic by displaying professionally made photographs intended to soothe "typical" American viewers.

What is the cultural impact of the landscape aesthetic devised by popular photographers, camera manufacturers, and photography magazines, and reinforced by news media and advertisements? Certainly it nearly overwhelms the efforts of professional photographers to reexamine rural landscapes; the photographs by David Plowden in his *Floor of the Sky: The Great Plains* appeal chiefly to an educated elite, not to the typical Americans who find the High Plains country disturbingly unphotogenic, and monotonous.[28] More important, the popular aesthetic shapes the public understanding of what the rural landscape ought to contain; if popular photography advice is any indication, beautiful rural scenery must have no utility poles, mobile homes, steel barns, oil wells, or even barbed wire fences. The new industrialized rural landscape, wholly alien to the dictates of the popular photography aesthetic, remains unnoticed by observers of postcard views and contemporary popular photography magazines.[29] The popular photography aesthetic endures as an intricate blend of hand-held camera formats and automobile viewsheds, a blend lacking precisely defined terminology, a blend challenging historians of painting and of serious photography. It endures as the prism that skews angles of vision, that casts glimmering distortions over visual assessment studies. How often does the visual assessment specialist recall that his subjects evaluate *photographs or slides of scenery,* not the scenery itself?

Notes

1. Edward Hungerford, *The Personality of American Cities* (New York: McBride, Nast, 1913), p. 199; Julian Street, *Abroad at Home* (New York: Century, 1914), p. 289; for another use of terminology, see J. Vildensky, "The Pictorialist," *Photo-Era* 55 (October 1925), 213. On industrial zones, terminology, and photography, see John R. Stilgoe, *Metropolitan Corridor: Railroads and the American Scene* (New Haven: Yale University Press, 1983), pp. 75–103.

2. William Gilpin, *Observations* (London: Blamire, 1789); Uvedale Price, *Essay on the Picturesque* (London: Robson, 1794); Richard Payne Knight, *The Landscape* (London: Bulmer, 1794).

3. Louis Hawes, *Presences of Nature: British Landscape, 1780–1830* (New Haven: Yale Center for British Art, 1982); Ronald Paulson, *Literary Landscape: Turner and Constable* (New Haven: Yale University Press, 1982); Christopher Thacker, *The History of Gardens* (Berkeley: University of California Press, 1979), pp. 181–227.

4. Luigi Salerno, "The Picturesque," *Encyclopedia of World Art* (New York: McGraw Hill, 1966), XI, 335–342.

5. See, for instance, Alvin Langdon Coburn, "The Future of Pictorial Photography" [1916], *Photographers on Photography,* ed. Nathan Lyons (Englewood Cliffs, New Jersey: Prentice-Hall, 1966), pp. 53–55; and Susan Sontag, *On Photography* (New York: Farrar, Straus, and Giroux, 1977), especially pp. 55–59. I emphasize that the distinction between popular and serious photography is my own, developed especially for analysis of landscape photography.

6. *Motoring With a Kodak* (Rochester, New York: Eastman Kodak Co., 1910), p. 27; on technological innovation, see Reese V. Jenkins, *Images and Enterprise: Technology and the American Photographic Industry, 1839–1925* (Baltimore: Johns Hopkins University Press, 1975).

7. David M. Steele, *Going Abroad Overland* (New York: Putnam's, 1917), p. 129.

8. See, for example, George H. Hazlitt, "What is Legitimate in Artistic Photography," *Photo-Era* 5 (August 1900), 46–49, and Henry Lewis Johnson, "Photography in Illustration," *Photo-Era* 13 (October 1904), 196–198.

9. John Tennant, "Landscape Photography," *Photo-Miniature* 111 (April 1901), 1–36.

10. Elizabeth B. Richardson, "Landscape Composition," *Photo-Era* 5 (December 1900), 178–184.

11. "The Lesson of the Chance Picture at the Salon," *Photo-Era* 4 (January 1904), 3–8; see also Denman W. Ross, "How Design Comes into Photography," *Photo-Era* 4 (January 1900), 1–2, and John L. Swayze, "Art and the Snapshot," *Photo-Era* 58 (May 1927), 243–248.

12. William S. Davis, "Tree-Studies," *Photo-Era* 29 (July 1912), 18–22. Some authors did address forest photography; see, for example, Thomas Sedwick Steele, *Canoe and*

Camera (New York: Orange Judd, 1880) and J. T. Coolidge, "Trapping with a Camera," *Country Life* 18 (September 1910), 535–536. On the photography of lone trees, see C. S. Luitwieler, "An Old Settler," *Photo-Era* 5 (August 1900), 29.

13. "A Kodak Incident," *Photo-Era* 12 (June 1904), 104.

14. Edward D. Wilson, "Beauty in Ugliness," *Photo-Era* 54 (June 1930), 303.

15. See, for example, Karen Tsujimoto, *Images of America: Precisionist Painting and Modern Photography* (Seattle: University of Washington Press, 1982) and *Buildings: Architecture in American Modernism* (New York: Hirschel & Adler Galleries, 1980).

16. Helen and Roland Beers, "Photography in West Texas," *Photo-Era* 65 (December 1930), 302–306.

17. Kenneth I. Helphand, "The Bicycle Kodak," *Environmental Review* 4 (Winter 1981), 24–33.

18. *Ibid.,* p. 10.

19. For sample illustrations, see advertisements on the back covers of the June 1907 *Century* and the June 16, 1910 *Life;* on the ramifications of speed and photography, see Cecilia Tichi, "Twentieth Century Limited: William Carlos Williams' Poetics of High-Speed America," *William Carlos Williams Review* 9 (Autumn 1983), 49–70.

20. "The Educational Value of the Camera: How it Develops the Power of Receiving and Classifying Impressions," *Craftsman* 17 (March 1910), 647–656.

21. On the stereograph aesthetic, see Oliver Wendell Holmes, "The Stereoscope and Stereograph," *Atlantic Monthly* 4 (June 1859), 738–748; John C. Bowker, "The Stereopticon in the Home," *Suburban Life* 7 (November 1908), 238–239; and William C. Darrah, *Stereo Views: A History of Stereographs in America and their Collection* (Gettysburg, Pennsylvania: Darrah, 1964).

22. On vacation photography, see A. Black, "Photography as a Vacation Resource," *Outlook* 51 (June 15, 1895), and C. H. Claudy, "The Vacation Camera: How to Use It," *Suburban Life* 10 (June 1910), 357–358. On actual practice, see S. Allan, "Camera in a Country Lane," *Scribner's* 31 (June 1902), 679–688, and "Amateur Landscape Photographs," *Country Life* 11 (March 1907), 602.

23. I base this conclusion upon my examination of turn-of-the-century family photograph albums held by museums and by antique dealers.

24. Wallace Nutting, *Connecticut Beautiful* (Framingham, Massachusetts: Old American, 1923); Wallace Nutting, *Pennsylvania Beautiful* (Framingham, Massachusetts: Old American, 1924); Nutting's "States Series" books remain in print and remain popular with tourists.

25. Wallace Nutting, *Photographic Art Secrets* (New York: Dodd, Mead, 1927), pp. 86–88, 100–101, 108.

26. On the early-twentieth-century view of abandoned agricultural land, see Stilgoe, *Metropolitan Corridor,* pp. 312–333.

27. *How to Make Good Pictures: A Book for the Every-Day Photographer* (Rochester, New York: Eastman Kodak Co., 1936), n.p.

28. David Plowden, *Floor of the Sky: The Great Plains* (San Francisco: Sierra Club, 1972); on the monotony of the High Plains, see, for example, Street, *Abroad,* pp. 365–376.

29. Roger Courtenay, "New Patterns in Alberta's Parkland," *Landscape* 26 (Winter 1982), 41–47, and "A New Class of Agricultural Landscapes" (unpublished paper read at the 1982 Council of Educators in Landscape Architecture national conference, Blacksburg, Virginia). See also Sally Schauman and Mary Pfender, *An Assessment Procedure for Countryside Landscapes* (Seattle: University of Washington, Department of Landscape Architecture, 1982).

PHOTOGRAPHED LANDSCAPE

BIKINIS, BEACHES, AND BOMBS

Human Nature on the Sand

Bikini. No other word more accurately connotes the intricate web of meaning infusing modern ocean recreation. *Bikini* suggests sun, tanning lotion, surf, and swimming, all mingled with a zesty vivacity, sexuality, and vague wantonness. It evokes California rock-and-roll music, a series of 1960s beach movies, and echoes of the long feminist struggle for abbreviated beach attire. And only rarely do contemporary Americans recall the other meaning of the word, as the name of the tropical island reduced to ashes in repeated atomic bomb tests. Sexuality and death, bronzed health and charred wreckage—do any more troubling dichotomies thrive in a single word? Do such searing dualities explain the American unwillingness to link the bikini with Bikini Atoll, to link natural vitality with thermonuclear fire?

Every beach is marginal; ocean beaches are more marginal than most. By definition, a margin is something like a boundary, something like an edge; but a margin is not a boundary, not an edge. It is a zone, a space, an empty area, in typographical terms usually thought of as the blank space separating the ends of lines from the edges of pages. By definition, everything within a margin is marginal, somehow on the edge, somehow hovering between proper and improper, between acceptable and unacceptable, between place within the text and no place at all. The word derives from the Latin *margo,* a word that sixteenth-century Englishmen knew as *marge* and used to designate what ecologists now call the littoral or coastal zone. In 1907, the Canadian poet Robert Service resurrected the anachronism in "The Cremation of Sam McGee," describing "the marge of Lake LeBarge" where the poetic narrator "cremated Sam McGee." Service perceived the continuing connotation of marginality intimately associated with any beach; where else could something as utterly marginal as the cremation of a living man more properly occur?

For centuries, mariners and landsmen alike distrusted the marginal zone as a place neither land nor sea, a zone of shipwreck, drowning, quicksand, and surf, the very lair of sea serpents, rocky hazards, and undertow.

"Bikinis, Beaches, and Bombs: Human Nature on the Sand" appeared in *Orion* 3 (Summer 1984): 5–15.

Mariners shunned the ledges and reefs they named "woes," and kept far offshore; farmers scorned the infertile sand and the fickle dune grass soon destroyed by grazing livestock. Throughout the American colonial era, indeed well into the middle of the nineteenth century, visitors to marginal zones saw only drifting sand, hazardous rocks, and an eerie barrenness. "Strewn with crabs, horse-shoes, and razor-clams, and whatever the sea casts up,—a vast *morgue*, where famished dogs may range in packs, and crows come daily to glean the pittance which the tide leaves them," and where "the carcasses of men and beasts together lie stately up upon its shelf, rotting and bleaching in the sun and waves," the unvisited ocean beach haunts Thoreau's 1865 travelog, *Cape Cod*. Thoreau saw only the grasping waves gnawing at the blowing, eroding dunes, felt only the suck of the surf, the sting of salt and sand. Nowhere in *Cape Cod* does the contemporary reader find the delicate love of nature that suffused *Walden*. To the visitor from inland Concord, the great barrier beaches evoked only fascination tempered by distrust.

Not for decades would American attitudes change. The national apprehension of the marge was reshaped gradually by a developing love of tropical scenery and lifestyle. As early as 1776, in "The Beauties of Santa Cruz," Philip Freneau extolled the voluptuous landscape of the island known now as St. Croix, a setting for a life of perfect ease. But Freneau explicitly omitted the island beaches from his catalog of beauties, noting that "the threatening waters roar on every side," and that "sharp craggy rocks repel the surging brine." Only inland, away from the marge, does he find scenery worthy of paradise; the littoral he dismisses as dangerous and barren. Fifty years later, when C.S. Stewart published his Hawaiian adventures in *A Residence in the Sandwich Islands,* the traditional attitude still shaped scenery assessment; Stewart described the entrance into the bay of Waikiki, the panoramic view of the south side of Oahu, the groves of coconut trees, the plain and hills beyond—and said not a word about the beach separating ocean from groves of trees. For Stewart, the beach existed as a mere threshold, sometimes dangerous, always unworthy of attention; only the lush inland scenery deserved remark.

Herman Melville heralded a shift in popular attitudes when he published his first two novels, *Typee* and *Omoo,* in the late 1840s. Melville appreciated more than the South Seas landscape. Unlike missionaries and explorers, he praised the ways of the natives, noting that "to many of them, indeed, life is little else than an often interrupted and luxurious nap," a lifestyle perfectly fitted to a luxuriant landscape. As a beached sailor, a deserter from his whaling ship, Melville lived among the natives, enjoying their idle, idyllic life, learning to mock the attempts of American missionaries to civilize the Marquesans. His books brought him success fired by scandal; conservative critics attacked his thinking on nearly every subject. According to their arguments, Melville had gone native and deserted the values of Western, genteel civilization as surely as he had deserted his ship.

Melville rejoiced in discovering a prelapsarian society, a society in which men and women lived more naturally than at home. His descriptions of people swimming scandalized and titillated his readers, because they explicitly legitimized nakedness. "The ease and grace with which the maidens of the valley propelled themselves through the water, and their familiarity with the element, were truly astonishing," he marveled. He tells how, on one occasion, he plunged in among them, "and counting vainly upon my superior strength, sought to drag some of them under the water, but I quickly repented my temerity." His readers learned quickly enough that the women swam nude; Melville describes one "beauteous nymph" who "for the most part clung to the primitive and summer garb of Eden. But how becoming the costume! It showed her fine figure to the best possible advantage." In Melville's books, the South Sea islands became the very paradisal place about which some readers dreamed, a place beyond social inhibition, a place beyond ill health, a place beyond work. To be sure, few Americans voiced their agreement with Melville, but the books kept on selling even as more missionaries sallied forth to terminate the wickedness he so enjoyed.

Despite the success of *Typee* and *Omoo,* an uneasiness born of prudery continued to shape American attitudes toward the South Seas margin. Victorian sensibility cowed even Mark Twain, whose 1872 *Roughing It* reveals the author's difficulties on Hawaiian beaches. As he approached the islands, Twain no more noticed Waikiki Beach than did Stewart; only later during his stay, when he tired of the luxuriant inland scenery, did he explore the margin. "At noon I observed a bevy of nude native young ladies bathing in the sea, and went and sat down on their clothes to keep them from being stolen," he remarks in the dry humor for which he was already known. "I begged them to come out, for the sea was rising, and I was satisfied that they were running some risk." But a closer reading of the final chapters reveals his profound discomfort with such local customs as "the lascivious hula-hula." He shied away from the innocent unclad native women he met with everywhere along the shore. In the Hawaiian marginal zone, even the iconoclastic Twain encountered a lifestyle of such unrestrained vigor that retreat became the only solution.

Until the beginning of the twentieth century, the South Seas marginal lifestyle remained the bane of missionary efforts and the secret delight of American men and women frustrated by the tightening strictures of Victorianism. Then slowly, but as certainly as the incoming tide, Americans discovered their own beaches. Books like *Typee* and *Omoo* may have predisposed some people toward beach-going, but other forces account for the throngs that soon wandered along the sand.

Fear drove many Americans to the seashore. Urban families found that summertime diseases were rampant in the burgeoning cities—diseases born of filthy streets, contaminated food, and unsanitary plumbing, diseases spread by overcrowding, foul air, and lack of exercise. Well-to-do families had long ago deserted the summer city for the healthful environment of rural villages, mountain hotels, and seashore inns, but by the 1890s, thousands of middle-class families had also begun taking out-of-city holidays, and even working-class families enjoyed day trips beyond suburban limits. Most frequently, wives and children abandoned cities for weeks or months on end, leaving husbands behind to endure the summer torment. Fortunate men visited their families on weekends, in the strange way William Dean Howells described in 1885 in *The Rise of Silas Lapham*. Families sacrificed togetherness for the seashore vacation in particular, for they believed that in the marginal zone lay the chance for health and longevity.

Many health experts drove home the near-miraculous advantages of beach life. In *Sea-Air and Sea-Bathing,* an 1880 guide to health and vigor, John Packard argued that the coastal zone offered dozens of advantages to the frail or sickly urban resident. Fresh, clean air refreshed the lungs and stimulated the appetite; sunshine warmed the blood and eased muscle strain; and—most important—salt water bathing refreshed the entire body. According to Packard and other authorities, bathing in fresh water leached precious salts out of the body, while splashing in salt water strengthened the saline concentrations. That medical advice alone sent millions to ocean beaches, prompted the donning of "bathing suits," and led to grown men and women jumping up and down in breakers. And it led to children being cajoled or dragged into the waves too.

Families eagerly embraced medical notions that beach play prevented childhood illness; in an age of high infant and child mortality, parents grasped at any theory, but the beach-life theory made common sense: sun, exercise, and salt water together would give old-fashioned vitality, the vitality of the farm of generations past. "A cleaner or more healthy occupation can scarcely be imagined," Packard argued, "and the only caution needful is the obvious one as to the mid-day heat." But other, deeper currents prompted parents to bring children to ocean beaches. Slowly, almost incredibly, considering the on-going racism directed against blacks and Indians, there developed the argument that sun, sand, and surf engendered the vitality usually associated by Caucasians with people of color. "Children of tender years, barefoot and with streaming hair, play for hours upon the beaches, now in and now out of the water with perfect immunity from colds," announced an 1896 Maine Central Railroad Company brochure advertising Casco Bay summer vacations. "Youngsters, after a season of such sports, look like young Indians; moreover they fare like Indians, at least three times a day." Sea-bathing, coupled with seashore exercise, consequently produced not only good health and good appetite, but an extraordinary vitality associated with sunburnt skin, or with the skin of races more vital than the white.

At first, only children enjoyed the luxury of sunburn and tanned skin; adults, particularly women, shunned the glare. "It is hard to picture nowadays the shell-like transparence, the luminous red-and-white, of those young cheeks untouched by paint or powder," recalled Edith Wharton in 1934, in her autobiography, *A Backward Glance*. "Beauty was unthinkable without 'a complexion,' and to defend that treasure against sun and wind, and the archenemy, sea air, veils as thick as curtains were habitually worn" by women summering in Newport in the 1870s. As late as 1901, in fact, *Collier's* and other magazines still published advertisements for Anita Cream and similar skin lighteners, although by then fashion too dictated change. For as long as Americans remained an agricultural people, upper-class women prized pale skin—"a complexion"—as proof of freedom from outdoor farm work; as the nation industrialized, pale skin began to suggest the pallor associated with factory labor, and men and women of leisure slowly embraced a tanned or "bronzed" skin as a sign of status, a sign announcing their ability to summer outdoors, usually along the seashore. Period paintings and photographs clearly reveal the change; in the 1860s, young women carry parasols above their hats and veils; by 1880 they wear only hats, and by 1905 they are hatless, and sometimes with streaming hair. Feminists championed the changes, for they argued that the abbreviation of beach attire announced a new value placed on health, not simple devotion to clothing fashions.

More than any other feminist, perhaps more than any other American, novelist Kate Chopin deciphered the changing attitude toward the sea. In *The Awakening,* a novel of 1899, Chopin details the summer life of a young mother visiting the seashore, wandering along the beach with parasol and long dress to defend her skin against tanning, and trying to learn how to swim while wearing a voluminous woolen suit intended for bathing, not swimming. "A certain ungovernable dread hung about her when in the water, unless there was a hand near by that might reach out and reassure her," Chopin writes of the woman she calls Mrs. Pontellier. As the summer passes, however, the woman begins to "loosen a little the mantle of reserve that had always enveloped her," and suddenly learns to swim. "She could have shouted for joy. She did shout for joy, as with a sweeping stroke or two she lifted her body to the surface of the water," writes Chopin at

BIKINIS, BEACHES, AND BOMBS

Celebrated turn-of-the-century illustrator Charles Dana Gibson understood that wearing abbreviated swimming attire somehow made women bold.

the climax of the novel. "She wanted to swim far out, where no woman had swum before. She would not join the groups in their sports and bouts, but intoxicated with her newly conquered power, she swam out alone." From that moment on, the woman becomes a different person; she casts off her parasol and becomes so sunburnt that her husband, arriving for a weekend visit, grows annoyed; she rebels against her role as a housewife; and eventually she moves away from her husband, leaves society, and commits suicide. "She cast the unpleasant, pricking garments from her, and for the first time in her life, she stood naked in the open air, at the mercy of the sun, the breeze that beat upon her, and the waves that invited her," writes Chopin of the woman now called Edna. "How strange and awful it seemed to stand naked under the sky! How delicious! She felt like some new-born creature, opening its eyes in a familiar world that it had never known." No longer does the sea terrify her. Bereft of woolen bathing suit, alone on the white beach, she strikes off into the waves and deliberately drowns, finally free of conventional lifestyle.

Swimming marked the height of the discovery period. After the Australian crawl entered American consciousness in the first years of the new century, men and women learned that exercise and bathing might be combined. And they learned too that in the water the sexes are equal in physical capacity, something that stunned men accustomed to dominating women. *The Awakening* shocked readers worse than *Typee* and *Omoo* had half a century before, and the novel disappeared from bookstores; but Chopin had perceived the awe-inspiring significance of beach life. On the seacoast women achieved more than the vigor acquired by children and men—they reaped a new understanding of themselves, an understanding laced with South Seas energy. In the ocean surf they glimpsed the physical prowess that had challenged Melville years before, when he swam among the lithe women of the tropics.

PHOTOGRAPHED LANDSCAPE

Despite the growing popularity of seashore recreation, salt-water bathing and swimming disconcerted many conservative Americans. Not only did men and women wear costumes considered abbreviated, but in the surf both sexes tumbled together wildly, limb touching limb, body touching body. In a turn-of-the-century essay, "The Beach at Rockaway," novelist William Dean Howells described the "promiscuous bathing" as something disturbing even to watch. "It was indeed like one of those uncomfortable dreams where you are not dressed sufficiently for company, or perhaps at all, and yet are making a very public appearance," he mused. He concluded that "all was a damp and dreary decorum"—a curious finale to an essay depicting "swarms and heaps of people in all lolling and lying and wallowing shapes" sprawled on the sand or "slopping and shouting and shrieking" in the waves. Being among so many people doing so many scarcely decent things sent Howells back inland in his carriage. Along with others of his years, the novelist retreated before the beach play of the younger generation.

Even as the retreat turned to rout, conservatives attempted to control what they perceived as the lazy morality of the summer beach, usually by controlling clothing. As late as 1930, Chicago police officers measured the hemlines of women's bathing suits, making certain that none swayed more than four inches above knees. Many states and municipalities passed ordinances prohibiting dressing and undressing in automobiles, although automobile manufacturers persisted in equipping large cars with curtains. And in Atlantic City, a resort dedicated to boardwalk promenades and bracing sea air, city fathers forbade men to remove bathing suit tops long after Malibu and other California communities had regarded male chests with disinterest. Advertising and corporate retailing quickly surmounted the conservative restrictions, however, and freed men—if not women—from the dictates of yesteryear.

So long as men swam in suits with long sleeves and pants, men drowned. Traditionally, boys and men had swum nude, enjoying the male-only conviviality of rural swimming holes, abandoned quarries and sandpits, or industrial waterfronts. Mixed bathing provided more freedom to women, but condemned men to paddling in heavy woolen suits almost as constricting as the female bathing dresses. By the early 1920s, however, men had discarded ankle-length leggings and long sleeves; ten years later, they swam in sleeveless tops. Underwear manufacturers anxious to broaden their markets recruited swimming champions like Johnny Weismuller to advertise ever more abbreviated suits intended for competitive sport. They understood the tremendous potential implicit in making swimming truly enjoyable.

Manufacturers of women's clothing knew the potential too, and

BIKINIS, BEACHES, AND BOMBS

vaguely discerned another. If bathing suit styles changed from year to year, fashion-conscious women would buy the latest design each spring, thus insuring a steady market for clothes that might otherwise last many seasons. Consequently, the Jantzen Company and other firms began styling women's suits—for swimming now, not for bathing. The Jantzen Company precipitated an uproar when, in 1924, it distributed millions of decals depicting a young woman in a sleeveless, nearly legless red suit, and suggested that motorists attach the logo to automobile windshields. In one of the first coups in modern advertising, four million motorists did, for unrecorded reasons; only in Massachusetts did motorists forego the pleasure, for the state legislature, fearful of collisions resulting from male drivers mesmerized by the young woman's form, outlawed the decal at once. In 1920, the Jantzen Company sold 26,832 women's bathing suits; ten years later, in one season it sold 1,587,338, a merchandising victory resulting from advertising, planned obsolescence, and an unanticipated cultural push.

Women adored the brief, one-piece suits that permitted genuine, effortless swimming. Exactly as Chopin had predicted, women delighted in enjoying water sports as equals with men. Charles Dana Gibson, the creator of the "Gibson Girl," caught the new enthusiasm early in the century, when he drew young women wearing not only ever briefer bathing dresses, but ever more arch expressions. Early Hollywood film makers, particularly Max Sennet, caught the mood in a number of "bathing beauty" films. But most important, Gertrude Ederle both caught and nurtured the love when she swam the English Channel in 1926, breaking the records set by the five previous swimmers, all men. Clad in trunks, brassiere, and axle grease, Eberle became a heroine overnight, proof of a new level of feminine physical competence. And her two-piece suit prompted more women to demand briefer one-piece garments.

A national swimming craze forced park commissions everywhere to build pools, level beaches, and confront the horrors of water-borne disease. Packed urban beaches—on some summer days in the late 1920s, Chicago authorities reported half a million citizens splashing in Lake Michigan—proved less healthful by the year. Health departments tried chlorinating water, building swimming pools (New York City built the first in 1901) and wading pools, or directing would-be beachgoers to distant beaches. New York City opened Jones Beach, some thirty-three miles from Manhattan, largely to draw unprecedented crowds away from polluted harbor water. On summer days more than 100,000 people crowded Jones Beach, partaking of a novel social experience in which sun, sand, and water seemed secondary, yet absolutely essential.

In the years just before the Second World War, Americans finally and fully accepted the active beach vacation, or the active day-at-the-beach. No longer did most visitors content themselves with a quiet stroll, or a lazy afternoon of sitting on a blanket reading magazines. Instead the typical beach visitor engaged the environment; he or she ran along the wet sand, climbed dunes, lay in the sun smothered with tanning oil, and—above all—swam. Sometime in the 1930s, being unable to swim became unacceptable, an embarrassing ignorance; being untanned in summer became unfashionable; and being too skinny or too plump became a summertime nightmare for millions bombarded with bathing suit advertisements featuring perfect-bodied, bronzed swimmers. Wartime slowed but scarcely stopped the drift toward abbreviated beach attire—Hollywood dispatched tens of thousands of "bathing beauty" photographs to servicemen, most of whom still recall Betty Grable posing in a risqué one-piece suit—and accelerated the active use of beaches. Swimming, as Depression-era experts had pointed out, cost almost nothing; in the early 1940s, many Americans found that the ocean offered cheap, unrationed enjoyment.

According to the magazine articles from 1946 and 1947, a French fashion designer created the bikini bathing suit "to lift the spirits" of a country shattered by war. No Paris model would wear the garment for photographers; the design firm hired a showgirl. The name came from Bikini Atoll, a hitherto unknown Pacific isle that was the site of atomic tests in 1946. Just as the bomb represented an "absolute," said the designer, so the bikini bathing suit represented an absolute of brevity.

While American men had shed their swimsuit tops by the late 1930s, emboldened largely by Tarzan films and the examples of advertising, American women embraced the two-piece suit more slowly, at least in public. Between 1945 and 1960, however, the ocean beach changed character once again as millions visited the seashore not to swim, but to sunbathe.

Despite the warnings of dermatologists, American women enthusiastically embarked on "the perfect tan," a deep, coppery or bronze tan produced partly by tanning creams or oil, largely by lying for hours in bright sunlight. Women sunbathed in backyards, on apartment house roofs, and on the beach; the beach provided more sunlight, reflected from water and sand, and thus a greater degree of tan achieved within a few hours. The bathing suit became a sunbathing suit, becoming briefer, and less suited to swimming; women chose strapless suits to eliminate the lines that marred the effect of off-shoulder dresses. California women led the march toward even briefer suits, toward the bikini that became popular in the late 1960s.

On the beach, 1960s young Americans confronted the medieval four elements almost directly. Sea air, sunlight, sand, and salt water—air, fire, earth, and water in the language of alchemists—touched skin scarcely encumbered by cloth. The ocean beach became the first environment encountered by all senses; it became a very proving ground of sensory experience.

As adults and children shed most of their clothing, they shed social inhibitions too. On the beach, men and women lay crowded together, grooming their near-naked bodies with lotions and oils, sleeping within touching distance of total strangers. Conversation began more easily on the beach; neighborliness found expression in the sharing of pepper, child care, and radios. Strangers united in sports ranging from touch football to volleyball, and gathered around cooking fires. Most of the subtle nuances of social rank and privilege vanished; a deep tan, trim physique, and accurate physical coordination mattered more than an expensive swimsuit or beach umbrella.

The "Bikini Beach" films of the late 1960s popularized the emerging image of the California beach as precursor to a better world. Nearly plotless, always zany, the feature films depicting scarcely clad teenagers surfing, singing, and flirting on broad sandy beaches nevertheless offer insights into a changing American culture—and changing attitudes toward seashore environments. The beach kids wage ceaseless struggle against middle-aged prudes convinced that near-nakedness engenders depravity; they struggle also against young men and women of their own age committed to a 1950s love of industrialism—the motorcycle gang attired in black leather jackets. Honest, friendly, open to natural living, the beach kids lead totally marginal lives beset by opponents invariably depicted as ignoble. *Bikini Beach, Beach Blanket Bingo, How to Stuff a Wild Bikini,* and the others present a teenage generation poised between the restrictions of the past and the uncertainties of the future. Indeed the films say nothing about the antecedents of the characters—or about their plans and dreams. The beach kids are simply "on the beach," enjoying a nearly natural life free of the developing problems that culminated in the student revolts of the late 1960s.

To watch the films twenty years later is to understand the marginality of the beach culture. The beach kids now seem to be waiting for something, seeking some mission or direction, and receiving no guidance from inland. Where did they go, the bronzed young men and bikinied women? The men went to Viet Nam.

In the "Bikini Beach" films, the beach is truly a liminal zone, an uncertain, momentary refuge between childhood and adult turmoil. On the beach blossoms a momentary awareness of pure nature that produces a carefree, loving existence threatened only by outsiders. The films spoke to a generation of teenagers already forgetting the Korean conflict, wary of the Cuban missile crisis, as yet unaware of Southeast Asia. They

PHOTOGRAPHED LANDSCAPE

Publicity photographs for the 1965 film *How to Stuff a Wild Bikini* perhaps unwittingly emphasized that bikinis forced women to mind both their posture and their carriage, at least out of the water. (Courtesy Museum of Modern Art, Film Stills Archive)

spoke to a generation aware of the atomic bomb, of the potential for a world of cinders and dry bones.

Consequently the films, and the actual life of the ocean beach that caught up children and adults as well as teenagers, embrace the youthful vitality that temporarily succeeds in blocking the specter of the bomb. More than half a century after *The Awakening,* Americans awakened to the wisdom of its author. "The voice of the sea is seductive; never ceasing, whispering, clamoring, murmuring, inviting the soul to wander for a spell in abysses of solitude; to lose itself in mazes of inward contemplation," wrote Chopin. "The voice of the sea speaks to the soul. The touch of the sea is sensuous, enfolding the body in its soft, close embrace." On the ocean beach, in the late 1960s, Americans fully embraced not only the four elements, but conflicting visions of the future. On the one hand, they glimpsed the future grounded in intimacy with nature, in equality of the sexes, in spontaneous friendship, sharing, and dreaming; on the other, they spied the future of the island paradise charred, the future of no future at all. In the rich mix of sun, sand, and surf, Americans rediscovered the long-lost vitality of the South Seas islanders. Literally turning their backs on inland civilization, they sojourned momentarily in an environment of possibility, in the marginal zone scorned by nineteenth-century critics. Wearing scarcely more than skin and sunglasses, they reveled in the magic of the littoral, thinking away the mushroom cloud hovering over Bikini Atoll.

And still today they dream, caring little for warnings about ozone layers and skin cancer, luxuriating in flesh alive to the elements, clad in bikinis far briefer than the post-war absolute. On the ocean beach, between land and sea, young Americans search for the paradise of innocence, the Eden found long ago by Melville, the Eden discerned by Chopin, the Eden of human life intimate with nature.

BIKINIS, BEACHES, AND BOMBS

SUNSET BEACH, STUDIO BEACH

Sunset over the ocean. In American culture the phrase almost invariably connotes sunset over the Pacific. Some Easterners travel to Key West to see the sun go down over the Gulf of Mexico, but the main event lies a continent away. The West Coast sunset, frequently spectacular, quickly came to symbolize not just the Gold Rush, but fertile soils and gentle climates that rewarded hard work, a sort of gold-in-the-sky recompense for the travails of covered-wagon pioneering. What the first farmers, ranchers, and loggers valued soon became a stock tourist icon. Railroad companies pushed the sunset notion, publishing brochures and even a magazine named *Sunset,* and in time an entire seashore resort industry evolved in the golden glow of the sun dropping slowly into the sea. But not until Hollywood grasped its subtler, sexier overtones did the Pacific Coast sunset reshape the way all Americans viewed beaches.

Who truly grasps the West Coast sunset? Millions see it every evening, and while most viewers accept it as a pleasant accent to the evening commute or something that enlivens west-facing windows, thousands throng parks not just to exercise or relax, but to enjoy the show. But the extraordinary East Coast bias of the national school system shackles most viewers who appreciate the beauty but know appallingly little about simple physics, optics, and meteorology that not only explain how the sunsets happen but make a handful of viewers aware of nuances most others miss. Our nation's East Coast bias originates in Britain, where most eighteenth-century educated observers lived in the environs of London and studied the sun rising from the sea. Unlike world-voyaging mariners, most British and American intellectuals fixated on the beauty and optics of the ocean sunrise, something that explains so many paintings, professional and amateur, and a lingering absence in schoolbooks and college curricula—the systematic method of analyzing the play of light over the sea.

Not surprisingly, a Dutchman wrote the premiere book on the subject. Long a favorite of deep-water mariners, M. G. J. Minnaert's *Light and*

"Sunset Beach, Studio Beach" appeared in *Mains'l Haul: A Journal of Pacific Maritime History* 38, no. 3 (Summer 2002): 42–51, copyright Maritime Museum of San Diego.

Color in the Outdoors appeared in Dutch in 1937, in English three years later, and in subsequent improved editions until 1968. Still in print in a handsomely illustrated paperback, the book deals with subjects often seen but rarely analyzed, say the color of diesel smoke against skies of different color, the nuances of mirage, and rainbows. The book is surprisingly useful for Pacific Coast observers of atmospheric effects over the ocean. "The following observations were carried out during a holiday on the flat, sandy coast of Holland, which runs virtually due north and south, and from where magnificent sunsets can be seen over the sea," Minnaert explains in the preface to a section called "Light and Color at the North Sea." "The phenomena are, of course, differently distributed over the day for differently oriented coasts: the essential point is the position of the sun relative to the surface of the sea." But the section based on his acute observations during a seashore vacation is only part of a larger whole in which the Dutch view of the sea—a sea that lies *to the west*—governs many observations.

In dealing with the green flash, the distortion of the sun setting over the sea, and above all with sunset over the sea, Minnaert makes clear his insistence that a bit of practiced observation yields tremendous dividends. In orienting sections of chapters around questions like "When is the color of the distant sky orange and when is it green?" he dissects the generic sunset into types that reward scrutiny. But his fascination with waves, reflection, and light-scattering produce a technique of analyzing the color of the sea too. "The color of the sea in the distance is therefore about the same as that of the sky at a height of 20–30 degrees, and therefore darker than the sky immediately above the horizon, and the more so because only part of the light is reflected." And always Minnaert is not merely a landsman, not merely an accomplished alongshoreman. He is something of a mariner too, and makes clear that the absence of surf means that sunsets seen from a ship at sea are fundamentally different from sunsets seen from a beach. He even explains, in the most casual way imaginable, why someone taking passage from the United States' West Coast to Australia will notice that above 40 degrees North latitude the sea seems olive green, that between about 30 and 40 degrees North the sea seems indigo, and that south of 30 degrees North it becomes ultramarine.[1] Anyone who follows his simple viewing procedures soon discovers that Pacific Coast sunsets vary by latitude as well as by local conditions.

What Minnaert explains once formed the armature of much public-school science teaching. Meteorology involved far more than predicting the weather: it included the whole range of mirage, and especially that phenomenon almost peculiar to the sea, looming. Physics meant Newtonian physics, and especially the Newtonian optics that once paralleled high-school geometry. Until about 1910 or so, liberal-arts college graduates knew at least something of the aesthetic superstructure built on such basics: the study of color in nature formed the skeleton of *gentleman's chromatics*—what a gentleman knew of looking around that made looking at paintings so valuable. Nowadays few observers of nineteenth-century marine art make much sense of the weather the artists depict, let alone the impact of the weather—or approaching weather—on either the colors on the canvas or the set of the sails the vessels carry. What happened to the old curriculum that taught American schoolchildren how to grasp a sunset, how to talk about it from both scientific and artistic angles combined?

Almost certainly, popular photography is the culprit, for it skewed entire angles of vision. After George Eastman put roll-film cameras in the hands of professionals and amateurs alike, and certainly by 1910, photography divided into thirds. A handful of professionals continued using tripod-mounted, large-format, glass-negative-based cameras while most Americans embraced the box-camera-and-roll-film approach still called *snapshot photography*. But thousands of professionals and serious hobbyists alike soon shared the sophisticated, medium-format Kodak cameras that quickly altered concepts of photography and concepts of looking too. In an odd way, Americans are still recovering from the shock of acquiring sophisticated cameras and are still ignorant of the limitations camera manufacturers secretly impose. Exactly a century ago, popular photographers struggled with beach photography. Despite ever more complex cameras, many photographers experienced only frustration.

"The lack of success, which has disappointed many, may usually be traced to a lack of familiarity with or understanding of the local conditions interfering with ordinary manipulations," wrote George D. Firmin in a July, 1901 *Photo-Miniature* essay entitled "Seashore Photography" that filled almost the entire magazine. "Atmospheric conditions, for instance, demand precautions unknown further inland. The intense illumination or light glare peculiar to the seashore and the strangeness of the subjects found there are real difficulties until known and mastered." Step by step, Firmin detailed what he knew of seashore photography using sophisticated cameras, both tripod-mounted and hand-held, in different atmospheric conditions. He warned readers about the corrosive effects of salt air on cameras and exposed film, suggested making cardboard screens to block stray light from viewfinders, and outlined at great length the

PHOTOGRAPHED LANDSCAPE

best combinations of lenses and shutter speeds when working with the long-distance views educated Americans appreciated.

For all its detail and seeming expertise, "Seashore Photography" in the end seems subtly biased, and indeed it is. Firmin worked from his experience along the New Jersey coast, and many of his suggestions derive from his locale. "The south Jersey beaches are usually flat and the breakers consequently small and distant, so that the camera will often be set up in the water," he wrote in a chapter devoted to surf photography. Placing the camera very low to the water sometimes produced images with what he called *sparkle*, something difficult to achieve if mist fogged a lens set only a few inches above the sea. But finding sunsets over the ocean meant heading south to Cape May and aiming his camera over Chesapeake Bay.

Firmin waited and watched for six weeks at Cape May before he saw a suitable sunset. "Evening after evening I would watch the sunset often, on the ground-glass, and decide it was not just what I wished. Beautiful beyond compare, maybe, in itself, but I knew that when translated into monochrome it would be robbed of most of its glory. And there was possibly nothing else to convey the impressions to the person viewing the print." In the end, Firmin concluded that "one must learn to forget color, or rather to see the colors as they will appear when photographed, in black and white," and that the photographer seeking a spectacular sunset should wait until after a stormy day. Anyone reading Minnaert's book carefully quickly discovers what so baffled Firmin: the lack of surf altered the whole appearance of the short-distance sunsets Firmin tried so hard to capture in black and white. Instead of watching sunsets over a bay, Firmin should have been watching sunrises over the ocean, and hoping for sunrises over the surf that magnifies the magnificence of sunrise and sunset. But however much he appreciated the beauty of his accidental efforts, in the end he admitted that "the whole effect is that of a warm summer moonlight night."[2] And in his perplexity, and in the puzzlement of thousands of other popular photographers, something changed along East Coast beaches.

Firmin and other savants suggested that popular photographers eschew making images of atmospheric conditions and instead concentrate on short-distance beach subjects. An extraordinary shift occurred by 1915 or so, as well-equipped, otherwise skillful photographers shifted their attention away from long- and even middle-distance views. Part of the shift occurred for a quite simple reason: few photographers enjoyed getting up before dawn, preparing their cameras in the dark, and then struggling to capture the sunrise. Daybreak is, after all, often uncomfortable along-

Beginning early in the twentieth century, Hollywood cinema producers routinely set films on beaches, and photographers quickly duplicated images they saw on screen.

In the 1920s and 1930s, West Coast chambers of commerce organized more and more events on beaches, many of which drew photographers.

PHOTOGRAPHED LANDSCAPE

shore. The air is cool and damp, and breezes prove unpredictable. But more important, the state of the sea itself is often difficult to discern before sunrise, simply because the photographer cannot see the sea. Since most photographers worked along East Coast beaches, and since so-called national photographic magazines catered to East Coast readers, West Coast sunsets received markedly little attention from any but West Coast photographers. Those photographers quickly learned the good fortune of location. Sunset photography not only allows the photographer to set up by daylight and scrutinize the state of the sea, but American West Coast sunset photography frequently involves spectacular sunsets most evenings highlighted by waves and surf. But another part of the shift occurred almost by coincidence. As Firmin and other experts counseled aiming at short-distance subjects, the fledgling film industry moved from New Jersey to California. The coincidence proved momentous.

"Seashore Photography" advises popular photographers to focus on short-distance subjects like pleasure boats close inshore, flotsam and jetsam strewn along the beach, anchored yachts, and above all, people. So also do many other period magazine articles, and an outpouring of advice from the Eastman Kodak Company and other manufacturers of cameras and film.[3] On both East and West Coasts, photographers began shifting their view sideways, ignoring atmospheric effects like sunsets, and ignoring ships offshore too. Instead they turned their attention and cameras to objects very close inshore—like a large rock of Rialto Beach or the tour boat off Catalina's Moonstone Beach—and in the middle distance alongshore—maybe the Point Fermin lighthouse. On-board photography of coastlines defeated many, even those equipped with sophisticated hand-held cameras. While West Coast photographers enjoyed the privilege of long afternoons and evenings when the setting sun illuminated the coast inshore from boats (East Coast photographers had to rise before dawn for such effects), they faced the enduring difficulties posed by over-exposure and an empty foreground—as at Santa Barbara. Not surprisingly, then, photographers shortened their attention-distance more and more, driven not only by limitations of equipment (perhaps especially by the lack of color film) but by the examples created in Hollywood. They focused on people.

Hollywood used West Coast beaches as film sets, but perhaps more important, as the locale for publicity photographs that in time reshaped much American beach photography. The publicity images nowadays so carelessly accepted as icons of the silent-film era do more than emphasize actresses in filmy costume and period pose: they make the beach and ocean only background, and the famed West Coast sunset mere sparkle in the lower left of the image, as in the image at left (above). By the 1930s,

SUNSET BEACH, STUDIO BEACH

Firmin's discovery that children make the best alongshore subjects had been subtly expanded and codified. Alongshore scenery had become the background of posed and candid portraits. Cropping period photographs, even slicing them up with scissors, very frequently converts them from carefully contrived portraits to images of close-inshore or nearby-alongshore subjects. By the beginning of World War II, popular beach photography, even snapshot beach photography, emphasized people, de-emphasized long- and even middle-distance views, and reoriented the design of cameras. More and more frequently, Americans purchased fixed-focus, snapshot cameras incapable of long-distance views. Camera manufacturers knew that snapshot portraits comprised most of the film being developed and printed, and they produced thousands of cameras that focused best on subjects between six and ten feet away.

World War II and Cold War morale-boosting efforts converted the Hollywood-publicity-office beach photograph into an odd cross between the sexy pin-up image and the spirit-lifting wholesomeness of photos of GI girlfriends. Men photographed women, and perhaps more important, women photographed each other, on beaches, since beach-going offered a proper reason for wearing revealing attire that so pleased far-off servicemen. Many sub-genres of beach photography combined in the early 1940s to create the morale-boosting snapshots so many elderly men keep in wallets and bureau drawers. 1930s West Coast beach athletics, especially races, for example, solidified the notion that men and women in at least some beach photographs ought to be doing something other than lying on blankets or staring out to sea. But not until the late 1940s did the power of West Coast beach culture become clear to the entire American public. "The one place where people of all ages and temperaments feel free to kick over the traces is a public beach," opined *Life Magazine* in its July 19, 1948 issue. "When hot weather comes Americans get beach fever and shed most of their inhibitions along with their clothes." *Life* wondered at the postwar willingness of Americans, especially men, to "show off" in almost nothing, and found all sorts of "extra-aquatic diversions" worth photographing.[4] Nothing of seascape, landscape, or atmospheric effects shapes the long *Life* article, only a focus on postwar exuberance during the Berlin airlift and an emerging openness toward frivolity, skin, sexuality, and image-making. Postwar Americans had become as unselfconscious as the children Firmin recommended as subjects a half-century earlier.

The willingness of West Coast beach-going women to be photographed, even by men unknown to them, jars the contemporary undergraduates whom I teach, ignorant of the postwar confidence of women and the freedom enjoyed by professional and popular photographers alike. For decades, American women and men often sought refuge in numbers when a friend asked to photograph them. Uneasy in bathing costumes, perhaps uneasy on the beach itself, they confronted cameras cautiously. But anyone scanning thousands of period images detects a greater easiness among West Coast subjects, an easiness born of greater familiarity with beaches perhaps, and one certainly assisted by their use by Hollywood as outdoor photography studios. In a September, 1950 *Popular Photography* article entitled "Your Summer Studio . . . The Beach," Herman Quick used the photographs of Peter Gowland to explain the revolution wrought by Hollywood and World War II, while offering straightforward techniques for photographing West Coast beachgoers.

In accompanying Gowland to the beach, Quick accompanied a master willing to teach advanced amateurs, the well-equipped and thoughtful photographers nowadays designated *popular photographers.* "The beach has everything, character studies, outdoor portraits, pinup boys flexing their big muscles; leap-frogging enthusiasts, gamesters of every variety, surrealists burying each other's bodies in the wet sand; teenagers, birds, fish, sea shells, clouds, boats, planes, rafts, colorful beach umbrellas and swimming gear . . . splashing waves and the mighty churning surf," Gowland announced, but he put the great surf last on his list. For Gowland, for Quick, and for the readers of *Popular Photography* by 1950, *beach photography* meant the photography of people. And for many young women, especially in California, beach photography meant the possibility of being discovered by acting agents or studios—just as eighteen-year-old Marilyn Hampton won a role in the Paramount film *Tripoli* after her photograph won the 1950 "Miss Photo Flash" contest.[5] Nowadays the 1945 to 1955 period of West Coast beach photography proves hard for university undergraduates to analyze. Many find themselves taken aback by the brief bikinis Gowland recorded for the 1950 *Popular Photography* article—they think that such brief suits materialized only in the late 1960s, after the wildly popular *Bikini Beach* films—and they cannot imagine young men and women being "discovered" on beaches and thrust into modeling and acting careers. To them, the beach culture of 1950 seems very long ago, almost beyond the horizon, yet subtly contemporary.

Beach snapshots turn up in dining-room closets, old suitcases, filing cabinets, and especially in antique shops. Sometimes dated, often not, they provide both professional scholar and enterprising adventurer with portals into rewarding subjects. Analyze any snapshot at random, say, "Looks Like Bob made out." Square format—120 or 620 film—and not well exposed, certainly, and perhaps the fixed-focus camera had begun to leak light. But where on the West Coast? Maybe more important, when? Consider the swimsuits, scrutinize the hairstyles, note that only one of the four subjects looks at the camera. What implications lie here, in this ordinary, poorly composed image? It is three thousand miles away from Firmin's *Photo-Miniature* advice and light years away from Minnaert's precise observations of atmospheric light and color, but is it 1938 or 1945 or 1960? In the end, Bob and his near-naked girlfriends show us something about how West Coast beaches changed American popular culture, as photography shifted our gaze from sunsets and surf to people.

Notes

1. M. G. J. Minnaert, *Light and Color in the Outdoors,* trans. Len Seymour (1937: rev. ed.: New York: Springer-Verlag, 1993), 337–345.
2. George D. Firmin, "Seashore Photography," *Photo-Miniature* III (July 1901), 151–177.
3. John R. Stilgoe, "Popular Photography, Scenery Values, and Visual Assessment," *Landscape Journal* 3 (Autumn 1984), 111–122.
4. "Fun on the Beach," *Life* 25 (July 19, 1948), 65–70. For an analysis of this period of beachgoing, see Stilgoe, *Alongshore* (New Haven: Yale University Press, 1994), esp. 335–367.
5. Herman Quick and Peter Gowland, "Your Summer Studio . . . The Beach," *Popular Photography* 27 (September, 1950), 34–39, 93–95.

SPARSE AND AWAY

About *sparse* lexicographers once disputed. Long before the Civil War, speakers of United States English used the word to designate something subtly lacking in the British word *scattered*. Now long forgotten, the dispute opens on openings, on sparseness, on the spaces between structures, on the arresting spaciousness in the photographs in this exhibition.

Samuel Johnson and other eighteenth-century English lexicographers omitted *sparse* because they did not know the word. Instead they offered *scatter,* what Johnson's 1755 *Dictionary of the English Language* defined as *to throw loosely about; to sprinkle: to dissipate; to disperse:* and *to spread thinly.* Yet something vaguely negative overshadowed that word, and perhaps kept Johnson from including it as an adjective. *Scattering* he defined as *a vagabond; one that has no home or settled habitation.* And about the word, Johnson admitted something in an editorial aside: *An elegant word but disused.* So far as he knew, it had been out of use for almost three centuries, and he could find printed reference only in Spenser, which he quoted: "Gathering unto him all the scatterlings and outlaws out of all the woods and mountains, in which they long had lurked, he marched forth into the English pale." While not outlaws, scatterlings live lonely lives, and their presence threatens, however obliquely, those who live together, those who live *not scattered,* those who live within the pale, in cities, those who make dictionaries.

But *sparse* existed despite English ignorance. In his 1846 *Dictionary of the Scottish Language,* John Jamieson identified it as *spars.* Meaning *to spread; to propagate* as a verb, and as an adjective, spelled both *spars* and *sparse,* in Scotland it meant *widely spread.* "*Sparse* writing," Jamieson explained, "is open writing, occupying a large space." Whatever its deep origin, Jamieson makes quite clear that the word connotes intention. Penmanship implies control, and a writer writing openly, sparsely, is one writing large, not wasting paper but making a point in the size of letters and words.

Much earlier, Noah Webster knew the word too. In his 1829 *American Dictionary of the English Language* the adjective meant *thinly scattered; set or planted here and there; as, a sparse population,* and it existed too as a transitive

"Sparse and Away" appeared in different form in *Reinventing the West: The Photographs of Ansel Adams and Robert Adams* (Andover, Mass.: Phillips Academy Addison Gallery of American Art, 2001), 73–79, copyright Addison Gallery of American Art.

verb—which he marked *not in use*—meaning *to disperse*. His unabridged dictionary included the word in the form of a noun too, *sparseness,* which it defined as *thinness; scattered state; as, sparseness of population*. More important, it directed readers to a major United States source for the use of the term, the 1833 *Commentaries on the Constitution of the United States* by the eminent jurist Joseph Story. The massive, three-volume work dissects the Constitution line by line, phrase by phrase, explicating issues Americans now take utterly for granted. But the issue underlying what Story referred to as "the frequency of elections" contemporary readers might well understand as a time-space continuum. "If the government be of small extent, or be concentrated in a single city, it will be far more easy for the citizens to choose their rulers frequently, and to change them without mischief, than it would be, if the territory were large, the population sparse, and the means of intercourse few and liable to interruption." Since some Americans chose to live far distant from others, elections must not be too frequent, lest people who live in towns and cities usurp the rights of others, the scatterlings. Our modern pattern of state and national elections rarely occurring at intervals less than two years derives from the late-eighteenth-century difficulty of assembling "the planters and farmers of the southern and western states," fur traders, and others who lived sparsely, who found trips to polling places difficult and time-consuming. As Story makes clear, the Constitution exists as it does because voters and representatives "are liable to be retarded by all the varieties of climate, and geological features of the country; by drifts of impassable snows; by sudden inundations; by chains of mountains; by extensive prairies; by numerous streams; by sandy deserts." In the new United States, living sparsely meant living in a perfectly correct way, one the Constitution had to accommodate to ensure equality under the law.

In 1859, when John Russell Bartlett published the second edition of his *Dictionary of Americanisms: A Glossary of Words and Phrases Usually Regarded as Peculiar to the United States,* lexicographers knew that *sparse* had begun to present genuine etymological difficulties. Bartlett defined it as *scattered; thinly spread; not dense,* but knew it connoted something slightly different than *scattered*. "This word has been regarded as of American origin; but it is found in Jamieson's *Dictionary of the Scottish Language*. It is in common use in America, though little used in England." Scottish or not, Bartlett followed Webster in tracing the word to a Latin root, *sparsus,* which one New York-published Latin-English dictionary, E. A. Andrews's 1857 *Copious and Critical Latin-English Lexicon,* defined as *to strew, throw here and there, scatter*. Andrews precisely grounded the term in such expressions as *with a [sparsely] freckled face* and in so doing suggested that it implied chance at least as frequently as it did intention. Looking to

In eastern New Mexico and elsewhere, a freight train becomes a mile-long moving wall, a sort of structure that appears, orders the landscape, then vanishes, making landscape seem even more empty.

Latin roots only deepened the mystery of United States usage, then, for while some citizens became scatterlings by intention, by design, their children lived as scatterlings by accident of birth, by chance. As London gathered in more and more rural English—and Scots too—the great frontier West attracted more and more United States citizens from East Coast cities and towns. Neither Latin origins nor English usage seemed much use to American dictionary makers therefore.

Bartlett found himself slewing away from why the English so rarely used the word toward trying to make sense of why Americans did. *Sparsely* he defined rather poorly, indeed using *sparse* to provide part of the definition: *in a scattered, or sparse manner; thinly.* He did find a quotation giving a better sense of the term, however, one that bears on Story's understanding of the Constitution as something that must work everywhere in the Republic.

"The river-bottoms, still lower than the general level, are subject to constant overflow by tide-water, and what with the fallen timber, the dense undergrowth, the mire-quags, the abrupt gullies, the patches of rotten or floating corduroy, and three or four feet of dirty salt-water, the roads through them are not such as one would choose for a morning ride," wrote Frederick Law Olmsted in *A Journey through Texas; or, A Saddle-Trip on the South-Western Frontier* in 1857 of a wilderness "completely terra incognita" to outsiders. "The country between Trinity River and the Mississippi is sparsely settled, containing less than one inhabitant to the

SPARSE AND AWAY

square mile, one in four being a slave," he continued of a place whose residents "live in isolated cabins, hold little intercourse with one another, and almost none with the outside world." While "steamboats land their coffee and salt on the Sabine and Trinity, at irregular intervals," he found that almost "no wheeled vehicles traverse the region" (in two weeks' riding he saw only a lone, two-wheeled peddler's cart) and discovered firsthand that travelers through the "boggy country" encounter "venomous water-snakes, four or five black moccasins often lifting at once their devilish heads above the dirty surface," and worse. "Beyond the Sabine, alligator holes are an additional excitement, the unsuspicious traveler suddenly sinking through the treacherous surface, and sometimes falling a victim, horse and all, to the hideous jaws of the reptile, while overwhelmed by the engulfing mire in which he lurks." The New Yorker did not like the place: "the avernal entrance might, I should think, with good probabilities, be looked for in this region." In such sparsely settled country, a sharp-eyed traveler might descry the entrance to Hell itself.

Implicit in Bartlett's *Dictionary of Americanisms* lurks the deepening suspicion that *sparse* is a term used by people on the far margins of density, people who might not be the scatterlings of Spenser exactly, but people deserving the most acute scrutiny of New York–based abolitionists. Olmsted rode through the slave states not only to understand slavery but to grapple with the immensity of a region becoming the new Southwest and West. Nowadays Americans all too easily forget that abolitionists wanted more than the end of slavery. They wanted to stop the westward advancement of slavery from the South and the Arkansas-based Old Southwest into a region many Northerners, especially urban Northerners, distrusted simply because of its vastness. By the beginning of the Civil War, city-dwellers content with urban and suburban living simply no longer understood the attraction of places like the bayou country between the Mississippi and the Trinity Rivers. Why did people want to live in such sparse places? Were they not lonely? Were they not overpowered by the proximity of alligators and snakes? Were they not drained of spirit and energy by the vast stretches of wilderness unaltered by human effort?

Two years after Olmsted published *A Journey through Texas* appeared Joseph Worcester's *Dictionary of the English Language,* the first United States–produced unabridged dictionary intended for both American and British readers. Worcester defined *sparse* simply: *scattered; thinly spread; not dense.* He traced its root to the Latin *sparsus,* and warned his readers that while the "word has been regarded as of American origin," Jamieson had found it alive and well in Scotland. But Worcester went a step further. He quoted the British *Penny Cyclopedia* on the emerging use of the word in Britain, especially in England: "'*Sparse* is, for any thing we know, a new word and

PHOTOGRAPHED LANDSCAPE

well applied: the Americans say a *sparse,* instead of a *scattered,* population; and we think the word has a more precise meaning than *scattered,* and is the proper correlative of *dense.*'" The preciseness that so appealed to the editors of the twenty-seven-volume *Penny Cyclopedia* goes unremarked in Worcester's lexicon, but appears to have something to do with intent.

Scattered connotes random distribution, the strewing implicit in the Latin root, but *sparse* suggests design, indeed perhaps fierce intent. Not until 1890, when the multivolume *Century Dictionary: An Encyclopedic Lexicon of the English Language* appeared, did any United States or British dictionary admit that *sparse* meant something other than *scattered,* and that the distinction had value for well-educated people delighting in nuance.

Thinly scattered; dispersed round about; existing at considerable intervals; as used of population or the like, not dense runs the *Century* definition of *sparse.* But then follows a remarkable editorial judgment: "*Sparse* has been regarded, falsely, as an Americanism, and has been objected to as being exactly equivalent to *scattered,* and therefore unnecessary. As a merely qualifying adjective, however, it is free from the possible ambiguity inherent in the participial form and consequent verbal implication of *scattered.*" Even Britons had noticed the ambiguity, and by 1879, Henry George, in *Progress and Poverty,* had begun using the term in its American way: "The earth as a whole is as yet most sparsely populated." By 1890 such usage was conventional in Britain, especially among people accustomed to thinking of the British Empire or the entire planet, and beginning to realize that sparsely populated territory might contain immense mineral wealth or present military conundrums. Charles Wentworth Dilke, in his 1890 *Problems of Greater Britain,* used the word precisely and pointedly in an imperial sense. "A group of colonies about as large as the Canadian Dominion, or as the United States, or as Europe; almost wholly settled by people from the United Kingdom, but still sparsely peopled, gives us Australasia." Educated Europeans had to revise their understanding of place, culture, and aesthetics to even begin to understand why Australians so loved their home. "The western part of the continent of Australia is as yet only a land of stones and flowers, and the great portion of the remainder, to the unaccustomed eye a kind of desert, almost mountainless, and consequently almost without permanent rivers." Despite "fiery mists" and a "red sun," Australians are anything but scatterlings. They are a united, peaceful, and intensely friendly people fiercely proud of their sparsely populated landscape. Dilke brilliantly explicated the cultural confusion implicit in British rule of vast, sparsely settled regions in which British travelers, colonial administrators, and even soldiers felt lonesome, uneasy, and at times disoriented, unaccustomed enough to see even a little beauty in regions with almost no people and ordinarily unable to imagine why the few inhabitants so loved where they had settled. Moreover, he analyzed why some Britons emigrated to places where they lived utterly different lives than most Britons imagined possible, at least in the British Isles themselves. Some people choose awayness, something *loneliness* misdesignates.

Sparse connotes intentional distancing, a lack of density by design, then, something other than anything *scattered* connotes. *Sparse* connotes the way people live who live beyond elbow room, people who value space for what it does to life, perhaps above all, to vision, to seeing, to imagining. It subtly informs familiar expressions like the line from the song "America the Beautiful." Spacious skies are skies seen only by people in spaciousness, people who leave behind density and move into another way of seeing, people who direct themselves into sparseness, who become part of sparse.

Whatever else it is, that way of seeing is not urban. It is not so much a wilderness way of seeing, although wilderness offers broad views indeed, and ocean wilderness offers perhaps the broadest. Nor is it so much a rural way of seeing, for all that vast fields and grazing land open on immense views too. It is not even suburban, for the suburban view is definitely not the same as a view of entire suburbs emerging from some locus, from some *other* point. The sparse way of seeing is something acutely, almost painfully special, especially in an urban age fixated on phosphorescent screens eighteen inches beyond the eyes. It is something that threatens many unfamiliar with it. It is the *other* vantage point.

Nowadays few American commentators remark on the statistical center of population. That in 1900 the United States Census Bureau placed it in Columbus, Indiana, no one much cares; nor does anyone much care that the 1920 census placed it only slightly further west in Indiana, in Whitehall. To drive west along Interstate 70 is to drive into statistical progression, but a progression that unnerves many urban intellectuals. Even as the center of national population moves westward, the great center of the United States becomes relatively less and less populated, for the Atlantic and Pacific coasts grow apace. Much of the High Plains, the region west of the ninety-eighth meridian, actually loses population as mechanization allows one farm family to manage the acreage eight families once worked, as the lure of big-city life draws more and more young people from small towns and crossroads hamlets. But what motivates those who stay behind? Do they value the vantage point the center-of-population markers obscure? Do they value sparseness? Do they associate sparseness with quiet, with great gores into which the human spirit flows? Do they associate it with an immense infusion of energy? Do they value the vision peculiar to sparsely settled, sparsely built places?

PHOTOGRAPHED LANDSCAPE

END

Only a few years ago great card catalogues dignified the first and second floors of Widener Library at Harvard University. Certainly the computer-driven replacement proves more efficient at ordering author, title, and subject information, and already students and even new junior faculty know nothing of the golden-oak file drawers around which everyone once clustered in some railroad depot–like way.

Automobile commuting is perhaps more efficient than commuting by train. The railroad industry watched riders abandon commuter trains in the 1920s, and by the 1950s many small suburban towns witnessed the end of service. Automobiles offered freedom from schedules, while providing garage-to-garage service. Less tangible commuter-train goods received little attention, even on last-run days. Commuter coaches brought together people who might exchange pleasantries or speak of deeper issues, help each other change jobs or find customers or deal with family crises, or now and then combine into start-up companies. Railroad commuting provided some physical exercise, since many passengers walked between homes and suburban depots and between urban terminals and offices. Commuter-rail service produced a periodicity in the suburban day, freedom from traffic jams, and reliable carriage on rainy and snowy days. As conservation trails become railroads again south of Boston, old-timers speak of the goods so thoughtlessly discarded in the 1950s.

Analyzing landscape means intensive library research. Observing landscape or images of landscape sooner or later produces questions about landscape constituents or long-ago attitudes expressed in an image, and the questions lead into libraries.

In libraries inquirers discover the maddening difficulties implicit in landscape inquiry. Landscape is nuanced and complex in ways that demand interdisciplinary scholarship, and those ways often confound the finest reference librarians and cataloguing systems. Even now, computerized catalogues notwithstanding, libraries order images badly. Struggling with seeming straightforward issues, the moment at which factory smoke no longer signified prosperity and productivity but air pollution, for example, forces the researcher into subjects all too rarely indexed then and now.

Only a few years ago, scholars gathered in the card-catalogue rooms and exchanged commuter train–like pleasantries. Sometimes they expressed frustration and offers to help and general observations on each other's research efforts. Many suggestions proved less than useful, but now and then a casual suggestion opened on discovery.

So did browsing. Until Harvard University opened a suburban storage library, students and faculty browsed in the stacks. Now most users key in the "browse" function and scroll titles across a screen. Perhaps serendipity decreases, as it did in the early automobile city. Only rarely now do I surprise colleagues and students in dim stack levels and learn that someone inquires into something that might have a landscape component. Browsing is far less practiced now, especially browsing in search of images.

In the old United States history classification, long-dead librarians ordered books according to the sequence in which colonies and then territories became states. The library user walks west along Four Stack through a physical monument to the westward movement. But then something jars. When Virginia split during the secession crisis, the new state of West Virginia confounded the sequencers of books just as it flummoxed mid-nineteenth-century cartographers coolly accustomed to an unspoken state coloring code. The library landscape, if landscape it is, still reflects the upheaval posed by a new eastern state.

When librarians dispatched almost everything published in Dutch to the robot-retrieval storage library, only a few scholars fussed. The Netherlands received little attention in coursework when librarians decided, and nowadays it receives even less, since the books have journeyed west. But then, while researching *Lifeboat: A History of Courage, Cravenness, and Survival at Sea,* I discovered that everything on Indonesia and its environs had gone west too. Indonesia, formerly part of the Dutch East Indies, vanished along with its mother country. So did some material on New York, formerly New Amsterdam. One day, my note cards in hand, suddenly realizing the enormity of whole Dutch sections vanished from the library landscape, I was startled by a colleague. Note cards in his own hand, he glared at me and said, "What happened to 'Netherlands'?" I shrugged my shoulders, and as he strode eastward I wondered how I would learn about the Dutch officials who welcomed Captain Bligh and his crew after their famous open-boat passage.

So much that landscape analysis requires is either gone from the library or turns out never to have been collected. Long-ago librarians excised advertising pages when binding periodicals, thus consigning many Kodak Company advertisements to a peculiar limbo. Learning how Kodak and its competitors taught women to use cameras proves frustrating in the absence of advertisements. But what archive collects mail-order

END

catalogues from the 1970s, especially clothing catalogues that used urban landscape to advertise clothing criminals fail to notice? What of the upscale catalogues from the 1980s that pose urban-attired models against suburban landscape images from the 1960s? Where are the maps gas stations once gave freely to motorists before the interstate highway system? Does the period photograph showing an astute observer of landscape gather force when the viewer realizes the observer rides astride, not side-saddle? How does one find other photographs of women in the saddle, or books on saddles?

Serendipity matters a lot in landscape analysis. Some landscapes and some libraries encourage it, and some seem inured to its vanishing. Learning to observe landscape, then to analyze it, now brings inquirers to analyze the landscape of learning, and especially the arrangement of books and other paper-based sources of knowledge. When the weather drives the landscape observer indoors, libraries prove rewarding places in which to look around, then read, then look around intently and grow suspicious about the shaping of knowledge. On the train going home, I wonder at the order in which I found the books I hold as I look through the windows at the darkening landscape.

END

FOUR MORNINGS, SEVEN AFTERNOONS

Cats communicate fire. Why else do prudent Americans put them outdoors before retiring to bed? "A cat should not be left in the house at
night," counseled an 1824 *New England Farmer* essayist. "They have often, by getting in the ashes, and having coals stick to them, communi-
cated fire to the house." Nineteenth-century Americans feared wildfire,
especially the fires of nighttime; farmers worried about hay moldering
in barn lofts, about lightning, about cats. Wise agriculturalists installed
lightning rods, dug "fire wells" next to back porches, and all winter kept
ladders propped against roofs leading to chimneys; they slept lightly,
boots, pants, and filled water buckets beside their beds. "Never give an
alarm of fire, unless you be pretty sure you cannot put it out without further assistance," the essayist warned, "for a small fire may be easier ex-
tinguished by one, than by twenty men." Warnings and precautions fill
the pages of antebellum farming journals.

Rows upon rows of agricultural periodicals rise upward in the Locked
Room beneath Cabot Library, brushing the ceiling eighteen feet above the
floor, walling in the historian blessed with a key to the collection. Like the
rifles rising organ-like in Longfellow's cryptic paean to the Springfield Ar-
senal, the volumes are silent now, rarely visited and less often read. Their
call numbers climb steadily through *The Cultivator* and *The Genessee Farmer,*
through *The Illustrated Annual Register of Rural Affairs* to *The Ploughboy,* leading upward into immense runs of farming pamphlets, and on into the
squat, bound reports of agricultural experiment stations from Maine to
Michigan. A miscellaneous collection, grounded in agriculture, but stretching down row after row into late-nineteenth-century holdings focused on
railroad engineering, on practical applications of electricity, on lighter-
than-air flight, and reaching in the other direction into the civil engineering, locomotive design, and urban design of nineteenth-century Europe,
North America, and Argentina. Not a chair, not a table punctuates the
room of crowded shelves; only a gigantic rolling staircase, scarcely ma-
neuverable in the narrow aisles, offers a precarious seat to the researcher.
High aloft, seated on the corrugated, non-skid top step just beneath the

"Four Mornings, Seven Afternoons" appeared in *Harvard Library Bulletin* n.s. 6 (Fall
1995), copyright by the President and Fellows of Harvard University.

humming fluorescent tubes, the historian of vanished landscapes gazes out upon a library landscape, one of canyons, peaks, and cliffs.

A trail of autumn leaves led into the Locked Room. Nineteenth-century reformers argued for the beautification of village streets; in an age enamored of environmental determinism, improvement of landscape seemed likely to foster improvement of public behavior. In 1849 and 1850, Andrew Jackson Downing lambasted the condition of village main streets, detailing a national shabbiness that mocked boasts of national spatial beauty. His *Horticulturist* essays endeavored to turn "neglected, bare, and lanky streets into avenues of fine foliage." Month after month, in the issues now ranked on Frances Loeb Library shelves, he equated street trees with morality. "A village whose streets are bare of trees, ought to be looked upon as in a condition not less pitiable than a community without a schoolmaster, or a teacher of religion," he asserted in some of the strongest language to enliven that staid journal of the first suburbanites, "for certain it is, when the affections are so dull, and the domestic virtues so blunt that men do not care how their own homes and villages look, they care very little for fulfilling any moral obligations not made compulsory by the strong arm of the law." The great street-tree crusade consumed Downing's energy certainly, and later that of others: landscape architects embraced the movement in the 1870s, in the 1890s, indeed into the twentieth century. Cities planted street trees, towns planted street trees, even farmers planted a tree or two before their houses, and in the Centennial years they set out maples and elms at regular intervals along the roads bordering their fields. Only villagers shunned the strident advice of Downing and the rest.

John Warner Barber discerned no trees in the villages he visited. From Massachusetts to Pennsylvania, he rode and walked, pursuing the raw material he distilled into his *Historical Collection* series. Each volume, a sort of local history/gazetteer/guidebook, he advertised as a complete description of all the communities within the chosen state. Unlike almost all of the extensive collection loosely titled "United States: Travel and Description" and shelved on Widener Four South, the Barber volumes contain nearly countless woodcuts, mostly views of cities, towns, and villages taken from nearby hilltops or from approaching roads. In the sunlight pouring through the south-facing windows the old illustrations regain their former liveliness and grow seductive. So nicely ordered, so intimately related to surrounding text, so detailed, the illustrations must be accurate, must they not?

Downstairs, through the tunnel, through the door held shut by air-conditioning back pressure, into Pusey, then upstairs to the Map Collection. Four volumes of Barber stacked on the large table prompt the

END

Early-nineteenth-century illustrations of villages rarely depict trees, and this is especially true in John Warner Barber's *Historical Collections of Every Town in Massachusetts.* Learning why something is not in an image often proves more challenging than analyzing the history of something obviously included.

librarian to suspect that many, many folders of maps will be lugged from the cabinets beyond the corner around which no scholar may ever pass. After consultation, and the selecting of certain sample village views, the "1820s series" begins to appear. The morning wears on, the great acid-free folders mount in a stack beyond the Barber volumes; atlases appear, then contemporary topographical maps, then 1830s sheets. Then Sanborn Company maps, immense, multi-colored sheets created for the use of fire insurance firms intrigued by the material, condition, and surroundings of industrial buildings. And therein lies the clue. Sanborn Company inspectors focused on brick walls, sprinkler systems, and the proximity of fireworks plants to lumberyards, but now and then they scrutinized trees. Why trees? Because lightning might strike them, igniting adjacent buildings (especially the fireworks factory) and causing claims? Trees are, after all, what is *not* present in the meticulously detailed, seemingly accurate Barber views of villages. Barber renders trees in cities and trees in towns, but much less often in villages. Is insurance involved?

At Baker Library even the students wear suits. Two future financiers listen momentarily to the historian interrogating the librarian about fire insurance firms, but decide nothing profitable can come of it. Down, down, down into stacks so cramped for headroom that two might fit easily into the towering basement of Cabot. Into A Stack, past rows of railroad volumes, the books and reports detailing the long forgotten financing and acquisition of the equipment and rights-of-way so carefully recorded in the Cabot Locked Room. A dead end, literally and figuratively; only one door, and nothing on pre-1850 fire insurance. Upstairs to the top floor for material in the Kress Collection, and there, the policies. "In Case Trees shall be planted before the Property above ensured after the Date of the Policy, the same shall be reported to the Society and an additional Deposit paid within One Year after they are planted or this Ensurance shall be void." In cities and towns, in 1815, street trees smacked of danger.

Policies are contracts, and contracts may have the force of law. In Langdell Hall prospective attorneys queue up at the reference desk, asking about cases, reports, needing the Very Latest Decisions. Early-nineteenth-century fire-insurance policies? The question appears a welcome change of pace, the librarian vanishes to consult, the queue grows restive, wondering about the value of such antiquated documents; the historian points out the age of the Constitution, and the queue falls silent. Downstairs again, down the stairs that twist, that surprise, that perhaps shape the reasonings of law students. More policies. Suits at law. Decisions and appeals. Street trees, like cats, communicate fire.

In cities and towns, street trees worried people of prudence, as did structures of wood. "Experience has proved that a wooden city is a vast tinder-box, kindling at every transient spark; an immense mass of phial'd phosphorous, blazing out by mere communication with the air," argued John Quincy Adams in an 1802 address to the Massachusetts Charitable Fire Society, an address carefully bound and secured in Houghton. As late as the 1760s, clergymen told parishioners that a wrathful Providence sent urban wildfire as punishment for urban vice; by the early years of the new century, Adams and other reformers blamed distinctly human causes. "But clapboards and shingles! What mysterious fascinations can they possess?" Building in brick, specifying firewalls, banishing hazardous manufacturing, and organizing fire brigades combined to lessen the peril of urban conflagration, indeed to diminish it so effectively that street trees appeared in Philadelphia, Boston, and in other cities, and even in large towns built almost wholly of wood.

New fire-fighting apparatus, the "engines" of early-nineteenth-century wonder, protected city folk and townsmen. Farmers lived too far from the technological wonders christened "Niagara" or "Extinguisher"; but farmers worried little about contagious fire. After all, however careless neighbors might be, the likelihood of fire consuming a house, then burning across fields and meadows to consume another, seemed so slight that even worrisome farmers worried more about their cats. But how effectively did the engines squirt? In the Cabot Locked Room stands the fire-

END

fighting collection, as dusty as the agricultural periodicals a few aisles away, as dry as tinder. Given an active crew heaving on the bars and an ample source of water, perhaps thirty feet high. Would street trees deflect the stream? What of the trees specified by Downing?

Upstairs at the Arnold Arboretum "visiting center," in one of the airiest, lightest reading rooms at Harvard, the historian finds not only volumes devoted to the complexities of street-tree planting, but an overwhelming collection of nineteenth-century photographs of trees of every species, all catalogued in Latin. At first a translation dictionary unlocks the images, then pure curiosity. Photograph upon photograph, revealing not only trees, but their habitats, their background buildings, their neighboring utility poles and trolley cars, their farms and fields over the whole of North America and, as the rows of cabinets suggest, the rest of the planet too. So, what of the twenty-year-old maple? Did it become a fire-department impediment only at forty? What of the elm? Outdoors then, out among the labeled trees and specimen groves, photocopies and notes in hand. Yes, a thirty-year-old maple shaded the residential street, but its crown stretched dangerously near abutting houses; two decades later the spark-catcher reached above chimney height and interlaced its branches with its neighbors. In the plantations Downing's love of beauty takes physical form; indeed, the elm is magnificent, so much so that fire-fighting concerns vanish, if only temporarily.

Downing, Olmsted, and other landscape architects labored almost fruitlessly. The street-tree movement bypassed villages because villagers knew the horror of wildfire among closely built frame houses, shops, and manufactories defended only by caution and bucket brigades. "There is not less danger from fire in country villages than in large towns," mused an 1825 *New England Farmer* writer. "Frequently the former are more combustible than the latter." Too few and too poor to afford a teacher or minister of religion, villagers looked enviously, and hopelessly, at the new fire-fighting inventions. Large towns and cities offered prospective residents educational and religious amenities, along with fire protection adequate enough to encourage even cautious families to dignify private and public space with trees that Americans now unthinkingly accept. Villagers, however, continued to fear wildfire, continued to eschew street trees, continued to appall Downing, Barber, and other visitors convinced of the morality of street trees. Prudent villagers struck aesthetes as vaguely immoral.

In the midst of it all, in trying to understand the twentieth-century American predilection for large-lot suburbs, street trees, and wooden houses secure from fire, and the corollary distaste for mobile-home parks, and treeless, 1950s ticky-tacky suburbs, notebooks fill with future projects, with detours and digressions. A farmers' bulletin on domestic uses of concrete, a business journal devoted to efficient cities, a book on the wooden-box industry and its relation to pine forests, and the Island of Navassa. A league or so off the Dominican Republic, off the Hispaniola of *Treasure Island* fame, lies Navassa, a tiny dot recorded in the leather-bound atlas idly turned in Houghton while the historian awaits Adams's fire-society address. A tiny dot, just offshore, named and marked "U.S." A prolonged squint, a hasty look at the atlas copyright (recent), then the delivery of the fire-society address next to the atlas. But the lingering, then nagging thought: Navassa? There, in the straits? A hastened lunch, a calculation of the interval (too short?) before tutorial, then the forced march to the Map Collection.

Navassa? The librarian frowns, bites off the question of its relationship to nineteenth-century villages, examines an atlas map, then unfolds the index to contemporary charts. A puzzled noise, then a gleam in his eye prompts the historian to peer over his shoulder: the island is printed in red. Out comes the massive, modern chart from its folder, a chart depicting some reefs and other hazards, and a large island, or rather, an outline, for the United States chart shows only blankness, and a red-printed warning to mariners. Only the southeastern commander of the Coast Guard may issue permission to land. Time in the Map Collection slows, then stops. A map of blankness, as blank as anything dreamed by Melville, Verne, or Conrad—a map of *deliberate* blankness. An undergraduate, assistant to the librarian and student of the historian, moves closer to see the "what in blazes." The librarian and historian scrutinize the document, trying to discern a channel through the ledges, a route for a motor whaler; the student stares, clears her throat, and suggests a helicopter. And then the librarian begins, finding first an eighteenth-century French-colonial atlas, then another volume, then nothing. Nothing. At least nothing of detail. The historian suggests an approach, the undergraduate, relieved for the moment of cataloging duties and willy-nilly drafted into the mission, suggests an approach. Nothing. And then time moves, time for tutorial.

Another undergraduate speaks of eighteenth-century Maine farms, of the paucity of period illustrations; the talk moves to images of landscape, to images made from sailing vessels entering port, to charts and their errors, to Navassa. And the undergraduate, after a question or two, suggests a gazetteer of Hispaniola, or, with rising excitement, the ocean collection; the historian muses aloud about the naval collection. Then tea and coffee half-drunk, and treeless, fire-prone villages and Maine farms temporarily abandoned, the tutorial shifts course into mischarted territory, veering south from Sever Hall into Widener, closing in on Navassa.

END

INDEX

landscape architecture: integration of architecture into, 189–90

landschaft, 29, 33–34, 35–44 passim

landschap, 29

landskap, 29

Lane, Robert E., 221

lanes, abandoned, 240

Lang, Andrew, 274–75, 277

Langewiesche, Wolfgang, 188

Langland, William, 52

La Salle, Sieur de, 67

laundry, drying of, 194, 210

law, higher moral, 292

lead, 109

Lemon, James T., 104

Leventhal, Herbert, 106

Lewis, Sinclair, 246

lexicographers, 153

light, 289; on bays, 159; blue, 253; electric, 274; emitted, 257; reflected from pages, 253, 257–58

limbo, 6–7; defined, 278–79; visual, 278–85

Lionel train, 15

littoral, 309–10

lizards, in mining, 110

London, Jack, 210

Longfellow, Henry Wadsworth, 339

looking, 1

looming, 83

Love, Edmund G., 18

lovers, meeting, 6

Loy, Myrna, 212

Lucretius, 279

Mabie, Hamilton Wright, 211, 214

magazines, photography, 300–301

magic, visual, 266–76

Maine Central Railroad Company, 313

making land, 27

Mann, Herman, 137

manufacturing, 94, 96

manuring, of fields, 94

maps, 2, 55, 134–50

marge, defined, 309

margo, defined, 309

Marsh, George Perkins, 181–82

Marx, Leo, 112

masks, 290

Mason-Dixon Line, 172

Mather, Cotton, 160–61, 206

Matthiessen, F. O., 288, 295

May Day Eve, 203

McKay, Donald, 288

McNally, Francis, 144

mechanics, 95

Mees, Kenneth, 276

Melville, Herman, 113–14, 310–11

men, meeting of, by women, 221, 224

metals, in theology, 110–11

meteorological phenomena, 82–83

meteorology, 321–22

microclimate modification, 170–91

Middletown, Pennsylvania, 19

minerals, colored, 109

mining country, defined, 108–10

Minnaert, M. G. J., 320–21, 328

mirrors, 268–69

miscegenation, 69

Mississippi River, 331–32

Missouri Compromise, 286

Mitchell, Donald G., 208–9

Mitchell, S. Augustus, 140, 142

Mittelberger, Gottlieb, 123, 126

Mobile, Alabama, 65

mobile homes, 228–29, 240

modification, of microclimate, 170–91

moisture retention, 185–86

Montauk Point, 153

Monteith, James, 144–46

Moodus noises, 110

moon, daguerreotyped, 293

moonlight, 280

morality, equated with beauty, 208

More, Thomas, 41

Morse, Jedidiah, 98, 110, 135–36, 141, 156

Morse, Sidney E., 143

moveable bridges, 215

Mowbray, H. Siddons, 275–76

Mowbray, J. P., 209

multi-plane universe, 274

names, of stores, 250

Nantucket, 11

Narragansett, vocabulary, 151–52

Narragansett Bay, 151–59

Navassa, 344

Nef, John Ulric, 104

neighbors, in site selection, 171

New Hampshire agriculturalists, 90
newspaper, view in, 17
New Sweden, 105
Newton, 276
New York, 12, 30
New York Central Railroad, 218
Nicklin, Philip Hulbrooke, 130
Niepce, Nicephare, 273
Nintendo, 258
Noble, Louis Legrand, 78
nodes, 27
nooks, for women, 197–98
Norden, John, 54
Norris Woods, 9
North River, Massachusetts, 57
North Truro, Massachusetts, 176
Northwest Passage, 268
Northwest Territory, 61, 105
Norway spruce, in windbreaks, 181
Novak, Barbara, 112
nudity, 311; power of, 319
Nutting, Wallace, 304–6

Oahu, Hawaii, 310
Old French Wars view, 68
Old Religion, 204
Olerich, Henry, 39
Olmsted, Frederick Law, 32–33, 81, 217, 219, 331
open country, defined, 119
open fire, 210–11
openness, valued, 119
optics, Newtonian, 322
order, in landscape, 92–93
Orford, Rosamond, 233
orientation, toward roads, 179
outdoor living, 190
Ovid, 204

Pace-Setter House, 189
Packard, John, 312
pagination, in atlases, 149n23
Pan, 203
Parish, Elijah, 137
Parker, Theodore, 292, 293–94
Parkman, Francis, 68
parlor, as exemplar of morality, 208
parts cars, 233–34
passenger cars, 262

Pawtucket River, 156
Peabody Museum, 287
peach trees, as indicators, 139
Pearson, John, 128–29
Peck, Bradford, 39
Penn, John, 126
Penrose, Margaret, 222
people, as photographic subjects, 325–26
perambulations, 51–52
Percy, Walker, 13
Philadelphia, 123
Phillips, Wendell, 293–94
photographic theory, 276
photographs, destruction of, 260
photography, 1, 7, 320–28; popular, 254, 298–307, 299; terminology, 259
physics, and crystalmancy, 275
Pickens, Buford L., 189
pickup trucks, 243
pictorial, defined, 299
picturesque, defined, 298–99
pit, 9
Place Congo, 71
place-names, Native American, 119
plains, 7
Plato, 47
Platte, Gabriel, 109
Plowden, David, 306
Plumer, William, 90, 91
Plutarch, 203
Poe, Edgar Allan, 86, 113
pool parties, 200
Poortvliet, Rien, 168
Pope, Alexander, 86
population, on seacoasts, 4–5
Port Royal, destroyed, 110
Post Office, 264–65
potholes, as creators of value, 232
Potosoi mines, 109
poverty grass, 107
Powell, Edward Payson, 194
prefabricated houses, 177
premiums, agricultural, 91
presentiments, 281
preservation, of landscapes, 218–19, 232–36
preserves, 217
Priapus, 213
Princeton, New Jersey, 219
prism, 13